John Sisco

CANADIAN
SECURITIES
INSTITUTE

D1368615

TEXTBOOK

Wealth

Management

Techniques

Names of individual securities mentioned in this text are for purposes of example only and are not to be construed as recommendations for purchase or sale.

Prices of individual securities given in this text are for the purposes of comparison and illustration only and were approximate figures for the period when the text was being prepared.

Every attempt has been made to update securities industry practices and regulations to reflect conditions prevailing at the time of publication.

While information contained in this text has been obtained from sources we believe to be reliable, it cannot be guaranteed nor does it purport to treat each subject exhaustively.

This publication is designed to provide accurate and authoritative information in regard to the subjects covered. It is distributed with the understanding that the Canadian Securities Institute is not engaged in rendering legal, accounting or other professional service. If legal advice or other expert assistance is required, the services of competent professional persons should be sought.

Canadian Cataloguing in Publication Data

The National Library of Canada has catalogued this publication as follows:

Main entry under title:
Wealth management techniques textbook

Includes index
ISBN 1-894289-55-2

1. Portfolio management.   2. Financial planners.
I. Canadian Securities Institute.

HG4529.5.W42 2000   332.6   C00-930671-4

First Printing 2000

Copyright © 2000 by the Canadian Securities Institute
Published by the Canadian Securities Institute

Wealth Management Techniques (WMT) is a trade mark of the Canadian Securities Institute.

Printed and bound in Canada
10 9 8 7 6 5 4 3 2 1

Wealth Management Techniques (WMT) *Textbook*

Prepared and published by

THE CANADIAN SECURITIES INSTITUTE

The National Educational Organization of
the Canadian Securities Industry

endorsed by

the Investment Dealers Association of Canada

The Montreal Exchange

The Toronto Stock Exchange

The Canadian Venture Exchange

**CANADIAN
SECURITIES
INSTITUTE**

Our Web Site: www.csi.ca

Toronto
121 King Street West Suite 1550, Toronto, ON M5H 3T9
Tel: (416) 364-9130 • Fax: (416) 359-0486

Vancouver
650 West Georgia St., Suite 1350, P.O. Box 11574, Vancouver, BC V6B 4N8
Tel: (604) 683-1338 • Fax: (604) 683-6050

Calgary
355 - 4th Avenue S.W., Suite 2330, Calgary, AB T2P 0J1
Tel: (403) 262-1791 • Fax: (403) 264-5304

Montreal
1 Place Ville Marie Suite 2840, Montreal, PQ H3B 4R4
Tel: (514) 878-3591 • Fax: (514) 878-2607

Halifax
1791 Barrington Street, TD Centre, Suite 1620, Halifax, NS B3J 3K9
Tel: (902) 423-8077 • Fax: (902) 423-0629

PROGRAMS FROM CSI

Canadian Securities Course & CPH Program
The Canadian Securities Course (CSC)
The Conduct & Practices Handbook Course (CPH)
CSI Prep Series

Financial Management Advisor Program (FMA)
Professional Financial Planning (PFPC)
Wealth Management Techniques (WMT)

Canadian Investment Manager Program (CIM)
Investment Management Techniques (IMT)
Portfolio Management Techniques (PMT)

Derivatives Program
Derivatives Fundamentals Course (DFC)
Options Licensing Course (OLC)
Futures Licensing Course (FLC)
Options Supervisors Course (OPSC)
Canadian Commodity Supervisors Exam (CCSE)
Technical Analysis Course (TAC)

Management Training
Branch Managers Course (BMC)
Effective Management Seminar (EMS)
Partners, Directors and Senior Officers
Qualifying Examination (PDO)

Specialty Learning
Trader Training Course (TTC)
Canadian Operations Course (COP)
Securities Law and Regulation Seminar
New Entrants Course (NEC)

Continuing Education (CE)
Compliance Program
Product Knowledge Program

Table of Contents

Introduction Introduction-1

1.0   A New Profession Introduction-1

2.0   The Role of the Wealth Manager Introduction-2

3.0   The Wealth Management Techniques Course Introduction-2
      Section I   The Wealth Management Process
                 and Dealing with the Client Introduction-3
      Section II   Advanced Financial Planning Introduction-3
      Section III   Investment and Portfolio Management Introduction-3
      Section IV   Practice Management Introduction-4
      Section V   Case Study Introduction-4

4.0   Financial Management Advisor Introduction-4

Section I

Wealth Management Process and Dealing with the Client

Chapter 1
The Wealth Management Process 1-1

1.0   Introduction 1-1

2.0   Understanding the High-Net-Worth Client 1-2

3.0   Formulating the Plan 1-3
      3.1   Advanced Financial Planning 1-4
              Retirement Planning 1-4
              Risk Management and Insurance 1-4
              Tax Planning 1-4
              Estate Planning 1-5
      3.2   Investment and Portfolio Management 1-5
              Risk and Return 1-6
              Asset Allocation 1-6
              Understanding Managed Products 1-7
              Measuring and Evaluating Managed products 1-7

4.0   Formalizing and implementing the Plan 1-8

5.0   Monitoring and Re-Balancing 1-9

Chapter 2

Understanding the Client

Understanding the Client 2-1

1.0   Introduction 2-1

2.0   Different Types of High-End Client 2-2
       2.1   The Owner/Manager 2-2
       2.2   The Entrepreneur 2-3
       2.3   The Corporate Executive 2-4
       2.4   Spouses and Other Family Members 2-4
       2.5   The Invisible Wealthy 2-5

3.0   Attitudes Toward Money and Wealth 2-6

4.0   Identifying Client Needs, Objectives, and Constraints 2-7
       4.1   Listen, Listen, Listen 2-7
       4.2   Asking the Right Questions 2-12
                    Return Requirements 2-14
                    Risk Tolerance 2-14
                    Liquidity Requirements 2-14
                    Legal Restrictions 2-15
                    Tax Issues 2-15
                    Time Horizon 2-15
                    Contingencies 2-15
                    Unique Circumstances 2-16
       4.3   Document Checklist 2-16

Appendix 2.1   Investor Profile Statement 2.1-1

Appendix 2.2   Risk Profile Statement 2.2-1

Chapter 3

Communication and Education

Communication and Education 3-1

1.0   Introduction 3-1

2.0   Communicating the Wealth Management Planning Process to the Client 3-1
       2.1   A Steadying Influence 3-2
       2.2   Keeping Clients Informed 3-3

3.0   Why Educate the Client? 3-4
       3.1   Types of Risk 3-5
                    The Risk of Not Investing or Investing too Conservatively 3-6
                    The Risk of Not Diversifying 3-6
                    Inflation or Purchasing Power Risk 3-6
                    Interest Rate Risk 3-6
                    Political Risk 3-7
                    Currency Risk 3-7
                    Default Risk 3-7
                    Risk of Uncertainty 3-8

		Market Risk	3-8
		Liquidity Risk	3-8
	3.2	Financial Comparisons and Illustrations	3-10
		Compounding	3-10
		The Rule of 72	3-10
		Volatility	3-11
		Market Timing	3-12

Chapter 4
Ethical Issues 4-1

1.0	Introduction	4-1
2.0	Essential Moral Attitudes	4-1
3.0	Ethics and Business Success	4-2
4.0	Trust and Trustworthiness	4-3
5.0	Loyal Agency	4-3
6.0	Moral Limits to Loyal Agency	4-5
7.0	Fiduciary Responsibilities	4-5
8.0	Client Education	4-8
9.0	Professional Standards	4-10
	9.1 Objectivity and Independence	4-12
	9.2 Understanding and Avoiding Conflicts of Interests	4-12
	9.3 Privacy and Confidentiality	4-16
	9.4 Honesty in Marketing Services and Fair Competition	4-16
10.0	Framework for Ethical Decision-Making	4-18

Section II
Advanced Financial Planning

Chapter 5
Retirement Planning 5-1

1.0	Introduction	5-1
2.0	The Retirement Independence Calculation	5-2
	2.1 Variables	5-2
	2.2 The Disclaimer	5-3
	2.3 The Budget	5-4
	2.4 Multiple Illustrations	5-4
	2.5 The Reality Check	5-5

3.0		Trends in Retirement Planning	5-6
	3.1	Level of Registered Retirement Savings	5-6
	3.2	Additional Uses for RRSPs: Home Buyer's Plan and the Lifelong Learning Plan	5-7
4.0		Should a Client Opt Out of a Company Pension Plan	5-9
	4.1	Opting Out of a DCP or Group RRSP	5-9
	4.2	Opting Out of a DBP	5-10
	4.3	Opting Out from the Client's Perspective	5-10
	4.4	Reviewing the Facts with a Client	5-10
5.0		Retirement Savings Beyond RRSPs and RPPS	5-12
	5.1	The Leveraged Deferred Compensation Plan	5-12
		How the LDCP Works	5-13
		Risks	5-14
	5.2	The Retirement Compensation Arrangement (RCA)	5-14
	5.3	Individual Pension Plans	5-15
	5.4	Supplemental Executive Retirement Plans	5-16
6.0		Preparing for Retirement	5-16
	6.1	Retirement Income Projection	5-17
	6.2	Choosing a Retirement Date	5-17
	6.3	Retiring from a Business	5-18
	6.4	Retiring from a Partnership	5-19
7.0		Financial Management during Retirement	5-19
	7.1	Getting Organized	5-19
	7.2	Maturing the RRSP	5-20
	7.3	RRIFs and Ways to Maximize a RRIF	5-21
		Make a final RRSP Contribution in Advance	5-21
		Claim the $2,000 Over-Contribution	5-22
		Base the Amount of the RRIF Withdrawal on the Age of a Younger Spouse	5-22
		Defer the RRIF Withdrawal Until the end of the Year	5-22
		Continue to Earn RRSP Room	5-22
	7.4	Annuities	5-22
8.0		Developing an Asset Allocation Strategy for Retirement	5-23
9.0		Tax Planning Strategies Available in Retirement	5-24
	9.1	Build a Tax-Effective Portfolio	5-25
	9.2	Tax Loss Selling	5-25
	9.3	File Quarterly Tax Instalments	5-25
	9.4	Work with a Client's Lifetime Tax Bill	5-25
	9.5	Split CPP Benefits	5-26
	9.6	Take Advantage of the Pension Income Tax Credit	5-26
	9.7	Use the Age of a Younger Spouse on the RRIF	5-26
	9.8	Integrate Charitable Giving	5-27
10.0		Strategies to Help Clients Keep More of their OAS	5-27

11.0   Integrating Retirement Planning with Estate Planning 5-29

12.0   Emotional Issues Surrounding Retirement..5-30
        12.1   There Is No "Perfect" Plan 5-30
        12.2   Planning for Mental Incapacity..5-31

13.0   Conclusion 5-31

Chapter 6
Insurance Planning 6-1

1.0   Introduction 6-1

2.0   The Insurance Needs of the High-Net-Worth Client...6-2
        2.1   Small Business Owners...6-2
        2.2   Senior Executives 6-2
        2.3   Professionals 6-3
        2.4   Independently Wealthy Clients 6-3
        2.5   Keeping Insurance Up to Date..6-4

3.0   Personal Insurance for High-Net-Worth Clients 6-4
        3.1   Life Insurance 6-4
        3.2   Critical Illness Insurance...6-4
        3.3   Homeowners' Insurance..6-4
        3.4   Travel Insurance 6-5
        3.5   Marriage Contract Insurance 6-5
        3.6   Annuities 6-5
        3.7   Funeral-Expense Life Insurance...6-6
        3.8   Keeping a Vacation Property in the Family...6-6

4.0   Property and Casualty Insurance for Business 6-9
        4.1   Business Property Losses 6-9
        4.2   Business Income Losses 6-10
        4.3   Business Liability Losses...6-10
                Directors' Liability 6-10
                Environmental Harm and Pollution 6-11
        4.4   Fraud, Criminal Acts, and Employee Dishonesty 6-12
        4.5   Product Recall Liability 6-12
        4.6   Workers' Compensation 6-12
        4.7   Kidnap and Ransom Insurance 6-12
        4.8   Key Person Insurance 6-13
                Multiple-of-Compensation Method..6-14
                Contribution-to-Profits Method..6-14
                Cost-of-Replacement Method..6-14
                Funding Key Person Insurance 6-14
        4.9   Standard Insurance Policies..6-16
                Business Owners' Commercial Package Policy 6-16
                Commercial General Liability Policy 6-16
        4.10   Buy-Sell Agreements 6-17

What Is a Buy-Sell Agreement..6-17
Funding a Buy-Sell Agreement..6-18
Structuring a Buy-Sell Agreement 6-19

5.0   Risk Management and Investments..6-21
    5.1   Segregated Funds 6-22
        How Maturity Guarantees Work...6-22
        Reset Dates...6-23
        Death Benefits 6-23
        The CompCorp Guarantee 6-25
        Creditor Protection..6-26
    5.2   Using Exchange-Traded Options as Insurance 6-27
        Selling the Portfolio..6-28
        Buying Put Options on Individual Stocks...6-28
        Buying Index Put Options 6-29
    5.3   Other Risk Management Options 6-30
        Covered Call Writing...6-30
        Combining a Put Purchase with a Covered Call Sale...................................6-30
        Index Futures Contracts 6-31

Chapter 7
Tax Planning

Tax Planning...7-1

1.0   Introduction 7-1
    1.1   Tax Planning and Customer Relationships...7-2
    1.2   How Much Do You Need to Know About Taxes 7-3

2.0   The Nature of Tax Planning 7-3

3.0   Average and Marginal Tax Rates...7-5

4.0   Tax Planning Strategies 7-7
    4.1   Income Deferral and Spreading...7-7
    4.2   Income Splitting and Attribution 7-8
    4.3   Registered Education Savings Plans (RESPs)...7-10
        Withdrawals from a RESP 7-11
    4.4   In-Trust Accounts...7-12
    4.5   Family Loans at Prescribed Rates 7-13
    4.6   Old Age Security Benefits 7-16
    4.7   The Principal Residence Exemption...7-16
    4.8   Tax Planning for Investment Income 7-17
    4.9   Flow-Through Shares 7-20
    4.10   Stock Option Plans 7-21
        Tax Treatment Prior to February 27, 2000 7-22
        Tax Treatment after February 27, 2000...7-22
        Stock Options Exercised After Employment Ceases....................................7-24
    4.11   Employee Loans 7-24
    4.12   Limited Partnerships 7-25

Tax Considerations of Limited Partnerships 7-26
Tax Filing and Limited Partnerships 7-29
4.13   Business Losses 7-30
Tax Consequences of Business Losses 7-30
Tax Filing Rules and Carry-Over Provisions 7-31
Tax Planning Implications and Methods 7-31
4.14   Trusts 7-32
Tax Consequences of Trusts 7-33
Tax Filing Rules 7-34
Tax Planning and Trusts 7-35

5.0   Taxation and Mutual Funds 7-37
5.1   The Adjusted Cost Base of Mutual Funds 7-37

5.2   Taxation and Churning inside Mutual Funds 7-37

6.0   Inflation and Taxes 7-39

7.0   Pension and Retirement Plans 7-39

8.0   Registered Retirement Savings Plans 7-40
8.1   RRSP Planning Opportunities 7-42
Spousal Spins 7-42
Early, Continuous, and Over-Contributions 7-43
8.2   Why So Few People Contribute to RRSPs 7-44

9.0   Paying Down a Mortgage vs. Contributing to an RRSP 7-46

10.0   Borrowing to Make RRSP Contributions 7-47

11.0   Tax Planning for Small Business Owners 7-47
11.1   Maximizing Deductible Interest and Other Expenses 7-48
11.2   Incorporation and Tax Deferral 7-48
11.3   Salary/Dividend Mix 7-49
11.4   Combined Employment and Business Income 7-49
11.5   Capital Gains Crystallization 7-49
11.6   Estate Freezing and Multiple Capital Gains Exemptions 7-50
11.7   Selling or Buying an Incorporated Business 7-50
11.8   Shifting Expenses Across Time Periods 7-51

Appendix 7.1   The Time Value of Money 7.1-1

Appendix 7.2   Accelerated Versus Gradual RESP Contributions 7.2-1

Appendix 7.3   RRSP Over-Contributions 7.3-1

Appendix 7.4   Paying Down a Mortgage Versus Contributing to an RRSP 7.4-1

Chapter 8
Estate Planning 8-1

1.0   Introduction 8-1

2.0   Approaching Estate Planning Issues With Clients 8-2

3.0   Dying Intestate: The Government's Solution 8-3

4.0   The Will 8-5
      4.1   Assets Covered by a Will and Assets Outside the Estate 8-6
      4.2   Reviewing the Will to Ensure it Meets the Client's Needs 8-6
      4.3   Special Clauses in the Will 8-9
      4.4   The Executor 8-9
                 The Wealth Manager as an Executor 8-10
                 Corporate Executors 8-10
                 The Powers of the Executor 8-11
                 The Legal List 8-12
                 Prudent Investor Standard of Care 8-12
                 Executor Compensation 8-13
      4.5   Appointing Guardians for Minor Beneficiaries 8-13
      4.6   The Common Disaster Clause 8-14
      4.7   Per Stirpes vs. Per Capita 8-14
      4.8   Restrictions on Testamentary Freedom 8-14
      4.9   Amending or Replacing a Will 8-15

5.0   Spousal Rights 8-16
      5.1   Ongoing Spousal or Child Support 8-17
      5.2   Common-Law and Same-Sex Spouses 8-17

6.0   Power of Attorney 8-17

7.0   Probate 8-18
      7.1   Reducing Probate Fees by Gifting Assets 8-19
      7.2   Reducing Probate Fees by Registering Assets as Joint Tenants
           With Rights of Survivorship 8-20
      7.3   Reducing Probate Fees by Naming Beneficiaries on Registered
           Plans and Life Insurance 8-22
      7.4   Reducing Probate Fees by Creating a Trust 8-22

8.0   Estimating the Client's Final Tax Liability 8-23

9.0   Techniques to Defer or Reduce Taxes 8-24
      9.1   Leaving Assets with Unrealized Capital Gains to a Spouse 8-24
      9.2   Naming a Spouse or Common-Law Spouse as Beneficiary on
           RRSPs or RRIFs 8-25
      9.3   Naming Financially Dependent Children as Beneficiaries on
           RRSPs and RRIFs 8-25
      9.4   RRSPs on Marriage Breakdown and Death 8-26
      9.5   Applying All Unused Capital Losses 8-27
      9.6   Life Insurance 8-27

9.7   Spending More before Death..8-27

9.8   Estate Freeze 8-27

9.9   Farm Properties 8-28

9.10   Falling Market Values after Death 8-28

10.0   Appropriate Use of Trusts 8-29

      10.1   Type of Trusts..8-29

                The Inter Vivos Trust 8-30

                The Testamentary Trust 8-31

                Spousal Trusts...8-31

      10.2   The Trust Agreement..8-32

      10.3   The Role of the Trustee 8-33

11.0   Segregated Funds..8-33

      11.1   Market Value at Death Greater than Original Investment.............8-34

      11.2   Market Value at Death Less than the Guaranteed Amount 8-34

12.0   Charitable Gifts 8-35

      12.1   Rules Regarding Charitable Donations...8-35

      12.2   Making Effective Charitable Gifts..8-35

      12.3   A Bequest in the Will..8-36

      12.4   Leaving a RRSP/RRIF to Charity..8-36

      12.5   In-Kind Donations 8-37

      12.6   Life Insurance 8-38

      12.7   The Charitable Remainder Trust...8-38

      12.8   Gifts of Cultural Property 8-39

13.0   Dealing with a Cottage or Family Business..8-39

      13.1   The Family Cottage 8-40

      13.2   A Family Business 8-40

14.0   Assessing Family Needs, Priorities, and Estate Planning Goals 8-41

15.0   Building The Estate Planning Team..8-42

      15.1   The Family 8-42

      15.2   The Lawyer 8-42

      15.3   The Accountant...8-42

      15.4   The Business Valuator..8-43

      15.5   Estate Appraiser 8-43

      15.6   Funeral Director 8-43

      15.7   The Gift Planner...8-43

      15.8   The Grief Counsellor..8-43

Section III
Investment and Portfolio Management

Chapter 9
Risk and Return 9-1

1.0	Introduction	9-1
2.0	Measuring Returns	9-2
3.0	Measuring Risks	9-3
4.0	Measuring Single-Security Returns	9-5
5.0	Measuring Single-Security Risk	9-7
6.0	Measuring Portfolio Returns	9-8
6.1	Covariance	9-9
6.2	Diversification	9-12
6.3	Efficient Portfolios	9-14
6.4	Evaluating Diversification	9-15

Chapter 10
Asset Allocation 10-1

1.0	Introduction	10-1
2.0	Strategic, Dynamic and Tactical Asset Allocation	10-2
3.0	Asset Classes	10-3
4.0	Strategic Asset Allocation	10-4
4.1	Identify the Investment Opportunity Set	10-5
4.2	Determine the Appropriate Investment Management Style	10-5
4.3	Develop Capital Market Expectations for the Asset Classes in the Portfolio	10-5
4.4	Develop Long-Term Asset Mixes	10-6
5.0	Dynamic Asset Allocation	10-6
6.0	Tactical Asset Allocation	10-7
7.0	The Efficient Market Hypothesis	10-7
8.0	Asset Mix Ranges for Different Portfolios	10-9
9.0	Taxes, Inflation, and Other Expenses	10-9
10.0	Client Needs	10-11

Chapter 11

Basic Managed Products

Basic Managed Products 11-1

1.0   Introduction 11-1

2.0   Investment Funds...11-2

3.0   Mutual Funds 11-2

        3.1   Structure of a Mutual Funds 11-3

                Mutual Fund Corporations 11-3

                Mutual Fund Trusts..11-4

                Corporations, Trusts, and Tax Efficiency...............................11-4

4.0   Types of Mutual Funds...11-5

        4.1   Cash and Equivalent Funds..11-5

                Canadian Money Market...11-6

                Foreign Money Market...11-7

        4.2   Fixed-Income Funds...11-8

                Canadian Bonds 11-8

                High-Yield Bonds 11-8

                Canadian Short-Term Bonds 11-8

                Canadian Mortgages 11-8

                Foreign Bonds 11-9

        4.3   Balanced Funds..11-9

                Canadian Balanced 11-9

                Global Balanced and Asset Allocation...................................11-9

                Canadian Tactical Asset Allocation 11-9

                Canadian High-Income Balanced 11-9

        4.4   Equity Funds 11-9

                Canadian Diversified Equity...11-10

                Canadian Large-Cap Equity 11-10

                Canadian Dividend 11-10

                Canadian Small-/Mid-Cap Equity..11-10

                U.S. Small and Mid-Cap Equity 11-10

                North American Equity 11-10

                International Equity 11-11

                European Equity 11-11

                Japanese Equity 11-11

                Asia ex-Japan Equity...11-11

                Asia/Pacific Rim Equity..11-11

                Emerging Markets Equity..11-11

                Latin American Equity 11-12

                Global Equity 11-12

        4.5   Sector Funds 11-12

                Country-Specific Equity 11-12

                Science and Technology...11-12

                Natural Resources...11-12

                Precious Metals 11-13

		Real Estate	11-13
		Specialty	11-13
		Miscellaneous	11-13
	4.6	Portfolio Funds	11-13
		Multi-Class Funds	11-14
		Funds of Funds	11-14
5.0		Mutual Fund Styles	11-15
	5.1	Active Funds	11-15
	5.2	Passive Funds	11-15
		Index Funds	11-16
		Index Funds Using Derivatives	11-16
		Active Index Funds	11-17
6.0		Closed-End Funds	11-18
7.0		Index Participation Units	11-19
	7.1	Canadian IPUs	11-19
	7.2	U.S. IPUs	11-20
	7.3	Global IPUs	11-21
8.0		Index-Linked GICs	11-22
9.0		Royalty and Income Trusts	11-23
	9.1	Royalty Trusts	11-23
		Cash-on-Cash Yield	11-23
		Reserve Life Index	11-24
		Other Factors Affecting Values	11-24
		Tax Consequences	11-25
	9.2	Income Trusts	11-25
10.0		Real Estate Investment Trusts	11-26
11.0		Segregated/Protected Funds	11-27

Chapter 12
Managed Products for the High-Net-Worth Client 12-1

1.0		Introduction	12-1
2.0		Separately Managed Portfolios	12-2
	2.1	Tax Advantages	12-2
	2.2	Separately Managed Account Fees	12-2
3.0		Pooled Funds	12-3
	3.1	Structure of Pooled Funds	12-3
	3.2	Portfolios of Pooled Funds	12-3
4.0		Wrap Accounts	12-4
	4.1	Advantages of Wrap Accounts	12-5
	4.2	Potential Disadvantages of Wrap Accounts	12-6

    4.3   Wrap Accounts for Active Traders 12-7

5.0   Hedge Funds 12-7
    5.1   True Hedge Funds 12-8
            Jones Model Funds 12-8
            Arbitrage Funds 12-9
            Macro Funds 12-9
    5.2   Nominal Hedge Funds 12-10
    5.3   Due Diligence on Hedge Fund Managers 12-10

6.0   Private Equity Investments 12-11

7.0   Managed Futures 12-11
    7.1   Managed Futures Fund 12-12
    7.2   Individual Managed Accounts 12-13
    7.3   Futures Linked Notes 12-13

Chapter 13
Performance Appraisal 13-1

1.0   Introduction 13-1

2.0   Performance Measurement 13-2
    2.1   Time-Weighted Returns 13-3
    2.2   Adjusting for Risk 13-3
    2.3   Management Fees and Expenses 13-4
    2.4   Operating Expenses and the MER 13-5

3.0   Performance Evaluation 13-6
    3.1   Benchmarks 13-6
            Composite Market Indexes 13-6
            Normal Portfolios 13-8
            Generic Investment Style Indexes 13-8
    3.2   Active and Passive Management 13-8
            Active Management 13-9
            Passive Management 13-9
    3.3   Cash Balances 13-10
    3.4   Diversification 13-10
    3.5   Performance Attribution Analysis 13-11
    3.6   Survivorship Bias 13-12
    3.7   Other Considerations 13-12
            Consistency of Performance 13-12
            Compatibility with Client's Portfolio Strategy and Objectives 13-13
    3.8   A Few Words of Caution 13-13

4.0   Mutual Fund Performance 13-14

Chapter 14
Formalizing and Implementing the Investment Plan..14-1

1.0	Introduction	14-1
2.0	Investment Policy Statement..	14-2
3.0	Choosing an Investment Firm	14-6
3.1	Step One: Define Your Client's Needs.............................	14-6
3.2	Step Two: Compile a Long List of Providers.....................	14-7
3.3	Step Three: Select a Short List for Further Investigation	14-7
4.0	Buying and Selling Individual Securities	14-7
5.0	Discretionary Investment Management............................	14-8
5.1	Investment Dealers..	14-8
5.2	Money Managers (Investment Counsellors)	14-8
5.3	Trust Companies	14-9
6.0	Mutual Funds	14-9
6.1	Advisor-Sold Funds (Commissioned)	14-10
	Acquisition Fees (Front-End Load)	14-11
	Redemption Fees (Back-End Load or Deferred Sales Charge)	14-12
	Trailer Fees..	14-12
	Distributor Incentives	14-13
6.2	Direct-Sales Funds (No-Load)	14-13
7.0	Evaluating Investment Firms That Offer Managed products...	14-14
7.1	Ownership..	14-15
7.2	Revenue	14-15
7.3	Growth Record..	14-15
7.4	Management and Staff Turnover	14-15
7.5	Staff Remuneration	14-16
8.0	When to Change Investment Firms.................................	14-16
8.1	Inability to Meet Stated Objectives	14-16
8.2	Turnover in Key Staff...	14-16
8.3	Changes in Written Reporting Packages	14-17
8.4	Change in Level of Service..	14-17
8.5	Changes in Trading Activity	14-17
8.6	Change in Investment Style...	14-17
8.7	Increased Frequency of Billings.....................................	14-17

Section IV

Practice Management

Chapter 15
Market Research and Business Planning 15-1

1.0   Introduction 15-1

2.0   Demographics, Trends, and Consumer Behaviour 15-1
    2.1   Understanding the High-Net-Worth Market 15-2
    2.2   Demographics Relating to the High-Net-Worth Market 15-3
    2.3   Consumer Behaviour 15-7
    2.4   Women in Perspective 15-9

3.0   Information Sources 15-10
    3.1   Internet 15-10
    3.2   Libraries 15-10
    3.3   Chambers of Commerce or Boards of Trade 15-10
    3.4   Universities and Colleges 15-10
    3.5   Municipal and Provincial Governments 15-10
    3.6   Suppliers 15-11
    3.7   Competitors 15-11
    3.8   Employees 15-11
    3.9   Consulting Firms 15-11
    3.10   Clients 15-11
    3.11   The Value of Information 15-12

4.0   Competitive Intelligence 15-13

5.0   Business Planning 15-14
    5.1   Defining Objectives 15-14
    5.2   Components of a Business Plan 15-15
    5.3   Ongoing Business Planning 15-17

Your Key Objectives 15-18

Appendix 15.1   Client Feedback Questionnaire 15.1-1

Chapter 16
Marketing Your Wealth Management Business 16-1

1.0   Introduction 16-1

2.0   Marketing Plan Checklist 16-2

3.0   Defining Your Target Market 16-2
    3.1   Targeting by Occupation 16-2
    3.2   Targeting by Outside Pursuits 16-3
    3.3   Targeting by Location 16-4

3.4	Building a Network of Professionals		16-4
3.5	How to Business Turn Down		16-4
4.0	Value Propositions		16-5
4.1	The Wealth Management Plan		16-5
4.2	Adding Value – Going the Extra Mile		16-6
4.3	Gaining a Competitive Edge		16-6
		Quality	16-7
		Speed	16-7
		Flexibility	16-7
		Competitive Pricing	16-7
		Personal Service	16-7
		Specialization	16-8
		Innovation	16-8
5.0	Fee Structures		16-9
5.1	Establishing Fees		16-9
6.0	Promotional Plan		16-10
6.1	Advertising		16-10
6.2	Public Relations		16-11
6.3	Seminars and Workshops		16-11
6.4	Sales Promotions		16-11
6.5	Newsletters		16-11
6.6	Prospecting		16-12
		Client Referrals	16-12
		Cold Calling	16-13
		Direct Mail	16-14
6.7	Keeping Clients		16-14
7.0	Marketing Plan Update		16-14

Appendix A
Future and Present Value Tables
....Appendix A-1

Section V

Integrated - Case Study

James & Laura Parker.. Case Study-1

INTRODUCTION

1.0 A New Profession

In the financial services industry today, some clients have more complex investment and financial planning needs, as well as higher expectations, than others. They may also have a higher net worth than the average Canadian, or be on their way to becoming wealthy. The wealth manager is a trained, experienced professional who can provide comprehensive, integrated wealth management services to meet the needs of these clients.

In the 1980s, the role of the comprehensive wealth manager did not exist. Clients had to go to different people and different financial institutions to meet their investment, insurance, trust and banking needs. Today, clients can expect to have all their financial needs met by one wealth manager who can coordinate and implement a strategy to meet their financial objectives. This is possible because of changing regulations and the fact that many financial institutions are focusing on wealth management. Wealth managers may work for investment dealers, banks, financial planning firms, insurance companies or investment counselling firms. They may also run their own businesses.

As a wealth manager, you will be the primary, if not the only, financial professional your clients deal with in the highly competitive financial services marketplace. This means you must assume a higher level of responsibility. You will need considerable expertise and insight. As the primary advisor, you will be responsible for technical analysis and strategic planning to achieve your clients' goals. This includes identifying and assessing their needs and helping them make sound financial decisions. Having the primary relationship also means you have the responsibility of not just meeting your clients' expectations, but exceeding them.

There are many challenges you will have to meet while building and running a wealth management business. Not all potential clients will see the value in your services or be willing to pay for them. Some people simply want someone to carry out transactions without providing advice, and will take their commission-based business to the lowest-cost provider. However, many people want to work with a highly qualified financial professional who can offer advice and recommendations. You must provide your clients with the guidance they need for their individual situations and possibly for succeeding generations of the family as well.

2.0   The Role of the Wealth Manager

What is wealth management? Although the term is not clearly defined within the financial services industry, from the client's perspective, the position integrates two key components of financial services:

- the ability to deal with complex financial planning issues;
- skills related to investment and portfolio management.

The wealth manager is generally compensated through fees based on the value of the assets being managed.

To fully manage an investment portfolio, you must address your clients' non-investment needs. In preserving and enhancing your clients' wealth, you must integrate retirement, tax, insurance, and estate planning into the investment management process. To do this, you must often coordinate a team of lawyers, accountants, and investment managers to identify tax-saving opportunities, establish family, lifestyle, and specialty trusts, and carry out professional money management.

The role of wealth manager is becoming more critical as the affluent population increases and high-net-worth individuals have more choice in all aspects of managing their wealth. According to industry estimates, the wealth of the world's very high-net-worth clients (those with financial assets exceeding $1 million) will grow by more than 50% between 1999 and 2003, to $32.7 trillion.

Wealthy and potentially wealthy clients today need strong advisors more than ever to help them negotiate the increased range of product, service, and provider choices available and to deal with complex financial planning issues. Today's wealth managers need to offer the best solution to their customers. The value, in part, of wealth managers, depends on their ability to coach and advise, bringing in experts where appropriate.

3.0 The Wealth Management Techniques Course

The Wealth Management Techniques (WMT) course builds on the basic financial planning issues dealt with in the Professional Financial Planning course. The WMT course takes you through more complex financial planning topics and also deals in more depth with investment and portfolio management. Through a case study, the course then integrates these two key components of wealth management.

In addition to hard skills, the course also gives you practical information on dealing with and understanding clients, as well as guidance on how to ensure that your wealth management business succeeds.

This course provides you with technical information, but it is not designed to give you the technical expertise of professionals in a specialized field. For example, the chapter on tax planning is designed to deepen your knowledge and understanding of some complex tax situations, but your clients will still need to deal with accountants on occasion. Similarly, the estate planning discussion will enhance your knowledge of estate planning, but your clients will still need to consult a lawyer/notary to draw up documents and get legal advice.

Some of the material in the course may be familiar to you. If so, we hope it is provided in such a way that you will see new connections and opportunities for serving your clients and taking your practice to the next level.

The course is divided up into five sections.

Section 1   The Wealth Management Process and Dealing With the Client

Clients with complex financial planning issues require a wealth manager with well-developed communication skills with whom they can establish and maintain a solid relationship. You will learn the skills you need to deal with clients who have higher net worth and/or complex financial planning needs through the stages of information gathering, ongoing communication, and education.

It is important for you to understand that although clients seek out wealth managers who are technically competent in the investment and financial planning areas, it's not enough to "know your stuff." You have to able to communicate it effectively.

This section describes the entire relationship you have with your clients, the process of gathering information and communicating with clients, as well as your ethical responsibilities toward your clients and others.

Section II   Advanced Financial Planning

As you build an investment policy statement for your clients, you must take into consideration your clients' financial planning needs. This section begins with retirement planning, from determining your clients' future needs in retirement to financial management during their retirement. It also includes a discussion of different types of insurance appropriate to the needs of high-net-worth clients, an overview of tax planning, and a chapter on estate planning.

Section III   Investment and Portfolio Management

Once you understand your clients' financial planning needs, you are ready to formulate an asset allocation strategy that will reduce unnecessary risk and offer the potential to earn the rates of return your clients need to achieve their financial goals. This section covers risk and return, asset allocation, the types of mutual fund products available, and managed products specifically designed for high-net-worth investors. Since, in order to choose a particular managed product for a client, you must be able to measure and evaluate the performance of the product, this section also includes a chapter on performance measurement and performance evaluation.

Along with a financial plan, your primary deliverable to a client is an investment policy statement (IPS). The IPS articulates the client's investment and non-investment goals and objectives, risk tolerance, and long-term strategy and establishes the guidelines for implementing and monitoring the plan. The final chapter in this section discusses the importance of the investment policy statement, what it should include, and what its objectives are, as well as information on choosing suitable managed products and their providers.

Section IV   Practice Management

This section of the course focuses on the skills needed to manage a wealth management practice, from carrying out market research, competitive intelligence, and business planning, to marketing and gaining a competitive edge.

Section V   Case Study

As a wealth manager, you must be a problem-solver and solution-provider for your clients. The last section of the course describes a specific case, designed to bring together the skills involved in dealing with clients, advanced financial planning, and portfolio management.

When you have worked through the case study and reached the end of the course, you will have the technical knowledge you need to recognize and address the more complex issues you will come across in your wealth management business.

4.0   Financial Management Advisor

Successful completion of this course and its prerequisites lead to the Financial Management Advisor (FMA) designation, which is the mark of a professional wealth manager who has demonstrated the proficiency needed to deal with complex client investment and financial planning issues.

We wish you well with the course.

Section I

The Wealth Management Process and Dealing with the Client

Although wealth managers must have strong technical compentence in the areas of financial planning and investment and portfolio management, that alone is not good enough. Wealth managers must be able to communicate their skills effectively. It is often an advisor's communication skills which will give him or her an edge on the competition.

In this section you will learn the skills you need to deal with clients who have higher net worth and/or complex financial planning needs through the stages of information gathering, ongoing communication, and education.

CHAPTER 1

The Wealth Management Process

1.0   Introduction

Wealth management is a continuous loop that involves relationship building, information gathering, formulating a plan that includes both investment and portfolio management and advanced financial planning considerations, implementation of the plan, reporting, reviewing, and re-balancing.

Primary Learning Objectives

By the end of this chapter, you should understand:

- **each step in the wealth management process;**

- **the significance of each step in the process.**

Schematically the wealth management process looks like this:

Figure 1.1 The Wealth Management Process

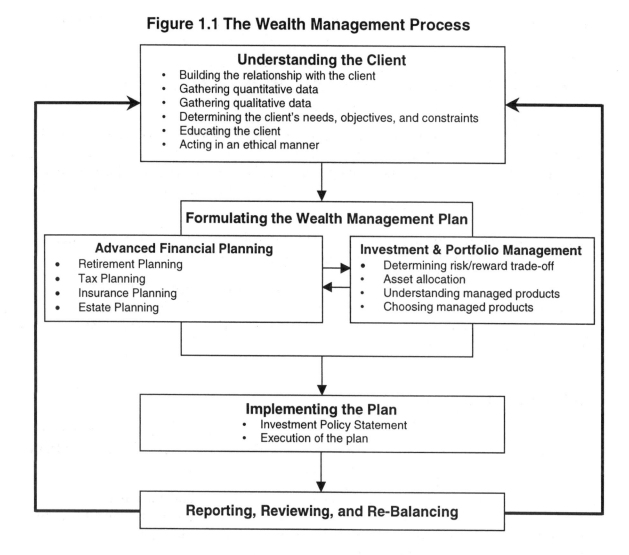

2.0   Understanding the High-Net-Worth Client

The wealth management process starts with the establishment of a strong relationship with the client, built on trust. Although as a wealth manager, your primary role may involve providing advice on investments, insurance, taxes, and other financial matters, you must never lose sight of the client's needs, goals, and constraints. You must find out the advanced suitability requirements of the client. This means going beyond what is recorded on the Know Your Client forms and getting a sense of the client's most closely held financial aspirations and attitudes.

Money brings out the emotions of anxiety, security, pride, satisfaction, fear, anger, loss, guilt, joy, hope, greed, lust, and sorrow in people. These emotions affect the wealthy man who inherited money from his father and the self-made woman who has earned every penny from her hard work, independence, and tolerance for risk. It is your job to help clients articulate these emotions and build a financial strategy to keep them under control.

Although you must be competent when it comes to managing wealth, including skills in investments and insurance, technical knowledge is often secondary to interpersonal skills for really successful wealth management.

Chapter 2 of this text discusses the importance of understanding a client and describes the various types of wealthy investors and how their motivations, needs, and expectations may differ. It also looks at the high-net-worth client from the perspective of personality types and emphasizes the importance of asking the right questions and listening for what the client leaves unsaid.

Chapter 3 emphasizes the importance of client education, particularly in understanding the risks associated with investments, including market, interest rate, and political risk.

Chapter 4 focuses on the ethical skills of wealth management, including a detailed examination of a wealth manager's responsibilities to clients and other morally significant parties, including professional colleagues, the investment industry, and the general public.

3.0 Formulating the Plan

Once a client has articulated his or her needs, objectives, and constraints, you can begin the process of formulating a plan. The plan sets out the steps that will take the client from where he or she is financially at present to where he or she wants to be.

The plan will draw on your knowledge and experience in investment and portfolio management and advanced financial planning. These are not separate steps in the wealth management process. Investment decisions affect the financial plan, and financial planning objectives influence the investment plan.

For example, suppose a client wants to maximize the after-tax income she receives in retirement and ensure there is no additional tax payable when she dies. You would need to implement a portfolio with an asset allocation mix that would minimize the risk for the particular level of return she needs. She would have to consider various personal tax planning strategies and decide where best to place her investments. She would also need to plan the timing of her withdrawals from the registered and non-registered accounts. While she is still saving for retirement, she would need to ensure that a disability or serious illness would not adversely affect her retirement plans.

3.1   Advanced Financial Planning

Wealth managers may have clients with complex retirement, insurance, tax, and estate planning needs. These clients may have a high net worth, or be on their way to becoming wealthy. Many clients are too busy to deal with these issues. They may also face unique situations that require you to come up with creative solutions.

The four pillars of advanced financial planning that are covered in Chapters 5 to 8 are:

- retirement planning;

- risk management and insurance;

- tax planning;

- estate planning.

Retirement Planning

Fewer than 45% of Canadians are currently members of a company pension plan. The rest are responsible for securing their own retirement. Retirement planning is a comprehensive process for determining how much money clients need when they retire. It is an essential part of any financial plan. Retirement planning also helps clients identify the best ways to save for retirement, given their financial situation.

Chapter 5 looks at the three phases of retirement planning: pre-retirement planning, preparing for retirement, and post-retirement financial management.

Risk Management and Insurance

The high-net-worth client may be a small business owner, a senior executive, a professional, or an independently wealthy person. Insurance allows them to be prepared for surprises and some inevitable expenses.

Chapter 6 describes various wealth preservation strategies using insurance products. These include personal forms of insurance, such as homeowner's insurance, and business insurance, including insurance against fraud, criminal acts, and international business losses. It also includes information on the protection of portfolios using derivatives, such as options contracts.

Tax Planning

You can better help your clients if you treat taxes as a controllable expense, and compare investment products on an after-tax basis.

For example, a client might insist on not cashing a Guaranteed Investment Certificate (GIC) while requesting a personal loan for non-investment purposes. On an after-tax basis, such a strategy is expensive, since interest income on the GIC is fully taxable, whereas interest expense on the personal loan is not tax-deductible (since it is not incurred to earn investment income). You can bring to your client's attention the cost (in terms of after-tax cash flows) of this strategy.

Chapter 7 provides an overview of the nature of tax planning, describes the major categories of tax planning, and explains the specific steps required in implementing some common tax planning decisions faced by taxpaying investors.

Estate Planning

From your clients' perspective, estate planning means making the most of what they have earned over their lifetime so that their beneficiaries receive the maximum allowed by law, without delay or unnecessary fees and taxes.

Since assets that a client spends during retirement, and assets that are transferred to heirs both come from the client's accumulated wealth, estate planning and retirement planning are closely linked. Estate and retirement planning should be done concurrently.

It is not necessary to become a specialist in estate planning, but you should be able to identify opportunities for your clients, help them solve problems before they occur, and make any necessary referrals to the appropriate tax and legal experts.

Chapter 8 describes the essential estate planning documents, ways to minimize the fees and expenses involved when a person dies, and advanced estate planning strategies involving trusts and charitable donations.

3.2 Investment and Portfolio Management

Once you understand your clients' financial planning needs, you are ready to start formulating an asset allocation strategy that will reduce unnecessary risk and offer the potential rates of returns your clients need to achieve their financial goals.

Portfolio management, which is covered in Chapters 9 through 14, encompasses five main subject areas:

- risk and return;

- asset allocation;

- knowledge of available managed products;

- performance appraisal;

- formalization and implementation.

Risk and Return

A client's investment objectives can be broken down into four types of return:

- capital growth;

- income generation;

- capital preservation;

- inflation protection.

You, as a wealth manager, must understand your clients' tolerance for risk. A questionnaire similar to the one in the appendix to Chapter 2 can be very helpful in getting clients to articulate their risk tolerance. You also need to know about constraints that may influence the composition of a portfolio. Examples of constraints include:

- liquidity—the need to convert investments into cash quickly and without loss of value;

- time limits—the period of time before money in the investment portfolio needs to be withdrawn (for example, five years is considered a short time horizon);

- family situations—for example, health care for an elderly member of the family, or education costs for a child.

Chapter 9 discusses risk and return and the appropriate trade-off between the two that may best suit a particular client.

Asset Allocation

Once you have a good sense of your client's needs, objectives, and constraints, you can create an investment plan. Probably the most important part of this plan is the asset allocation program. Research indicates that asset allocation may be responsible for as much as 90% of the returns generated by a portfolio. Asset categories are generally broken down as follows:

- cash and equivalents;

- bonds, mortgages, and preferreds;

- foreign currency bonds;

- Canadian equities;

- U.S. and other international equities;

- hard assets, such as real estate or gold.

Chapter 10 discusses asset allocation in detail, focusing on strategic, dynamic, and tactical asset allocation.

- Strategic asset allocation means choosing the target mix of assets among the various asset categories.

- Dynamic asset allocation refers to re-balancing the actual mix to return the portfolio to the target mix.

- Tactical asset allocation involves adjusting the target mix based on the manager's current view of the market.

Understanding Managed Products

Over the past ten years, as more and more Canadians have accumulated liquid assets, managed investment products have proliferated, the most popular being mutual funds. According to the Investment Funds Institute of Canada (IFIC), which includes more than 95% of the mutual fund dealers in Canada as its members, at the end of January 2000, the total of assets under management in IFIC-member mutual funds was $382.7 billion divided among approximately 2,000 funds. This compares with $20.3 billion in 1987 and $114.6 billion in 1993.

After becoming familiar with the benefits of professional management through mutual funds and other investment funds, many investors have turned to other managed products, including segregated funds, realty and income funds, index participation units, hedge funds, wrap accounts, pooled funds, and separately managed accounts. Chapter 11 describes basic managed products such as mutual funds, and Chapter 12 focuses on managed products geared toward the high-net-worth client, such as separately managed products and hedge funds.

Measuring and Evaluating Managed Products

Once you have made the asset allocation decision, you must choose a specific managed product. This decision will be based mostly on past returns and the risk level of available products. You must compare these results with equivalent figures for benchmark managed products to establish whether or not the portfolio is producing satisfactory results.

Consistency of performance, year in and year out, is important. Portfolio appraisal involves performance measurement and performance evaluation.

- Performance measurement involves calculating the return achieved by a single portfolio manager over certain time period. Four types of transactions are measured— purchases, sales, income, and distribution. Although measuring return sounds relatively straightforward, it can sometimes be complicated.

- Performance evaluation is an appraisal of how well a managed portfolio has done over the evaluation period in relation to the cost of management. It is both expensive and time-consuming to analyze and select securities for a portfolio, so the portfolio's sponsor must determine whether the investment performance justifies the cost of the service.

Together, performance measurement and evaluation provide a cost-benefit analysis of a managed product. Performance appraisal, which also includes consideration of the managed product's investment process and personnel, is covered in Chapter 13.

Once a decision is made with respect to a particular managed product, you must decide where to buy the product. Managed products are available from investment dealers, investment counsellors, banks, and trust and mutual fund companies.

4.0   Formalizing and Implementing the Plan

Once you have formulated a wealth management plan, it must be formalized into a written document. It may actually be two documents, one a financial plan and the other an investment plan, or the financial plan may be incorporated into the investment plan, which is then known as an investment policy statement. The length of the document will vary with the complexity of a client's individual situation. Whether it is one or two documents, the items that should be included are:

1. Introduction;

2. Goals;

3. Plan summary;

4. Assets available to reach goals;

5. Assets required to reach goals;

6. Any gaps between the two;

7. Insurance plans;

8. Health, elder care, and incapacity plans;

9. Estate plans;

10. Target rates of return;

11. Limits on risk;

12. Investment constraints;

13. Asset allocation plan;

14. Managed product selection;

15. Implementation instructions;

16. Criteria for reviewing and evaluating managed product performance.

A wealth management plan is valuable only if the recommendations are acted upon. However, the decision to implement, modify, or reject the recommendations in the plan remains the sole responsibility of the client. He or she may ask for your help in implementing the recommendations, including coordinating with other professionals.

It is usually a good idea to set up an appointment with the client to discuss the plan and to send the plan to an existing client about a week before the date of the appointment. This gives the client plenty of time to review it and come to the appointment fully prepared with questions and comments.

Implementing the plan may take several months or even years. You must ensure that the client has full, true, and plain disclosure of all pertinent facts related to the plan.

Chapter 14 describes the investment policy statement and discusses the different types of managed product providers from investment counsellors to mutual fund companies to investment dealers. The chapter looks at the services they provide and how they charge for services.

5.0   Monitoring and Re-Balancing

Monitoring the plan is an ongoing process. You must evaluate the performance of the plan by analyzing how closely it meets your client's objectives. You must also be aware of changes in the client's personal situation and economic conditions, as these may warrant revision of the plan.

The investment policy statement should include a process for ensuring adherence to investment policy and monitoring the effectiveness of the policy. For example, it could require a monthly portfolio report, and specify criteria against which each fund manager or managed product is to be evaluated.

CHAPTER 2

Understanding the Client

1. Introduction

A wealth manager can do far more than just manage the financial affairs of clients and provide advice to help them achieve their financial goals. A client may ask you for a combination of services, some of which go beyond providing investment advice or financial planning. Some clients need you to provide a financial framework for their lives. For these clients, no decision is too big or too small to be undertaken without advice from their wealth manager. Others will see you as a confidant. Still others will see you as someone off whom they can bounce new ideas.

Just as companies employ a Chief Financial Officer to coordinate and execute their financial strategies, individuals and families may rely on a wealth manager to act as CFO for their personal finances. Therefore, you must understand your clients' motivations. Sometimes you will have to dig deep to find them, because they may not be readily apparent. Once you understand your clients, you can help them articulate their needs, objectives, and constraints and start to build a financial strategy. Of course, you must constantly encourage clients to re-examine their needs and objectives in the context of their evolving business and personal lives.

Primary Learning Objectives

By the end of this chapter you should understand:

- **the classifications of wealthy investors and how their motivations, needs, and expectations may differ;**

- **the nine types of high-net-worth personalities;**

- **the importance of listening to clients;**

- **the types of questions you should ask your clients.**

2.0 Different Types of High-End Client

High-net-worth clients come in all types, some of them more predictable than others. Owner/managers, entrepreneurs, corporate executives, and other family members all have different expectations, attitudes, and needs. So do people who inherit wealth or individuals who receive a large sum of money in a divorce settlement.

How individuals accumulate their wealth affects their financial approach. As a wealth manager, you must appreciate the differences between an individual whose personal goals are inseparable from his or her business goals and an individual who maintains a strict separation between his or her private life and work life.

Many clients expect you to provide far more than investment advice or financial planning. In many cases, they have already made up their minds about investing and planning for the future (although their decisions may need re-examining). They want you to help them manage their financial programs in detail, clarify their financial goals, and help them achieve those goals. In the process, you must be prepared to question decisions they have made and further their understanding of the contribution made by each element of a financial strategy to their well-being and that of their families.

In making decisions about a client's financial well-being, you cannot make assumptions about the client's expectations. You must ensure that these expectations have been clearly articulated before you present a course of action. You must also know how to present ideas in a way that will make sense to your clients. The following is a list of the different types of clients that you will encounter as a wealth manager.

2.1   The Owner/Manager

Owner/managers may buy or inherit a business and feel happy just letting it operate as it did before they came along. They may know how to manage the business, but may not care if it gets bigger. Nor may they be looking for opportunities to expand or start a spin-off venture.

Owner/managers may approach decision-making cautiously. They evaluate every opportunity before choosing one, and make a clear distinction between their business and personal lives. Nevertheless, the financial decisions they make about their businesses determine their ability to meet personal objectives. Although they are often guided by personal goals when they make decisions about the business, they may place a higher priority on their achievements within the context of their chosen industry than they do upon status or social class membership.

In helping owner/managers determine their personal goals, you may also be helping them run the business more effectively. Although owner/managers often make good clients, only a few sales professionals are proficient at selling to affluent business owners.[1]

2.2   The Entrepreneur

Entrepreneurs will form the fastest-growing segment of high-net-worth Canadians over the next two decades.

For an entrepreneur, the distinction between personal and business finances is arbitrary and possibly even misleading. In deciding to start a business, an entrepreneur makes an intensely personal decision. Many factors influence that decision, and few of them have anything to do with business. Entrepreneurs bring to bear the full force of their personalities to the business. As much as any other attributes, the founder's personality distinguishes one entrepreneurial business from another.

Entrepreneurs' primary personal investment is their own business. Nevertheless, they recognize the need for financial security, especially as their families grow.

"What does someone who has made himself rich expect from his financial advisor?" asks Bob Pennington, Vice-Chairman and President of Capital Guardian Trust in New York. "He is searching for individuals supported by organizations to assist him in facilitating and maintaining his wealth; someone as smart as or smarter than he is; a leader. He is searching for someone he can trust, not only on his own behalf but on behalf of his family as well."

Of all new businesses started every year, at least half are started by entrepreneurs who have failed at least once before in another business, according to some estimates. These people learn from their experience, persevere, and start again. "I regard what some people term a failure as a lesson," says Ron Foxcroft, President of Fortron International Inc. in Hamilton, Ontario. "There's no such thing as failure in my eyes."

According to Professor David McClelland of Harvard and Prof. John Atkinson of the University of Michigan, entrepreneurs are motivated by three main needs:

1. the need for achievement: they strive toward self-defined goals and look for indications of success or failure along the way;

2. the need for power;

3. the need for affiliation: they want to build warm relationships with other people and enjoy mutual friendships.

---

[1]   Dr. Thomas J. Stanley, *Selling to the Affluent: The Professional's Guide to Closing the Sales that Count*, McGraw-Hill, 1997.

Contrary to conventional thinking, entrepreneurs often feel isolated and lonely. Your job as a financial advisor to an entrepreneur may include providing solace in difficult times. "There are a lot of moments when entrepreneurs question whether or not they can do it," says Michael Grenier, President of Star Data Systems in Markham, Ontario. "It's the feeling of laying everything on the line." Entrepreneurs cherish anything that helps boost their spirits during critical times, he says.

2.3   The Corporate Executive

Corporate executives must put aside their personal likes and dislikes for the sake of the organization. They need to know how to delegate responsibility and ensure that the people around them live up to their expectations.

Corporate executives who spend time making business decisions using detailed economic and political analysis may not need a wealth manager to explain the opportunities of investing in Brazil. But they may need help managing the family finances, since they have so little time to do it themselves.

Executives may feel tempted to take a risk, to prove their entrepreneurial mettle. Often your job will involve tempering their enthusiasm for risk with their—and their families'—need for security.

Pension plans, bonuses, and stock options may form a large part of an executive's wealth. In many cases, this wealth is not readily accessible. The discretionary wealth that they accumulate may, in many cases, be managed by a spouse.

2.4   Spouses and Other Family Members

Also called multigenerational planning, providing financial advice to spouses and family members has become a mainstay for some financial advisors. "The only way to help a family, and really make the help stick, is to counsel the whole family—all of its living generations," says author Nick Murray in his book *The Excellent Investment Advisor*.[2] Otherwise, "either the account gets lost, or the message gets lost, or both do."

Some high-net-worth individuals do not have time to pay much attention to their personal financial lives. They delegate much of the responsibility to their spouses. Like a corporate vice-president, the spouse makes the decisions and reports to the overworked and under-involved partner on the results. That's why it is essential to involve the whole family in developing and monitoring a financial strategy.

Murray takes an all-or-nothing approach to multigenerational counselling. "Counsel the whole family, or don't counsel anybody," he says. "Don't take a piece of the account and hope the plan you make will stick." Murray holds a family conference to develop and

---

[2]   Nick Murray, *The Excellent Investment Advisor,* The Nick Murray Company Inc., 1996.

execute a financial plan that takes each member into consideration. At regularly scheduled family financial conferences, he identifies sources of potential conflict that may affect the plan's success.

"I can save myself a lot of time, and save these people a lot of time and grief, by saying at the outset: 'I want to make a plan that works for everybody in the family or I will walk into the sunset,'" says Murray. "You may not get the outcome you were looking for, but you know exactly where you stand—and in many cases, you know just how fast you want to get out of there."

Despite some financial advisors' efforts to counsel entire families, a 1997 Trimark Mutual Funds/Environics Research Group poll revealed that only 3% of people between 35 and 55 use the same financial advisor as their parents.

2.5   The Invisible Wealthy

Most individuals build their wealth with their own hands through hard work, determination, and passion. They don't inherit their wealth, acquire it through marriage, or even win it in a lottery.

In many cases, this kind of wealth is invisible. Despite the focus in the media on individuals like Jimmy Pattison, Peter Monk, Bill Gates, and Donald Trump, most wealthy people don't flaunt their wealth.

"You can learn a lot from these people," says financial author and planner Larry Waschka, "but they aren't featured in magazines or television. They may live next door to you and have an incredible knowledge about building wealth, but you'd never know to ask."

Most really wealthy people do not own fancy cars or huge mansions, says Waschka. Like Sam Walton, founder of Wal-Mart, they drive older vehicles, fly economy class on commercial airlines, and wear ordinary clothes. They live well within their means in average-sized houses and avoid large mortgages and car payments by paying cash.

Once in a while, the news media discover one of the invisible wealthy. In 1996, for example, Frank Lalli wrote an article about Anne Scheiver in *Money Magazine*. Beginning in the depths of the Depression, when she was 38 years old and earning only a little more than $3,000 a year, Scheiver invested most of her life savings in stocks. She lost her initial investment, but started again in 1944 with $5,000. By the time she died in 1995, at the age of 101, she'd accumulated more than $20 million. With growth of 17.5% a year, the rate of growth on her portfolio exceeded that of some of the best-known investment professionals in the world, including John Neff and Ben Graham.

"More than 80% of millionaires are not born into wealth; they are ordinary people who have accumulated their wealth in one generation. . . . About two-thirds are self-employed. They live beneath their means—on about 7% of their wealth."[3]

3.0   Attitudes toward Money and Wealth

Wealthy individuals can be differentiated according to their passion as well as their occupation. People's occupations make them a living; their passions make them tick. Wealth managers can earn their clients' trust more effectively by understanding their clients' passions rather than their jobs.

"I find our industry far too concerned with how investments and portfolios work, and not nearly concerned enough with how real people feel," says Nick Murray. "Feelings are to facts as 19 is to one."

By understanding a client's passions, you can also understand how a client feels about money. According to Russ Alan Prince and Karen Maru File, authors of *Building Your Business: Marketing Your Way to a $100-million Investment Advisory Business*, there are nine main types of high-net-worth personalities:

- **Family stewards** feel that the purpose of investing is to let them take proper care of their families.

- **Financial phobics** hate being involved in investment decisions. They rely completely on investment advisors to take care of things.

- **Independents** think that investing is a necessary evil. They like to set their own objectives and investment styles.

- **The anonymous** are very secretive and believe investment success is crucial for their personal comfort. They focus on privacy and confidentiality and want long-term relationships.

- **Moguls** identify investing as a means of attaining personal power. They like to be in charge and they want financial products and services that allow them to have control and power over their affairs.

- **VIPs** like the status that successful investing can confer. They seek prestige as well as respect and deference from others.

- **Accumulators** simply want to be rich. They like tracking their investment returns.

- **Gamblers** treat investing as an enjoyable hobby and are quite happy managing part of their personal portfolios. They also like to set their own risk levels.

---

[3]   Thomas Stanley and William Danke, *The Millionaire Next Door: The Surprising Secrets of America's Wealthy*, Pocket Books, 1998.

- **Innovators** want to be on the cutting edge of investment technology. They like access to new investment management approaches.

4.0   Identifying Client Needs, Objectives, and Constraints

4.1   Listen, Listen, Listen

From the outset of a relationship with a client, your role is to provide clients with comfort and assuage their fear of losing financial control. If the client does not want to work with you, the relationship will not work. You must ensure that clients really want to get involved, and that they do not hold back information, or try to second-guess your decisions. You are building an all-or-nothing relationship and, in the initial stages, you are interviewing the client, not being interviewed by the client.

In a healthy relationship, you need the following things:

- full information on all pertinent aspects of the family's finances;

- total stewardship of the family's entire investment portfolio;

- the time and effort necessary to arrive at a complete understanding of investment goals.

If the client grants you these things, you must respond with complete trustworthiness, which means devoting yourself to the client's best interests, and creating and maintaining an investment plan that will, within reasonable probabilities, achieve the client's lifetime goals.

A good wealth manager is, by definition, a good listener. Listening is the basis of all good client relationships. There is simply no other way to serve a client well than to listen to his or her concerns. If you do not understand those concerns, ask questions until you do. As Stephen Covey says in his book, *The Seven Habits of Highly Effective People*, "first seek to understand, then to be understood."[4]

---

[4] Stephen R. Covey, *The Seven Habits of Highly Effective People*, Fireside, 1990.

Case 2.1   Listen to What Isn't Being Said

Elaine Hammond sat quietly as her husband John told their financial advisor, Robert Faulkner, about their plans.[5] Elaine and John were in their fifties with two grown children. John's imminent retirement and their plan to sell off the family printing business meant that their profiles as investors were about to change drastically. They would have a huge amount of capital to invest. Robert knew he would have to help them reassess their goals and financial plan. He had set up the meeting to discuss these changes.

John Hammond talked excitedly about his plans for the freed-up cash. He was a keen market watcher and was excited about a number of new-media companies he'd heard about. Although he had been a conservative investor, he was now considering investing a large chunk of their assets in a start-up Internet company.

As John talked, Robert noticed Elaine's silence. It wasn't unusual; he'd been in many situations in which the man had done all the talking. In fact, it was John who had taken care of the financial decisions for as long as Robert had known the Hammonds. He also knew that it often occurred when he talked to clients of this generation. The wives usually knew little about, and concerned themselves even less with, finances. Still, Elaine's body language—she kept her eyes averted, lightly clenching the hands that rested in her lap—told Robert that she wasn't fully comfortable with what her husband was saying.

"You must be excited about all these opportunities too, Mrs. Hammond," he said. She responded politely that, yes, it did sound exciting. He knew that she was still holding back and decided that a straightforward approach would be best. "Is there a dream that you have for retirement?" he prodded.

Elaine finally admitted that she felt that her husband's plans would put too much of their capital at too great a risk. Although the couple had agreed that, in retirement, they would give up the business, their plans for their golden years had not gone much beyond this agreement. She wanted to have some fun in retirement, but was equally concerned about maintaining some of the wealth for their children and grandchildren. Travel, trust funds, and real estate investments were among her desires.

Previously, the couple had had the same goals—making the business successful and funding their children's education. Although they still shared a common goal—that of comfortable retirement—their aspirations diverged in other respects. Faulkner explained to John Hammond that wealth preservation doesn't mean forgoing investment opportunities, and that both sets of objectives could be achieved.

When working with a couple, it's a good strategy to focus on the person who does the least talking. Failing to hear what the less vocal person has to say could mean missing half of what's being said.

---

[5]   The names of characters for cases in this course are fictional and chosen to represent the diversity of Canada's population. No stereotypical references are intended.

By listening, you will avoid mistakes. As most clients feel frightened and apprehensive about letting an advisor handle their financial affairs, even if they don't say so directly, the only way to ascertain the client's feelings and address them is to listen to their observations.

"Money is uncomfortable and intimidating. If you don't get your signals right by actively listening, it will cause headaches if the client later finds the investments unsuitable," says Jeanne Kaufman, a Calgary investment executive.

"Listening involves being sensitive to nuance and gesture," says business journalist Harvey Schachter. "It requires understanding differences, be they individualistic or tied to such factors as gender and ethnicity. And, above all, it demands that wealth managers understand themselves, so their own psychological needs don't clutter or derail the process."

It's your job to learn everything possible about your clients, so you can decide on appropriate recommendations. Yet the demonstration of expertise is a prime psychological need—one that can create conflict, particularly during getting-acquainted sessions. As Harvey Schachter says, "Instead of learning what the client requires, too many advisors spend early meetings signalling their own brilliance. It's tough to listen when you're doing all the talking."

Opportunities to ask questions arise not only in the initial stages of a relationship, but much later as well. If you give advice to a client and it is rejected, you have a golden opportunity to find out why. In the process, you will find out more about your clients. The key is to ask the question and listen to the answer.

Case 2.2   Ensure Your Clients Feel Comfortable with Your Advice

Angus Hogg is a likeable young man, thought Laura Evans. She and her husband, Frank, had chosen him as their financial advisor as much for his enthusiasm as for his expertise. Not only was he knowledgeable, he also seemed to be genuinely interested in helping them reach their goals.

But a recent discussion with Angus had left Laura feeling unsure about whether he could really fulfil her needs as an advisor. Although it wasn't a huge sum, the money that Laura had inherited when her mother died five years ago had given her the strongest sense of security that she'd ever felt. Now he was insisting that keeping that money outside the overall plan wasn't the right thing to do.

No doubt Angus's intentions were good, but Laura suspected that he had no idea how important it was to her to have that nest egg in her own name. It was clear from their previous conversations that he had had all the advantages in life—including private schools, social club membership, and all the right business connections.

Case 2.2   **Ensure Your Clients Feel Comfortable with Your Advice**
(continued)

As for Laura, the fact that she had come this far in life—she had a comfortable home, a good marriage, two small children, and both she and her husband held secure, well-paying jobs—was a tribute to her mother. When Laura's father died in an industrial accident in 1969, Laura was just seven years old. Her mother had struggled to raise Laura and her two brothers. Their upbringing had involved much hardship and sacrifice on her mother's part, and a lot of worrying about not having enough money.

Sure, she understood that a savings account in her name wasn't the best place for her money, and if she were making the decision on purely logical grounds, she wouldn't hesitate to make her inheritance money part of the larger financial plan that Angus had mapped out. But it wasn't that easy. The memory of her mother's constant worrying, of never having enough was hard to erase. Laura wished that Angus could understand why she needed to keep this money outside the general family finances.

Listening is a sign of respect. If clients sense that they are not being listened to, they will feel angry, resentful, and hurt.

Clients often say one thing and mean another. Your job is to decipher the meaning behind people's words, not just by listening to the words themselves, but by observing the gestures and behaviour that accompany them. Asking the right questions helps. Open-ended questions, such as: "What's important to you about your money?" While the client answers, you have to assess the client's degree of comfort with money and finances.

"Body language is often more revealing than words," says Harvey Schachter. The client may cross his hands, for example, indicating resistance. Or the client may simply look bored."

"Men are harder to read," says Wayne Crowder, an advisor in London, Ontario. "They're not as vocal. They often don't say anything. They grunt. Women seem to express themselves more easily. They have a better ability to communicate. They may be willing to say something a man won't."

You and your clients communicate in more ways than one. Your clothes, your office, your attitude—all deliver a message to clients that either encourages or discourages them from talking. Once clients start talking, you should take notes. Not only will your notes help you later to remember what was said, they also indicate to clients that you take their words seriously.

In addition to asking questions to clarify statements, you should repeat to clients what you think you've just heard them say. Don't try to rush the conversation and focus your attention on the client, by setting aside the rest of your work.

Studies show that many advisors either underestimate or overestimate their abilities. "Planners who overestimate are prone to not listening," says Harvey Schachter. "They're either too busy anticipating the glorious future ahead for the prospect, or too preoccupied with whether the prospect appreciates his or her greatness as an advisor." Those who underestimate their abilities are often afraid they'll make a mistake. Anxious about their own performance, they don't focus on the client.

"Of course," says Schachter, "the client will also bring his or her psychological inclinations to the table. Some want quick closure, others are expansive and tangential. Some react intuitively to suggestions, while others want carefully formulated action steps. Understanding such character types can aid your listening."

Jan Lowenthal is now dealing with her fifth investment advisor. A consultant herself, she's an attractive client financially and has worked with advisors from some of the country's top brokerages. But she has abandoned four of them because until now she hasn't found one who would listen to her. "They had their own agenda," she says. "I had to fit into their system. Most of them didn't ask enough questions to find out about me and what I want."[6]

Remember, you're not selling something to your clients; you're letting them buy it. The easier you make it for clients to join in your enthusiasm about their future, the better they will feel. That doesn't mean that you have to toss out the bar charts and throw away the technical reports. Some clients take great comfort in knowing that an advisor's advice is based on hard facts. But most clients value trust as well, and trust is not earned from a bar chart.

In her book, *How Not To Take It Personally: 10 Action Strategies For Communications Success*, author Vera Held[7] suggests some principles for interactions with clients:

- clarify the facts;

- clarify the feelings;

- restate;

- be neutral;

- summarize;

- prepare;

- avoid saying "You should…";

- appreciate and value the message.

---

[6] *Advisors Edge Magazine*, September 1998.

[7] Vera Held, *How Not To Take It Personally: 10 Action Strategies for Communications Success*, VNH Publications, 1998.

Case 2.3   Clients Don't Always Say What They Mean without Prompting

Most standard investor questionnaires, including the one used by Eva Sinhala's firm, include exercises to determine a client's risk tolerance and investment objectives. Eva, however, prefers talking to her clients to gauge their attitudes to investing.

Lately, Eva's business has been booming and she's been spending most of her extremely busy days getting to know new clients. She met with one such client, Paul Bergeron, in between an appointment with a money manager and a training session for the new data system that was being installed on her computer. Meanwhile, the phone messages were piling up on her desk.

"How much do you expect your portfolio to earn?" she asked Paul. It was a question that she posed to all her clients. Considering that his GICs were earning barely 5%, a return of about 10% a year was all he hoped for, he replied. Eva believed that this range of expectations and the risk that it implied was acceptable for her client. She constructed a suitable asset allocation model for Paul's portfolio and helped him choose from a number of equity and fixed-income mutual funds. Paul seemed happy with the recommended portfolio.

A few months later, Eva returned to her office from a morning meeting to find three phone messages from Paul. He had received his monthly statement that day and his account's value was down almost 15% from its original purchase price. There was a tone of panic in his voice. "I thought we agreed that I'd be making about 10% on my investments," he said.

What Eva, in her haste that day, had failed to ascertain was the degree of volatility that Paul was willing to accept in earning 10%. He had not stated explicitly that he was unwilling to risk sharp short-term losses. Although Eva felt that the investments in the portfolio were likely to rebound, and that the average annual return over a full market cycle would probably be close to the originally targeted return, she knew that she had misinterpreted Paul's real objectives. She would have to revisit the issue of risk tolerance with Paul, and this time not cut corners in asking questions.

4.2   Asking the Right Questions

You need information from your clients, including:

- age, family situation;

- total wealth;

- funds available for investment;

- investment objectives, including the return required, investment time horizon, and need for liquidity;

- need for contingencies;

- tax status;

- risk tolerance;

- constraints.

Appendix 2.1 contains an Investor Profile Statement that captures the information that you need to know about your client.

Once you have this information, the next step is to determine how that wealth is distributed and the funds available for investment. For some people, money is not an easy topic to discuss and, in some instances, it is almost taboo. It is your job to encourage clients to speak frankly about their financial position and goals. Only then will you have a clear picture of your client's financial status and be able to work with the client in developing objectives (for example, a specified average rate of return for life with no depletion of capital).

Financial objectives can include short-term and long-term goals, each one with a corresponding target date. For example, a short-term goal might be to buy a cottage in three years' time, while a long-term goal might be to retire in 30 years at age 60. The more detailed the description of the objective, the more constraints on the investment policy. Finally, you need to establish short-run goals for the coming year that are consistent with the longer-term objectives. These form the basis for an operating cash budget that should be reviewed annually.

Long-term goals should have associated benchmarks to indicate whether or not the client is on target. For example, if you estimate that a client will require $500,000 in 30 years' time to supplement company and government pensions, then the client must make a regular annual contribution to an RRSP. Based on an assumed investment return of 8% a year, the required contribution would be about $4,400 a year in order to create a value of $26,000 in 5 years, $64,000 after 10 years, and $202,000 after 20 years. If the client is unwilling or unable to make this commitment, then either the objective must be revised or you may have to recommend a riskier portfolio that will offer a higher expected return.

Your clients' tax status plays an important part in the financial plan. The current tax laws tend to penalize fixed-income securities and favour equity investments through the dividend tax credit and the tax deferral of unrealized capital gains. You should aim to make the maximum use of your clients' RRSPs and other tax shelters where possible.

Finally, you must determine your clients' risk tolerance before finalizing an investment policy. You can ask a client to complete a questionnaire that will place him or her in one of several risk tolerance categories. For each category there is a model portfolio with a different balance of asset classes. Risk-averse investors fall into a category that corresponds to a portfolio that emphasizes cash and fixed-income securities. The model portfolio for more risk-tolerant investors include higher proportions of equities and possibly investments in international emerging-market equities.

In some instances, you may have to revise the financial plan as the implications of your initial recommendations may not be acceptable to a client. You may need to review the goals and the constraints before making a final recommendation.

Here are some sample questions that can be used to help clients articulate their objectives.

Return Requirements

Individual investors have different return requirements depending on their age and where they are in their careers. Younger clients tend to focus on growth; older clients on liquidity and capital preservation. Ask:

> *What level of income do you require from the portfolio on an annual basis?*

> *What returns do you expect to get on your investments?*

Risk Tolerance

There are various methods for determining and quantifying risk tolerance. For institutional clients, a statistical approach may be appropriate, whereas for individual investors, you may need a highly customized approach. Questionnaires have been designed that assign individual investors to categories in the risk spectrum and recommend model portfolios for each category. A sample risk profile questionnaire is found in Appendix 2.2. Ask:

> *How many quarters of negative returns can you withstand?*

> *How much of a drop in your portfolio can you withstand annually?*

Liquidity Requirements

Clients may want to make a major expenditure in the future, such as acquiring a property or a business. Ask:

> *How much cash do you need for an expected major expenditure?*

> *When do you expect this would be needed?*

Legal Restrictions

You should take into account any legal or policy constraints on the portfolios. For individual clients, this may simply mean restrictions on registered (such as RRSP/RRIF) portfolios. In the case of foundations, endowments, segregated funds, and funds whose source is legally controlled, you must identify your fiduciary responsibilities and, through the investment objective-setting process, uphold the intended use of the funds. Ask:

Are there any legal constraints on the investments made by the foundation?

Tax Issues

Your client's tax status will affect the choice of investment policy. Properly managing gains and losses within portfolios can significantly reduce the tax a client must pay in a year. For example, if large gains have been realized during the year, you can trigger losses to reduce the value of realized capital gains. You should make the maximum use of the investor's RRSP and other tax shelters wherever possible. Ask:

What rate of tax do you pay on interest, dividends, and capital gains?

What kinds of tax liability would your spouse/children face upon your death?

Time Horizon

Clients of different ages have longer or shorter time horizons. You must identify their time horizons, as it affects the choice of asset mix. Ask:

How long will your money be invested?

When do you expect to need income from the portfolio?

Contingencies

Ask what would happen if the client could no longer work:

Have you made arrangements for your children's financial security?

Have you appointed someone to act on your behalf in case you became incapacitated?

Do you have a Power of Attorney document?

Do you have a will?

Have you tried to minimize probate fees?(Not applicable in Quebec)

Unique Circumstances

Investors may have preferences that they would like included in the policy statement. Examples may involve including a "socially responsible" statement, or excluding particular securities from the portfolio.

Do you have any particular instructions related to your portfolio, or any preferences or constraints about types of investment?

The appendices to this chapter present a sample questionnaire that can be used to assess the financial situation of a client as well as the client's needs, objectives, constraints, and risk profile.

4.3   Document Checklist

In addition to the client questionnaire, you should also receive from your clients' the following documentation:

- tax returns for the past 2-3 years and notices of assessment;

- wills;

- powers of attorney;

- statements of liabilities such as mortgages or lines of credit;

- trust agreements;

- pre-nuptial agreements;

- life insurance policies;

- pension and benefits statements from employers;

- latest statements from banks, investment dealers, trust companies, or other financial institutions;

- financial statements and tax returns from private businesses with which the client is involved.

APPENDIX 2.1

Investor Profile Statement

Assante Capital Management Inc. has generously given the CSI permission to reproduce, in part, their Investor Profile Statement for the purposes of illustrating to students the types of client information that wealth managers should be gathering. The statement is divided up into two sections. Section One is designed to help the client and the wealth manager assess the client's financial situation and investment needs and objectives. Section Two gathers personal background information.

Section One

Investment Needs & Objectives

This section has been designed to help you better evaluate your overall financial situation, along with your investment needs and objectives. This includes a review of issues such as liquidity needs, investment time horizon, tolerance for risk, current income requirements, growth expectations, tax considerations, and various other essential elements.

1. This question deals with the element of investment time horizon, which is an important consideration when looking at investment objectives. The length of your time horizon, or the period you intend to stay invested, will influence the asset allocation or mix of your portfolio. The longer an investment remains in place, the greater the probability that market variations will even out.

   The table below demonstrates that as investment periods are lengthened to 3, 5, 10 and 25 years, the variability of returns was reduced and negative returns were eliminated.

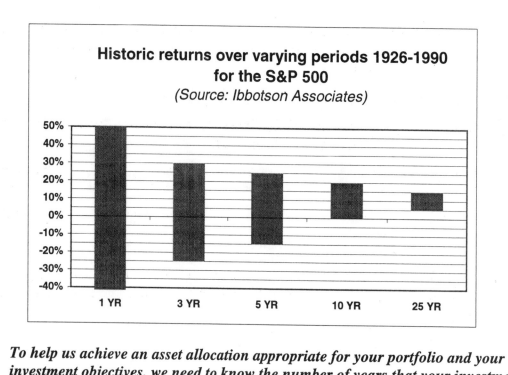

To help us achieve an asset allocation appropriate for your portfolio and your investment objectives, we need to know the number of years that your investment funds will be available:

☐ 0 – 3 years   ☐ 3 – 5 years   ☐ 5 – 10 years

☐ 10 – 15 years   ☐ over 15 years

2. Major changes to an investor's lifestyle can also have an impact on the structure of an investment portfolio. This question helps us to anticipate significant developments in the lives of our clients, and to factor them into our investment recommendations and strategies. Remember, it is a dynamic and fluid process.

Do you anticipate any major lifestyle changes over the course of your investment time horizon (i.e. retirement, sabbatical, extensive travel, career change, etc.)? If so, please indicate them below along with when you would expect these changes to occur:

_____

_____

_____

3. This question deals with the fact that your own personal experience with investing, and knowledge of the process itself, can have a bearing on the structure and management of your portfolio.

   How would you rate your level of investment experience?

   ☐ *Minimal* - You have little, if any, investment experience and consider your knowledge base to be limited.

   ☐ *Moderate* - You have some investment experience but are still on a learning curve.

   ☐ *Excellent* - You are a seasoned investor with a thorough understanding of the capital markets.

4. What is the dollar value of the assets you are placing under the management of ____. What percentage of your total investment assets does this represent? (Further details will be requested in Section Four.)

   $ _____   _____ %

5. It is important for us to know about all of your investment assets, and not just those under our management. The answer to this question will help ensure that our investment recommendations will be made with a complete understanding as to your entire financial picture.

   Are there any investment assets that will not be managed by ____?

   ☐ Yes   ☐ No

6. Your investment objectives are important and we want to help you reach them. Sometimes goals have to be placed in order to increase the probability that they will all be met and this question helps to give priority to your objectives.

   Financially speaking, if you could accomplish one thing in the next year, what would that be?

   _____

   The next 5 years?

   _____

   The next 10 – 15 years?

   _____

7. This question deals with the issue of investment risk as reflected in the volatility of return. This means that over the course of your investment time horizon, your portfolio can experience wide fluctuation in annual value, including downturns.

    Which of the following best describes your attitude towards investment risk?

    ☐ **Conservative:** You have a low risk threshold and can only tolerate modest, short-term fluctuations in the value of your portfolio during rough phases in a market cycle.

    ☐ **Moderate:** You are prepared to assume some risks and can tolerate one year of negative total returns during rough market cycles.

    ☐ **Aggressive:** You accept risk in the pursuit of portfolio growth and can tolerate more than one negative year of total returns during rough market cycles.

THE EFFICIENT FRONTIER

The point of minimum risk for every level of return is called the "Efficient Frontier." Please indicate with an "X" the position on the "Efficient Frontier" that best reflects your tolerance in balancing risk and return.

8. This question deals with the need you may have to receive income from your portfolio over the course of your investment time horizon, through interest-bearing instruments or dividends.

    Do you have a requirement for regular income from your investment?

    ☐ Yes   ☐ No

    If yes, please indicate the total dollars that you will need.

    $ _____ total per month ☐   per quarter ☐   per year ☐

9. Your liquidity requirements, or short notice access to cash, are an important consideration in your investment planning. They are a direct function of purchases such as a home or automobile. By keeping a sufficient portion of your investments in cash equivalent securities, a forced sale of investment assets at an inopportune time can be avoided.

   Please list any large expenditures you are planning for the coming year:

   $ _____ in which month(s) _____ for _____

   $ _____ in which month(s) _____ for _____

   $ _____ in which month(s) _____ for _____

   Are sufficient liquid reserves maintained outside your managed portfolio to fund these special expenditures?

   $ _____ in which month(s) _____

   $ _____ in which month(s) _____

10. There are many needs and variables that must be balanced in order to achieve the portfolio that is ideal for you as an investor. This question has been designed to help further define the parameters of your investment portfolio.

    Please assign a number to each of the following, ensuring that the overall total of the numbers does not exceed 10:

Liquidity	Low	0	1	2	3	4	5	High
High Income	Low	0	1	2	3	4	5	High
Growth	Low	0	1	2	3	4	5	High
Time Horizon	Short	0	1	2	3	4	5	Long

11. Throughout this Investor Profile you have seen the interrelationship between risk and return. You have also seen that staying with an investment management program, even through difficult years, has historically proven to be a wise and prudent strategy.

    In order to keep pace with taxes and inflation, an investor must achieve a return in excess of what's known as the "risk-free rate" (the return delivered by T-Bills), over the course of his or her investment time horizon. Portfolios can be created that will produce return premiums ranging from 2% - 6% over T-Bills in the long-term.

    However, in order to produce these premiums an investor must be prepared to accept some degree of short-term risk in the form of fluctuations in portfolio value. There is a direct relationship between the size of the premium return and the degree of fluctuation. For example, assuming T-Bills earned 5%, a portfolio designed to generate a premium of 3.5% over T-Bills in the long-term (an overall return of 8.5%)

will under-perform T-Bills in 3 out of every 10 years. This question will help to further determine how much fluctuation in value you are prepared to accept.

Assuming once again that T-Bills earned 5%, what is the lowest return in any one year that you could tolerate before the fluctuation in your portfolio's value caused you to reevaluate your investment strategy? (Please keep in mind that greater tolerance for an under-performing portfolio in the short-term will afford greater overall return in the long-term.)

<u>Overall Annual Return</u>	<u>Measured Against T-Bills Return (on average)</u>
☐ 2.0%	(3.0% below T-Bills)
☐ 1.0%	(4.0% below T-Bills)
☐ 0%	(5.0% below T-Bills or Break Even)
☐ -1.0%	(6.0% below T-Bills)
☐ -2.0%	(7.0% below T-Bills)
☐ -3.0%	(8.0% below T-Bills)

12. Although we believe that the preceding series of questions and scenarios is comprehensive, it is possible that we may not have addressed every single area that we should have relating to your own unique investment situation. This question has been designed to allow the inclusion of additional information that may have been overlooked up to this point.

Is there any other information you believe to be relevant to your investment situation, or to the management of your portfolio that we should know about? If so, please indicate below:

_____

_____

_____

_____

Section
Two

PERSONAL BACKGROUND INFORMATION

Now that we have reviewed your investment needs and objectives, we would like to receive some personal information from you. This will provide us with important data which will also be used in the preparation of your IPS, and ensures that our files are current for client contact, and any appropriate regulatory requirements we may have to fulfill.

1. Please provide us with the following information:

Name _____

Address _____ City _____

Province _____ Postal Code _____

Mailing Address (if different from above) _____

_____ Postal Code _____

Date of Birth _____ Res. Phone _____

Occupation _____ Employer _____

Business Address _____. City _____

Province _____ Postal Code _____

Bus. Phone _____ Fax _____

Language Preference: _____ French _____ English

Bank (s) _____ Account # (s) _____

Branch (es) _____

Lawyer _____ Firm _____

Accountant _____ Firm _____

Insurer _____ Policies _____

Number of Dependents/Children _____ Ages _____

Are any married? _____ (Yes) _____ (No)

Have you been previously married? _____ (Yes) _____ (No)

Do you have a will? _____ (Yes) _____ (No)   Power of Attorney? _____ (Yes) _____ (No)

Date of last update _____

Do you utilize other Brokers/Dealers/Agents? If so, please list:

Firm _____ Service provided _____

Firm _____ Service Provided _____

Send duplicate statements to _____

2. Please provide us with your spouse's information:

Spouse's Name _____ Date of Birth _____

Occupation _____ Employer _____

Bus. Address _____

City/Province _____ Postal Code _____ Bus. Phone _____

Section
Three

INCOME TAX PROFILE

The following chart has been designed to develop an Income Tax Profile, which will be utilized to allocate the assets within your portfolio so as to maximize your after-tax return. Some of the information requested is highly technical. Accordingly, you may wish to consult your accountant for assistance in completing this section. Alternatively, you could provide copies of income tax returns for all related individuals, companies, partnerships and trusts which we will analyze on your behalf.

Income Tax Profile

Name	Marginal Tax Rate	Capital Losses Carry Forward	Capital Gains Exemption Claims	Operating Losses or ABILS
Self:				
Spouse:	.			
Related Accounts (i.e. corporations, partnerships or trusts)				

Section
Four

NET WORTH – ASSETS

Please list the current values of your assets and provide your most recent statements where available:

	Self	Spouse	Joint	Other
Liquid Assets				
Cash & Chequing				
Savings Account				
Short-Term Deposits				
Canada Savings Bonds				
Cash Value of Life Insurance				
Treasury Bills				

	Self	Spouse	Joint	Other

Non-Registered
Investment Assets

	Self	Spouse	Joint	Other
Short-Term/Money Market Funds	_____	_____	_____	_____
Term Deposits & GIC's	_____	_____	_____	_____
Canadian Fixed Income	_____	_____	_____	_____
Global Fixed Income	_____	_____	_____	_____
Canadian Equity	_____	_____	_____	_____
US Equity	_____	_____	_____	_____
International Equity	_____	_____	_____	_____
Real Estate Investment Trusts	_____	_____	_____	_____
Limited Partnerships	_____	_____	_____	_____
Other Investments*	_____	_____	_____	_____

*(Please describe here) _____

_____

Registered Retirement
Assets (RRSP/RRIF)

	Self	Spouse
Short-Term/Money Market Funds	_____	_____
Term Deposits & GIC's	_____	_____
Canadian Fixed Income	_____	_____
Global Fixed Income	_____	_____
Canadian Equity	_____	_____
US Equity	_____	_____
International Equity	_____	_____
Real Estate Investment Trusts	_____	_____
Limited Partnerships	_____	_____
Other Investments*	_____	_____

*(Please describe here) _____

_____

Personal Assets

	Self	Spouse	Joint	Other
Residence/Cottage	_____	_____	_____	_____
Furnishings	_____	_____	_____	_____
Vehicles	_____	_____	_____	_____
Other*	_____	_____	_____	_____

*(Please describe here) _____

_____

Total _____ _____ _____ _____

Other Assets

Do you own an interest in a private business corporation, partnership, professional practice or rental properties? If yes, please describe and provide latest financial statements and tax returns, if applicable.

_____

_____

_____

Section Five

Please list any short-term and long-term obligations for you and your spouse, and place a star beside those loans for which interest is tax deductible.

LIABILITIES – SELF

	Current Balance	Interest Rate	Monthly Payment	Final Payment
Short-Term Obligations				
Consumer Credit Obligation				
Borrowings on Life Insurance				
Installment Loans				
Personal Loans				
Income Taxes				
Other Short-Term Obligations				
Long-Term Obligations				
Investment Loans				
Business Loans				
Mortgage on Residence				
Personal Vehicle Loans				
Loans for Other Personal Assets				
Other Long-Term Obligations				
Contingent Liabilities				

LIABILITIES – SPOUSE

	Current Balance	Interest Rate	Monthly Payment	Final Payment
Short-Term Obligations				
Consumer Credit Obligation				
Borrowings on Life Insurance				
Installment Loans				
Personal Loans				
Income Taxes				
Other Short-Term Obligations				
Long-Term Obligations				
Investment Loans				
Business Loans				
Mortgage on Residence				
Personal Vehicle Loans				
Loans for Other Personal Assets				
Other Long-Term Obligations				
Contingent Liabilities				

Section Six

INCOME & EXPENDITURES

Please indicate your annual level of income and expenditures for the current year:

Income

	Self	Spouse	Total
Gross Salary			
Bonuses/Commissions			
Self-Employment			
Pensions, CPP, and OAS benefits			
Other Earnings			

Investment Income

	Self	Spouse	Total
Interest			
Dividends			
Rental Income			
Partnerships			
Other Investment Income			
Capital Gains			
Annuities			
Total Income			

Expenses
(Please identify what % is deductible for tax)

	Amount	Self % Tax Deductible	Spouse % Tax Deductible
Shelter			
Transportation			
Food			
Clothing			
Insurance Premiums			
Alimony/Maintenance			
Vacations			
Debt Reduction			
Income Taxes			
Other Expenses			
Total Expenses			

Section Seven

DOCUMENT CHECKLIST

This section helps to ensure that any documentation that may be relevant to the management of your portfolio is included for our review and consideration. Many of the documents asked for may not be applicable to you. If this is the case, please disregard our request. However, if you feel that any important material pertaining to your financial situation has not been listed, please include it with the rest of your submissions.

*If applicable, please submit the following documentation for you **and** your spouse:*

☐ Tax returns for the past two years

☐ Wills

☐ Powers of attorney

☐ Individual statements of liabilities, examples of which are:
- Mortgage
- Investment Loans
- Lines of Credit
- Unpaid Taxes

☐ Family trust agreements and related financial statements and tax returns

☐ Spousal or pre-nuptial agreement

☐ Pension & benefits booklet and statements from your employers

☐ Disability insurance contracts and latest statement

☐ Life insurance policies (group & private) including any annuity contracts

☐ Latest statements from brokerage firms, trust companies, banks and investment companies with respect to all investments, including RRSP's

☐ Statement of Adjusted Cost Bases of all assets listed in Section Four

☐ Past two years of financial statements and tax returns from any private businesses that you are involved in (including corporations, partnerships and professional practices)

☐ Past two years of financial statements from other investment entities such as limited partnerships, real estate holdings and co-ownerships

☐ The original and amended prospectus from any of the other investment entities

☐ Other documentation:

_____

_____

_____

_____

_____

_____

_____

_____

Section Eight

INVESTOR PROFILE CONCLUSION

To the Investor:

You have now completed the Investor Profile and have provided our analysts with the information they require to prepare your Investment Policy Statement. The Investment Policy Statement and the Investment Management Services we will provide to you, will be based solely on the information gathered in this Investor Profile. To the extent that the information is inaccurate or incomplete, we cannot be confident that our services will be appropriate to your circumstances. Please sign below and record the date, confirming for our staff that you have answered the questions accurately and completely, and are satisfied to the best of your knowledge with the answers you have given.

Self _____   Date _____

Spouse _____   Date _____

To the Advisor:

You have now reviewed the Investor Profile with your Client(s) and you have both completed it together. Please sign below and record the date, confirming for our staff that you are satisfied the information provided is thorough and accurately reflects the personal financial situation, attitudes and investment objectives of your Client(s).

Advisor _____   Date _____

Section Nine

NOTES

_____

_____

_____

_____

_____

_____

_____

_____

_____

_____

_____

_____

_____

_____

_____

_____

_____

_____

_____

_____

APPENDIX 2.2

Risk Profile Statement

A risk profile is a key component of the investor profile. The following is an example of a sample questionnaire that could be used to assess a client's attitude towards risk.

With investing, a general rule is that the greater return you seek, the greater your exposure to risk. With this in mind, please answer the following questions.

1. Which of the following best describes how you view your investment portfolio?

    a. Seeking to protect account value, which implies low returns and minimal chances for short-term losses.
    b. Seeking moderate returns, which implies moderate chances for short-term losses.
    c. Seeking high returns, which implies high chances for short-term losses.

2. Which of the following best describes your expectations for your portfolio?

    a. I want a portfolio that will primarily provide me with supplemental income.
    b. I want a portfolio that offers both moderate long-term growth potential and current income.
    c. I want a portfolio that will maximize my long-term growth potential.
    d. I want a portfolio that will make me rich very quickly

3. Suppose you had most of your money invested in one mutual fund and your last statement showed that the value of the fund decreased by 2%. (For example, your $100,000 investment was now worth $98,000.) What action are you most likely to take?

    a. Sell all shares of the fund.
    b. Sell some, but not all, of the fund shares.
    c. Continue to hold the shares.
    d. Purchase more shares to take advantage of the low price.

4. If your tax rate is 50% and the inflation rate is 2.0%, your investments must return at least 4% to retain their purchasing power. With this in mind, which of the following best describes your attitude toward taxes and inflation?

   a. I am primarily concerned with protecting my investments. So I want investments designed to minimize risk and to keep pace with inflation on an after-tax basis.
   b. I want investments designed to moderately outpace inflation on an after-tax basis. I am willing to accept some additional risk to do so.
   c. I want investments designed to significantly outpace inflation on an after-tax basis. I am willing to accept substantial risk to do so.

The following table lists several different types of investments. For each type, please indicate the status that applies to you.

Type of Investment	Previous or Current Investment Would Invest Again	Previous or Current Investment Dissatisfied	No Previous or Current Investment
Short Term Assets – T-bills, money market accounts, GICs ect..			
Government bonds or Government bond mutual funds			
High-Grade Corporate Bonds or Corporate Bond mutual funds			
Blue-Chip Stocks or Blue-Chip mutual fund			
Small-Cap stocks or mutual fund			
Hedge Funds			
Derivatives – Futures or Options			

5. The following table shows potential one-year gains and losses for four different portfolios with an initial investment of $250,000. The number above each bar is the potential high return for each portfolio in a given year. The number below each bar is the potential low return for each portfolio in a given year. The number to the right of each bar is the average return in a given year. Which portfolio would you invest in?

Portfolio	Potential Low Return	Potential High Return	Potential Average Return
A	-4%	+11%	+7%
B	-8%	+20	+9%
C	-11%	+28%	+12%
D	-20%	+45%	+18%

   a. Portfolio A
   b. Portfolio B
   c. Portfolio C
   d. Portfolio D

6. I can tolerate substantial short-term fluctuations in my portfolio value in order to increase the likelihood of long-term after-tax gains that outpace inflation.

   a. Strongly agree
   b. Agree
   c. Neutral
   d. Disagree
   e. Strongly disagree

CHAPTER 3

Communication and Education

1.0 Introduction

The job of gathering information about the client is only the start of the client communication process, a process that includes regular contact and education.

Clients rely on wealth managers for a number of reasons, but almost all of them share one characteristic: they want someone to attend to the details of their financial lives. Clients may be too busy or simply disinclined to attend to these details themselves, preferring to let you do the job for them.

That doesn't mean, however, that they don't want to understand the ramifications of your recommendations. By explaining your recommendations and the reasons for them, you make life easier for the client and for yourself.

Primary Learning Objectives

By the end of this chapter you should understand:

- **the importance of client communication;**
- **the importance of client education;**
- **the types of risks with which a client should be familiar.**

2.0 Communicating the Wealth Management Planning Process to the Client

Simplicity is critical in communicating with a client. The more you simplify the concepts in financial planning and how they contribute to achieving a client's objectives, the more thoroughly the client will understand them. This means that you must be able to tell a story, with a beginning, a middle, and an end, and explain effectively how the planning process will contribute to your client's well-being. The effort spent on effective communications is usually rewarded with increased client loyalty.

Case 3.1   Tailor Your Communications to Your Clients

When Montreal financial advisor Frank Vernon takes on wealthy elderly clients who are discouraged by the returns on their life savings, which are invested in low-interest GICs and Treasury bills, he sympathizes with them.

"There was a time," he says, "when I would have said beware of the market, but that's when interest rates were juicy. It behoves these clients to look at other investment opportunities in today's market."

Vernon eases his older clients into the market through conservatively managed mutual funds, but not before he has spent hours making them feel comfortable with their investments. For example, he uses pie charts to show risk scenarios and realistic expected returns based on these historical models. He also speaks their language: he calls the low-risk, low-return example the Chevrolet model, and the high-risk, high-return portfolio the Ferrari.

He avoids the tendency to lump all elderly investors together. One client, a 68-year-old widow who holds a Ph.D. in education, had more than $250,000 to invest. She was the heir to her husband's estate. His financial assets had been held mainly in segregated funds and other life insurance policies. Unlike many members of her generation, she was able to discuss financial matters knowledgeably and comfortable investing portions of her portfolio in blue-chip stocks and a well-diversified global equity fund.

2.1   A Steadying Influence

Professor Robert Bloomfield at Cornell University advises financial advisors to keep their clients' overconfidence under control. "Imagine a client is in your office saying, 'I've heard great things about ABC Company.' You should remind the client that it's not a sure thing, especially if the decision to buy is based on a small bit of information," he says.

A study by Professor Bloomfield and two fellow faculty members at Cornell University, Professors Robert Libby and Mark Nelson, has shown that the amount of information an investor gathers about a particular investment has little effect on his/her confidence and aggressiveness in making it.[1]

In laboratory experiments, the study leaders created 'less informed' investors by giving them small amounts of information about a company and compared their confidence and trading decisions to another set of more-informed subjects who were given more data.

---

[1]   Study by Robert Bloomfield, Robert Libby and Mark Nelson of the Johnson Graduate School of Management at Cornell University, May 21, 1998.

The study found that rather than be less confident, the less-informed investors were every bit as confident as those who really did know more. When they had a little good news, they acted as if they had a lot. They bought aggressively from more-informed investors, driving prices up too high, and losing money as a result."

The experiment showed that it isn't simply a lack of information that can hurt less-informed investors. Rather, it is their tendency to overestimate the quality of their information. "More-informed investors are better off because they get information from so many sources," Bloomfield observed. "Serious investors get lots of good news and bad news. All of these conflicting signals lead them to be a little more careful in drawing conclusions. But casual investors often rely on just a few pieces of information, such as an earnings report or a personal experience with a company. If all they see is one piece of good news, they are much more likely to buy aggressively which will ultimately drive prices up and they could loose money as a result.

2.2   Keeping Clients Informed

Calling your clients regularly reassures them that you are keeping their interests in mind. You should call them with news about their investments, whether it's good news or bad. In fact, by telling them bad news before they hear it from some other source, you will strengthen the client relationship. "Clients want to know they have an advisor who is watching out for their interests—who is thinking about them and is prepared to take the time and effort to call them, even when the news is sour," says Dan Richards, author of *Getting Clients, Keeping Clients: The Essential Guide for Tomorrow's Financial Advisor.*

Case 3.2   Keep Clients Informed Whether the News is Good or Bad

For every demanding client who second-guessed his recommendations, Adam Silver had a client who was happy to relinquish all control and cared little about the ins and outs of investing. Either way, results that don't measure up to expectations inevitably take a lot of explaining, and a portfolio that underperforms, even in the short term, is an easy way to lose clients.

Arnie and Stan Berman are brothers who own an import-export business that has grown steadily over the 15 years that Silver has managed their pension plan. Although the plan is now worth about $2 million, substantially more than when he first acquired the account, his diligence in giving his clients thorough reports has changed very little.

Arnie and Stan were neophytes to investing when Silver acquired their account and are still relatively unsophisticated when it comes to financial matters. In the 1980s, they had been quite happy to hold a "laddered" portfolio of high-quality bonds of varying maturities; in the 1990s, they felt forced into equity markets by the low bond yields. Now they hold a portfolio of bonds, trust units, foreign mutual funds, and index-linked notes.

Case 3.2   Keep Clients Informed Whether the News is Good or Bad
(continued)

Silver knows that people can have unrealistic expectations because of the benchmarks or even the particular stocks that are highlighted in the media. The upcoming review with the Bermans was sure to be a tough one. At a time when record-breaking stock gains led the nightly news on a regular basis, the Bermans' pension plan had returned a very modest 3%.

A couple of months ago, before the scheduled portfolio review, Silver contacted the Bermans to update them on their portfolio. A lot of the news was bad: bond yields were low, income trusts were under pressure from falling commodity prices, and many foreign markets had failed to perform as expected.

As always, the Bermans' accountant, Louise Reed, who was also a loyal friend of the brothers, attended the regular review. Silver showed them a market commentary published by his company's research department as well as a personalized outline of market conditions as they related to the Bermans' own holdings. He presented line graphs to show the effect of falling interest rates on interest-sensitive securities, using one of the portfolio's holdings as an illustration. He showed them how the same conditions had made for the same pattern some years back, and how that trend had turned around in subsequent years. Finally, he illustrated that the portfolio's performance was actually not bad when compared to an appropriate benchmark.

As his clients listened and nodded, Silver still wasn't sure how much they really understood, but he remained as diligent as ever in his presentation. This time, he got some unexpected back-up from the Bermans' accountant. She said that the same thing had happened in her portfolio and that she too believed that the modest returns were acceptable for a conservative, balanced portfolio. The Bermans confidently accepted Silver's recommendations for the next period.

3.0   Why Educate the Client?

The ultimate point of informing and educating clients is not to enhance their store of knowledge or for you as a wealth manager to display your insights into the world of investing. The point is to make your clients feel comfortable and prevent them from worrying about their families' financial future. "If [a client] pays for my investment counsel, and then worries about it, he hasn't really accepted my advice, which in effect means he doesn't trust me," says author Nick Murray.

Your job will be easier if your clients understand why you have made specific decisions. You can explain in simple terms the technical nature of each element of the plan. (For example, "A global equity fund invests in stocks on markets around the world.")

The greater challenge is to earn your clients' full cooperation and trust in making these decisions. In fact, without your clients' cooperation, you can't do your job. That means you have to explain how an investment will help your clients achieve their goals.

Case 3.3   Explain the Basics of Investing in Plain Language

Wayne Franklin takes his mutual-fund analysis seriously. Before recommending funds to his clients, he screens them not only for past returns, but for risk. Among other things, he looks at beta scores, standard deviation, and the Sharpe measure, all of which help him determine how well the fund manager is performing on a risk-reward basis.

He appreciates the input he gets from his firm's research department and from the independently produced fund software product to which he subscribes. "I use all the research and quantitative tools at my disposal to assess how well the fund manager copes in both bull and bear markets," he says.

But when it comes to communicating his opinions to his clients, Franklin keeps the esoteric risk-measurement jargon to himself. "Clients want to know what it means to them in dollar terms," he says. "If you talk in terms or percentages, they'll have a tough time trying to follow what you're saying. Risk may be easy to quantify, but it's also very abstract."

Franklin still makes use of a wide range of risk measures. But he takes the trouble to translate them into an estimated dollar impact. To make things even easier to understand, he uses the dollar amounts applicable to the clients' own situation as a reference point.

For instance, when a client was contemplating a $10,000 investment in an aggressive growth fund that he'd heard great things about, Franklin asked him: "How would you feel if this fund was worth only $7,500 a year from now?" The client said that he would be "extremely disappointed, unhappy, and nervous." After further discussion, the client indicated that he would find acceptable a potential risk of a $1,500 loss over a year.

That was what Franklin needed to know to go back to his company's list of available funds and look for a less volatile alternative. "And when I find one, it's a sure thing that I'll be again discussing the down side in terms of dollars, not ratios."

3.1   Types of Risk

There's an old saying: "We all want to go to heaven, but nobody wants to die." Many Canadians take the same attitude when it comes to investing. We all want to double our money, but nobody wants to take a financial risk. In fact, only about 1 in 10 Canadians ever invests directly in the stock or bond markets.

One of your jobs as a wealth manager is to determine your clients' tolerance for risk (the questionnaire appended to Chapter 2 can help). Before you do that, however, your client must understand the types of risk above and beyond market risk.

The Risk of Not Investing or Investing too Conservatively

Believe it or not, the biggest risk to financial security is to do nothing. A $1,000 investment in the U.S. stock market in 1950 would be worth around $700,000 Canadian today.[2] The same $1,000 invested in Canadian 90-day Treasury bills would be worth only $21,300 today. It has been very costly to stay out of equity markets, particularly the U.S. market.

The Risk of Not Diversifying

One example of how costly a strategy of not diversifying your investments can be is particularly relevant to Canadian investors. A $1,000 investment in Canadian stocks[3] in 1950 would be worth $165,507 Canadian dollars today (compared with the U.S. investment of $700,000 discussed above). The opportunity cost of putting a client's investments solely in Canadian equity markets was huge.

Inflation or Purchasing Power Risk

Since 1950, inflation has averaged 4.2% a year. It dropped to about 2% in the late 1990s, but there is no certainty that it will stay at that level. At 4%, the cost of living doubles every 18 years.

An investment in 90-day Canadian Treasury bills would have yielded an annual real return of only 2.2% since 1950, compared to a 6.4% nominal rate of return. It is important to have exposure to investments such as equities and real estate that provide a hedge against inflation.

Interest Rate Risk

When inflation slows down, interest rates fall. If a client's fixed-interest investment, such as a GIC or a Canada Savings Bond, matures during one of these periods, it would be reinvested at a lower rate.

---

[2]   Includes all common stocks on the NYSE, AMEX, and NASDAQ markets, assumes all income reinvested and no commission costs or taxes.

[3]   Toronto Stock Exchange 300 Total Return Index.

During 1981 and 1982, for example, the rate of interest on Canada Savings Bonds fell rapidly from 19.5% to 10.5%. Senior citizens, whose fixed income was derived from their investments in CSBs, found their incomes cut in half.

To protect against interest rate risk, a client should keep some money in short-term investments, like a money market fund, so they will have the cash on hand to invest when rates start to rise again.

Political Risk

When a nation becomes politically unstable, the value of investments in that nation decreases because of the political risk of turmoil, revolution, radical changes in tax policy and other disturbances. For example:

- In 1939, German troops marched into Czechoslovakia. Stock prices around the world fell 20%.

- In 1974, the Watergate scandal in the United States contributed to a stock market decline of 28%.

- In March 1994, the leading candidate for the Mexican presidency, Luis Colosio, was assassinated. In the following two weeks, the Mexican stock market fell 10%.

For investors who understand the nature of political risk, these occurrences can present excellent buying opportunities.

Currency Risk

When the value of the Canadian dollar falls from $0.89 U.S. to $0.70 U.S. in two years, Canadians experience the effects of currency risk. When a Canadian hands a bank teller a Canadian $100 bill and gets back $65 in U.S. dollars, that is currency risk.

Likewise, if a client invests in Greece, and the Greek drachma suddenly loses value, the client suffers a loss when selling the investment and converting the proceeds to Canadian dollars.

There are ways that investors can protect themselves against currency risk. You can explain these methods to your client, if the client's portfolio warrants it.

Default Risk

This is the risk that the issuer of a debt instrument, such as a bond, will not pay the semi-annual interest payments or the face value at maturity. With Canadian government securities, this risk is remote, but with debt instruments issued by corporations and less industrialized governments, there is always some risk.

Risk of Uncertainty

Market pundits sometimes blame downturns on uncertainty, which they say the market hates. Some of possible future risks might include:

- Housing markets lose value, so that the value of your clients' house may be lower when they sell it than it was when they bought it—a simple risk of home ownership that may happen when aging baby boomers become empty-nesters and begin putting their family houses on the market en masse.

- The government changes the rules for Old Age Pensions and the Canada Pension Plan/Quebec Pension Plan. Your clients may not get as much as they thought they would from their government pensions. See Chapter 5, Retirement Planning, for a more thorough discussion.

- A recession occurs, as it did North America in the early 1980s and in Asia in the late 1990s.

- A war or natural disaster upsets the North American economy.

Market Risk

Investing in equity markets entails two types of risk: stock-specific and overall market risk. Even if your stock selection is good, your portfolio may not be immune from the effects of an overall market decline.

In Chapter 6, there is a discussion on the various ways in which investors can insure portfolios. As your clients near retirement they will probably become more risk-averse. The demand for portfolio insurance products is likely to grow.

Liquidity Risk

Your clients put their money in seemingly conservative investments like GICs but then, suddenly, need the cash back. They will probably lose gains to prepayment penalties.

Case 3.4   Address Your Clients' Concerns about Risk and Volatility

Marvin Owen, 55, an avid reader of the financial pages, has overcome his former compulsion to check the stock and mutual-fund listings every day to see if he has made or lost money. His financial advisor, Tamara Clift, has convinced him that the daily ups and downs of the market are irrelevant to his long-term portfolio strategy and that his time would be better spent on more productive activities.

But even though he now checks his holdings only monthly, the risks of investing still weigh heavily on Marvin's mind. He is single, with no dependants, but also without sources of retirement income outside his own retirement savings and the government pension plan. He thinks that investing in the securities markets will put him ahead of the game in terms of savings for retirement. But he wants some assurance that after a 10-year period—he plans to retire at 65—he would at least break even.

From his reading of personal finance articles in the media, and from discussions with Tamara, Marvin has learned the basics of segregated funds issued by insurance companies. Though the management fees and expenses associated with these insurance contracts are higher than regular mutual funds, they hold attractions too. Marvin likes the maturity guarantees that provide for the return of original amounts deposited and held for at least 10 years. But he doesn't have dependants or other obvious beneficiaries, so the death benefits are of no use to him. Nor does he have any foreseeable use for the creditor-proofing and probate-bypass provisions associated with segregated funds.

Marvin decides that, all things considered, segregated funds aren't the best safety net for him. Is there some other way he can get in on the higher returns available from equity markets, while safeguarding his nest egg against a repeat of 1929 or 1987?

In coming up with a solution for Marvin, Tamara emphasizes the need to look at his investment portfolio as a whole. "Don't get caught up in what a particular holding might do over the short term. Even if it's losing money at some point, it can still be doing its job."

In keeping with that philosophy, she convinces Marvin to look at the components of his portfolio as members of a team working together. One component's job, for example, might be to provide regular income, while another's task would be to create capital growth that would exceed what would be feasible in a portfolio consisting solely of deposit instruments.

The component that Marvin wants to keep the closest eye on is the one that will ensure that he at least breaks even. Tamara assigns that role to high-quality strip bonds, which can be purchased at a discount to their face value at maturity. For Marvin's $325,000 portfolio, she ensures that it holds enough assets in strip bonds so that in 10 years' time, the combined maturity value of the bonds would be at least $325,000. This gives Marvin the safety net that he wants.

Case 3.4   Address Your Clients' Concerns about Risk and Volatility
(continued)

> With Marvin's break-even position reasonably secured, Tamara is able to place the remainder of her client's portfolio in more growth-oriented securities, in this case a combination of blue-chip stocks and foreign equity funds. Marvin has the growth potential that he wants to improve his chances of a more comfortable retirement, and the security of knowing that there is a solid foundation that will hold up if worst came to worst.

3.2   Financial Comparisons and Illustrations

It is important for clients to understand how financial concepts affect their financial plans and how they enhance or detract from their ability to achieve long-term objectives. It is sometimes useful to use financial comparisons and illustrations to help clients grasp an essential concept.

Compounding

Compound interest is calculated on an accumulating balance, which consists of both the capital invested and the interest earned. A $100 investment earning 6% compound interest would increase by $6 in the first year and by $6.36 in the second year (6% of $106).

To reinforce the meaning of compound interest, it's helpful to use a graphic example. A $1,000 investment in an RRSP, for example, made by an 18-year-old at 20% a year and compounded annually would be worth $5,266,463.20 when he or she turns 65. An even simpler comparison is a snowball rolling down a hill. The farther it rolls, the bigger it gets, as its surface increases and it picks up more snow.

The Rule of 72

A surprising number of clients may not know this simple rule:

> *Divide 72 by your annual investment return to get the number of years it will take to double your money.*

Say you earn 6% on an investment. Divide 72 by 6. You get 12. It will take 12 years to double your money.

If you earn 20% on your money, you'll double it every 3.6 years: 72 divided by 20 equals 3.6.

Volatility

Clients must understand that the stock market goes up and down in value. So do individual stocks. Between 1960 and 1999, for example, the TSE 300 declined significantly eleven times. Those periods of decline lasted from a few months to several years, and the biggest drop occurred between June 1981 and June 1982, when the TSE 300 fell 39%.

Despite those eleven declines, clients would have made money in the market if they had held on to their investments, even those bought at the peak. Your job is often to reassure clients that volatility is normal, although not always predictable, and that there is no need for panic.

The most recent volatile period was the stock market correction of 1998. The Toronto Stock Exchange (TSE) index declined by 29.3% between April 22, 1998, and August 31, 1998. Those who had invested a large portion of their investments in Canadian equities suffered large setbacks, which caused many individuals to question their future investment strategies. "Should I sell? Should I hold? Should I buy? What should I do?"

At times like this, remind your clients of the following facts:

- equities have and will continue to provide a higher rate of return than other investments over the long term, but with more risk (volatility);

- without risk, investors would not earn higher rates of return;

- long-term investors will inevitably encounter setbacks, and they should not despair when these setbacks occur: it's an essential part of investing in equities.

The table below illustrates the eleven major setbacks in the TSE 300 index, and the length of time it took the market to recover.

Table 3.1   TSE Market Corrections Since 1960

Market Correction	Toronto Stock Exchange 300 Decline	Number of Months to Recover Loss
December 1961 to June 1962	17.0%	10
January 1966 to September 1966	15.1%	7
May 1969 to June 1970	25.4%	33
October 1973 to September 1974	35.0%	44
February 1980	17.6%	4
June 1981 to June 1982	39.0%	10
December 1983 to July 1984	14.4%	6
July 1987 to October 1987	29.0%	23

Table 3.1   TSE Market Corrections Since 1960
(*continued*)

December 1989 to October 1990	20.1%	35
March 1994 to January 1995	15.2%	6
April 1998 to August 1998	29.1%	15

Market Timing

Market timing is simply the strategy of being in the market when it is going up and being out of the market when it is going down. Despite its apparent simplicity, it's almost impossible to execute this strategy consistently. There are simply too many variables that influence market behaviour, and no investor can accurately predict the impact of each variable.

Nevertheless, clients may feel confident that now is the time to follow a strategy based on market timing. As a wealth manager, you may want to reassure them that no matter how well or poorly they time the market, the achievement of their financial goals depends on consistency and disciplined investment, not on catching a lucky wave. You may suggest that they consider the following example.

A perfect market timer will invest his or her yearly contribution at the market low; the worst market timer will make his or her annual contribution at the market high.

The following table illustrates the growth of a portfolio invested in the TSE 300 from January 1962 to February 1998, using different market timing strategies, as well as a comparison with investment in Treasury bills.

Table 3.2   Market Timing Strategies

Strategy	Return
Market low	$511,910
Monthly plan	$469,317
Market high	$433,254
T-bills	$211,155

Investors who consistently made their annual contributions at the market low had a portfolio valued at $511,910, while investors who contributed at the market high had a portfolio value of $433,254. An investor who invested every month without fail would have had a portfolio valued at $469,317. Finally, investors who put all their money in T-Bills would have generated a portfolio valued at $221,155, significantly less than a poor market timer.

"Thus, even an investor who has poor market-timing skills can improve his performance by investing systematically in equities and holding for the long term," says analyst Wilfred Vos. "Systematic investing in equities over time brings superior results to any fixed-income investment held over the same period."[4]

[4] Wilfred Vos and Bruce McDougall, The Best of the Best: Mutual Funds and Blue-Chip Stocks for Canadians, Prentice-Hall, 1999.

CHAPTER 4
Ethical Issues

1.0   Introduction

In this chapter we focus on the ethical basis of wealth management. We will discuss your responsibilities to your clients and other parties, including professional colleagues, the securities industry, and the general public.

Primary Learning Objectives

By the end of this chapter, you should understand:

- **the moral foundation required in wealth management;**

- **the importance of trust in wealth management;**

- **the fiduciary and other moral responsibilities you owe to clients, colleagues, the securities industry, and other interested parties;**

- **the duty and limits of loyal agency;**

- **the role of objectivity, independence, and conflicts of interest;**

- **the importance of honest marketing and fair competition.**

At the end of the chapter, we present a framework for ethical decision-making that you can use to analyse situations from an ethical standpoint.

2.0   Essential Moral Attitudes

Psychologist James Rest[1] has identified four components of moral or ethical behaviour[2]

1. The ability to recognize a situation as having moral significance;

---

[1] James Rest, editor, *Moral Development in the Professions: Psychology and Applied Ethics,* Lawrence Erlbaum Associates, 1994.
[2] The terms "ethical" and "moral" will be used interchangeably in this chapter.

2. The ability to judge which action is right, fair, just, and appropriate;

3. A commitment to taking morally appropriate action;

4. The possession of appropriate personal qualities, such as perseverance and courage, to carry out morally appropriate actions.

All four components must be in place for a person to act morally. Let's look at an example.

A wealth manager, Betty Stuart, is considering recommending that a client, Henry King, invest in a small but promising Internet company, NetTrack Enterprises. Betty's brother-in-law, Fred Barber, is NetTrack's main shareholder and CEO. In this situation, Betty needs to:

1. Recognize that she faces a moral issue if she makes an investment recommendation in a situation in which she has a potential or actual conflict of interest.

2. Assess her options in terms of moral criteria and develop a morally appropriate strategy for managing conflict-of-interest situations, such as disclosing to Henry that one of her relations has a major interest in NetTrack. She must consider whether her professional objectivity regarding NetTrack's promise might be compromised or appear to be compromised by her relationship to Fred.

3. Make a commitment to a morally appropriate strategy such as disclosure.

4. Have the courage to carry out the moral strategy by letting Henry know that Fred Barber is her brother-in-law.

The first two challenges can be described as "cognitive." Betty must recognize that this situation has moral significance and then make an intelligent judgement about what to do. In other words, her **moral insight and judgement** as a wealth manager are being tested.

The second two components have to do with carrying out her decision by acting morally. Here, Betty's **moral character** as a wealth manager is at issue.

Although this chapter focuses on issues of moral judgement, remember that moral character is essential for moral action.

3.0   Ethics and Business Success

Although some people in business and professional life profit by unethical behaviour, acting ethically generally has a favourable effect on business and professional success. Ethical firms and individuals tend in the long run to be more successful than amoral firms and unethical individuals. Ethical firms and individuals build a reputation by earning and deserving the trust of their stakeholders—customers, suppliers, employees, and the general public. The reputation of unethical firms elicits distrust.

At a market level, ethical firms and individuals have a distinct advantage over unethical firms and individuals, since they reduce the transaction costs of doing business with them. If, for example, you know for certain that Jones's word is his bond, then you won't need performance bonds, elaborate credit checks, extensive character references, and so forth to be confident that Jones will live up to his promises. You are more likely to continue doing business with the scrupulously ethical Jones than the double-dealing and deceitful Smith.

The same can be said at the level of society as a whole. A society in which people treat each other according to the Golden Rule ("Do unto others as you would have them do unto you") or even the Copper Rule ("Do not do unto others what you would not have others do unto you") will prosper more than one in which people generally follow the Cynic's Rule ("Do unto others before they do to it to you").

4.0 Trust and Trustworthiness

Wealth managers help clients think through their financial goals and educate clients about options. Wealthy clients not only have a higher net worth than other clients, but they also have higher expectations of their financial advisors. Their financial situations are likely to be more complex. They expect you to demonstrate an advanced skill set and specialized knowledge.

Beyond your knowledge of the client and the market, you need your clients' trust. Your clients should see you as a person who understands and helps them realize their financial goals. They need to know that you are working to promote their best interests and not simply your own.

When clients trust you, they don't personally have to verify everything that you tell them. For example, they don't have to check the tax and estate implications of every investment recommendation or ask for details about its risk or volatility. They certainly don't waste time wondering if you made the recommendation to enrich yourself rather than them. Clients also rely on you to seek the help of other professionals, such as lawyers, accountants, or insurance brokers, as needed.

There are two parts to a trust relationship: trust in your **competence** and trust in your **integrity**. Both are essential. Competence without integrity leaves clients at the mercy of a self-serving professional. Integrity without competence puts clients in the hands of a well-meaning but inept professional.

5.0 Loyal Agency

Wealth managers have an **agent-principal relationship** to their clients. These relationships are found in many areas of business life. For example, corporate managers are agents of the company's owners. Lawyers and accountants also act as agents of their clients. The agent-principal relationship is one of delegated authority. The agent is delegated to act on behalf of the principal to serve the principal's interests.

There are two main types of agent-principal relationship.

1. In the first type, the agent acts according to the **express delegated authority** of the principal. That is, the principal gives explicit instructions to the agent and expects the agent to follow these instructions to the letter. The agent is a kind of instrument or extension of the principal. For example, wealthy and financially knowledgeable clients may seek the services of a wealth manager to handle routine financial transactions following their explicit instructions.

2. In the second type, **discretionary delegated authority,** a principal asks an agent to do what the principal lacks the expertise to do himself or herself. In this relationship, clients may rely heavily on the advice and counsel of the wealth manager in arranging their financial affairs.

In general, most wealth management work falls into the second category—discretionary delegated authority. Clients want a wealth manager to be a competent and trustworthy professional. They need someone with considerable expertise to manage their affairs. However, discretionary authority raises much more complex moral challenges than express delegated moral authority. With express authority, the agent simply follows the principal's orders, whereas discretionary authority requires the agent to use his or her judgement about what is in the principal's best interests.

Discretionary authority relationships are open-ended in a way that express authority relationships are not. For example, consider a simple buyer-seller relationship. You go to the corner store to buy a lottery ticket. What you expect of the clerk as your agent is quite straightforward. You expect her to sell you the lottery ticket that you order. While you may jokingly ask, "Is this one a winner?" or even ask the clerk to "pick out a winner," you have no particular expectations as to the clerk's expertise. As to integrity, your expectations are quite simple—that she will sell you a valid ticket and give you the correct change. It would be easy to write up a simple contract that describes in full the buyer-seller relationship in such a case.

It would be much harder to write a contract for the ethical relationship between wealth managers and their clients. While there would be some obvious expectations, such as "No lying" or "No conflicts of interest," there would also be many areas that would be harder to pin down, such as the client's knowledge and tolerance for risk, the available financial options, the degree of involvement by other professionals in the client's financial affairs, and other variables.

For example, some clients will have clearly thought through their financial goals; while for others, the initial meeting with a wealth manager will be the first time they have paid serious attention to these matters. Moreover, clients' needs change over time. At certain times in their lives, they will depend more on their wealth manager's advice and expertise than at other times.

6.0   Moral Limits to Loyal Agency

Whether the agency relationship is of the express or discretionary type, there are moral limits to being a loyal agent of the principal. For example, it is obviously wrong to help a client do something illegal, such as money laundering, cheating on income tax, or defrauding a former spouse of court-ordered maintenance payments. In such cases, the rights of others limit the wealth manager's loyal agency to a client. If it wrong for the principal to engage in fraud, it is also wrong for his agent to do so at the principal's request.

There is a second and more complicated type of moral limit on loyal agency, especially discretionary agency. An agent with discretionary authority is morally bound to serve the best interests of the principal. If the principal asks the agent to act in a way that appears to seriously compromise those interests, the agent has a responsibility to warn the principal and may even have to resign as an agent. For example, physicians may refuse to provide a treatment to patients if the treatment has been shown to be harmful. Even though a patient may mistakenly believe that such a treatment is beneficial and may demand it, the physician has a professional obligation to not provide such a treatment.

A general ethical and legal standard here is that of professional practice. Ask yourself: would other wealth managers see the client's request as clearly contrary to the client's interests? If the answer is yes, then you should decline to act on the client's instructions. If the answer is no, but you have good reason to believe that the request is nonetheless imprudent, then you should consider advising the client to have another professional carry out the request. Although you may lose the client, you will have acted with integrity by following your own best judgement about the client's good.

7.0   Fiduciary Responsibilities

When trust relationships are open-ended and involve "caring for" or "looking after" a client's interests, there is a **fiduciary relationship** between wealth managers and their clients. Fiduciary or trust relations in ethics and law are needed where there is an imbalance of knowledge or control between two morally related parties, such as a parent and a child, a guardian and a ward, a trustee and a beneficiary, a physician and a patient, or a lawyer and a client. Fiduciary relationships are agent-principal relationships in which the principal has a certain vulnerability and the agent has greater expertise or authority.

You should have particular concern for any vulnerable clients. Clients can be vulnerable for a variety of reasons including limited understanding of financial options and circumstances such as bereavement or illness. The *Rhoads v. Prudential Bache Securities Canada Ltd.* case illustrates the sort of fiduciary care that courts expect in such cases.

The Rhoads were a retired couple with little financial experience. They depended on their investments for their monthly income. However, their financial advisor advised them to invest in equity funds. When the market collapsed in October 1987, the couple suffered serious financial losses. The court found liability on the part of the Rhoads' financial advisors. The court might have found otherwise if the Rhoads had been more knowledgeable investors, less dependent on their investments for income, or if they had a greater time horizon to recoup their losses. Client vulnerability was central to the court's decision.

In the 1994 *Hodgkinson v. Simms* case, Justice LaForest of the Supreme Court described the variables that affect whether or not a relationship is a fiduciary relationship:

> *What is required is evidence of the mutual understanding that one party has relinquished its own self interest and agreed to act solely on behalf of the other party... There must be something more than a simple undertaking by one party to provide information and execute orders for the other for the relationship to be enforced as fiduciary. The relationship of an investor to his or her discount broker will not likely give rise to a fiduciary duty, where the broker is simply a conduit of information and an order taker. There are, however, other advisory relationships where, because of the presence of elements such as trust, confidentiality, and the complexity and importance of the subject matter, it may be reasonable for the advisee to expect that the advisor is in fact exercising his or her special skills in that other party's best interests, unless the contrary is disclosed.*

Here as elsewhere, it is important to observe the Know Your Client rule. There is a spectrum ranging from clients who are highly knowledgeable and who take an active role in investing to clients who have little knowledge and who are passive. Nevertheless, you should treat clients as the ultimate decision-makers by making them aware of the options and acting on their instructions. If a client is incapable of taking charge of his or her own financial affairs, then an independent third party must be appointed by the courts to act as a legal guardian.

Case 4.1   Be Aware of a Client's Vulnerability

Sometimes Ron Springfield must advise a surviving spouse about what to do with inherited assets. But the time immediately following the death of a loved one is a time for grieving, not decision-making, says Springfield, who over the years has guided many widows and widowers through this difficult period.

His widowed clients include Martina, whose retirement life in a peaceful small town in the B.C. Interior was shattered by the sudden death at age 67 of Ivan, her husband of 35 years. Amid the flurry of contacting friends and relatives and making funeral arrangements, Martina also worried about what to do about her husband's RRSP and his other investment accounts. It was all overwhelming, particularly since it was Ivan, and not her, who had been the main overseer of the family's finances.

Martina felt some relief when she contacted Springfield by phone at the brokerage office. He assured her that no immediate action was required on her part. "Most people in your situation believe that things need to be done very quickly," Springfield told Martina. "The reality is that as long as you have enough cash on hand to pay the bills, there is no great rush. When you're ready to sit down and talk, give me a call."

Though the timing of Ivan's passing was unexpected, the couple's financial plan had provided for this eventuality. Ivan's death triggered the payment of a life insurance policy designed to cover the cost of any tax liabilities on his death. The two largest tax payouts had to do with the termination of his RRSP, and the deemed sale of a portfolio of stocks, most of which had been held for at least 10 years.

The life insurance policy had been overfunded to ensure that Martina, the beneficiary, would have a cash reserve to cover the one-time expenses associated with a death. These included the cost of plane fare to enable her son and his young family to make the trip to the West Coast from their home in southern Ontario.

While the mourners gathered to comfort Martina, Springfield was quietly taking care of business. Shortly after the death, his assistant produced an estate-evaluation report listing the market value of Ivan's investment and RRSP assets as of the date of his death, and the maturity dates of his bond and GIC holdings.

The report clearly laid out the information that the executors would need to do their job. "This is a lot easier to do right after the death than several weeks later," says Springfield.

Springfield also reviewed Martina's own investment account, which he has been looking after for many years. He saw that a five-year GIC was just about to expire, and that some stocks and mutual funds had recently paid quarterly dividends into her account.

Case 4.1   Be Aware of a Client's Vulnerability
(continued)

In the weeks and months to come, as the probate process played out, Martina would need advice from Springfield on investing her existing and inherited assets. But now was hardly the time for reinvestment decisions. Springfield knew from his conversation with Martina that she would need the money for short-term travel, funeral, catering, and other related expenses. So he transferred the available cash from Martina's investment account to her daily chequing account at her bank.

Less may be more when it comes to helping clients who are bereaved or going through a period when they are feeling vulnerable. "A death in the family immediately changes a client's profile," says Springfield. "People have a lot more need for liquidity. You try to get everything accumulated and make it easier for them."

8.0   Client Education

Since clients have the right to make final decisions about their own affairs, your main responsibility is to help your clients make good decisions. You should be knowledgeable about their income and assets, short- and long-term financial goals, and tolerance for risk. You must regularly update this information, since their circumstances can change.

Perceptive wealth managers understand that what is at stake for clients is not simply wealth (that is, dollars in an investment portfolio or an annuity), it is significant life-opportunities (education for a child, a dignified retirement, or taking care of a disabled relative). They appreciate the weighty responsibility of having in their hands clients' hopes and dreams.

Nevertheless, your expertise as a wealth manager has limits. You are a wealth manager, not a lifestyle counsellor. Although you need to understand what clients want to do with their money, your clients have the final decision about what sort of life they want to lead. If their lifestyle is causing problems, they should seek help from psychiatrists, counsellors, friends, and family members. As a wealth manager you may have to gently probe a client's aspirations to see if the goals they have set are consistent with their assets. But you should not try to act paternalistically, treating your clients like immature children who must be tricked or cajoled into doing what is in their long-term best interest.

You must also educate your clients about their options. This means "doing your homework" so that you can identify the options and the pros and cons of each one. You should not, however, go beyond the limits of your expertise. Bring in other experts if necessary. For example, if your main expertise is mutual funds, not inheritance tax planning, get help from an expert in that area or advise your clients to seek specialized help on their own.

You should inform your clients about changes in markets or regulations that could significantly affect their financial situation. Legally and ethically, there can be significant liabilities for negligence in this regard. At the same time, clients may need to be reminded to tell you about any important changes in their life circumstances, such as an inheritance, the birth of a child, or a change in career.

Morally your goal should be to help clients make well-informed choices. On the information side, your responsibility is to tell the truth candidly. Avoiding deception is insufficient; it is essential to be forthcoming with the information and guidance that the client needs to make good decisions.

You must also make sure that information is provided in a form that the client can understand, by avoiding technical or academic jargon. This does not, however, mean that you should over-simplify information by leaving out significant details that are part of a complex investment strategy, such as trading in derivatives.

If you have any reason to doubt that a client understands the information you have provided or its importance (especially its relevance to the client's financial aims), you should test the client's knowledge. Ask clients to repeat in their own words what they understand the choices to be. If they can't do this, then you must try again to explain the options clearly. When clients are making important decisions, it is a good idea to review the client's long-term goals to provide context for clients to make a well-informed choice.

It is of course essential to speak truthfully and not to make deceptive or misleading statements. For example, the securities industry requires advisors not to make unjustified promises of specific results, such as by stating or implying that the past performance of an equity fund is a sure-fire indicator of its future performance. Avoid presenting information selectively, for example, pointing to the strong performance of a mutual fund without mentioning that its experienced management team has just moved to another company and has been replaced by a team of neophytes. Don't present the opinions of financial commentators as statements of fact.

But there is more to client education than providing bare information. Clients want to know more than just facts and figures. They need to know how various options will affect their lives and the achievement of their financial goals.

As a financial professional, you have an obligation to make sure that the context you provide for financial and other information is accurate and not misleading. Go beyond asking yourself if what you are saying, "Is true and to the point?" Ask yourself: "What is the client hearing and understanding?" Enormous problems can be avoided when professionals carefully work to close the gap between what they are saying and what clients are hearing. If you are in doubt about a client's understanding, ask the client.

When you need clients to make a choice, remember:

- To have a choice, clients must understand that there *is* a choice. Make the options explicit if a client seems passive or non-responsive.

- Don't force clients to make a decision. Give them time to think it over. It is sometimes better to schedule an additional meeting with clients so that they can sleep on a decision rather than to force a premature decision.

- The same information can often be presented in ways that favour a particular option or in ways that inhibit it. For instance, presenting the choice with a double or nothing bet as "a 50% chance of doubling your money" is likely to have a far more positive effect than pointing out there is "50% chance of losing your stake." There have been famous experiments in which experts have been by fooled by the same data presented in alternative forms. Pointing out hidden similarities can be crucial in ensuring that a client makes an informed choice.

9.0   Professional Standards

The standard of professional behaviour is tested by the question, "What would a well-informed wealth manager advise?" This test is built on the idea that within each profession, there is a broad area of professional agreement about standards. Although areas remain in which professionals may reasonably disagree, professional standards represent a substantial area of agreement. Both ethically and legally, professionals are required to use due diligence to uphold these standards in their own practice. Among other things, this means that they are expected to keep their knowledge current through, for example, continuing professional education. Ignorance is no excuse for poor advice. It is not just what you know, but what a qualified professional should be expected to know.

The standard of professional responsibility and liability is a modified subjective standard. It differs from an objective standard, which would require a professional to "get it right" or produce certain results, no matter how hard it would be to guarantee those results in advance. An objective standard for a professional is like demanding that a physician cure a patient, whereas a subjective standard requires the physician to diligently follow professional practice guidelines and standards. Professional standards are not, however, completely subjective standards, since they require professionals to meet or exceed professional criteria for competence and integrity. Therefore a professional may not excuse his or her behaviour by arguing, say, that he or she lacks certain professional knowledge.

A related area of concern with professional standards is the development of appropriate professional virtues. Moral character is essential for moral behaviour. It is not just a matter of knowing what is right, but of acting on that knowledge. It is particularly important for professionals like wealth managers to have insight into their own characters and their own professional practices to identify morally sensitive areas. Part of this self-examination involves figuring out what the incentives and disincentives are in the area of professional practice.

Take the simple but important matter of how wealth managers are compensated. Different methods of compensation have different incentives. Commissions, either direct or indirect, create an incentive for "running up the meter." The same problem occurs when managers are compensated on a fee-for-service basis. On the other hand, fixed fees provide no incentive to go the extra mile for clients. Awareness of these structural incentives and disincentives can alert astute wealth managers to areas in which extra moral effort is necessary. Good wealth managers develop the virtues and character to do the right thing, regardless of monetary incentives or disincentives.

Professional standards for wealth managers have a variety of sources. Wealth managers are often qualified financial planners or investment advisors. Canadian financial planners have a *Code of Ethics and Standards of Conduct for Financial Planners*. The Code sets out seven key principles:

- integrity;
- objectivity;
- competence;
- fairness;
- confidentiality;
- professionalism;
- diligence.

Wealth managers who are also accountants (CAs, CGAs, or CMAs) have a particular code of conduct that is relevant to wealth management. Wealth managers may also come under other professional or regulatory rules, such as those set by self-regulating organizations (like stock exchanges), securities commissions, or other professional bodies. Across these various sources, there is broad consistency with regard to the seven principles set out in the *CFP Code of Ethics*.

There may also be specific requirements or regulations specific to a particular profession or regulatory authority, such as rules in accounting codes for the establishment of a professional practice or a stock exchanges rules for trading stocks. If there are inconsistencies between the rules of one body and those of another, it is prudent to consult experts in both groups to find a satisfactory resolution.

Professional standards for different groups in the financial planning sector are relevant in another way to wealth managers. You will need to work with professionals and experts from a variety of areas, including law, taxation, accounting, insurance, and investments. Seek out trustworthy individuals who meet and, ideally, exceed the ethical standards required in their particular areas of expertise. You will acquire an understanding of the standards in related professions and how they are applied and enforced.

9.1   Objectivity and Independence

Objectivity and independence are essential values for wealth managers. According to the *CFP Code of Ethics*, objectivity requires "intellectual honesty and impartiality." Wealth managers who are objective seek solid evidence to back their judgements. They don't rely on opinion, idle speculation, or emotion. Objective advisors try to hear both sides of a dispute or disagreement and do not seek to limit prematurely the expression of opposing points of view. They are not "know-it-alls," nor do they claim to be infallible. They recognize their own limitations and seek the advice and assistance of others in areas where they do not feel competent to judge. In the complex and ever-changing area of wealth management, objectivity is an essential virtue.

Independence means remaining free of the control of others and not bending or compromising professional judgements out of fear of retaliation or in the expectation of receiving favours. Independence reinforces objectivity by creating a space for the exercise of objective judgement. Being independent does not mean you should isolate yourself from others and refuse to consider their points of view. Rather, independence is a habit of mind that allows you to reach your own conclusions on particular matters, including, for example, whether or not to accept another person's claims or assertions.

9.2   Understanding and Avoiding Conflicts of Interest[3]

A conflict of interest is "a situation in which a person, such as a public official, an employee, or a professional, has a private or personal interest sufficient to appear to influence the objective exercise of his or her official duties."[4] There are three key elements in this definition.

1. Private or personal interests. Often this is a financial interest, but it could also be another sort of interest, say, to provide a special advantage to a spouse or child. There is nothing wrong with private or personal interests in themselves, for instance, changing jobs for more pay or helping a child get a university education.

2. An official duty. This is the duty you have because you act in an official capacity. As a wealth manager you take on certain official responsibilities, thereby acquiring obligations to your clients, employers, and others. These obligations should take precedence over your own private or personal interests.

3. Conflicts of interest occur when private or personal interests collide with objective and independent professional judgement. Clients and employers value professionals because they expect professionals to be objective and independent. Private and personal interests that either interfere or appear likely to interfere with objectivity or

---

[3] Parts of this subsection are taken from Michael McDonald's article, "Ethics and Conflicts of Interest" (1994), which is posted at http://www.ethics. ubc.ca/mcdonald.

[4] Kenneth Kernaghan and John W. Langford. *The Responsible Public Servant,* Institute for Research on Public Policy, 1990.

independence are a matter of legitimate concern to those who rely on professionals—be they clients, employers, professional colleagues, or the general public.

It is also important to avoid apparent and potential as well as actual conflicts of interests.

•   An **apparent** conflict of interest is one in which a reasonable person would think that the professional's judgement is likely to be compromised.

•   A **potential** conflict of interest is a situation that may develop into an actual conflict of interest.

It is important to distinguish a conflict of obligations from a conflict of interest.

In a **conflict of obligations**, an individual faces a *right versus right* choice. A classic example of a conflict of obligations is whether to tell a dying accident victim that his spouse has just perished in the same accident or let him die in peace, thinking that his spouse survived the accident. There isn't an easy right answer in such a case, and people disagree about which option is preferable.

An example in the investment area would be a situation in which a wealth manager comes up with a financial strategy that can be offered to only one client (for example, to buy the controlling interest in a specific business), but the manager has two clients, A and B, both of whom would benefit by such an investment. Assuming both clients have an equal claim on the wealth manager's time and efforts, the best that can be done is to make a judgement call as to which client should benefit.

In a **conflict of interest**, the conflict is a matter of *right versus wrong*. Typical examples of conflict of interest include self-dealing (in the example cited earlier, Betty could have recommended her brother-in-law's firm as an investment without telling the client about the familial relationship). Another would be using your employer's office or contact lists without permission to conduct your own private business. A third example would occur when you change jobs. You leave one firm to take up work with another firm, taking your old firm's client list with you.

There are three strategies for managing conflicts of interest.

1.   Disclosure to all interested parties. If everyone knows what your interests are, then they can take appropriate precautions. Your actions are out in the open, subject to the scrutiny of others. This is the strategy that Betty adopted.

2.   Bring in outside experts to evaluate the situation and advise interested parties.

3.   Vacate or give up the conflicting interest. For example, when you change jobs, you simply leave the old client list behind and start afresh.

Wealth managers must be alert to possible conflicts of interest not only for themselves but also for others.

For example, Bill Chow asks his wealth manager, Cindy Yurko, to manage the affairs of his senile father James Chow, over whom Bill has legal guardianship. Cindy must treat James's affairs as separate from those of Bill. If Bill urges investment and other decisions that are designed to favour his own interests at the expense of his father's interests, it is not appropriate for Cindy to accept these instructions. She should try to persuade Bill that other investments are more appropriate for his father and, if necessary, remind him of his moral and legal obligation as a guardian to promote his father's interests, not his own. If this approach does not work, Cindy may have to take further actions, such as involving other members of the Chow family or even legal authorities.

Another example: Daniel Armstrong, who serves on the board of a closely held company, Jazz Enterprises, Ltd., calls his wealth manager Tom Peterson and places a substantial purchase order for Jazz shares. Tom is puzzled by Daniel's buy order. Jazz shares have been in the doldrums for weeks, and in Tom's view, Daniel's portfolio is already overloaded with Jazz shares. At the very least in these circumstances, Tom should check to see if Daniel is engaging in insider trading. Tom might even ask for an explicit written disclaimer from Daniel in these circumstances. (It would be wise for Tom's employers to have a policy requiring such disclaimers, since this should discourage insider trading and help reduce the wealth management company's potential liabilities.)

Another potential conflict of interest involves the regulation that investment advisors are not allowed to receive direct or indirect benefits from mutual funds. However, conferences and seminars organized by mutual fund companies for dealer sales representatives are permitted, but restricted to locations within Canada and the continental United States.[5]

Case 4.2   Mutual Funds and Conflicts of Interest

Mutual fund M has a lavish seminar each year in a resort location for educational purposes—spouses and kids included. Although there are no explicit requirements regarding qualifications for the trip, such as selling so many dollars' worth of M units per year, there is the implicit expectation that all those going advise clients with significant investments in M.

Wealth manager Carl Davis and his family very much enjoy this annual junket, which this year will be a trip to Bermuda in February with all travel and golfing fees covered. Alan Rudanya, who is arranging the seminar for M, calls to ask Carl to give a talk on the relative advantages of investing in M and asks for "as many illustrations as possible."

Carl agrees to give the talk, even though he hasn't been recommending M very much to clients this year. Carl is now feeling that perhaps he should be recommending M more often to clients—a clear conflict of interest situation.

---

[5] *Conduct and Practices Handbook,* The Canadian Securities Institute, 1999, p. 103.

Case 4.3   Relationships and Recommendations

Sam and Dana Windfield are retired and comfortably wealthy, confident that they will be able to maintain their lifestyle throughout their retirement years. They also want to help their handicapped nephew, who is unable to manage his financial affairs independently. A trust arrangement would be ideal, since it would ensure that his financial needs were provided for, while leaving the trust account's assets outside his control.

For advice on which trustee to select, the Windfields—who are themselves childless—turned to their own broker, Randy Mercer. His bank-owned firm is one of the biggest in the country. Wanting to ensure the best for their nephew, the Windfields were a little uneasy at first when Mercer suggested that the Windfields take their business to the bank's own trust company, whose nearest branch also happened to be on the main floor of the office tower where Mercer works.

It was certainly convenient, particularly for expediting the paperwork of arranging the transfer of assets to the trust. But the Windfields wanted to be satisfied that this was the right course for the long term. Mercer, and the trust company would have to make their case if they wanted the responsibility of looking after their nephew, whose special needs had severely strained the financial resources of his parents.

The Windfields wanted the trust's assets to be managed prudently, with an eye toward capital preservation and mitigation of risk, and in this regard they felt assured by the strength and stability of the bank's trust subsidiary. Yet, recognizing that their nephew was now only in his late 30s, they also recognized the need to have a growth component in the portfolio.

Upon further investigation, including an interview with the portfolio manager who would be overseeing their nephew's trust account, the Windfields felt satisfied that the trust's investment objectives could be attained. In doing some comparison shopping on fees, they found potentially cheaper alternatives, but not considerably cheaper, given the level of advice and service that they wanted.

For his part, Mercer acknowledged to the Windfields the obvious corporate relationship between the two firms. He also explained that this type of cross-referral happened all the time, stressing that the two related companies were distinct entities that operated separately from one other. "The bank-owned trust should be accepted or rejected on its own merits, and not because it has a similar corporate name and logo," he said.

The Windfields agreed, and eventually decided to go with the bank-owned firm. As part of the parent bank's policy, clients who want to transfer between one financial-services subsidiary and another are required to sign a disclosure form. The form states that the common corporate ownership has been explained to them, that they understand the affiliation, and that they are in favour of the transfer. When the Windfields signed, they felt that they were doing so with their eyes wide open.

9.3   Privacy and Confidentiality

The general principle regarding privacy is that client information gathered in confidence may be shared with others only with the client's authorization. Thus, in marketing services, it would be wrong for a wealth manager to tell a potential client that he manages the affairs of a well-known wealthy recluse. It is, however, acceptable to ask existing clients to recommend you verbally or in writing. However, an endorsement should not be demanded as a condition for continuing to provide first-class professional services.

Disclosing client information to other professionals (such as asking an accountant for tax advice on a client's file), is acceptable on a "need-to-know" basis with trustworthy individuals. Confidential information should be protected through appropriate security arrangements for confidential files, including encryption for files transferred electronically.

It is inappropriate to use confidential information from a client for your personal benefit or the benefit of other clients. Ambiguous situations may nonetheless arise in which information arises from both a confidential source and a public source. In such cases, you can use the "newspaper test": "How would this look if it were reported in tomorrow morning's newspaper?" You may also want to get a colleague's advice.

A regulatory authority may have the legal authority to order the disclosure of confidential information. If you are in doubt about the regulator's authority, you should seek a legal opinion. There may also be occasional cases in which breach of confidentiality is necessary to protect third parties from harm. Some of these cases may raise the issue of "Who is the client?" especially in situations of internal family conflict over divorce and separation, for example, or in which there is possible financial abuse of a dependent relative.

9.4   Honesty in Marketing Services and Fair Competition

Wealth management is not just a way of providing valuable services to clients; it is also a business. Properly managed, there need be no ethical conflict between providing services to clients and customers and making a profit. Ethical management includes not only guarding against conflicts of interest and protecting confidentiality, but also proper marketing of management services and fair competition.

There is more to marketing ethics than care in seeking client endorsements. As in all dealings with clients, representations made to potential clients must meet the standards of honesty and candour. Wealth managers as individuals and as a group will not retain their credibility over the long run if they fail to meet these standards. Not only must you avoid outright misrepresentations, but also misleading half-truths, hidden disclaimers, deliberately ambiguous statements, or claims of having greater expertise than you actually possess. A good test for marketing services is to ask, "Is this an honest and fair representation of what I as a wealth manager can do for these potential clients?"

Marketing services can take many forms. Not all marketing takes place in electronic or print media. Some of the most effective marketing in the world of wealth management will be of the informal soft-sell variety rather than the hard sell associated with mass-market consumer products. Educational seminars and informal contacts in business or in community service provide low-key and often highly effective opportunities to market yourself as a wealth manager. But just because they are low-key, soft-sell opportunities do not make standards of honesty and candour irrelevant. In fact, they are even more important, since in casual settings most people have their guards down and are more inclined to trust each other.

Wealth managers work in a competitive environment. Competition is one of the cornerstones of a free market economy. However, despite the rhetoric of some business media, competition cannot be a free-for-all—the "dog-eat-dog" or "no-holds-barred" approach. Free market competition is built on both negative and positive moral standards. The basic negative rules are "No coercion" and "No fraud." The basic positive rule is "Keep your word."

It is easy to forget in the flurry of day-to-day business activities that the market is built as much on cooperation as it is on competition. The essence of business success is building cooperative arrangements with customers, employees, colleagues, and other parties including the general public. A company can't stay in business unless customers freely choose to buy its products. The company also needs managers, employees, investors, creditors, suppliers, and others to maintain its operations. Companies need a secure operating environment created by effective social norms and resting on public confidence.

Fair competition has two main elements.

1. Fair treatment of competitors. This includes not engaging in marketing practices that misrepresent one's competition or in industrial sabotage and espionage, for example, stealing confidential information.

2. Genuine competition. In certain types of markets such as oligopolies, it is easy for businesses to collude by fixing prices, limiting innovations, or keeping out new competitors through lobbying for government restrictions. The consumer loses in such situations, and others are denied the opportunity to enter the market to offer their services.

Maintaining both elements of fair competition requires both individual and collective (industry-wide) action. So the wealth management entrepreneur should be sure that his own actions are both fair and competitive and work with others in the industry to ensure that this standard prevails generally.

10.0 A Framework for Ethical Decision-Making

This is a framework for ethical decision-making used in many professional training programs and postsecondary institutions.

A Framework for Ethical Decision-Making, Version 5.2: Ethics Shareware[6]

1. Identify the problem.

1.1. Be alert; be sensitive to morally charged situations. Look behind the technical requirements of your job to see the moral dimensions. Use your ethical resources to determine relevant moral standards [see Part 3 below]. Use your moral intuition.

1.2. Gather information, and don't jump to conclusions. While accuracy is important, there can be a trade-off between gathering more information and spending so much time on research that morally significant options disappear. Sometimes you may have to make supplementary assumptions because there is insufficient information and no time to gather more information.

1.3. State the case briefly with as many of the relevant facts and circumstances as you can gather within the decision time available.

1.3.1. What decisions have to be made? There may be more than one decision to be made.

1.3.2. By whom? Remember that there may be more than one decision-maker and that the interactions between decision makers can be important.

1.3.3. Be alert to actual or potential conflict of interest situations. If you have a conflict of interest, you should declare the conflict openly. In a conflict of interest case, it is often appropriate to also let others make the decision without your input or direction.

1.4. Consider the context of decision-making. Ask yourself why this decision is being made in this context at this time? Are there better contexts for making this decision? Are the right decision-makers included?

---

[6] Author of this framework is Michael McDonald. Students should feel free to share this framework with others. If you reprint or distribute it, please let the author know. Comments are welcome. Send comments and requests to the author at mcdonald@ethics.ubc.ca. An earlier framework is posted on the Unversity of British Columbia's centre for Applied Ethics web page: http:// www.ethics.ubc.ca.

2.   *Specify feasible alternatives.*

State the options at each stage of decision-making for each decision-maker. You then should identify the likely consequences of various decisions. Here, you should remember to take into account good or bad consequences, not just for yourself, your profession, organization or clients, but for all affected persons. Be honest about your own stake in particular outcomes and encourage others to do the same.

3.   *Use your ethical resources to identify morally significant factors in each alternative.*

3.1.   Principles. These are principles that are widely accepted in one form or another in the common moralities of many communities and organizations.

- Respect autonomy. Would I be exploiting others, treating them paternalistically, or otherwise affecting them without their free and informed consent? Have promises been made? Are there legitimate expectations on the part of others because I am a professional person or family member?

- Don't harm. Would I be harming someone to whom I have a general or specific obligation as a professional or as a human being?

- Do good. Should I be preventing harm, removing harm, or even providing positive benefits to others?

- Be fair.

3.2.   Moral models. Sometimes you will get moral insight from modelling your behaviour on a person of great moral integrity.

3.3.   Ethically informed sources. Consult policies and other source materials, professional norms such as company policy, legal precedents, and wisdom from your religious or cultural traditions.

3.4.   Context. Consider contextual features of the case that seem significant, such as the past history of relationships with various parties.

3.5.   Personal judgements. Your judgements, your associates, and trusted friends or advisors can be invaluable. Of course, in talking a tough decision over with others, you have to respect client and employer confidentiality. Discussion with others is particularly important when other decision-makers are involved, such as your employer, co-workers, clients, or partners. Professional or business associations may provide confidential advice. Experienced co-workers can be helpful. Many forward-looking organizations have ethics committees or ombudsmen to provide advice. A good friend or advisor can also help you by listening and offering their advice.

4.   Propose and test possible resolutions.

4.1.   Perform a sensitivity analysis. Consider your choice critically: which factors would have to change to get you to alter your decision?

4.2.   Impact on the ethical performance of others. Think about the effect of each choice upon the choices of other responsible parties. Are you making it easier or harder for them to do the right thing? Are you setting a good example?

4.3.   Would a good person do this? Ask yourself what a virtuous professional— one with integrity and experience—would do in these circumstances.

4.4.   What if everyone in these circumstances did this? Formulate your choice as a general maxim for all similar cases.

4.5.   Will this maintain trust relationships with others? If others are in my care or otherwise dependent on me, it is important that I continue to deserve their trust.

4.6.   Does it still seem right? Are you still satisfied with your choice? If you are still satisfied, then go with your choice. If not, consider the factors that make you uncomfortable with a view to coming up with a new general rule with which you are satisfied.

5.   Make your choice.

5.1.   Live with it.

5.2.   Learn from it.

This means accepting responsibility for your choice. It also means accepting the possibility that you might be wrong or that you will make a less than optimal decision. The object is to make a good choice with the information available, not to make a perfect choice. Learn from your failures and successes.

Section II

Advanced Financial Planning

This section focuses on the four pillars of advanced financial planning: retirement, tax, insurance, and estate planning. Although it has not been designed to be a legal or tax guide, it gives a general, practical and objective overview of the key financial planning issues within these four categories. Together with an understanding of your client's needs, objectives, and constraints, you can use the information in the section to build a financial and investment plan that will help take your clients from where they are to where they want to be.

CHAPTER 5

Retirement Planning

1.0 Introduction

Retirement planning involves building up a nest egg for retirement. It is not always easy to make the transition from saving for retirement to living off those savings. Some people restrict themselves to spending only the earnings on their portfolio. Others try to live within their pension earnings.

This chapter will look at pre-retirement planning, preparing for retirement, and post-retirement money management. Each phase has its own issues. We will also look at ways to integrate a client's life goals with retirement planning strategies and techniques.

Primary Learning Objectives

By the end of this chapter, you should understand:

- **the assumptions, and their importance, required in a retirement independence calculation;**

- **the difference a slight change in an assumption can make in planning a client's retirement and why there should be a disclaimer regarding its limitations;**

- **trends in retirement planning that affect the level of registered retirement savings and additional uses for RRSPs;**

- **how to determine whether or not a client should opt out of his or her company pension plan;**

- **alternative retirement savings options beyond RRSPs and RPPs, how they work, and the risk factors associated with each option;**

- **retirement income projections and how to use them to explain retirement planning principles to clients;**

- **issues faced by clients who are retiring from a family business or partnership;**

- **useful financial strategies during retirement that involve clients' RRSPs and asset allocation strategy;**

- **strategies that will maximize a client's RRIF;**

- **tax planning strategies that are available in retirement;**

- **how retirement planning is integrated with estate planning;**

- **the emotional issues surrounding retirement.**

2.0   The Retirement Independence Calculation

Before you can help your clients plan their retirement, you should ask them what retirement means to them. Clients in a corporate or government position might see retirement as their reward for having put up with the job for all those years. Some people feel they are being put out to pasture before they are ready. Others believe that retirement is something they can never achieve because of misfortune or lack of planning. Still, others do not see themselves as retired, but rather as cutting back on work gradually as time goes on.

Traditional retirement planning starts with the assumption that everyone retires at 65, which is the age at which Old Age Security (OAS), the Canada Pension Plan (CPP), and government benefits usually start. Although there is uncertainty about whether government benefits will continue in the form we know them today, it is unwise to use this uncertainty as a way to market retirement planning services. Wealth managers provide guidance to clients, but it is up to the clients to determine the level of risk they are willing to accept in their retirement projections.

The retirement projection helps clients understand the choices they have and illustrates what they need to do to achieve their retirement goals. Many clients do not understand these calculations, the assumptions that are used, and the difference a slight change in an assumption can make in their retirement planning. You need to explain these issues to your clients in detail. Chapter 9 of the Professional Financial Planning Course (PFPC) textbook illustrates a typical retirement projection calculation. As well, there is an abundance of retirement planning calculators on the internet.

2.1   Variables

The variables in a retirement independence calculation include:

- A client's likely life expectancy. Add more years if the client's family has a history of longevity. Most clients would rather save too much than run out of money before they die.

- The age at which the client wishes to retire.

- The amount needed to support the lifestyle a client expects in retirement.
- The likely inflation rate between now and the beginning of the client's retirement, and the rate likely to prevail during the client's retirement.
- The appropriate asset mix between now and the beginning of the client's retirement and the appropriate asset mix during the client's retirement.
- The rates of return for each asset class in the asset mix.
- The marginal tax bracket of a client before and during retirement.
- The mix of registered assets and investment assets.
- The additional savings a client plans to make.
- The amount a client will receive from government benefits, including OAS and CPP.
- The tax rules in force during a client's lifetime. The income projection should be based on the tax rules as they stand at the time the retirement projection is done.
- The client's company pension plan, if any, and the retirement income the client expects to receive under the terms of the plan. If the plan is a defined benefit plan, the terms can be found in the employee pension handbook. If it is a defined contribution plan, the retirement benefit will be based on the rate of savings, the types of investments, and the actual returns on those investments.
- Any estate planning goals a client may have.

2.2   The Disclaimer

Given all the variables required in the calculations, all retirement income projections should be accompanied by a disclaimer such as the following:

> *These retirement calculations are based on certain assumptions and on the government benefits in effect at the time the projection was prepared. The information is for illustration purposes only. There is no guarantee that the assumptions in the document are accurate, nor is there any guarantee that the government benefits used in these calculations will be in effect throughout the retirement period. The retirement calculation should be reviewed and recalculated every two or three years, so that the assumptions and savings rate can be adjusted if necessary. Although this retirement projection is prepared using assumptions that are considered appropriate within the financial planning industry at present, there is no certainty that this illustration will reflect the future.*

2.3   The Budget

The closer clients get to their retirement date, the more realistic their income needs must be, since they must be able to prepare an accurate retirement budget. However, it would be a mistake to assume that their expenses in the first decade of retirement will be similar to their expenses in the last decade of retirement.

In the first decade of retirement, clients are likely to have a more active lifestyle, with its related expenses. Later, they may be less active but have higher expenses, particularly if they need to move into a nursing home, rather than relying on whatever support government programs will provide. Some clients may be looking for ways to shelter their assets if they expect to enter a government-funded nursing home. Although they could give away their assets or put them into a trust, the government does not support individuals who have the ability to pay, and will apply means tests.

As much as clients generally dislike budgeting, they need to estimate how much their retirement lifestyle will cost. They also need to understand how much they will spend in the last few years before retirement and think about their expenses in retirement. If clients are planning to move to a smaller home or a different country, it will be harder for them to do this exercise. But without it, the retirement income projection is just a 'guess-timate'.

2.4   Multiple Illustrations

To help clients understand the retirement projection and how different assumptions affect the result, you should carry out multiple calculations to illustrate the differences. The rate-of-return assumptions make an important difference to the retirement projection and should be tied to the long-term historical rates of return, the economic outlook, and a client's personal risk tolerance. The following example illustrates the rate-of-return assumptions:

Client details: Lesley Shapiro

Sex:	Female
Current age:	52
Life expectancy:	90
Current income:	$65,000
Company pension plan:	None
Current value of RRSP:	$150,000
Current value of non-registered account:	$50,000
Projected inflation rate:	2%
Marginal tax rate:	50%
Target retirement income:	70% of pre-retirement income
Eligibility for CPP and OAS:	Maximum benefits payable
House:	Fully paid for as of the beginning of the year

If the annual rate of return between now and age 90 is 8%, Lesley will need to save about $260 a month. However if the annual rate of return is 6.5% between now and age 90, she will need to save about $927 a month.

Although the difference in the rate of return might not seem significant to clients, how it affects the amount they need to save will be obvious to them. You could also compare the amount of interest a person would pay over a 25-year mortgage at 6.5% compared to a mortgage at 7% to help your client understand the effect of a change in rate of return.

Suppose Lesley wanted to retire at 60. Assuming a 6.5% annual return, she would have to maximize her annual RRSP contribution and save more than $2,000 a month outside her RRSP. Even assuming an 8% annual return, she would still have to save $1,274 a month outside her RRSP, as well as making the maximum RRSP contribution. This is more than a third of her salary—a very unlikely scenario. Although she was planning to redirect all of the money that had been going to the mortgage payment, these numbers are larger than her budget allows.

2.5   The Reality Check

Retirement income projections may be the first time clients see that their retirement goals and dreams are too ambitious. You need to help clients find solutions, financial or otherwise, that will help them come to terms with the choices they have made in their lives to date, as well as the available options.

The four traditional options for clients are:

1. Save more before retirement.
2. Retire later and save for a longer period.
3. Accept less income during retirement.
4. Increase the risk in the portfolio to achieve a higher rate of growth.

Other options are possible. For example, Lesley might be able to retire at 60 if she is willing to get a reverse mortgage. In this way she could tap into the equity she has build up in her house after she has used up her investment and RRSP portfolios. It may not be an ideal solution, but it is another option.

Some clients may be on track to reach their retirement goals. They have strong RRSPs and company pension plans, good cash flow, and many years to save before retirement. While you can encourage them to keep up their rate of savings, you can also ask them to reflect on what they want their money to do for them over their lifetime. If the retirement projection shows that they will have a surplus in retirement, there are several questions you and they should consider. Should they cut back on their savings rate? Should you encourage them to continue to build their retirement savings in case the market drops? What are their goals and tolerance for risk? If you discover that some clients are saving for retirement at the expense of their lifestyle today, you should consider helping them find a better balance between their current lifestyle and their future needs.

3.0   Trends in Retirement Planning

In a world driven by ideal financial planning decisions, all individuals would live within their means and set aside a portion of every dollar they make for retirement. In Canada, every working Canadian is eligible to receive Old Age Security and Canada Pension Plan benefits. In 1999, these two benefits would give a working Canadian a maximum annual income of more than $12,000, or a couple more than $25,000. Some Canadians will have more disposable income in retirement at these income levels than they had during their working years. Others are not prepared to live on these income levels.

The government either does not assume that this income will be enough for Canadians to enjoy their retirement years, or does not want Canadians to depend too heavily on the continuation of these benefits. This is why, in addition to the basic benefits provided, the government offers tax deductions for contributions to a company pension plan or to a Registered Retirement Savings Plan (RRSP). Eligible contributions provide tax savings today in exchange for tax-deferred growth and a future taxable retirement benefit. Although the government wants Canadians to be responsible for providing more of their own income needs in retirement, and to depend less on government benefits, it does not mean that government benefits will be eliminated. Rather, the trend is to give with one hand, and, when certain income levels are exceeded, to take back some or all benefits with the other hand.

3.1   Level of Registered Retirement Savings

While Canadians are using the Registered Retirement Savings Plan (RRSP) to save for their retirement, the introduction of the enhanced Registered Education Savings Plan (RESP) will redirect some dollars away from the RRSP in households with young, growing families. This does not necessarily put a family's retirement at risk. It reflects two considerations:

- the value of post secondary education to Canadians; and
- the fact that the time horizon for education is shorter than that for retirement, so a family can take care of first things first.

Retirement planning needs to be sensitive to clients' changing values and goals over a lifetime. The closer people get to retirement, the more important it becomes. Financial goals often conflict, particularly for educated consumers who feel that they should pay down their mortgage, educate their children, maximize their RRSP, and enjoy their life, all at the same time. Some clients try to do a little bit of everything. Others try to pay off their mortgage and get the kids educated before they tackle saving for retirement. As a wealth manager, you can help clients prioritize their goals based on their financial projections and their emotional needs.

Human behaviour, being what it is, suggests that clients should make their RRSP contributions or prepay their mortgage on a regular basis. Some wealth managers want their clients to get into the habit of making their RRSP contributions, but is this the best financial choice for clients who also have the option of prepaying their mortgage? Like many financial decisions, it depends on a number of variables, such as:

- The rate of return a client might earn inside the RRSP, based on their risk profile. If the rate of return a client can make is higher than the interest rate charged on the mortgage, then the RRSP contribution makes more sense.
- The after-tax interest rate on the mortgage.
- The spread between the interest rate on the mortgage and the anticipated rate of return.
- The number of years remaining on the mortgage. The earlier a client is in the mortgage schedule, the greater the benefit will be of prepaying the mortgage rather than contributing to an RRSP.
- The number of years to retirement. The closer a client is to retirement, the better the RRSP appears, because they have only so many years left to take advantage of the RRSP tax savings.
- The client's marginal tax bracket. The higher the marginal tax bracket, the better the RRSP option looks.

3.2   Additional Uses for RRSPs: Home Buyer's Plan and the Lifelong Learning Plan

The purpose of the RRSP has always been, first and foremost, a tax-assisted retirement savings program. However, RRSPs have also been used over the years for income splitting, in preparation for retirement, as well as during the working years. The spouse in the higher income bracket would make a contribution to a spousal RRSP on behalf of the spouse in a lower-income bracket. Although this is allowed, there is a waiting period of three calendar years before the amount can be withdrawn from the RRSP and taxed exclusively in the hands of the lower-income spouse.

More recently, the government has introduced the Home Buyer's Plan (HBP) and the Lifelong Learning Plan (LLP), which allow annuitants to withdraw money from their RRSP, without penalty, to buy a home or to pay educational expenses, if certain qualifications are met. If the annuitant repays less than the annual amount, the difference is included in the taxable income for that year.

If clients intend to withdraw money from their RRSP for either of these uses, they should understand the limits on the deductibility of RRSP contributions for the year. Any contributions made to an RRSP in the 89-day period just before the HBP or LLP amount is withdrawn from the RRSP may not be eligible for deduction in any year.

Summary of HBP and LLP		
Program	**Home Buyer's Plan**	**Lifelong Learning Plan**
Maximum withdrawal	$20,000	$20,000 (maximum $10,000 a year)
Death of annuitant	Balance is taxed unless spouse took out plan for same property	Balance is taxed
Maximum loan period	15 years	10 years
Amount that must be included as income following each tax year	Any portion of the 1/15th required payment you do not make is added to your income.	Any portion of the 1/10th required payment you do not make is added to income

You must find out if your clients intend their RRSP money for long-term retirement savings, or if some or all of it will be applied to one of these two shorter-term uses. If clients intend to use either the HBP or the LLP, the investments will need to be turned into cash before they can be withdrawn.

These programs give clients more flexibility for their money in the registered plan. However, like any tax-assisted planning program, just because they *can* do these things does not mean they *should*.

Clients may see the HBP as a way to give themselves an interest-free loan. Although the withdrawal may trigger redemption and administration fees, the direct cost of the loan from inside the RRSP is zero interest on a $20,000 loan (assuming no tax is due, because the client repays the HBP on schedule). By comparison, a $20,000 mortgage with a 15-year term at 7% would create an interest cost of $13,194. However, clients may not see that taking the loan reduces their opportunity for tax-sheltered growth on their investments if they had left the money in the RRSP. In other words, the loan is not free—it has an opportunity cost.

The financial implications of the LLP program are slightly different. Would a client have had access to money to fund further education without the LLP? If the educational program enables clients to find work when they might otherwise have been unemployed, or if it helps them get a promotion or a job in which they can earn more money, then its value will probably be greater than leaving the money in an RRSP.

4.0 Should a Client Opt Out of a Company Pension Plan?

Detailed descriptions of different types of company pension plans and how they work are illustrated in the more basic financial planning texts including the PFPC textbook. In this section we will discuss some of the factors that determine whether clients should opt out of a company pension plan.

Less than 45% of working Canadians are members of a company pension plan. The trend has been to replace the Defined Benefit Pension Plan (DBP) with either a Defined Contribution Plan (DCP) or a Group Registered Retirement Savings Plan (GRRSP), or to leave retirement options up to the individual employee. Some employers offer a deferred profit-sharing plan, whereby employees receive a share of the company profits.

The DBP plan may provide the richest benefit to employees. The amount of pension they receive is based on a formula tied to their years of service and salary. Since the benefit amount in a DBP is based on a predefined formula, rather than investment returns, the employer is responsible for ensuring the pension plan is adequately funded and can meet its obligations to today's and future retirees. Every three years, employers must have the pension plan reviewed by an actuary to determine if it is adequately funded. If there is a deficit, the employer must make additional contributions. If there is a surplus, the employer may take a contribution "holiday" or withdraw the surplus from the plan and use the money for other purposes.

With the DCP and GRRSP, the retirement income employees receive is based on the market value of their investments when they retire. When employees retire or leave a company, they take the value of their pension plan with them.

4.1 Opting Out of a DCP or Group RRSP

If the company pension plan is a DCP or GRRSP, the amount employees can transfer is generally equal to the contributions they made, plus any earnings. If your clients are retiring and they leave the money in the DCP, they may be entitled to receive ongoing benefits, such as extended health and dental coverage, as well as group life insurance.

Before opting out of a DCP or GRRSP, your clients need to ensure that they will not be giving up any company benefits. They should also be confident that they could manage the money more successfully than the managers of the pension plan would before they transfer the money to their own locked-in RRSP (for a DCP) or to a self-directed RRSP (for GRRSP).

Generally, a locked-in RRSP provides a wider range of investment options. Clients should compare the costs of managing the money if it is left inside the DCP with the costs of managing the money in the RRSP. The cost of having the money managed inside a DCP can be as low as 25 basis points (0.25%) compared to 100 (1%) to 200 (2%) basis points for managing money in an RRSP.

4.2   Opting out of a DBP

If the company pension plan is a defined benefit plan, the amount employees can transfer to a locked-in RRSP is the commuted value, which is the present value of the pension benefit earned to date. The present value is tied to the yield of a Government of Canada long-term bond. When interest rates are low, the commuted value of the pension plan is greater than when interest rates are high. If your clients are retiring and stay in the DBP, they may be entitled to ongoing benefits, such as extended health and dental coverage.

The key difference to employees is that with a defined benefit plan, they do not have to bear any investment risk. The retirement benefit they receive does not depend on market performance. If your clients transfer the commuted value of their pension plan from the employer to their own locked-in RRSP, the employer no longer has any obligations to them and their retirement income. Sometimes employers will enhance the package they offer to employees on retirement or severance, if in return employees are willing to take out the commuted value, rather than staying in the plan.

4.3   Opting Out from the Client's Perspective

Some of your clients may want to "get their money out of the hands of that company." This may be an emotional response to having been terminated or it may reflect fears about the company's solvency. However, company pension plans are not "owned" by the company. For example, when Confederation Life Insurance Company went out of business, the pension plan was separate from the company's assets. Not only did the retiring employees receive their pensions, but they also received healthy bonuses from the pension surplus when the pension plan was wound down.

Some clients may be looking at a substantial sum of money that they have never had to deal with before. They may not be experienced investors, since their retirement savings have until now been tied to their company pension plan. Their vulnerability at this point increases your fiduciary responsibility as a wealth manager. Although there are some situations in which clients should opt out of a defined pension plan, there are many situations where opting out is not in a client's best interest.

4.4   Reviewing the Facts with a Client

Explaining to your clients the financial differences between staying in a defined pension plan and opting out can be difficult. You must make the differences clear by drawing up a scenario.

In the scenario, you need to use a rate of return comparable to a long-term Government of Canada bond rate. Although this will not duplicate the way the commuted value was calculated, it will show your clients the basic benefit under the plan and make the commuted value more meaningful. The scenario should also consider the clients' risk profile. If the clients are not risk-averse and have some investment experience, their asset mix over the long term would result in a larger income benefit. However, if your clients are risk-averse and have limited investment experience, their asset mix over the long term might not earn much more retirement income. You should also include a worst-case scenario, supposing that the investment markets fell dramatically.

If your clients stay with a pension plan, they will begin receiving pension income at 65 or before, unless they finance their income needs in retirement from other sources. The scenario should show the clients the income they would receive if they converted their locked-in RRSP to a Life Income Fund (LIF) at 65. Unlike the RRIF, the LIF has minimum and maximum amounts that can be withdrawn each year. If the clients start withdrawing money at 65 or earlier, compare the income they would receive from a pension and from a LIF.

As a rule of thumb, clients might be better off taking the commuted value of the pension plan if:

- they are more than seven years from the date at which they would start to receive the pension income, since the pension income is likely "frozen" and not linked to inflation during that time;
- the pension plan does not offer indexing, either guaranteed partial or occasional adjustment;the client (and his or her spouse) have a shorter-than-average life expectancy;
- the client is single and wants to leave a larger estate.

For some clients, anomalies in the calculation of the pension plan will make the commuted value much larger than it would otherwise be. This may be the case for clients who have had a year or two of unusually high income, because of a high performance bonus or some other reason.

Before recommending whether or not these clients should opt out of a defined pension plan, you need to:

1. Consider any company benefits, such as health and dental care or group life insurance, the clients would receive if they stayed in the plan.

2. Determine when the clients want to begin receiving income. The closer they are to that date, the more risk they must be prepared to assume, and the better the pension plan looks.

3. Determine their investment experience and risk profile.

4. Assess how this benefit will affect their lifestyle in retirement. A client who has a spouse with a generous guaranteed pension that would be more than adequate to support both of them in retirement has more flexibility in making the decision. However, a client who is the sole supporter of his or her family may want a more reliable income stream.

5. Estimate how long your clients will live. The greater a client's longevity, the longer the income has to last. With the DBP, the income stream will last as long as they do, even if they live to 95 or more. With a self-managed account, there is no such guarantee.

6. Determine if the pension income is indexed, either fully or partially, to accommodate inflation.

You also need to decide whether your client's spouse will be adequately provided for if your client opts out of the pension plan. Spouses are entitled to receive a benefit from a pension plan of no less than 60% as a survivor benefit, unless they waive their right to this entitlement. Clients should consider whether they want the spouse to receive a guaranteed income or to be responsible for managing an investment portfolio.

You should outline all your recommendations to your clients in writing and ensure that they understand that all numbers are possible scenarios only, not a guarantee of future returns. Give your clients time to consider those recommendations and recommend that they get a second opinion. You should never recommend that a client opt out of a company pension plan unless this course is clearly in the client's best interest. Impartial advice will go a long way in enhancing your reputation and the likelihood of referrals.

5.0   Retirement Savings beyond RRSPs and RPPs

RRSPs and RPPs are not the only retirement savings options. Leveraged Deferred Compensation Plans (LDCPs), Retirement Compensation Arrangements (RCAs), Individual Pension Plans (IPPs), and Supplemental Executive Retirement Plans (SERPs) may offer alternative methods of funding retirement goals for some clients.

5.1   The Leveraged Deferred Compensation Plan

The leveraged deferred compensation plan (LDCP) combines the features of the universal life insurance policy with a loan in retirement. A universal life insurance policy, sometimes called an insured retirement plan, has two components:

*   term life insurance; and

*   a savings or investment fund, in which investments accumulate on a tax-sheltered basis.

The investment growth depends on the premiums and contributions paid into the universal life insurance policy:

Investment growth = investment earnings − insurance expenses

One drawback with life insurance is that it does not pay out any tax-free death benefits until after death. The LDCP is marketed as a creative way for clients to grow an investment pool that is tax-sheltered and allows them to tap into the investment value of the life insurance policy tax-free while they are alive.

How the LDCP Works

In an LDCP, the owner of the life insurance policy uses the investment value of the life insurance policy as collateral for a loan with a financial institution when he or she retires. The financial institution uses the value of the life insurance policy to secure the loan and advances payments to the owner of the life insurance policy on a tax-free basis. Interest is charged at the going rate—currently between prime + ½% and prime +1%. The interest can either be paid every year or left to accumulate, increasing the value of the loan and decreasing the estate value of the life insurance policy. When the owner of the policy dies, the proceeds of the policy are used to pay off the loan and any interest that has accumulated. The remaining value of the policy is then paid out tax-free to the beneficiaries.

Case 5.1   Maurice Thom and Leveraged Deferred Compensation Plans

When Maurice Thom is 45 years old he begins to pay $10,000 a year into this policy. He makes payments for 20 years, for a death benefit of $1 million. He will have contributed $200,000, less the cost of insurance. This net amount is growing tax-free.

When he turns 65, Maurice assigns the policy to the bank for a loan (between 75% and 90% of the value of the death benefit). The bank makes the payments, tax-free. During retirement, he uses $300,000 as income. When he dies, the policy pays out $1 million, less $300,000, less the interest on the loan. Maurice's beneficiary receives about $625,000. Maurice has received tax-free income (from a third-party financial institution) from the universal life insurance policy during his lifetime.

This strategy works best for a client who:
- is in the top tax bracket;
- is not risk-averse;
- needs life insurance;
- has used up all available RRSP contribution room;
- has other investments to supplement income in retirement;

- is sophisticated enough to understand the limitations of the arrangement.

Risks

The LDCP plan is not without risk. The following risks must be considered:

- Tax laws could change. Current tax rules allow the universal life policy to be used as collateral without a deemed disposition. (Deemed disposition occurs when property is treated as though it were sold, when in fact it is not.) Revenue Canada could change the rules at any time and require the policy to be treated for tax purposes as if it had been disposed of at the time of the first payment under the loan.

- Financial institutions may refuse to accept the universal life policy as collateral for this type of loan. To avoid this risk, some wealth managers make the loan arrangements when the life insurance policy is bought, years in advance of their clients' retirement.

- The strategy needs time to work. Since the cost of the insurance is built heavily into the first years of the policy, if a client is too close to retirement, the cost of the policy will interfere with the investment growth of the policy. A client needs enough market growth to cover the cost of the insurance over their lifetime and the interest cost of the loan. Depending on market performance, this strategy usually requires at least ten years before it can begin to work.

- Changes in rates of return on investments and loan rates in the future may reduce the strategy's attractiveness. The difference between the growth rate on the investments and the interest rate charged on the loan greatly affect the outcome. The greater the difference you assume in a scenario, the less risky the strategy appears.

This strategy is most attractive for clients who have a long time before retirement. Unfortunately, the length of time between constructing scenarios and actual retirement increases the inaccuracy of your projections about investment returns and about the cost of the future loan. Leverage always increases potential risk.

5.2   The Retirement Compensation Arrangement (RCA)

A Retirement Compensation Arrangement (RCA), as set out in the *Income Tax Act*, enables employers to pre-fund retirement benefits without using a registered pension plan. Since the RCA is not a pension plan, it does not affect the individual's ability to contribute to an RRSP.

The RCA is a taxable trust set up by an employer to hold funds for retirement. The investments in an RCA arrangement are governed by the trust agreement, not the *Income Tax Act*. A wide range of investments are eligible for inclusion in the RCA trust, including tax-exempt life insurance, stocks and bonds, mutual funds, and deferred annuity contracts.

The employer pays an amount of tax that is refundable, based on:

- 50% of all contributions made to the RCA during the year;
- **plus** 50% of the net profit on the investments for the year;
- **minus** 50% of the benefits paid out during the year.

Each year, the custodian of the RCA sends Revenue Canada the 50% refundable tax, along with a report summarizing the accounting of that tax. The tax is refunded when retirement payments made to the employees are greater than the income earned inside the RCA trust.

Costs to set up and administer an RCA include the legal cost of setting up the trust, the cost of filing the annual trust tax return, and the services of the RCA custodian. RCA arrangements are often used by:

- owners of privately held corporations who want to build up funds for retirement;
- corporate executives with salaries of more than $85,000;
- individuals who might retire outside Canada.

5.3   Individual Pension Plans

An Individual Pension Plan (IPP) is a registered pension plan structured for one person.

It is a defined benefit plan and therefore specifies a certain level of payments to the plan holder. The employer is responsible for making annual contributions. Set-up and administrative costs, while tax deductible, are high.

An IPP permits higher tax deductible contributions than those allowed under an RRSP. Compared to an RRSP, the increase in retirement savings provided by an IPP can be substantial.

There are two types of IPP's: a Shareholder Pension Plan for owner-manageres who own more than 10% of the shares of the company and an Executive Pension Plan for those who are not shareholders or who own less than 10% of the shares.

Executive Pension Plans are often used as an executive prerequisite to attract or retain senior management personnel.

IPP's are not available to a partner nor the proprietor of a company nor those who are self-employed and have no employees.

Based on actuarial projections and the high costs of setting up and administering such plans, IPP's are generally attractive only to those in the 40-60 age group earning in excess of $100,000 annually.

IPP's are more restrictive than other spousal plans. However, an IPP plan holder is still permitted to make an RRSP contribution to his or her own RRSP or a spouse's plan. No RRSP contribution is permitted in the first year the IPP is in existence and a maximum of $1,000 is allowed for each succeeding year. Since there is a limited ability to contribute to a spousal plan, there is little opportunity for income splitting as provided through spousal RRSP's.

Unlike RRSP funds, which may be withdrawn at any time, IPP funds must remain "locked in". As retirement approaches, the IPP plan holder could elect to transfer the funds to a "locked in" RRSP. This could further defer tax until age 69 when the "locked in" RRSP must be used to purchase a life annuity or a Life Income Fund. In contrast, an RRSP provides for a variety of options on termination or retirement.

While IPP's may provide greater benefits and higher contribution limits, they are complex, costly to set up and require a considerable amount of costly administration. Owner-managers should explore their appropriateness with competent financial advisers.

5.4   Supplemental Executive Retirement Plans

The *Income Tax Act* attempts to give group pension plans and registered retirement savings plan parity and comparable tax benefits. However, once employees reach an income of $75,000, they have maximized their tax-assisted savings under the RRSP and when their income reaches $86,000, they reach the maximum benefit under a defined company pension plan. Some corporations use a supplemental executive retirement plan (SERP) to increase the retirement benefits for senior executives and employees.

6.0   Preparing for Retirement

Clients whose income is not based on government benefits or a defined employer pension plan may have difficulty envisioning how to take retirement savings and turn them into a stream of income throughout retirement. How you turn savings into a tax-effective income stream for clients involves new strategies and a variety of investment vehicles. Some of these strategies may be new to your clients and you will need to explain how they work.

Clients also have to give themselves permission to spend their savings in retirement. This involves a change in direction. Going from a savings mentality, to a situation in which they are no longer having to save and can actually spend the money they have accumulated, requires a certain psychological adjustment. Clients need a retirement income projection that gives them some idea how long the money will last.

Some clients never make the adjustment and scrimp their way through retirement. Others decide they will withdraw from their portfolio only the earnings that the portfolio makes in any given year. Unfortunately, this strategy chains them to the ups and the downs of the market. Others budget how much of their portfolio they will allow themselves to withdraw each year.

6.1   Retirement Income Projection

In many ways, the retirement income projection is similar to the retirement independence calculation. It makes a number of assumptions about the future, including the future of government benefits and tax rates. The retirement income projection is intended to illustrate:

- the most tax-effective way for clients to use the assets they have accumulated;
- the impact of additional withdrawals on their income throughout their retirement;
- the value of their estate at different ages, which may require some additional estate planning;
- how long the money will last, given the clients' anticipated level of consumption.

It is not unusual for a person retiring today to spend 25 to 30 years in retirement. No one can anticipate what the world will look like even 5 to 10 years from now, so it is important that your clients understand the strengths and limitations of a retirement income projection. The more guaranteed income streams in the projection, including government benefits, annuities, and company pensions, the greater the certainty of the income projection.

Like the retirement independence calculation, the retirement income projection should be presented to clients with a disclaimer and reviewed every two or three years.

6.2   Choosing a Retirement Date

Some clients have to retire; others choose to retire. For clients who are members of a company pension plan, the "normal" retirement date is the date at which they are entitled to full retirement benefits. If they retire before this date, the pension income they receive is reduced. If an employee wants to retire at 55, the pension he or she would receive would be about half of what the pension payable at age 65 would be. This is because the pool has to pay out the income for 10 more years and because the employer has either 10 fewer years to contribute to the plan or 10 fewer years of service on which to base the benefit. Under certain plans, employees can retire on full pension benefits when the sum of their age and their years of service reaches a particular number.

In the last few years, some employees have been able to retire early on full benefits. This usually happens when a company wants to downsize while maintaining good public relations. Suppose a company enhances its retirement program for two years and gives eligible employees the option of retiring five years early. What does this cost the company? It saves five years of salary and related government costs and reduces its staff without having to pay expensive severance packages. On the other hand, it may have to make a one-time payout to the pension plan (unless it can tap into a surplus inside the plan).

The closer employees get to the normal retirement date, the more they are focused on preparing for retirement. When a company announces an early retirement program, some employees are taken by surprise and need intensive retirement preparation, both financial and psychological. Many employers provide retirement preparation courses to these employees to allow them to work through the implications of early retirement. Employees who still have children at home that they are supporting, or who are still paying off a mortgage may not be financially ready to retire. In this case, they would have to weigh their employment options, either with their current employer or elsewhere. They may also be interested in "double-dipping": taking the pension and going into consulting or working for a new employer.

6.3   Retiring from a Business

Clients who retire from their own business have to plan their retirement income, but they also need to find a tax-effective way to divest themselves of the business. They might sell it to a family member or to someone else. If the business is a qualified small business, they may be eligible for the $500,000 capital gains exemption. This $500,000 exemption is available to all eligible shareholders. If the client, his or her spouse and two adult children are registered shareholders of the business, the family may be able to receive $2 million profit on the sale of the business without paying tax on that capital gain. Of course, if the shares of the family business were held in a family trust, the trustees of those shares would still be responsible for managing the money.

The shareholder or related shareholders must hold shares in the corporation and pass the following tests in the two years before the sale of the shares:

- more than 50% of the fair market value of the business assets were used primarily in an active business carried on primarily in Canada or invested in other small business corporations (or any combination) (50% test); and

- all or substantially all of the Canadian-controlled private corporation's assets were used in carrying on active business in Canada or be shares and debt in other small business corporations (or any combination)(90% test).

The client's accountant should be able to structure the transaction and help the client prepare the business so that it will qualify for the $500,000 capital gains exemption. Business owners who sell a business and retire from it may be eligible for a retiring allowance that can be rolled into an RRSP, not just for themselves, but for other employees, possibly including their spouses and children.

6.4   Retiring from a Partnership

Clients may receive various types of payment when they retire from a partnership and the other partners acquire their interest in the partnership. The two most common options are:

- a capital payment, which could be paid out on a tax-free basis, if the tax is paid by the partners;

- an income payment, which is taxable in the year it is received, but is not classified as earned income for RRSPs.

7.0   Financial Management during Retirement

Clients have different needs during retirement, depending on their sources of income. Some need you to turn their investment assets, RRSP, or RRIF into a predictable income stream for them. They may also need to make withdrawals from the RRSP before they turn 69. Others do not require much or any income from their portfolios and want you to preserve their capital and ensure that their assets grow. They may want to postpone taking money out of their RRIF until the last possible moment.

7.1   Getting Organized

Working people may have their assets spread among different financial institutions and advisors. For some, this is their definition of "diversification." When they retire, however, many people want to feel that their financial situation is organized and well taken care of. They may want to consolidate some of their accounts with a single wealth manager. They may also be looking for ways to simplify the task of managing their money. Others find they have more time on their hands and want to take a more active role in managing their money.

You need to assess a client's needs when it comes to money, not just in terms of capital preservation or growth, but also in terms of control and delegation. Clients who are willing to delegate their portfolio management to a discretionary money manager, for example, have less need for control. Sometimes the investment policy statement provides enough "control" for these clients, sometimes it does not.

One approach that has worked with clients who have a high need for control is to set them up with a low-fee trading account and a discretionary managed account. The client can focus on the investments in the trading account, giving them a sense of control and day-to-day excitement, while most of their money is managed in a more disciplined manner.

Some clients may not be interested in consolidating their accounts. However, they may want to make sense of the accounts they have set up over the years and rationalize those accounts where possible. They may also want to simplify their financial affairs to make their executor's life easier. If your clients have not already done so, recommend that they set up a filing system so their executor will know where to find all their important papers and the history of their financial lives. This will help their executor when the time comes.

Reducing the number of RRIFs to one could make it easier to plan and track the annual withdrawal. However, there are several reasons why clients might need more than one RRSP or one RRIF. For example:

- their accounts have different beneficiaries;
- they want one held by a financial institution and another by a life insurance company;
- they want a qualified RRIF and a non-qualified RRIF;
- they want to take advantage of the $60,000 limit under the Canadian Deposit Insurance Corporation (CDIC).

A client might have an RRSP and a spousal RRSP. Under Revenue Canada rules, an individual can combine these plans if he or she is the annuitant under both plans. However, once the plans are combined, clients must follow the rules as if the combined plan were a spousal RRSP, so it is not advisable for them to continue making RRSP contributions. However, once they convert the combined spousal RRSP to a RRIF, it becomes a spousal RRIF. Any withdrawals over the minimum amount within three years of a spousal contribution would be taxed in the hands of the contributor rather than the annuitant. If a client combines a spousal plan with a non-spousal plan, it is a good idea to have the client sign a release stating that no further contributions will be made, so that he or she will not be adversely affected by the rules relating to spousal plans.

7.2   Maturing the RRSP

The RRSP must mature no later than December 31 of the year the client turns 69. The maturity date for a client should be no later than this date, but if clients in their sixties require additional income and have an RRSP that will support this, they may be interested in early withdrawals from their RRSP.

There are three maturity options for the RRSP:

- Cash it in and pay the tax in that tax year. This is the default option if a client fails to transfer the funds to a RRIF or an annuity. This may be the most appropriate option if the value of the RRSP is small and a client wants the money.
- Transfer the funds to a RRIF.
- Transfer the funds to an annuity.

The rules for these three options are covered in more basic level financial planning texts, including Chapter 8 of the PFPC text. A client can also use a combination of maturity options. Most clients will transfer the funds either to a RRIF or to an annuity. The income from the RRIF or from an annuity that was created with RRSP/RRIF dollars is taxed in the year it is received.

The merits of an RRIF vs. an annuity depend on the client's financial situation. The RRIF may be more appropriate when investment returns are in double digits. However, the investment profile of a client is particularly important in determining which option to select. Many wealth managers are licensed to offer both investments and insurance products.

7.3   RRIFs and Ways to Maximize a RRIF

A Registered Retirement Income Fund (RRIF) is a fund registered with Revenue Canada established by an individual for the purpose of receiving retirement income. RRIFs are discussed in detail in chapter eight of the Professional Financial Planning Course textbook.

A self directed RRIF is suitable for clients who are both comfortable in making their own investment decisions as well as having some of their money in investments with no performance guarantees but which might give them income they need over the long term. A RRIF has the following advantages for clients:

- They do not have to turn their investment portfolio into cash when they turn 69.
- Clients have maximum flexibility in the amount of income they can withdraw in any one year—although if they take out too much too soon, they could outlive the money.
- They continue to control the investment choices in the portfolio.
- On the death of the owner of the RRIF, the value is transferred to the beneficiary.

Your clients can make the most of a RRIF in the following ways:

Make a Final RRSP Contribution in Advance

If your clients choose the RRIF option and do not require the RRIF to provide a regular income stream, they can maximize the continuing benefits available from the RRIF by making their final RRSP contribution before December 31 of the year they turn 69. In any other year, they have 60 days after year-end to make their RRSP contribution and deduct it on the tax return for the previous year. However, since they cannot own a RRSP after December 31 of the year they turn 69, this is the last date they can make a RRSP contribution.

Clients who have earned income in the year they turn 69 do not actually create RRSP contribution room until the following year. In anticipation of the RRSP contribution room available in the year they turn 70, they could make an over-contribution in December of the year they turn 69 equal to the amount of RRSP contribution room they will have one month later, in January of the new year.

There is a penalty of 1% for each month a client's account is in over-contribution, in this case, one month. But the penalty is usually modest compared to the tax savings from the

RRSP deduction. Suppose your clients are in the 50% tax bracket and expect to earn $10,000 of RRSP contribution room the year they turn 70. If they make a RRSP contribution in December of the previous year, they will have to pay a penalty of $100 (1% of $10,000), which will be more than offset by the $5,000 saved by taking the $10,000 RRSP deduction.

Claim the $2,000 Over-Contribution

Clients who have over-contributed to their RRSP should be sure to claim that amount out of any remaining RRSP contribution room they have. Suppose a client, Roland Masters, is retiring at age 65 and has $2,000 in over-contributions inside a RRSP. Since he does not anticipate having any earned income in the future, he should include that $2,000 as part of his regular contribution. If the unused RRSP contribution room for the year is $5,000, Roland would contribute only another $3,000 to his RRSP and claim the $2,000 from the amount that was over-contributed.

Base the Amount of the RRIF Withdrawal on the Age of a Younger Spouse

The RRIF withdrawal can be based on the age of the annuitant or the age of his or her spouse or common-law spouse. Using the age of the younger spouse requires that less be withdrawn from the RRIF each year, allowing more to remain in the RRIF for longer.

Defer the RRIF Withdrawal until the End of the Year

Although the RRSP has to mature by December 31 of the year the annuitant turns 69, the first withdrawal does not have to be made until the end of the following year for clients who do not require the amount for their cash flow. The money stays inside the RRIF and remains tax-deferred for up to 12 more months. Alternatively, the withdrawals can be made monthly, quarterly, or semi-annually.

Continue to Earn RRSP Room

Clients who continue to earn income after age 69 and who have a spouse or common-law spouse who is still eligible for a RRSP (because they have not yet reached 69), can make a contribution to the spousal RRSP and take the deduction on their own tax return.

7.4   Annuities

If clients do not want to make ongoing investment decisions or want to ensure the money lasts as long as they do, they might consider one of the following options:

- purchase an annuity with a portion of the value of the RRSP; or

- convert the RRSP to a RRIF for a few years and then convert some or all of that RRIF to an annuity.

An annuity has the following main advantages:

- It creates a steady, predictable income.
- It relieves a client from making ongoing investment decisions.
- The client cannot outlive the income.
- The Canadian Life and Health Insurance Compensation Corporation (known as CompCorp) guarantees monthly annuity income of up to $2,000.
- If a client dies before the guarantee period is up (if there is one), the estate receives the remaining value of the annuity.

Annuities also have some disadvantages:

- There is no flexibility in the amount of income to be received once it is set up.
- Cash is required to buy the annuity. If investments have to be liquidated to buy an annuity, the purchase could result in a market value adjustment or redemption fees.
- There may be no estate value. If there is no guaranteed period, the annuity payments may not continue to your client's estate or beneficiary.
- Inflation protection is not automatically built in.

8.0 Developing an Asset Allocation Strategy for Retirement

Today, investor risk profile questionnaires are designed to determine clients' risk tolerance based on their attitude to risk, their age, and their time horizon. Most of these questionnaires, however, miss one key aspect of developing the asset allocation strategy. How much risk do clients need to assume in order to meet their financial objectives?

Clients who have accumulated large portfolios and have modest income needs during retirement may be able to meet their financial objectives with a relatively low-risk portfolio. On the other hand, there are no guarantees that clients with greater income needs would be better served with a more aggressive portfolio. Tolerance for risk generally decreases with age and retirement.

How does risk tolerance change? Most wealth managers prepare retirement independence calculations and retirement income projections assuming that their clients will have a consistent risk profile throughout their lives, but this may not be an accurate assumption. When clients are working and bringing in employment income, they may not pay much attention to temporary losses in their portfolio. After all, a drop in the value of their long-term retirement portfolio does not affect their day-to-day lifestyle, unless it requires them to save more money each year. However, when clients stop work and their retirement income depends on withdrawals from the portfolio, they are less tolerant of the impact of an investment loss.

It is not unreasonable to assume that clients who retire at 60 may still have an investment horizon of 25 or 30 years. Clients whose retirement income needs are covered by their government benefits and pension plan may not need any money from their portfolio in their retirement. In fact, they may continue to save once they are retired. These clients might want you to consider their pensions as the fixed-income portion of their portfolio and the investment portfolio to be the growth portion. This, however, is a risky approach for the wealth manager to take. You run the risk of being fired when the markets are not going in your clients' favour, because even though they do not really need the money, they are unhappy when they see losses.

Clients who need a retirement income stream from their investment portfolio have an investment horizon that is only a few months long. To meet both the practical and psychological needs of these clients, you should design a portfolio to meet both their long-term and short-term needs. Some wealth managers do this by dividing the portfolio into two components: one for long-term investments and the other to meet the monthly pension "payroll." The "payroll" component of the portfolio would consist of shorter-term investments that are not affected by drops in the stock market, and the riskier investments would remain in the long-term portfolio.

Clients who have accumulated a portfolio that will last longer than they do, regardless of the assumptions you use, can select the level of investment risk they consider appropriate. These clients might use their grandchildren's time horizon rather than their own.

Some clients need growth in the retirement portfolio if they are to stand any chance of having the money last as long as they do. The financial projection may illustrate that without enough growth, they will run out of money. Although investment research indicates these clients have a higher probability of meeting their income needs by keeping an adequate proportion of equity holdings, the outcome is not guaranteed. Clients may have to choose between a guarantee of running out of money and a high probability that a portfolio with higher weighting in equities will mean they do not run out of money.

Asset allocation is discussed in detail in Chapter 10.

9.0   Tax Planning Strategies Available in Retirement

Since taxes do not stop just because a client stops working, tax planning can help a client keep more of what they earn. Although the opportunities to minimize tax get more and more limited every time the tax rules change, some tax planning strategies are related directly to the retirement years.

9.1   Build a Tax-Effective Portfolio

You can help clients build more tax-effective portfolios by adjusting the target asset allocation. Equity investments that offer tax-preferred treatment, dividends, and capital gains should be held outside the clients' registered plans. This strategy should increase the risk level in your clients' portfolios.

If your clients do not already have tax-effective portfolios, you can swap long-term fixed-income investments held outside the registered account with investments earning dividends or capital gains income held inside the registered account. The short-term fixed income investments, the ones clients are planning to live on, are normally held outside the RRSP.

9.2   Tax Loss Selling

In years when a client has earned taxable capital gains income and has investments with unrealized capital losses, year-end tax loss selling can reduce the client's tax burden. In other words, a client could sell an investment that will incur a capital loss (for example, selling stock in XYZ Co. that was purchased for $95 a share but is now worth only $45 a share) and use the capital losses to offset capital gains from other investments. Although there is a risk that the client will become focused on those losses, the ability to use the loss to reduce their overall tax bill for the year can be attractive.

9.3   File Quarterly Tax Instalments

If clients are required to file quarterly tax instalments, it may be helpful if their portfolio automatically deposits the cash required directly into their bank account each quarter, so they can be made on time.

9.4   Work with a Client's Lifetime Tax Bill

During clients' working years, the focus of much of their tax planning is to defer taxes for as long as possible. Once clients retire, you should start to look at balancing out your clients' need for income, their annual tax bill, and the tax bill payable when they die. If a client is in the top tax bracket today and expects to be there still at the end of his or her life, there may not be much you can do to help. But if a client will change tax brackets over the years, you may be able to reduce their overall tax bill.

For example, Jeremy Simeoni retires at 55 with a company pension. Five years later, he could start to receive CPP, then in five more years the OAS. At 70 he would begin to receive income from a matured RRSP. Jeremy would effectively be "getting a raise" every five years. If the RRIF is worth $200,000 at age 70, his "raise" that year would be $10,000.

You may be able to even out the stream of income in your clients' early retirement, when they can probably enjoy it more, and thereby reduce their lifetime tax burden. Your retirement income projection should illustrate this possibility to your clients.

9.5   Split CPP Benefits

The rules of the Canada Pension Plan allow spouses to split their benefits. As a way of lowering your household tax bill through income splitting, you may direct up to 50% of your CPP benefits be paid to your spouse, provided both of you are over age 60. If either of you does this, a portion of the other spouse's CPP is assigned automatically back to the first spouse. The amount that can be split is based on the length of time you and your spouse have lived together as a proportion of your total contributory period to a maximum of 50%. This is useful when spouses are in different tax brackets. It allows the higher-income spouse to transfer some of his or her CPP benefits to the spouse with the lower income.

For example, if Pam Farquharson is eligible to receive $8,000 a year and her husband Neil $4,000 a year, each would receive $6,000 a year. In this example, $2,000 of income would be shifted into the lower tax bracket. Both Pam and Neil must be eligible to receive CPP benefits (that is, over 60 and no longer in the full-time work force) and they must apply in writing for this arrangement.

9.6   Take Advantage of the Pension Income Tax Credit

Clients who are 65 or older and do not have any pension income from a company pension plan, an annuity, or a RRIF are missing out on the $1,000 pension tax credit. Even if they do not require the income, recommend they convert enough of their RRSP or spousal RRSP to a RRIF or an annuity to create $1,000 worth of eligible pension income.

Clients who do not have a pension plan, who have never worked, or who have held most of their assets inside a holding company often miss this opportunity.

9.7   Use the Age of a Younger Spouse on the RRIF

If a client has a younger spouse or common-law spouse and does not need the income from the RRIF to live on, base the RRIF withdrawals on the age of the younger spouse. This would allow the couple to keep more in the RRIF for longer, enhancing the tax-deferral properties of the RRIF.

9.8   Integrate Charitable Giving

Contributing to charity can be an effective way for clients to reduce their tax bill and make a difference. When the type of gift and the timing of the gift is planned to make the most of the potential tax savings using the non-refundable tax credits, charitable donations become a "planned gift." Clients can make charitable gifts now, over time, or on death. However, remember that some retired clients may be afraid to give away assets or cash until they are sure they do not need the money themselves.

Some clients are required to make withdrawals from their RRIF even when they do not need the income. They might be interested in offsetting some of the tax that would otherwise be due by using the non-refundable tax credit for charitable donations.

10.0   Strategies to Help Clients Keep More of their OAS

All Canadians who meet Canada's residency requirements qualify for Old Age Security benefits, but not all of them get to keep it. When a client's net income reaches $53,213, 15% of every dollar is clawed back when he or she files an annual tax return. When the net income is over $80,000, the entire amount has to be repaid. Most Canadians feel entitled to the social benefits. There are a number of strategies that could help clients keep more of what they get.

Each strategy described in this section focuses on ways clients can manage to keep their income below $53,213 or at least below $80,000, so not all of the OAS is clawed back. Each strategy has its own advantages and disadvantages, not all will apply to every client.

1. If the taxable income cannot be kept under the target level every year, then plan the income to minimize the taxable income in some years.

2. To reduce the annual income received from CPP, start CPP benefits at age 60, so the clients can collect a few years of benefits before OAS benefits start.

3. If your client's spouse or common-law spouse is in a lower tax bracket, apply to the Income Security Office of the federal government to split CPP benefits as soon as the spouse is eligible for CPP benefits.

4. Maximize the tax savings from RRSP contributions. A client might consider making RRSP contributions but defer claiming the deduction until he or she starts to receive OAS.

5. Clients who participated in the RRSP Home Buyer's Plan or the Lifelong Learning Plan should repay any outstanding balance, if they can. This moves open investments back into the tax-sheltered RRSP for a few more years.

6. Before the client turns 64, consider realizing capital gains on investments that would likely have to be realized within the next five years. Although this would result in an

immediate tax bill, selling the investment after age 64 would increase the client's net income and the amount that would be clawed back.

7. Consider a prescribed annuity as an alternative to traditional fixed-income investments. The income payment is part income and part return of capital. The taxable income from a prescribed annuity would be lower than for traditional fixed-income investments.

8. Consider the effect of withdrawals from the RRSP or RRIF on a client's taxable income. If a client has a spouse in a lower-income bracket who also has an RRSP or RRIF, make the withdrawal from that plan (since on the death of one spouse, the plan will transfer to the surviving spouse if he or she has been named as the beneficiary).

9. Consider having clients pay off all debts before they turn 64 instead of investing the money and getting investment income, so they do not have to incur more taxable income than is necessary.

10. Review the investments in your client's portfolio. If investments in an open account are generating interest or dividend income that the client does not need, consider shifting some money into investments that focus on deferred capital gains, so the taxable gain can be deferred until the asset is sold, or until the client dies.

11. To meet short-term cash flow needs, recommend that clients use their line of credit, rather than an unplanned RRSP/RRIF withdrawal.

12. Consider transferring the investment portfolio to an investment holding company where the income can be taxed in the name of the corporation. Although the income tax rules try to deal equally with the income earned by a corporation and the income earned by an individual, the investment holding company may be useful to the individual whose income would otherwise fall into the OAS clawback. The size of the portfolio must be able to deal with the annual administrative costs of setting up and maintaining a corporation.

13. Consider transferring the investment portfolio to an inter vivos trust where the income can be taxed in the trust (at the highest marginal tax rate) but could then be paid to the beneficiary tax-free. The clawback does not apply to income earned inside an inter vivos trust.

14. If a client does not require the income to live on, an inter vivos trust could pay the tax and the assets in the trust could continue to grow until the death of a client. On the client's death, the assets could be transferred to the beneficiaries, following the instructions in the trust, without probate and with a bonus of added privacy.

15. Clients could consider a reverse mortgage as a way to withdraw income tax-free from their home. You can help your client weigh the costs associated with setting up a reverse mortgage and the associated interest costs against the amount clawed back.

Although no one should pay more in taxes than is necessary, clients should not make all decisions based on their tax implications. If you feel clients are letting tax rules dominate their lifestyle and financial decisions, you should say so. You should also review any tax-avoidance strategy every few years. Sometimes a strategy put in place based on the current rules can go amiss if the rules change.

11.0 Integrating Retirement Planning with Estate Planning

Retirement planning and estate planning often go hand-in-hand. While clients are getting their finances organized for retirement, they often reassess their estate plan. Estate planning is described in detail in Chapter 9.

Although clients may not be focused on their life expectancy when they are saving for retirement, the idea of life expectancy has clearer meaning when it is discussed within the context of the retirement income projection. This issue needs to be handled with sensitivity. It is also a good door-opener for a solid estate planning review.

Clients have three options:
- to preserve as much as possible for their beneficiaries;
- to spend as much as possible on themselves; or
- something in between.

This is no right or wrong option. The option appropriate for your clients will depend on their personal value system and how they have lived their lives to this point. Clients who plan to spend as much as possible on themselves may have already given generously to their children and know that the children are successful in their own right. Clients who want to preserve as much as possible for their beneficiaries may be attempting to make up for lost time or may be concerned about their beneficiaries' future.

You must ask your clients what their goals are. There is no point in presenting life insurance as an estate preservation option to a client who is on a spending spree. On the other hand, a client who wants to preserve as much as possible for his or her beneficiaries may require income and may be interested in a life insurance option that would replace the value of the estate that he or she has spent.

If your clients are setting up RRIFs, they should review the beneficiary designations. If the beneficiary is not a spouse, ensure that all their documents, the ways their accounts are registered, and their beneficiaries' designations all contribute to their estate planning objectives. Clients should also be sure that their estate plans will last if they become incapacitated and unable to make any further changes to them. This includes ensuring that they have named a back-up executor in their will and a back-up attorney in their power-of-attorney document. The documents should be worded in a way that covers the "what-ifs" of life. On the death of a spouse or common-law spouse, your client should review the estate plan to ensure that it is still current.

12.0   Emotional Issues Surrounding Retirement

In the pre-retirement planning phase, some clients find it difficult to put a plan in place and commit to saving for the future. In some ways, clients who are members of a company pension plan may have an advantage over those who do not. Those inside a company pension plan cannot procrastinate about saving for retirement.

Some clients retire successfully and some do not. The rate of success can be increased if retirement planning also includes counselling about what clients will do with their time. Clients who end up retiring earlier than they had planned may feel as if they have been put out to pasture. They may find it hard to make the adjustments needed to feel that life still has meaning. Although they have the same amount of time as they did when they were working, they are responsible for filling that time. While they were working, not only was time taken up on the job, but also by commuting back and forth to work and lunches. You can tell when a client is enjoying retirement, or just getting through the days. Retirement is also a time when clients are most likely to have a serious illness or to lose their spouse.

Some retired clients have time to talk with others about investing and managing money. They also have more time to read the daily papers and surf the Internet. Their wealth management strategy may be prudent and working well for them, but they may feel that it lacks excitement. The person with a balanced portfolio often feels they are being too conservative during a strong bull market or perhaps too aggressive during a bear market.

12.1   There Is No "Perfect" Plan

A client who is very close to retirement may be looking for the "perfect" retirement plan. You will have to explain that no one has the perfect retirement plan, because no one can predict how the future will turn out. However, a retirement income plan can show a client the impact of different financial decisions.

The retirement independence calculation may present a scenario that some clients find hard to balance with their current lifestyle. If the calculation suggests that they should be saving more for the future, they may need to work with you to rethink their expenses. You may be able to help by working with them on budgeting or by finding ways for them to reduce the amount of interest they pay to service their debt, and eventually pay it off. Other clients may be too focused on living for today to plan for the future. If they are completely unable to understand the need to save for the future, they may turn out to be a professional liability for you.

Some wealth managers deal with these situations by being prepared to discuss anything financial with their clients, to help them isolate what is relevant to them from the general advice and information that is available. This helps the wealth manager to develop the client relationship and anticipate problems before they arise.

12.2   Planning for Mental Incapacity

The longer clients live, the more likely it is that they will find themselves in a situation where they are unable make their own financial decisions. It is important that clients have power-of-attorney documents appointing someone to make decisions on their behalf, if necessary. The person appointed may be a family member or friend; it could be a professional with whom the client may or may not have a working relationship.

The person assigned power of attorney is responsible for making decisions in the best interests of the individual. The person appointed may continue to have you manage the account if it appears that the incapacity will be temporary. If the incapacity appears to be long-term, he or she may want the account to be managed where his or her own assets are managed.

To ensure that clients continue to have their accounts managed by a person of their own choosing, and not a public guardian, encourage your clients to have proper power of attorney documents drawn up.

13.0   Conclusion

Retirement is the time in a person's life when he or she starts to picture a world without him or her in it. If you have a long-term relationship with your client, retirement planning may include a succession plan for who will take care of a dependent spouse. If you have not already done so, you should expand the wealth management relationship to include the spouse so you can get to know each other. If you are not managing the spouse's money, he or she may transfer your client's assets to another firm after his or her death.

CHAPTER 6

Insurance Planning

1.0   Introduction

Canada has about 600,000 millionaires and many more thousands of Canadians have a net worth of $250,000 to $400,000. Over the next few years, the number of high-net-worth individuals is expected to increase further. The shrinking market of "old money," that is, investors with a significant amount of money in the family for at least one generation, and the growing group of newly wealthy Canadians present new opportunities in insurance and financial planning.

In this chapter, you will become familiar with the insurance needs of high-net-worth clients, including their business and personal needs. The chapter describes personal property and casualty insurance as well as commercial and general liability insurance for business owners. We will also look at wealth preservation strategies using insurance including kidnap and ransom insurance, funeral insurance, annuities, key person insurance, and buy-sell agreements. Finally, we will discuss the protection and insurance of portfolios through the use of derivatives, particularly options contracts.

Primary Learning Objectives

By the end of this chapter, you should understand:

*   the business and personal insurance needs of different clients such as small business owners, senior executives, and independently wealth individuals;

*   types of insurances appropriate for high-net-worth individuals and families, including life insurance, critical illness insurance, homeowners' insurance, travel insurance, marriage contract insurance, annuities, and funeral expense insurance;

*   how to use insurance to ensure that a vacation property does not need to be sold by the family after the original owner's death;

*   the property and casualty insurance needs of businesses, including risks associated with business income, property and liability losses, fraud and

employee dishonesty, international business loss exposures, kidnap and ransom insurance, key person insurance;

- the use of buy-sell agreements to ensure the smooth transition of business ownership after the death of a partner or major shareholder;

- how to use segregated funds, exchange-traded securities, options, and other risk management techniques to hedge risks associated with a client's investment portfolio.

2.0   The Insurance Needs of the High-Net-Worth Client

Insurance allows your clients to be prepared for surprises and for the inevitable (death and taxes). Unfortunately, many people find that they are underinsured when they make a claim and that their policy does not cover the losses they have sustained. You must help your clients identify their insurance needs in a systematic manner and then choose the most appropriate policies to cover each major type of need, rather than trying to find all-inclusive coverage.

Clients may have both personal and business-related insurance needs. These include life and health insurance as well as property and casualty insurance. Insurance needs may be as basic as addressing concerns regarding disability, or as complex as cross-border coverage for people who have a second home in another country or for "snowbirds" who spend long periods outside Canada.

2.1   Small Business Owners

Small business owners usually need commercial insurance. The requirements of insurance companies may also influence the security measures they use. For example, some insurance companies require shops to have secret silent alarms, high-quality safes, and laminated glass to protect against entry by force.

Small business owners in the manufacturing sector also need product liability insurance to protect them against allegations that their manufactured goods are faulty.

2.2   Senior Executives

Senior executives are often compensated in a different way from other employees. Also, they and their families may be accustomed to a certain lifestyle that they want to maintain. Although these clients may have generous insurance packages as part of their company benefits, you should consider their need for additional insurance. For example, is their life insurance adequate for the lifestyle to which their spouse and children are accustomed?

2.3   Professionals

Sound financial planning allows professionals to concentrate on their careers. However, self-employed professionals who work from their homes may be vulnerable to a disaster, such as a burglary or fire, that can seriously impair their livelihood.

Homeowners' insurance is the starting point for coverage, but few homeowners' policies cover business liabilities and there may be only limited coverage for items such as mobile phones and cameras. Endorsements to homeowners' policies may provide additional coverage for business risks incurred in residential premises.

Professionals such as consultants may need errors and omissions/professional liability insurance to cover them if they are alleged to have provided the wrong advice to one of their clients.

Self-employed individuals also need disability insurance. Disability insurance policies pay out a regular income if the insured is unable to work because of an accident or illness.

2.4   Independently Wealthy Clients

Standard insurance policies such as homeowners' policies may not fully insure large homes containing luxury items. Insurance policies specifically designed for high-net-worth individuals tend to be more flexible and usually offer coverage at attractive premiums. These policies provide coverage for items such as antiques, fine art, rare books, collectors' cars, jewellery and other contents such as valuable carpets, entertainment centres, designer clothes, and furs. They include a broad range of situations including liability, fire, and theft. You should also recommend that these clients get a comprehensive appraisal of their homes, and seek advice on security arrangements.

Depreciation coverage for antiques and art, which covers loss of value and restoration of any damaged articles, should be built into these insurance packages. You should also check the provisions of standard homeowners' policies. Some require that the insurance money be used to buy replacements for any lost or damaged items, whereas customized policies may allow the insured person to retain the insurance money for other purposes.

You should also look at the dollar limit for single articles. Every item over the limit must be listed separately. You also need to consider the maximum period under the policy during which a house can be left empty and still have coverage. In many cases, theft and malicious damage to a property left empty for more than 30 days is not covered.

High-net-worth individuals may have second homes or vacation properties. Coverage is usually more limited for these properties than for dwellings that are occupied throughout the year. For instance, the policy may cover burglary but not simple theft; for a claim to be admitted, the client would need to prove that there had been forcible entry to or exit from the property. Vacation properties may also require special policies to cover trees and shrubs, hedges, outbuildings, fences, garden furniture, and statues. Specialty insurance products may also cover yachts and horses. Horses are typically covered under livestock insurance policies.

Independently wealthy clients have a duty to disclose to their insurance company any material changes in circumstances related to the risks that have been insured. Additional risks arising as a result of individuals carrying on business in their vacation homes should also be covered, generally by way of an endorsement to the policy.

2.5   Keeping Insurance Up to Date

You should regularly re-evaluate your clients' insurance needs and coverage to keep abreast of changes in their lifestyles. This may include reviewing the amount of the deductible and liability limits, and considering new, more flexible types of coverage as they become available. You also need to ensure that your clients' life insurance is adequate and will preserve the existing lifestyle of their dependants and family members.

3.0   Personal Insurance for High-Net-Worth Clients

3.1   Life Insurance

Life insurance is important, especially for clients with children. The amount of coverage really depends on the client's circumstances. Term life insurance is the cheapest form of insurance for people under 40. In determining the appropriate amount of life insurance, you should consider estate obligations such as estate taxes, funeral expenses, an outstanding mortgage on the principal residence or vacation home, the education of dependent children, and the amount required to replace the loss of the deceased's income.

3.2   Critical Illness Insurance

Critical illness insurance (CII) policies provide coverage, generally by way of a lump sum, if the policyholder suffers a specific health problem during the term of the policy, such as a heart attack, cancer, stroke, kidney or other organ failure, or coronary thrombosis requiring bypass surgery. CII policies are discussed in detail in the Professional Financial Planning course.

3.3   Homeowners' Insurance

Most high-net-worth clients need homeowners' insurance, but it must be tailored to the client. For example, some high-net-worth clients have valuable homes, but the contents of their homes are not as valuable. For these clients, you should look for an insurance policy that does not focus on the contents of the home.

3.4 Travel Insurance

Many high-net-worth clients need travel health insurance to cover unforeseen emergencies resulting from illness or accidents when they are abroad. Travel insurance policies may cover a family including up to three children. Some policies are for personal travel; others cover business trips only. Coverage for high-risk activities, such as parasailing, hang-gliding, or scuba diving, may also be available for an additional premium. Clients should be aware of the various restrictions, including pre-existing conditions, amount maximums, duration of coverage, and destinations covered when they buy travel insurance.

3.5 Marriage Contract Insurance

Marriage contract insurance has recently been introduced in Canada. It protects the assets of the party who is applying for the coverage as well as the lawyer who drafts the insurance contract.

The application for marriage contract insurance must be submitted before the wedding, along with a copy of the marriage contract. The amount of insurance on the marriage contract policy will be 50% of the assets of the person applying for coverage as set out in the Schedule of Assets, which must accompany the application. The policy term is 10 years, with a guarantee of renewal if the same insurance company is still underwriting the product.

3.6 Annuities

An annuity is a contract that converts a pension or retirement fund into an annual income for a certain term or for life. It is sold by a life insurance company and provides payments to the annuitant at specified intervals, usually beginning when the annuitant retires. The funds in a Registered Retirement Savings Plan (RRSP) must be converted to an annuity when the RRSP holder turns 69, unless they are transferred to a Registered Retirement Income Funds (RRIF) or cashed. Some of the benefits and drawbacks of annuities were described in Chapter 5, section 7.4.

An annuity can be useful for retired high-net-worth individuals as a form of tax planning. The retiree surrenders the capital to the life insurance company, and buys an annuity generating an annual income for a fixed period of years or for life. If, however, the annuitant dies, any monies remaining in the fund on the death of the annuitant belong to the insurance company and do not go to the estate of the deceased.

Payments made under an annuity are based on the rate of interest/return earned on the investment as well as a mortality calculation that takes into account the health and lifestyle of the annuitant and the average likelihood of death in a particular year.

Different kinds of annuities are available from life insurance companies:

- In a **level-paying annuity**, the amount that the annuitant receives is the same every year.

- In an **annuity with an escalating option**, the amount the annuitant receives may rise by 3 to 5% a year or may be indexed to inflation.

- A **single-life annuity** can be guaranteed such that it is paid out for a fixed period of years, usually five or ten years, even if the annuitant dies.

- Under a **joint and last survivor annuity**, the spouse receives a percentage of the annuity of the deceased, or the entire amount.

Investment annuities, often called unit-linked policies, have been gaining greater recognition in recent years as retirees aim to boost returns through the stock market. Although they have higher potential for growth, they are riskier because of the exposure to the stock market. In contrast, traditional annuities invest in conservative, fixed-income securities.

3.7   Funeral-Expenses Life Insurance

Many people pre-arrange funeral services to help cut the cost of funerals and ensure that their families are not required to carry out the administrative work of organizing a funeral at a difficult time. Insurance-based funeral plans, usually whole life insurance policies, have been available in Canada for several years, and tend to be bought mainly by individuals in their sixties.

For example, the Guaranteed Funeral Plan underwritten by Westbury Canadian Life Insurance Company provides coverage for funeral expenses. Application packages are available from funeral directors. In order to buy funeral-expense life insurance, decisions must immediately be made about such things as whether the person wants to be buried or cremated, what type of coffin should be used, and how many limousines must be hired to follow the hearse. The premium for funeral-expenses life insurance can be paid in a lump sum or it can be subject to a time payment plan.

3.8   Keeping a Vacation Property in the Family

Thousands of Canadians own vacation properties such as cottages. Most cottage owners want to keep the property within the family so that children and grandchildren can continue to enjoy it. The ultimate concern of cottage owners with heirs is to ensure that the property can be passed on to future generations in a tax-effective manner.

When a property owner dies, there is a deemed disposition of all capital property immediately before death at fair market value. Capital gains arising as a result become subject to tax in the final income tax return of the deceased. If a cottage purchased in 1983 for $30,000 has a deemed disposition in 2000 upon the owner's death and it is now worth $150,000, then a capital gain of $120,000 has occurred; 2/3rds of that amount must be included in the deceased's final tax return.

If a cottage property is designated as the owner's principal residence on death (for example, if the owner does not own a house in the city but rents a condominium or apartment), then it can be fully exempt from capital gains tax under the principal residence exemption.

Before 1982, spouses could hold their house in one spouse's name and a cottage or other vacation property in the other spouse's name and each could designate one property as his or her principal residence. This way they could sell or transfer both properties without paying tax on the capital gains from the sale. As of 1982, however, only one property can be designated by a family unit (considered to be the two spouses and any unmarried children under age 18) as its principal residence for a particular year. However, for properties acquired before 1982, the portion of the capital gains on a second property that dates from the period before 1982 is still exempt.

If there are not enough liquid assets in the surviving spouse's estate to cover the income tax liability, the heirs may be forced to sell the property to pay the taxes. In the example above, capital gains tax would be payable on 2/3rds of $120,000. Without readily available cash to pay these taxes (which could be between $45,000 and $50,000), the heirs would have to borrow funds or sell the property to fulfill the tax obligations. Nowadays, it is not uncommon for many cottage properties to be worth between $500,000 and $1,000,000, which means that taxes can be very high.

To avoid a huge tax liability on death, the owners of the cottage could purchase a "joint and last to die" life insurance policy to provide funds to pay the tax liabilities that arise when the owners die. This policy would pay off on the death of the surviving spouse. The heirs could continue to enjoy the property without having to find cash to pay taxes or decide which assets to sell to raise the required funds. This strategy would provide an orderly and trouble-free transfer of property to the next generation. The heirs can pay all, or a portion of, the premiums on the life insurance policy, thus sharing the financial obligation. A potential risk in this strategy is that the capital gains tax exposure on the cottage property may keep rising, if the property grows in value. Therefore, the amount of life insurance that is taken out today may not cover the entire capital gains tax exposure in the future.

Case 6.1   Keeping a Cottage in the Family

Gord and Vera Dunn have been married 40 years and have two adult children, Peter and Nancy. Gord is 70 years old and Vera is a year younger. In 1971, they purchased a cottage property overlooking Lake Simcoe for $25,000. They have been enjoying it every summer and fall, first with their young children and now with their 2 grandchildren. Both Gord and Vera and their children have strong emotional ties to the cottage and want to keep it in the family for coming generations.

The area where the cottage is located has experienced a phenomenal boom in property values and their cottage is expected to be worth an astounding $400,000 by the time that both Gord and Vera are dead. Clearly, Gord and Vera are concerned about the financial implications of passing this property on to their children after their death.

Analysis:

The pre-1982 portion of the capital gain amount on the cottage is $15,000, (i.e., the property appreciated by that amount between 1971 and 1981. This gain is exempt from taxation based on the then prevailing rules of the principal residence exemption.

The post-1981 capital gain on the cottage would be $360,000, calculated as follows:
    Property purchased at $25,000 in 1971.
    Property worth $40,000 as of 1982, the time of the rule change on capital gains.
    Property's projected value when both Gord and Vera are dead: $400,000.
    Therefore, the capital gain is $400,000 - $40,000 = $360,000.
    Taxable capital gain would be 2/3rds of $360,000 = $240,000.

The heirs, Peter and Nancy, would have to come up with enough to cover the tax liability on their portion of the $240,000 taxable capital gain. This amount may be too large to fund. Without adequate preparation it could compel them to sell their cherished cottage just to pay Revenue Canada (Canada Customs and Revenue Agency).

To solve the impending liquidity problem, Gord and Vera buy a "joint and last to die" term-to-100 life insurance policy that would pay out on the second death, giving Peter and Nancy the funds required to meet the substantial tax liability.

A general agreement can be established to split the premiums on the policy three ways. Gord and Vera would pay one third, and Peter and Nancy would each pay one-third. This leads to an equitable sharing of the premiums payable on the policy and demonstrates a tangible commitment from the next generation to retain the property within the family.

4.0 Property and Casualty Insurance For Business

Most businesses need insurance for property and casualty risks. Liabilities arising from corporate operations, international loss exposures, corporate fleets, property losses, and industry-specific risks should be covered by special insurance policies.

Property and casualty insurance companies underwrite risks and issue policies designed to help policyholders cope with the financial consequences of sudden, unpredictable events. Property insurance is defined as "insurance against the loss of, or damage to, property and includes insurance coming within the class of forgery insurance but does not include insurance coming within the class of aircraft insurance, automobile insurance and hail insurance."

Property and casualty insurance companies offer a variety of types of insurance, including automobile insurance, fidelity insurance, property insurance, liability insurance, and surety insurance. Insurance companies can be licensed for more than 40 classes of insurance, such as credit insurance, earthquake insurance, fire insurance, guarantee insurance, inland transportation insurance, mortgage insurance, and theft insurance.

4.1 Business Property Losses

Property losses may arise as a result of fire, natural disasters, or theft. Business property insurance policies usually cover:

- commercial property such as buildings, equipment, and stock;
- tenants' legal liability;
- crime and employee fidelity.

Commercial property insurance may be purchased separately, with several different policies for each property, or may be purchased as a commercial package. Commercial property insurance packages are covered in more detail in section 4.9.

Insurance companies have also developed specialized coverage for computer business equipment. Insurance policies are often tailored to cover both the costs of replacing hardware and reprogramming lost data.

Tenants' legal liability coverage provides protection against losses to the property should the property owner be held legally liable for losses. Typical insurable losses covered by tenants' legal liability insurance result from fire or explosions caused by company equipment.

Crime and fidelity coverage protects business owners from criminal acts such as burglary and kidnapping that may arise from dishonest employees. Crime and fidelity coverage is discussed in more detail in section 4.4.

4.2   Business Income Losses

Business income losses may arise for businesses in all sectors of the economy, from the manufacturing industry to mercantile and service industries. Business income losses are covered under the Business Interruption Insurance Endorsement to property insurance policies. Different versions, from those that use gross earnings as the basis of coverage and loss calculations to those that use profit, are available to meet different client needs.

4.3   Business Liability Losses

Directors' Liability

All incorporated businesses should have directors' liability insurance and should regularly reassess the directors' liability policy limits to ensure that the policy remains appropriate in today's changing legal environment. Directors' liability may include executive directors as well as non-executive or outside directors.

In 1973, the Supreme Court of Canada, in *Canadian Aero Service v. O'Malley*, set out the leading Canadian decision on the duties of directors. The court held that directors have "duties of loyalty, good faith, avoidance of conflict of interest between duty and interest and avoidance of personal profit."

Canadian federal and provincial statutes also create responsibilities and liabilities for directors. Under corporate legislation such as the *Canada Business Corporations Act* and the *Ontario Business Corporations Act*, directors have a duty to act honestly and in good faith with a view to the best interests of the corporation as well as a duty to exercise the care, diligence, and skill that a reasonably prudent person would exercise in comparable circumstances. Allegations of breach of duty of care and claims for damages for negligent mis-statement and misrepresentation are examples of litigation that may result in directors' liability.

Under the *Competition Act (Canada)*, which came into force in 1985, the types of misconduct that could lead to directors' liability include conspiracy, bid-rigging, agreements or arrangements to fix interest rates or charges, illegal trade practices, exclusive dealing, tied selling and market restrictions, misleading advertising, double ticketing, pyramid selling, bait-and-switch selling, price fixing, and the abuse of a dominant market position.

Directors' liability may also arise as a result of directors failing to remit tax, employment insurance contributions, or pension plan contributions, or to pay wages owing to employees under the *Income Tax Act (Canada)*, the *Canada Pension Plan Act*, the *Employment Insurance Act (Canada)*, the *Canada Pension Benefits Standards Act*, and the *Canada Labour Code*.

Generally speaking, coverage under a directors' and officers' liability policy is for "corporate reimbursement." There are two basic insurance clauses.

1. A clause that indemnifies the corporation to the extent that the corporation is required to indemnify its own directors and officers for their own liability, either for the costs of defence or for damages, or both.

2. A clause that generally indemnifies the directors and officers directly if the corporation is unable to indemnify them.

In the past, directors have not been liable for a corporation's debts. However, there seems to be a trend developing in Canada whereby courts are holding directors of a corporation liable to creditors of the corporation if the directors knew or should have known that the corporation was or would be unable to honour its obligations to creditors when the obligations were incurred. The Quebec Superior Court in the *Peoples Stores* case, held directors of a corporation liable to the corporation's creditors. Although the judgement has been appealed, the decision of the Quebec Superior Court is significant in that it opens the door to greater responsibility of directors towards creditors of a corporation.[1]

Environmental Harm and Pollution

Under environmental law, "environmental harm" is the release into the environment of a toxic substance by someone who owns the toxic substance, is in charge of it, or causes or contributes to its release into the environment.

Certain federal and provincial statutes impose personal liability on directors and officers for environmental harm or damage. Environmental liability arises under numerous statutes including the *Environmental Protection Act (Canada)*, *Environmental Protection Act (Ontario)*, and the *Waste Management Amendment Act (British Columbia)*. Directors can also face liabilities for environmental mismanagement. For example, a company could be accused of operating a hospital incinerator in breach of its licence. Chemical and engineering companies may also be liable for environmental clean-up operations. Directors of shipping companies may also face environmental liability in the event of shipping disasters.

Generally speaking, the directors' and officers' insurance policy covers only economic loss resulting from the announcement of a pollution liability or from problems with government regulators and bureaucrats regarding an environmental hazard.

---

[1] Under the *Civil Code* of Quebec, the duties of directors are similar to those set out above; they must act with prudence, diligence, honesty, and loyalty in the best interest of the company.

4.4   Fraud, Criminal Acts, and Employee Dishonesty

Businesses may suffer losses arising from fraud, criminal acts, and employee dishonesty. An insurance company licensed to write fidelity insurance will generally provide coverage for these kinds of losses under a Dishonesty, Disappearance, and Destruction ("3D") policy.

The comprehensive 3D policy provides coverage for employee dishonesty, loss inside the premises, loss outside the premises, money orders, counterfeit paper currency, and depositors' forgery. The policy can be custom-tailored. For example, certain 3D policies cover organizations that have a benevolent, social or political purpose (such as the United Way or Scouts Canada) against the fraudulent or dishonest acts of employees, campaign solicitors, and volunteer workers. Others can be issued to a partnership to provide coverage against fraudulent or dishonest acts of the insured's partners. The 3D policy can also provide coverage for property or securities in safety deposit boxes.

Theft insurance, which is insurance against the loss of or damage to property caused by theft or robbery, includes insurance against losses caused by forgery.

4.5   Product Recall Liability

Many companies today buy product recall liability insurance. Recently, many companies have been affected by product contamination scares and high-profile recalls (for example the identification of dioxins in Belgium's milk and meat products, which led to a recall of these products from store shelves). Product recall insurance compensates for a drop in sales due to product tampering or contamination.

4.6   Workers' Compensation

In Canada, workers' compensation insurance is provided by provincial boards, which focus on workplace safety. Most of the workplace compensation boards operate with significant unfunded liabilities. A number of initiatives are under way in provinces such as Ontario and Alberta to lower unfunded liabilities.

In the United States, workers' compensation insurance is a specific class of insurance offered by insurance companies, which focus on employee health.

4.7   Kidnap and Ransom Insurance

Kidnapping is rare in Canada but a growing number of abductions in other countries raise fears for business people who work abroad. During the 1990s, more than 7,000 people were reported kidnapped around the world. The highest number of incidents occurred in Colombia, Mexico, Brazil, the Philippines, and Pakistan. Wealthy and high-profile individuals who undertake a significant amount of travel to high-risk destinations buy kidnap insurance. So do organizations that send employees to dangerous locations.

The Hiscox Group at Lloyd's of London is the largest kidnap insurance company in the world, followed by American International Group (AIG). Marsh & McLennan and Sedgwick are insurance brokers that specialize in kidnap insurance policies. Kidnap insurance covers ransom payments, money lost in delivery, the cost of victims' salaries, and travel and other expenses for the victim's family, as well as additional expenses such as legal fees, interpreters' fees, and medical and psychiatric care for victims and their families.

A fundamental condition of a kidnap and ransom insurance policy is that its existence must not be disclosed. The identity of the policyholder is kept strictly confidential. Employees who undertake business travel for a global organization may not be told that they are covered by a kidnap and ransom insurance policy.

4.8   Key Person Insurance

"Key person" insurance, also known as "key man" or "key employee" insurance, protects a business from the negative impact, mostly financial, of the death or disability of a highly valued employee who is integral to the survival and success of the business. This insurance gives a business funds to hire and train a qualified replacement and thereby restore a key employee's contribution to profits, growth, and success. It can also be used to provide continuity in operations during a period of ownership transition.

The untimely death of a key employee can have a disastrous effect on a business. For example:

- A company's credit rating may get downgraded.
- The company's suppliers and customers may lose confidence in the company.
- The organization's other employees may become overburdened and distracted, resulting in unmet deadlines, poor morale, or disagreements.
- Finding, hiring, and training a suitable substitute is expensive and time-consuming.
- Precious cash may have to be set aside, at an inopportune and difficult time, to fulfil financial promises made to the deceased employee's spouse or family.
- The company may miss a major business opportunity, because senior management is preoccupied in dealing with the employee's absence or because scarce cash reserves must be devoted to conducting a search for a replacement.

Determining the value of a key employee is not easy. Several methods can be employed to come up with a reasonable value. The most common are:

- the multiple-of-compensation method;
- the contribution-to-profits method;
- the cost-of-replacement method.

Multiple-of-Compensation Method

This method assumes that an employee's value is accurately represented by his or her total annual compensation (including benefits). A multiple is applied to that amount (usually two or three) that varies according to the industry, type of business, current profitability, and the estimated difficulty in finding a qualified substitute.

Contribution-to-Profits Method

This method focuses on the estimated impact of a key employee on the company's net profits. The firm initially comes up with the expected profit from a normal return on investment. Profit exceeding the normal return is then assumed to flow from the contribution of the key employee or employees. Once the percentage of profit attributable to each key employee is determined, it is multiplied by total excess profit to determine the dollar amount of excess pertaining to each key employee. The resulting sum is multiplied by a factor that takes into account the time it is likely to take to find and train a competent replacement.

Cost-of-Replacement Method

This method focuses on the direct, out-of-pocket costs incurred in searching for, hiring, and bringing a replacement up to speed, and the estimated opportunity costs of this process. Search costs, especially for a senior executive or professional, can run into tens of thousands of dollars. Lost opportunities can also be substantial, particularly when business is moving rapidly and critical decisions have to be made quickly.

Funding Key Person Insurance

Financing the replacement of a key person can be accomplished by putting funds aside for such a contingency, borrowing funds when the contingency arises, or using the proceeds of a life insurance policy.

Putting funds aside is not an ideal use of resources, especially when they could be used more profitably in operating or expanding the business. Borrowing funds when a key employee dies may not be feasible. It might be difficult to convince a financial institution to lend money to the business when it is in a state of flux and possibly in jeopardy due to the death of the key employee.

Life insurance is the most feasible and efficient means of protecting a business from the problems that arise when a key employee dies or is disabled. The premiums are relatively minor compared to the lump sum that would have to be set aside out of earnings, or to the cost of borrowing.

The business is usually the owner of the policy on the life of a key employee. It pays the premiums and is the beneficiary. Premiums are not deductible and the proceeds received on death are not taxable. If the employee dies, the proceeds are paid to the business to use as it wishes. If permanent life insurance is purchased, there will also be an accumulation of cash value that can be used by the business as and when needed.

Case 6.2   Key Person Insurance at Computers R Us

Rohit Kapoor, a 35-year-old MBA from Queen's, is the vice president of marketing at Computers R Us, a burgeoning chain of computer hardware and software "big box" outlets. Last year, the company had sales of $12 million and profits were $3 million. Rohit has been instrumental in increasing market penetration since he started at the company three years ago. He is constantly on the go, promoting Computers R Us with manufacturers, distributors, and resellers. Getting the big-name players to offer their merchandise for sale at its outlets is a constant challenge and Rohit excels at it.

The President, Caleb Strom, considers Rohit to be an invaluable employee of the rapidly growing company. Without Rohit looking after the all-important marketing end, the company would, indeed, be in dire straits. Rohit is without a doubt a key employee of Computers R Us and should be appropriately insured to protect the company in the event of his death or disability. Caleb contacts his insurance agent, Greg Tridel, and together they discuss the issues involved.

Analysis:

Rohit earns a base salary of $150,000 and is eligible for bonuses that relate directly to the profits made by the company. While Computers R Us can estimate Rohit's value using a multiple of his yearly compensation, Caleb feels that his value is more intrinsically related to the profit side of the equation.

As such, Caleb estimates Rohit's impact on the bottom line of Computers R Us to be around 30%. In other words, 30% of the profits made by Computers R Us can be attributed to Rohit's superb performance as the marketing vice president. Consequently, close to $1 million of life insurance is needed to replace Rohit's contribution to the company's profitability.

The company agrees to purchase a 10-year renewable and convertible term insurance policy on Rohit's life with a face amount of $1 million. The premiums are payable by Computers R Us and the company is also the beneficiary.

Caleb knows that it would be difficult to replace Rohit because of the relationships he has cultivated with the company's primary suppliers, but a $1 million cushion would prove very useful in the event of tragic circumstances. Computers R Us would at least have the resources to continue operations and the wherewithal and time to look for a suitable replacement without being strapped for cash.

4.9   Standard Insurance Policies

Business Owners' Commercial Package Policy

The business owners' commercial package policy is an example of property insurance that insures for loss to property, including building, equipment, and stock. As the name implies, the commercial package policy will cover various types of losses, including property losses as well as liability losses.

Endorsements can also be added to a property insurance policy, including:

*   inflation protection endorsement;

*   earthquake endorsement;

*   replacement cost endorsement (receiving a settlement of claim without any deduction for depreciation). This was originally intended to provide coverage for buildings only, but it has been extended to personal property. Replacement cost coverage depends on the items listed on the declaration page of the property insurance policy.

Generally, losses under the property insurance policy are payable to the insured, subject to the Standard Mortgage Clause, which provides that fire losses are payable to the mortgagee (lender), and that the mortgagee's interest as payee is not invalidated by any act, negligence, omissions, or misrepresentations of the insured. The Standard Mortgage Clause is essential to protect the rights of the mortgagee in residential as well as commercial mortgage transactions. It creates a "separate contract" of insurance between the mortgagee and the insurer. Without it, the mortgagee would be at the mercy of the mortgagor.

Commercial General Liability Policy

Commercial general liability insurance provides coverage against business liability exposures. This includes coverage for situations in which:

*   negligent acts and/or omissions result in bodily injury and/or property damage on or away from the premises of the business;

*   someone is injured as a result of using a product manufactured or distributed by the business;

*   someone is injured in the general operation of the business.

Commercial general liability policies can be occurrence-based or on a claims-made basis:

*   In an **occurrence-based policy**, the insurance covers claims arising from an event that occurred while the policy was in force, regardless of when the insured submits the claim.

*   In a **claims-made policy**, the insurance covers only those claims made while the policy is in effect, as long as the event occurs during the policy period.

In recent years, there has been a shift from occurrence-based policies to claims-made policies.

4.10   Buy–Sell Agreements

Upon the death of a business partner or major shareholder in a closely held business, the remaining partners/owners have four main choices:

1. Liquidate the business and distribute the remaining assets. This is not a very desirable option, since the survivors would be giving up their major source of income and a business in which they have likely invested a lot of time and money. Also, under "fire sale" circumstances, the business assets might only fetch a fraction of what they are worth.

2. Sell the business to the heirs of the deceased partner. The same problems arise.

3. Bring in the deceased partner's spouse or adult children as new business associates. This, too, is a difficult choice to make and implement successfully. A strong working relationship among partners or owners takes time to develop. Except in rare situations, bringing on board a deceased partner's spouse or heir can cause more problems than it solves and could even result in the failure of the business.

4. Buy out the surviving heirs' share of the business, using a previously executed buy-sell agreement. This is, in most cases, the most practical course of action. Although it can be difficult to place a value on each partner's share of the business, the terms and funding mechanisms can be negotiated before the event with proper planning and consultation. Professional advice should be sought at each stage of the agreement and by each party to the agreement.

What is a Buy-Sell Agreement?

A buy-sell agreement is a legally binding agreement that ensures that either the business or the remaining owners will buy one owner's portion of the business for a mutually agreed-upon price under predetermined and mutually acceptable terms and conditions. It can be used when an owner dies, retires, becomes disabled, or just wants out. Buy-sell agreements also permit the orderly transition of ownership when the owners of a closely held business or partners in a partnership split up. Buy-sell agreements may be drawn up between owners or shareholders of a corporation, partners of a partnership, or between an employer and a key employee.

The agreement protects remaining owners by guaranteeing that they can buy the shares when another owner dies or leaves the business. It prevents outsiders from purchasing the outstanding portion of the business and allows for continuity in operational and managerial control.

A buy-sell agreement is a necessity for a partner or shareholder in a private company. It puts a relatively objective value on the shares or partnership interest, a value that is established in the capital market for shares of public corporations. In a private corporation, at the time of death or divorce of a principal owner or shareholder, the emotions of the heirs and the remaining owners can stall discussions about the value of the business. On occasion, these discussions have led to expensive litigation, thereby reducing the value of the business.

A well-thought-out and carefully constructed buy-sell agreement is not a guarantee of protection against discord. However, the agreement does provide a way to value the shares if an owner opts out or dies. The heirs of a deceased owner or partner may feel that the value of the deceased's share of the business, as set forth in the buy-sell agreement, is unreasonable and may challenge the valuation in court. However, a buy-sell agreement is evidence of the thinking of the principals at a relatively stress-free time and provides a benchmark for further negotiation and discussion.

A buy-sell agreement is like a prenuptial contract between business partners, in that it specifies what happens to a partner's or owner's share of the business when he or she departs. A properly executed and funded buy-sell agreement benefits everyone. The surviving family has cash and no concerns about the future of the business. The remaining partners have a business about which they feel secure. The business's employees keep their jobs. Customers and creditors are assured of the continuity of the business.

A variation on the buy-sell agreement is the disability buy-out agreement, which helps a business survive if one of the partners or owners becomes disabled and unable to work. The disability buy-out agreement is either among the business owners themselves or between the owners and the business organization. The agreement establishes a predetermined price and a buyer for the business interest. Disability buy-out insurance is commonly used to provide the funds needed to fund the buy-out.

Funding a Buy-Sell Agreement

A buy-sell agreement can be funded in several different ways:

1. Using current cash flow. Some agreements state that the deceased's share will be paid in instalments from the cash flow of the business. Heirs typically dislike such arrangements, because future payments depend on the continued success of the business. This can be a considerable risk if the past success of the business was due principally to the skills and talents of the deceased owner or partner. This option may also result in a significant drain on the key operating resources of a business at a time when it is least affordable.

2. Creating a sinking fund. It is hard for most businesses to set aside money for a sinking fund.

3. Selling existing assets. Unfortunately, this may leave the business vulnerable at a critical time.

4. Borrowing. Borrowing can be expensive. Given the tenuous nature of the business after an owner's death, it may be difficult to secure a substantial loan without offering considerable collateral or accepting more stringent guarantees.

5. Life insurance. Cash value life insurance is the most effective funding option.

Using a life insurance or disability insurance policy is the most common way to fund a buy-sell agreement. Cash is paid out to the deceased partner's beneficiary or estate and shares are transferred to the remaining owners in an efficient and methodical manner. Other advantages include:

- ironclad payment guarantees;
- tax-free funds payable on death;
- cash values under a permanent policy that can be used for a buyout on retirement or disability;
- the strengthening of the business's credit position.

Insurance coverage must be maintained at all times and periodic adjustments should be made to the amount insured to reflect increases in business values. The buy-sell agreement should be flexible enough to permit quick and relatively easy changes.

Structuring a Buy-Sell Agreement

Under cross-purchase agreements, the partners or shareholders agree to purchase one another's business interest in the event of death, disability, retirement, or termination. Insurance funding of a cross-purchase agreement requires that each partner or shareholder purchase a policy on every other partner or shareholder's life. Business ownership of life insurance is not involved.

Under corporate-redemption agreements, the corporation agrees to purchase the shares of a departing shareholder. The business entity owns the insurance, pays the premiums, and is named the beneficiary. Redemption agreements are generally simple and easy to administer. For example, only one insurance policy is required for each shareholder to fund a redemption agreement. Hybrid agreements combine elements of both.

There are numerous tax, estate, and financial planning issues to be considered in deciding which type of buy-sell agreement is most beneficial. Consulting a professional with expertise in this area would be worthwhile.

Case 6.3   Jerry, George, and Kramer's Buy-Sell Agreement

Jerry, George and Kramer are co-owners of Funny Bone Inc., a successful comedy club operation across Canada, with an estimated worth of $10 million. They are all in their late thirties. Jerry and George are married and each has two children. Kramer is single.

Jerry is the creative genius of the business. He is a devoted family man and loves to race fast cars. Kramer and George are huge draws in the comedy club circuit and perform together. They live sedentary lives, eat a lot of fast food, and both have hypertension and high cholesterol.

Kramer cannot see eye-to-eye with Jerry's wife, Alanna. He thinks she is too meddlesome and aggressive. Jerry is aware that there is no love lost between Kramer and Alanna. If something were to happen to him, Alanna would inherit his entire estate including his share of Funny Bone Inc. Alanna has expressed an interest in joining and even running Funny Bone Inc., which terrifies George and Kramer.

Their wealth manager, Susan Bestworth, has suggested that they enter into a buy-sell agreement. She is concerned about the lifestyle, health, and interpersonal relationships of the three partners. Without a carefully planned and drafted agreement, she fears the business could be in jeopardy on the death of any one of them.

Analysis:

The first issue she raises is the value to be placed on each person's share of the business. While they began informally as equal owners, it has become abundantly clear in the last two years that Jerry has been, by far, the biggest contributor to the growth and success of the business. Therefore, there is general agreement that he should be assigned half of the estimated value of the business. $5 million for Jerry share and George and Kramer's shares would be worth $2.5 million each.

The three also agree to have a professional business valuation undertaken at 5-year intervals to ensure that the funding mechanism in place takes into consideration changes in the worth of the business.

To fund the buy-out at death, Funny Bone Inc. purchases permanent life insurance policies on the lives of Jerry, George and Kramer, pays the premiums and is named the beneficiary. Guaranteed insurability options are included in each of the policies so that more life insurance can be purchased (if needed) at standard rates at a future stage, irrespective of the state of their health.

Case 6.3   Jerry, George, and Kramer's Buy-Sell Agreement

(continued)

Four years later, while racing at the Molson Indy, Jerry loses control and crashes his car into a concrete embankment. He is rushed to hospital for emergency surgery, but dies on the operating table.

Funny Bone Inc. collects the death benefit of $5 million and uses the funds to buy out Jerry's share of the business from Jerry's estate, in accordance with the terms of the buy-sell agreement. The transition occurs without any financial hitches. Although George and Kramer are devastated by their partner's death, they have by now established themselves as a successful comedy team and feel that they can continue successfully in the business on their own.

George and Kramer execute a revised buy-sell agreement and use the guaranteed insurability options to increase the amount of life insurance on their lives to reflect the fact that each of them now owns half of Funny Bone Inc.

5.0   Risk Management and Investments

As equity investments have become a larger and larger component of an individual's net worth, insurance has been extended to cover investment portfolios. This type of insurance is likely to become even more popular as members of the baby-boom generation approach retirement and become increasingly risk-averse.

This insurance may be embedded in the particular managed product, such as a segregated or protected fund, or purchased separately through exchange-traded options.

Some may question the need for portfolio insurance. In historical terms, there is virtually no risk of losing money in North American stock markets over a holding period of 10 years. The TSE 300 total-return index has never had a negative return over a span of 10 years. Therefore, many financial advisors and observers conclude that insurance premiums may constitute an unwarranted drag on an investor's returns.

The potential value of maturity guarantees should not to be taken lightly, however. As the performance of the Japanese market during most of the 1990s suggests, even the largest and most developed markets are vulnerable to capital loss over a 10-year period. The Nikkei 225 index, from its peak in 1989 to the end of 1999, lost more than 50% of its value.

Moreover, maturity guarantees safeguard individuals against any catastrophic losses triggered by an unanticipated external shock to the economy, such as a major natural or a man-made disaster. For this reason, some actuaries have suggested that rather than insurance premiums being too high, the premiums charged for maturity guarantees in segregated funds may be too low in relation to the guarantees provided. In the late 1990s, the apparent scarcity of re-insurers willing to take on the risk of maturity guarantees for Canadian segregated funds lent credence to the notion that the insurance premiums have been underpriced.

5.1   Segregated Funds

Segregated funds offer maturity protection, death benefits, creditor protection, and the ability to bypass probate. With the availability of maturity guarantees of up to 100% and death benefits, the risks associated with capital markets become less of an investment constraint. Segregated funds enable older clients to invest in higher-growth asset classes, knowing that the principal amount of their contributions is protected.

Because of the insurance benefits that they offer, segregated funds are a costlier form of managed investment than uninsured funds. In recommending a segregated fund to a client, the wealth manager should weigh the benefits of segregated funds against their added costs. There is more information on segregated funds in Chapter 11.

How Maturity Guarantees Work

Maturity guarantees, particularly those that offer full protection after 10 years, alter the normal risk-reward relationship. With a maturity guarantee in place, clients may participate in rising markets without capping potential returns while protecting their invested capital from loss.

The Ontario Superintendent of Financial Institutions requires that the maturity guarantees cover at least 10 years. Most individual segregated fund policies sold in Canada carry a 10-year term, although longer terms are possible.

Under provincial securities legislation, the amount payable by an insurer under a 10-year maturity guarantee must be a minimum of 75% of the premiums paid. Given past trends in financial markets, there appears to be no likelihood that a contract holder will need to collect on a guarantee that requires a decade-long holding period, because financial markets tend not to lose over 10-year periods.

The statutory 75% guarantee is therefore mainly a regulatory requirement that must be fulfilled in order for a fund to be structured as a segregated fund and exempted from regulation under securities legislation. Many insurers have even increased the guarantee for some funds to a full 100%. Maritime Life, for instance, offers the full maturity guarantee on all but three of its funds. (Not surprisingly, the three Maritime Life funds carrying only 75% protection are in asset categories that have traditionally been risky: global equity, Asian equity, and small-cap U.S. equity.)

The maturity protection of segregated funds can be thought of as an embedded put option on the fund itself. At maturity, assuming 100% protection, the fund investor automatically receives the higher of the fund's market value or original value (which is the exercise price). If the market value of the fund is less than the original value, the embedded put option is in-the-money and is automatically exercised so that the holder receives the original value. If the market value is higher, the embedded option expires without value, and the investor receives the full market value of the fund.

Reset Dates

Although segregated fund contracts have at least a 10-year term, they may be renewable, depending on the annuitant's age. If renewed, the maturity guarantee on a 10-year contract would "reset" for another 10 years. Resets provide additional flexibility in investment strategy and financial planning.

Many insurers offer more frequent reset dates. In some cases, holders of segregated fund contracts may lock in the accrued value before the original 10-year period has expired and thereby extend the maturity date by 10 years.

Depending on the insurance company, resets may be initiated by the policy owner or may be automatic. If resets are optional, there are generally limitations on the number of resets allowed each year.

Death Benefits

The death benefits offered by a segregated fund guarantee the contract holder's beneficiary or estate a payout amounting to at least the contract holder's original investment, minus sales commissions and certain other fees. The amount of the death benefit is equal to the difference, if any, between the net asset value of the fund and the original amounts invested.

Table 6.1 illustrates the death benefits when the market value of the units held in the segregated fund are below, the same as, or higher than the original purchase price. To simplify the illustration, it is assumed that the fund has been held long enough that any deferred sales charges no longer apply.

Table 6.1: Death Benefits for Segregated Funds

Guaranteed amount	Market value at death	Death benefit
$10,000	$8,000	$2,000
$10,000	$9,000	$1,000
$10,000	$10,000	None
$10,000	$11,000	None

Death benefits provide reassurance to clients who want the potential for higher returns offered by equities and long-term fixed-income funds, but are concerned about preserving the value of their investment for their heirs. The death benefit enables these clients to pursue a long-term investment strategy while not having to lock in capital losses if they die during a period when the fund is losing money. In this respect, segregated funds can be compared with other guaranteed investments such as index-linked GICs.

Segregated funds can be useful in estate planning. For example, through the use of provisions relating to irrevocable beneficiaries, contract holders can control the timing of bequests to their surviving children.

For example, John Chin is the terminally ill single parent of Rachel, aged 10. He wants to leave money to Rachel, but postpone her access to the funds until she is 21. Through a segregated-fund contract, John could designate one of Rachel's grandparents as the irrevocable beneficiary of the contract, with the proviso that the contract would be reassigned when Rachel turns 21.

Unlike some life-insurance policies, clients do not have to submit to medical examinations or any other health-related conditions to receive the death benefits offered by segregated funds. However, the death benefits usually have other conditions or exclusions that may eliminate or reduce payouts to the beneficiary. The most common exclusion is based on age. Once the insured person reaches a certain age, the beneficiary may lose eligibility for death benefits, or be required to accept a reduced percentage of benefits.

For example, Maritime Life's guaranteed death benefits are based on a graduated scale according to age. Annuitants who are younger than 77 at the time of the deposit qualify for 100% death benefits. The percentage benefit declines to 95% at age 77, 90% at age 78, 85% at age 79, and 80% for annuitants 80 or older.

When deposits have been made over a period of time and benefits vary according to the client's age, the death benefit is calculated according to a formula that factors in the amount of deposits and the client's age when they were made.

Using the same Maritime Life schedule of benefits, consider the example of Rose Macklin. She opened the account when she was 67 with a deposit of $20,000, deposited another $10,000 at age 70, and a further $5,000 at age 77. (Assume that all the deposits were made with an initial sales charge, so no redemption fees apply.)

Rose dies at age 79, when the market value of the policy is $34,000. Her policy's death benefit is based on the following formula:

$$\$20,000 + \$10,000 + (95\% \times \$5,000) = \$34,750$$

The formula is based on 100% of deposits made before age 77, plus 95% of the deposit made at age 77. Rose's beneficiary receives a death benefit of $750, which is the difference between the guaranteed amount and the policy's market value at death ($34,750 – $34,000). The payment is made in the form of cash, not fund units, since the concept of units in a segregated fund is notional and serves only to determine the amounts payable under the terms of the policy rather than to indicate ownership.

The CompCorp Guarantee

The maturity guarantees and death benefits offered by segregated funds are only as good as the creditworthiness of the insurer issuing the contracts. There is, however, a level of protection outside the company itself. The Canadian Life and Health Insurance Compensation Corp., known as CompCorp, is a non-profit industry organization that backs policies sold by its members. At present, CompCorp has more than 190 members.

If the insurer defaults, CompCorp will make up any shortfall in the amount payable on policies issued by its members. Although CompCorp provides additional protection of capital to contract holders, in practice this contingency fund has never been used.

The CompCorp guarantee covers only the death benefits and maturity guarantees of a segregated-fund contract. The assets of the funds themselves are not eligible for CompCorp protection, because they are segregated from the general assets of the insurance company. Segregated fund holders therefore enjoy a built-in form of protection against an insurance company's insolvency. CompCorp's role is to top up any payments made by a liquidator to fulfil the insurance obligations under a segregated fund contract.

The CompCorp guarantee applies only in the event of the death of the contract holder or at the end of the contract term. Clients who surrender their policies at any other time before the maturity date have no protection against capital loss. The amount they can redeem will vary according to the investment performance of the funds, and any applicable redemption or transfer fees.

To qualify for protection by CompCorp, the segregated-fund policy must be written in Canada by a member company, or be shown on the books of a Canadian branch of a member company. The contract holder, however, does not need to be a Canadian resident to be eligible for CompCorp coverage.

The maximum amount of any compensation awarded under an individual segregated fund policy is $60,000 for each insurance company. This amount has remained unchanged since CompCorp began operations in 1990. The CompCorp-guaranteed amount is not indexed to inflation, nor does it provide protection against fraud on the part of the insurance company.

The $60,000 limit applies both to amounts held by individuals in registered plans, such as RRSPs, registered retirement income funds (RRIFs) and life income funds, and to contracts held outside registered plans.

Up to $60,000 in protection is also available for segregated fund policies held through group plans, whether registered or non-registered. This protection limit is separate and distinct from the one for individual plans. For example, an individual who held both an individual policy and a group policy from the same insurer would qualify for $60,000 in protection under each policy, for total coverage of $120,000.

Creditor Protection

Segregated funds offer protection from creditors that is not available through other forms of managed investment products, such as mutual funds. Creditor protection stems from the fact that segregated funds are insurance policies and ownership of the fund's assets resides with the insurance company, rather than the contract holder. Insurance proceeds generally fall outside bankruptcy legislation.

Creditor protection can be a valuable feature for clients whose personal or business circumstances could make them vulnerable to court-ordered seizure of assets to recover debt. Business owners, entrepreneurs, professionals, or clients who have concerns about their personal liability might welcome the creditor protection offered by a segregated fund.

For example, Renée duBois, a self-employed professional, dies, leaving a non-registered investment portfolio of $300,000, and business-related debts of $150,000. If the portfolio were made up of mutual funds, Renée's creditors would have a claim on half of her portfolio, leaving only $150,000 for her family. Furthermore, the remaining $150,000 would be subject in most provinces, except Quebec, to probate fees based on the size of the estate. In high-fee provinces such as Ontario and British Columbia, the probate fees would be more than $1,500. Had Renée's portfolio been held in segregated funds, the full $300,000 portfolio would be payable directly to her beneficiaries. Creditors could claim nothing, and the beneficiaries would receive their money promptly and without having to deduct probate fees.

Creditor protection does not apply under all circumstances. In order for the assets held in the contract to be eligible for creditor protection, a beneficiary must be named. If the named beneficiary is revocable, he or she must belong to a designated class of individual:

- In Quebec, the contract holder's rights under the contract are protected from creditor seizure if the beneficiary is a spouse, child, or parent of the *contract holder*. The beneficiaries receive the full amount of any benefits to them under the contract, regardless of any claims by creditors against the contract holder.

- In other provinces, the beneficiary must be related to the *annuitant*, the person whose life is being insured. (The annuitant is not always the same person as the contract holder.)

5.2   Using Exchange-Traded Options as Insurance[2]

Exchange-traded put options can be used as insurance to protect investors in the event of a decline in the value of their equity investments, while call options provide insurance against the risk that the price of an equity investment rises before it can be purchased.

The price of the option—whether it is embedded in a fund, as it is with segregated and protected funds, or on its own—is calculated taking into consideration the following factors:

- time to maturity or expiration;
- market price;
- exercise price (in a segregated or protected fund this would be the original value);
- volatility;
- risk-free rate of interest;
- dividends (if any).

The decision to purchase an option for insurance purposes should take into account the following considerations:

- The cost of the option versus the perceived risk of being unprotected;
- The correlation between the option and the underlying equity investment being protected. If the insurance is for an individual stock, an option on that particular stock will provide full insurance in case of a decline in the exercise price of the option. If, however, the portfolio insurance is in the form of an index option, the investor must take into consideration the portfolio's sensitivity to the index underlying the index option.

The following table summarizes the similarities between buying an index put option and a standard insurance policy on a home or car:

Table 6.2 Features of an Index Put Option

Insurance Policy	Purchase of a Put Option
Risk premium	Option time premium
Value of asset	Index level
Face value of the policy	Option strike price
Maturity	Time until expiration
Amount of deductible	Index level minus strike price (out-of-the-money portion)

---

[2] This section assumes readers have a basic level understanding of the derivatives knowledge that is found in the Canadian Securities Course (CSC). If a refresher is needed, students should review the derivatives section of the CSC.

The following example illustrates the use of index options to provide portfolio insurance.

Mike Carrel is one year away from retirement. He has a sizeable equity portfolio, which, except for a small amount of trading money, he intends to switch to fixed-income products when he retires. The size of Mike's portfolio is $500,000, made up of five Canadian blue-chip stocks that closely track the S&P Canada 60 stock index. Mike has 1,000 shares of each stock and each stock price is $100.

As he is bullish on the market, Mike wants to keep the portfolio for one more year. At the same time, however, he cannot afford a significant loss of equity, as his portfolio will form the bulk of his retirement income.

Mike has three options:
1. sell the entire portfolio;
2. purchase put options on the five stocks held;
3. buy index put options.

Selling the Portfolio

Selling the portfolio is the ultimate insurance policy. However, if the market increases in value (and Mike expects that it will), he could incur a sizeable opportunity loss. As well, if he sells the portfolio and the market starts to increase, he will be tempted to buy back some or all of the portfolio, thereby incurring transaction costs and market timing risks.

Mike also has to consider taxes. If he has held the portfolio for a long time and has large capital gains, selling might lead to high taxes. He would be better off selling after he retires, when his income may be lower.

Buying Put Options on Individual Stocks

As each equity option contract represents 100 shares of the underlying equity, Mike would need to buy 10 put option contracts on each of his 5 equity holdings for a total of 50 contracts.

If he wanted to protect the full value of his portfolio, he would need to buy at-the-money options. If he did, and the price of any of the equities he held fell below the option strike price at expiration, he could sell the stock at the strike price.

Since at-the-money puts provide full downside protection, they can be expensive. Mike would have to weigh the cost of the options versus the perceived risk of being unhedged.

Mike could also consider buying out-of-the-money options. For example, he could purchase put options with strike prices 10% below the current stock price. This strategy protects 90% of the portfolio (versus 100% for at-the-money options), and is cheaper to implement. The 10% loss is in effect comparable to the deductible on an insurance policy.

However, this strategy involves transaction expenses. The commission for the purchase of 50 options can be quite expensive, particularly when they are divided up among 5 stocks. Also, not all of the stocks for which insurance is required may have options listed on them. And even if they all have listed options, the options may have different expiry months, which makes management of the hedge more difficult.

Buying Index Put Options

Index options address some of the difficulties of purchasing multiple equity options. As the index option covers the entire portfolio, fewer option contracts are needed, the transaction costs are lower, and the hedge is much more manageable.

Mike's portfolio tracks the S&P Canada 60 index (i60), which is a capitalization-weighted index of the 60 largest and most liquid stocks in Canada. Mike could buy put options on this index. As regular options have a maturity of 9 months or less, and Mike is looking for one-year insurance, the long-term equity anticipation securities options (LEAPS), which have terms between 9 months and 2 years, 8 months, would make sense. The i60 LEAPS, along with other LEAPS and equity options, trade on the Montreal Exchange.

The size of the option contract is $100.00 times the level of the index, which we assume to be 500, for a total value of $50,000. If Mike's portfolio tracks the i60 index perfectly, the number of i60 put option contracts Mike would need for full protection would be:

Size of the portfolio/value of 1 option contract = $500,000/$50,000 = 10 contracts

The purchase of 10 one-year i60 LEAPS with an exercise price of 500 will give Mike full protection. If in one year's time the index fell to 450, the put options would be worth $50,000 ($500 − $450 × 100) x 10 contracts. The $50,000 worth of the options will offset the $50,000 portfolio loss.

The one disadvantage of using index options is that the result of the hedge is uncertain (at least relative to the hedge using individual equity options). If Mike's portfolio of blue-chip Canadian stocks does not perfectly track the i60 index, the payoff on the index option will not match the portfolio loss.

To minimize this risk, the hedge should be done on a beta-adjusted basis. If, for example, Mike's portfolio has historically been shown to be 20% less volatile than the i60, rather than buying 10 put option contracts, he could buy only 8 (10 contracts × the beta of 0.8). If the index fell to 450 (that is, by 10%), the options at expiration will have a value of $40,000, which would offset the $40,000 decline in the value of the portfolio (8%).

5.3   Other Risk Management Options

Covered Call Writing

Another way to gain some downside protection for a portfolio or an individual stock, while at the same time creating some additional income, is through covered call writing. Covered call writing is the selling of a call option against the underlying stock when an investor's view for that particular stock is neutral to slightly bullish. The premium received from the sale of the call creates additional income and provides a buffer in case the stock or portfolio declines in value. If the price of the stock or portfolio rises above the exercise price of the call, the investor does not profit from this increase.

If Mike felt that the portfolio was likely to experience only modest appreciation, he could sell either the individual call options or the i60 call options with a strike price of 520. If the premium for each i60 one-year call was $15, for example, he would have picked up total premium of $15,000 on 10 calls. This adds 3% to his return.

With a strike price of 520, Mike has given up the opportunity to profit from a rise over this level. If the index rises above this level, he must pay the difference between the index value at expiration and the exercise price. If the level of the index rises to 530, Mike would have to pay $10,000 to his broker in settlement of the contract. The most Mike could earn over the year would be $35,000 or 7% ($20,000 on the portfolio and $15,000 on the option). By writing the 520 call, he has given away the opportunity to earn a return over this level.

Combining a Put Purchase with a Covered Call Sale

Buying a put option can be expensive. At the same time, covered call writing gives an investor only limited downside protection (3% in the example above). A strategy that is becoming increasingly popular for portfolios or individual stocks is a combination of a put purchase and call sale.

This strategy, known as a "collar," gives the investor full protection against losses at a cost that is reduced by the sale of the call. The catch, of course, is that if the market rises above the exercise price of the call, the investor has given away the opportunity to profit over this level. The exercise prices of both the put and call, however, depend on the investor's view of the market.

If Mike thought there was a good chance the market would rise 6% over the course of the year and wanted full protection against losses, he could buy the i60 500 put option while at the same time sell the i60 530 call option. If the put option costs $25, and the call option sells for $10, Mike has achieved this protection for only $15. If he bought 10 option contracts, the total cost would be $15,000 or 3% of his entire portfolio.

Index Futures Contracts

Another way to hedge an equity portfolio is by selling index futures contracts. For example selling 10 S&P Canada 60 futures contracts with one year to expiration at a price of 530 (assume the portfolio perfectly matches the index), will lock in that price for one year's time, whether the portfolio declines or rises in value. Although there is full protection against loss, there is no chance of windfall gains using futures contracts if they are held to expiration. Options, on the other hand, leave this possibility open. If the market rises, the put options will merely expire worthless, leaving the investor the opportunity to profit from this gain once the original cost of the option is covered.

The price of the one-year index futures contract ($530) represents the cost of carrying the stocks that make up the index for that period (6%). The cost is merely the difference between the costs of financing the portfolio (the risk-free borrowing rate) minus the dividends received from holding the portfolio (the dividend yield). This price ensures that there is no advantage to buying the portfolio and holding it for one year (paying the 6% carrying cost) over buying and holding the index futures for one year. If one of these ways of gaining exposure to the market is more attractive than the other, an arbitrage opportunity exists. The collective actions of arbitrages will ensure that if the futures contract is mispriced, it will not remain so for long.

As a futures hedge offers no opportunity for windfall gains and futures are priced at their cost of carry level, the short futures hedge does not offer an advantage over selling the portfolio and putting the proceeds into Treasury bills. The returns would be the same. The futures hedge would be more complicated, however, as the futures system of mark-to-market could dictate frequent margin calls.

Since a perfect index futures hedge is no better than selling a portfolio and using the proceeds to buy Treasury bills, a futures hedge would be used for only two reasons.

- If the portfolio is expected to outperform the index, the sale of index futures contracts would reduce or eliminate systematic (market) risk. In other words, if the stocks do outperform the index, the futures hedge will produce greater returns than the Treasury bill rate.

- An investor may want to take a dynamic approach towards the hedge. As the investor becomes increasingly concerned about market overvaluation, particularly following substantial market gains, the futures can be used to insure against market corrections. This market timing approach is very difficult, however, and is often unsuccessful.

CHAPTER 7

Tax Planning

1.0 Introduction

Taxes should be considered as an integral part of investment and financial decision-making, rather than a separate function to be dealt with only by tax lawyers and accountants. Over the long run, such a focus can result in loyal and satisfied clients.

As a wealth manager, you can better assist your clients by treating taxes as a controllable expense and by comparing investment products on an after-tax basis. Since most investors pay taxes, cash flow before tax should have little effect on their choice of investment products.

Tax planning involves shifting taxable income from higher to lower tax rates through:

- income deferral or spreading across time-periods;

- income splitting or spreading across individuals;

- choosing the appropriate form of investment income.

This chapter provides an overview of tax planning, describes the major categories of tax planning, and explains the specific steps in implementing some common tax-planning decisions faced by tax-paying investors.

Primary Learning Objectives

By the end of this chapter, you should understand:

- **the multiple objectives of the Canadian tax system and how the tax planning process relates to it;**

- **the difference between average and marginal tax rates;**

- **how changes in marginal tax rates affect income recognition or deferral;**

- how to determine whether a client should accelerate contributions to an RESP or delay them to maximize the government's annual grants;

- effective tax strategies involving the transfer of assets among family members;

- how family loans at the prescribed interest rate can be used to split income and save taxes;

- strategies for reducing retirement income and avoiding OAS clawbacks;

- the principal residence exemption and how it can be used to shelter capital gains on both a principal residence and vacation property;

- the use of flow-through shares in reducing taxes;

- the tax consequences of employee stock option plans and employee loans;

- limited partnerships and their tax considerations;

- the tax implications of business losses, including allowable business investment losses;

- how to use trusts, including offshore trusts, in tax planning;

- the importance of maintaining the adjusted cost base in mutual fund investments and how it can reduce overall capital gains tax liability;

- how asset churning inside mutual funds triggers taxes that can erode an investor's returns;

- the effect of inflation on investment income;

- RRSP strategies involving spousal spins; early, continuous, and over-contributions; paying down a mortgage vs. investing in an RRSP; borrowing to make RRSP contributions;

- tax planning strategies for clients who own a small business.

1.1   Tax Planning and Customer Relationships

Understanding your clients' needs will help you suggest appropriate products and services. By matching their objectives to available investment products, you can develop a loyal clientele. Some clients, however, are unclear about their investment objectives and may rely on you to help them articulate their goals. At times this may mean educating them about the consequences of their decisions, including the tax consequences.

For example, you may have an experienced client who refuses to cash a Guaranteed Investment Certificate (GIC), but who wants to take out a personal loan for non-investment purposes. This is not a wise move in terms of its tax implications, because interest income on the GIC is fully taxable, whereas interest expense on the personal loan is not tax-deductible, since it is not being used to earn investment income. You can explain to the client the cost (in terms of after-tax cash flows) of this approach to saving money. Even though your financial institution may lose the value of both the GIC and the potential loan, you will benefit in the long run from remaining committed to customer satisfaction.

Offering sound financial planning advice may also create dilemmas for you if you are subject to pressure relating to sales quotas and other short-run performance measures. However, selling only the most "profitable" products, regardless of the effects on your clients, will eventually damage your reputation and that of your firm.

1.2   How Much Do You Need to Know About Taxes?

Financial planning involves selecting an appropriate investment strategy, consistent with your clients' objectives, to help clients accumulate an estate during their working lives and preserve the accumulated amount upon retirement as well as upon death. Tax rates in the range of 40-50% affect the accumulation and preservation of wealth.

Keeping abreast of detailed tax laws and changes imposed by federal and provincial budgets may be difficult. However, this does not mean that you should refer all tax issues concerning investment products to professional advisors outside your financial institution. Although tax accountants and lawyers understand the technicalities of taxes, they may not be as familiar with your clients' specific needs as you are.

You should be able to explain tax regulations to your clients, so that you and they do not inadvertently overlook fundamental aspects of taxation during investment selection. The competition for retail clients means that you will need enough tax sophistication to understand the tax features of individual products as well as the tax consequences of cross-selling more than one product.

The approach to taxation suggested in this chapter is to consider tax aspects of financial planning as inseparable from good financial planning. Although investment and financial decisions should not be made for tax reasons alone, ignoring taxes can lead to poor product choices and failure to maximize after-tax wealth. Investments are subject to different tax treatments and investors are subject to different marginal tax rates. An appropriate investment selection process should therefore view tax as a controllable expense, similar to variables such as the maturity, liquidity, and expected yield of investments.

2.0   The Nature of Tax Planning

The tax laws in any country reflect the unique blend of its social, economic, cultural, and political forces. In general, the Canadian tax system is designed to:

- raise revenue to finance public projects such as national defence, and social objectives such as Medicare;

- redistribute income with progressive tax rate schedules and tax credits for the poor;

- provide incentives for economic activities such as saving for retirement or investing in Canadian securities;

- discourage taxpayers from certain activities such as tobacco and gasoline consumption.

These objectives often conflict with each other, and individual tax provisions are rarely able to satisfy all objectives simultaneously.

The multiple objectives of the tax system impose varying tax rates. Taxes discriminate among different economic activities, different assets, and different individuals. Tax planning involves taking advantage of the different rates of taxation imposed on various returns by shifting income from economic activities, assets, and individuals that are taxed at a high rate to those subject to a lower rate of taxation.

Such tax planning or tax avoidance (as opposed to tax evasion, which is illegal) means taking full advantage of the provisions of Canada's *Income Tax Act* to reduce one's tax liability. The incentive to undertake tax planning or to find legal loopholes is greatly enhanced by the high marginal tax rates within Canada's tax structure where higher income earners pay a higher fraction of their income in taxes than lower income earners do. Lord Tomlin's dictum in the famous Duke of Westminster case in 1936 established the following principle:

> *Every man is entitled if he can to order his affairs so that the tax attaching under the appropriate Acts is less than it otherwise would be. If he succeeds in ordering them so as to secure this result, then, however, unappreciative the Commissioners of Inland Revenue or his fellow taxpayers may be of his ingenuity, he cannot be compelled to pay an increased tax.*

> *(I.R.C. v. Duke of Westminster, [1936] A.C. 1, p.19)*

Judge Iacobucci reaffirmed this principle in a 1998 Supreme Court of Canada decision by stating that:

> *Taxpayers can arrange their affairs in a particular way for the sole purpose of deliberately availing themselves of tax reduction devices in the Income Tax Act.*

> *(Melville Neuman v. Her Majesty the Queen, 98 DTC p.6302)*

On the other hand, tax restrictions are essential if the revenue objective of the government is to be fulfilled. Without RRSP contribution limits, for example, taxpayers could eliminate their entire tax liability by contributing all of their employment income to an RRSP and then borrowing against the RRSP fund to finance their living expenses. Therefore, the government imposes contribution limits and does not encourage using RRSP funds as collateral for personal borrowing.

Schematically, the above description can be summarized as follows:

Multiple objectives of the tax system	$\equiv$	Varying tax rates	$\equiv$	Tax planning opportunities	$\equiv$	Tax restrictions

The tax-planning process involves shifting income over time, across individuals, and over different forms of investments through:

- Income deferral: these opportunities arise because a taxpayer is subject to different rates of taxation at different times. The differences can be the result of different levels of income, which are taxed differently in a progressive tax system, or may simply relate to the time value of money[1].

- Income splitting: these opportunities arise because two or more taxpayers may be subject to different rates of tax in the same time period.

- Investment income tax planning: these opportunities arise because the tax liability of investment returns depends on whether returns are in the form of interest, dividends, or capital gains.

If there were a single rate of tax on all types and sources of income, then tax-planning opportunities would largely disappear (except for time value deferment) and there would be no lucrative employment opportunities for tax accountants and lawyers. Although the move to a single, flat-rate tax is unlikely, recent tax reforms in Canada and other industrialized countries have reduced the range and number of tax brackets, and narrowed the tax differentials for different types and sources of income. The result of these reforms has been the decline in tax planning (or tax avoidance) opportunities for most taxpayers.

3.0   Average and Marginal Tax Rates

An **average tax rate** is computed by dividing the total income tax liability by the total income. For example, a tax liability of $23,100 on income of $55,000 implies an average tax rate of ($23,100/$55,000) or 42%. Average tax rates are useful in comparing tax burdens across different jurisdictions. For example, the average tax rate on $300,000 of income is about 42% in Alberta, and about 49% in British Columbia. Tax preparation software can illustrate these differences effectively—by changing the province of residence while keeping all other information constant, you can immediately see the effect on total taxes.

---

[1] Please see Appendix 7.1 for a detailed discussion of the time value of money and accompanying tables.

A **marginal tax rate** is the rate of tax payable on incremental income. For example, if earnings of $100,000 triggers $45,000 in taxes and earnings of $102,000 triggers $46,000 in taxes, then the marginal tax rate on the $2,000 incremental earnings is: ($46,000 – $45,000) / ($102,000 – $100,000) = 50%.

It may be useful to think of incremental income in units of $1 and the marginal tax rate as the taxes paid as a proportion of those additional units of $1. Using tax software, you can easily see the changes in the marginal tax rate by increasing the total income by $1 at a time and watching the change in total taxes payable.

The relevant rate for most financial planning decisions is the marginal tax rate, since most financial planning decisions are undertaken at the margin and involve incremental rather than drastic changes in income. Consider the following questions:

- Should I invest an additional $1 in an RRSP or a non-RRSP instrument?

- Should I use $1 to pay down my mortgage or contribute to an RRSP?

- Should I withdraw $1 from my RRSP to increase my down payment?

- Should I borrow $1 from the bank to increase my RRSP contribution?

- Should I work an extra hour of overtime or not?

Marginal tax rates are generally higher than average tax rates, and they increase with income much faster than average tax rates. Once a certain level of income is reached, the marginal tax rate will no longer change as income increases, but the average tax rate will continue to increase with income (at least in a progressive tax structure).

In a U.S. survey,[2] only a third of the respondents knew their marginal tax rate within plus or minus 5 percentage points, and the number of taxpayers who overestimated their marginal tax rates was about the same as the number of taxpayers who underestimated it. The study also found that respondents with higher incomes or with investment advisors had a more accurate estimate of their marginal tax rates.

A 1993 study[3] calculated 515 different marginal tax rates at the federal level in the Canadian personal tax rate system. The different rates reflected differences in the tax treatment of ordinary income, dividend income, and capital gains, with and without deductions, credits, and clawbacks.

---

[2] Rupert, T.J. and C. Fischer. "An Empirical Investigation of Taxpayer Awareness of Marginal Tax Rates." *Journal of American Taxation Association*, vol. 17, 1995, supplement, pp. 36-59.

[3] Perry, D. "A Buck Is Never a Buck." *Canadian Tax Highlights*, Vol. 1, No. 4, April 1993, 20, pp. 26-27.

4.0   Tax Planning Strategies

The following tax planning techniques involve strategies ranging from income deferral and spreading, income splitting and transferring assets among family members, using Registered Education Savings Plans (RESPs) and in-trust accounts for funding post secondary education, family loans at prescribed rates, the principal residence exemption, tax planning for investment income, using flow-through shares, stock option plans, employee loans and limited partnerships. The wealth manager should be familiar with these techniques to better assist client in reducing taxes payable.

4.1   Income Deferral and Spreading

If marginal tax rates remain constant over time, taxpayers will want to delay the recognition of income due to the time value of money. If marginal tax rates decrease over time, taxpayers have a good incentive to delay receiving income until it can be taxed at the lower rate. The major vehicles for this kind of delay are well known:

*   the Canada Pension Plan;

*   employers' pension plans;

*   Registered Retirement Savings Plans (RRSPs).

All three provide deferral until retirement, although RRSPs can provide short-term deferrals as well. Investing in education, which usually leads to higher future returns (wages) can also be viewed as a form of income deferral.

If marginal tax rates increase because of budgetary deficits, a change in the government, or the clawing back of benefits, then it pays to receive income now rather than later. However, this strategy must be viewed in light of the after-tax opportunity cost of funds.

For example, if surtaxes are expected to increase marginal tax rates from 44.4% to 48.2% by next year, the taxpayer has a choice: either receive the income this year and pay this year's taxes on it, or invest $44.40 this year in a way that will yield at least $48.20 in after-tax return next year. The investment opportunity would have to offer at least 8.5% after-tax return, or 16.5% in pre-tax return. Other factors such as liquidity and risk will also affect the decision. Managers opting for deferred compensation arrangements should consider these issue carefully.

The typical beneficiaries of income-deferral strategies are families in which the income-earners will retire at some point and experience a drop in income because of the loss of employment, business, or professional earnings. Families living entirely on investment income may not qualify for income-deferral strategies.

Registered Retirement Savings Plans (RRSPs) are the most popular tax-deferral instruments. The two significant tax benefits of RRSPs are:

- the immediate tax savings of being able to deduct contributions from taxable income;

- the compounding of returns at pre-tax rather than after-tax rates.

Although withdrawals from RRSPs are fully taxable, the compounding of returns at pre-tax rates and over long periods results in a reduction of the total tax liability in present-value terms.

Making RRSP contributions at the beginning of a tax year rather than at the end can magnify the compounding effect, provided that the cash for making a contribution is available at the earlier date.

4.2   Income Splitting

The unit of taxation in Canada is the individual,[4] who faces progressive marginal tax rates. For example, the combined federal and provincial tax on a single person with a $50,000 income is more than three times the tax on an individual with a $20,000 income. All else being equal, taxpayers subject to high tax rates benefit from having some of their income attributed to a spouse, child, or children in a lower tax bracket.

The easiest and most common strategy is for the higher-income spouse to pay all the family living expenses, thereby allowing the lower-income spouse to accumulate investment assets and earn investment income at a lower tax rate. If the marriage breaks down, the equalization provisions of the *Family Law Act* generally require assets accumulated during the marriage to be equitably divided between the spouses, regardless of legal ownership.

Family members may transfer assets within the family in the form of gifts or direct sales. In both types of non-arm's-length transaction, the transferor is deemed to have disposed of the assets at their fair market values and is liable for tax on any resulting capital gains, unless the transfer is to a spouse or a spousal trust. However, some asset transfers or asset swaps between spouses may offer modest income-splitting opportunities.

Income earned on assets transferred from a high-tax-bracket spouse to a low-tax-bracket spouse is generally attributed to the high-tax-bracket spouse. However, the secondary earnings (or earnings on earnings) could be reinvested by the low-tax-bracket spouse without attribution. Such a strategy can build up the capital base of the low-tax-bracket spouse over time.

Another strategy requires the low-tax-bracket spouse to take a home equity loan on his or her share of the family home and invest the funds. The gain from such a strategy is

---

[4] In the United States, married taxpayers can elect to file joint tax returns that are subject to a separate tax rate schedule.

limited to the spread between investment earnings and interest expense (on the home equity loan).

Another option is for spouses to swap assets. For instance, a low-tax-bracket spouse could give up some jewellery (non-income-generating assets) in exchange for income-generating stocks or bonds of the same value from the high-tax-bracket spouse. However, this strategy could trigger a capital gain. For such strategies to be successful, the details of the transactions must be properly documented.

One of the most popular income-splitting strategies is when a spouse and/or children contribute to the operations of the business. They may draw reasonable salaries and thereby accomplish some income splitting. If the spouse and children are in a lower tax bracket relative to the business owner, then income splitting can save taxes by reducing the amount of income taxed at a higher rate and increasing the amount taxed at lower rates.

If the spouse has little or no other income, then the tax benefits of income splitting should be compared with the potential tax cost of losing the dependent spouse tax credit (worth approximately 27% of $5,718 or $1544). Children who work in a business can earn up to $6,794 (the current level of the personal exemption) without paying any taxes. The resulting tax savings through income splitting can therefore amount to $3,397 if the amount paid to the child would have otherwise been withdrawn as salary by the business owner at a marginal tax rate of 50%.

Income-splitting activities with children are subject to a different set of provisions in the *Income Tax Act*. The *Act* requires that income earned on outright gifts (with no strings attached) to children younger than 18 must be attributed to the parent, while capital gains are taxed in the child's hands. When the children reach the age of 18, the income earned on the gifts (which are not loans) is not attributed to the parent. Loans to children over 18 years trigger attribution rules. In all cases, secondary income is considered to have been earned by the child. Table 7.1 summarizes the attribution rules.

Table 7.1 Attribution Rules

Type of Transfer	To spouse	To child, sibling, niece, or nephew under 18	To child over 18
Gift	Investment income/losses and capital gains/losses attributed to giver	Investment income/losses attributed to giver; capital gains/losses not attributed	No attribution
Sale	Must elect to sell at fair market value, otherwise investment income/losses and capital gains/losses attributed to seller	Sale must be made at fair market value, otherwise investment income/losses (but not capital gains/losses) attributed to seller	No attribution
Loan	Loan must bear interest at prescribed rate, otherwise investment income/losses and capital gains/losses attributed to lender	Loan must bear interest at prescribed rate, otherwise investment income/losses (but not capital gains/losses) attributed to lender	Loan must bear interest at prescribed rate or greater, otherwise investment income/losses (but not capital gains/losses) attributed to lender

4.3   Registered Education Savings Plans (RESPs)

Registered Education Savings Plans (RESPs) are designed to make saving for postsecondary education more attractive. A parent can contribute up to $4,000 a year for each child, up to a cumulative total of $42,000 per child.

RESPs are not subject to foreign-content restrictions, and may include mutual funds, segregated funds, stocks, bonds, and cash deposits. Contributions to an RESP are not tax-deductible, but the interest accumulates tax-free until the child enters a postsecondary institution and starts to receive payments from the fund. In addition, the federal government contributes an additional 20% of the first $2,000 of annual contribution in the form of a Canada Education Savings Grant (CESG), to an annual maximum of $400 per child for each year the beneficiary is under 18.

Once the child starts attending a postsecondary program that is at least three months long and has a minimum of 10 hours of courses a week, and starts withdrawing the funds, the interest portion is taxable (the capital portion is not taxable, since it was not tax-deductible when contributed). However, since most postsecondary students have little or no taxable income, the tax burden is usually very low. All RESPs must be terminated within 25 years.

The maximum annual grant of $400 per child applies to RESP contributions of $2,000 a year. If the RESP grows at a rate of 8% annually, the government grants alone add up to $14,980. If a full-time student who has very little other income withdraws the money, the

RESP may have been not only sheltered from tax during the 18 years, but also sheltered when it is withdrawn.

The major benefit of RESP is the tax-free compounding of returns. The government grant is more heavily advertised, but is actually less valuable. If they have the cash, parents would do better to accelerate their contributions so they can reach the plan limit of $42,000, rather than delaying contributions in order to maximize the government's annual grants.

For example, annual contributions of $4,000 will yield government grants of only $4,400 ($400 annual maximum grant × 11 years), whereas $2,000 annual contributions will yield government grants of $7,200 ($400 annual maximum grant × 18 years maximum period). However, if contributions earn an 8% return and withdrawals begin when the student is 21 years old, the accelerated contributions (with its corresponding government grants) will have grown to about $166,000, whereas the gradual contributions (with the larger government grant) will accumulate to only about $129,000. Please see Appendix 7.2 for proof of this.

Withdrawals from a RESP

A family-plan RESP allows for the listing of multiple beneficiaries, as well as multiple and joint contributors, as long as they are related by blood or adoption. The beneficiaries can use the funds in any proportion, as long as each beneficiary does not receive more than $7,200 of grant money. If there are no beneficiaries who want to pursue postsecondary education, the government grant must be repaid (without interest). The contributing (non-retired) parents can transfer up to $50,000 of RESP income to their RRSPs or spousal RRSPs, subject to the availability of contribution room and as long as the plan has been in existence for at least 10 years. If no RRSP contribution room remains, the investment income can be withdrawn at the contributor's marginal tax rate plus a 20% tax penalty. The original capital portion can be withdrawn tax-free, since it was not deductible when it was contributed.

Case 7.1   Maximizing RESP Grants vs. Maximizing RESP Contributions

The Felthams want to maximize their RESP annual grants received, and therefore contribute $2,000 a year into Northern Bond Fund, registered as their 8-year-old son's RESP. This allows them to get a $400 grant each year for 18 years. They also contribute an additional $2,000 per year into Northern Growth Fund held as an in-trust account (not part of the RESP). Ms. Feltham, the contributor, has a marginal tax rate of 52%.

The Paquettes contribute $4,000 a year into the Northern Growth Fund as part of their 8-year-old son's RESP. This earns them an annual grant of $400 for 11 years only ($42,000 lifetime maximum/$4,000 a year = 10.5 years).

The Northern Growth Fund is expected to earn 5% a year over the next 10 years, until the children reach the age of 18 and are ready to withdraw the RESP funds for postsecondary education.

Which family has the better strategy? If the children do not end up pursuing postsecondary education once they turn 18, what will be the consequences to their parents? Both the Felthams and the Paquettes have been making maximum contributions to their respective RRSPs each year.

Analysis:

After 10 years, the Felthams will have accumulated:
- $30,187 inside their RESP (FV of an annuity = [5%, 10 years, $2,400]);
- $22,304 outside their RESP (FV of an annuity = [5% (1 − 0.52), 10 years, $2,000]);
- for a total of $52,491.

In contrast, the Paquettes can shelter investment income on the entire $4,000 each year, and therefore accumulate $55,343 after 10 years (FVA[5%, 10 years, $4,400]).

If the children do not attend postsecondary education, and the parents' RRSP room has been used up, then the income earned inside the RESP (but not the principal) will be taxed at 1.20 times the contributing parent's marginal tax rate, and all of the government grant has to be repaid (without interest). The additional 20% represents a penalty.

4.4   In-Trust Accounts

The 20% penalty for withdrawing RESPs for any purpose other than postsecondary education may drive some taxpayers away from RESPs and toward in-trust accounts. An in-trust account belongs to the child in whose name it is registered, and the parent can make non-deductible contributions of any amount for the child's benefit. The contributor relinquishes all access to the income earned by the trust, and the trust forgoes all CESG grants. Although dividend and interest income earned by the trust is attributed to the contributor, any capital gains are taxable in the hands of the child.

The main advantages of an in-trust account are that there are no limits on contributions, and no restrictions on the use of the funds, as long as they are used for the benefit of the child. Some taxpayers use both RESPs and in-trust accounts to accomplish income splitting. A comparison of RESPs and in-trust accounts is summarized in Table 7.2.

Table 7.2   Comparison of RESP and In-Trust Accounts

	RESP	In-Trust Account
Withdrawals used for	Postsecondary education only	Any purpose benefiting the child
Contribution limits	$4,000 per child	No limit
Tax deductibility of contributions	No	No
Tax implications on income earned	Tax-free compounding for income, dividends, and capital gains	Dividend and interest attributed to contributor; capital gains taxable in the hands of the child
Fund accessibility to contributor	Can be rolled over to RRSP or Spousal RRSP; withdrawn in cash at 1.20 multiplied by marginal tax rates	None
Eligibility for government grants	Yes; 20% of contribution, to a maximum annual grant of $400	No

4.5   Family Loans at Prescribed Rates

Income earned on a family loan from a high-tax bracket family member to a low-tax bracket family member is generally attributed to the high-income individual. However, attribution rules do not apply if investment loans are made at prescribed rates, and if the interest is collected by January 30 of the following calendar year. The investment income generated is taxed in the hands of the borrower, not the lender. The interest paid on the investment loan can be deducted by the borrower and is taxed in the hands of the lender.

Prescribed rates for non-arm's-length loans are based on the 90-day Treasury bill rate in effect at the beginning of the preceding calendar quarter. If interest rates are expected to increase, taxpayers may want to lock in a family loan indefinitely at the current prescribed rate in a written agreement.

For example, Elise Khan, a business owner, lends $100,000 to her daughter Shana at the current prescribed rate of 5%. Elise has to report only $5,000 in annual interest income, as long as the interest is received by the following January 30. Any investment return in excess of 5% earned by Shana is reported on her tax return, thereby indirectly splitting income.

This arrangement could be maintained indefinitely if interest rates are expected to increase. If the prescribed rate falls below 5%, on the other hand, the loan could be repaid and a new loan could be arranged at the lower rate. Elise may also wish to hold the investment as a security, thereby ensuring that the prescribed interest payments are made on time.

Case 7.2   The MacNaughtons' Spousal Loans

Alan MacNaughton recently inherited $400,000 from a distant aunt. Alan faces a marginal tax rate of 54%, while his wife Bonnie's effective marginal tax rate is 35% for the next $25,000 of income, and 54% thereafter.

Alan is considering investing the $400,000 in a mutual fund that offers a 10% annual rate of return. Alan has heard something about splitting income through loans at prescribed rates. Prescribed rates are 5% this year, and expected to be 6.5% next year. The MacNaughtons would be able to invest in the mutual fund for only two years, since they want to use the accumulated amount to buy a farm property in the United States and move there at the end of two years.

What is the appropriate tax-planning strategy that will allow the MacNaughtons to use loans at prescribed rates to maximize their after-tax returns over the two-year planning horizon?

Analysis:

Alan can lend $400,000 to Bonnie at the prescribed rate of 5%, thereby avoiding attribution rules. For simplicity, we will assume only annual (simple) interest payments on December 31 of each year and a discount rate of 10% (although a 5% discount rate may also be possible).

The expected increase in the prescribed rate to 6.5% is irrelevant, since the applicable rate is the one in effect at the time the arm's-length, bona fide loan was arranged. If the prescribed rate decreased, then the appropriate strategy would be to pay off the loan and arrange a new loan at the lower prescribed rate.

Alan's income inclusion = $400,000 × 5% = $20,000

Bonnie's income inclusion = $400,000 × (10% − 5%) = $40,000 − $20,000 = $20,000

Effectively, $20,000 of income has been split with *annual* tax savings of:

$$[\$20,000 \times (54\% - 35\%)] = \$3,800$$

Case 7.2   The MacNaughtons' Spousal Loans
(continued)

Present value of tax savings = $20,000 (54% − 35%) (PVA, 10%, 2 years) = $6,595

This tax-planning strategy, however, runs the risk of certain non-tax consequences:

- The MacNaughtons are more likely to be reassessed by Revenue Canada.

- Their tax returns will be more complicated.

- If the marriage breaks down, the situation will become more complex and will be subject to family law provisions.

Alternative solution:

Alan lends $400,000 to Bonnie.

Alan's after-tax return = $400,000 × 5% × (1 − 0.54) = $9,200

Bonnie's after-tax return = $400,000 × (10% − 5%) × (1 − 0.35) = $13,000

Total after-tax return = $9,200 + $13,000 = $22,200

Benchmark (if Alan had invested the money himself):

After-tax return = $400,000 × 10% × (1-0.54) = $18,400

Incremental family return = $22,200 − $18,400 = $3,800 in year 1.

At the beginning of the second year, the portfolio would be worth $440,000.

At the end of the second year, the portfolio worth $440,000 (1.10) = $484,000.

The return for the second year = $44,000.

Alan's after-tax income = $400,000 × 5% × (1 − 0.54) = $9,200 (same as year 1)

Bonnie's after-tax income = ($44,000 − $20,000 interest deduction) × (1 − 0.35) = $15,600

Total after-tax return = $9,200 + $15,600 = $24,800

Benchmark (if Alan had invested the money himself):

After-tax return = $44,000 (1 − 0.54) = $20,240

Improvement in family after-tax return = $24,800 − $20,240 = $4,560 in year 2

Total incremental return over two years = $3,800 + $4,560 = $8,360

4.6   Old Age Security Benefits

Old Age Security (OAS) benefits are clawed back for individuals who earn more than about $53,000. Individuals close to the $53,000 threshold may want to split their investment income with their spouses or their deceased spouse's estate or with their children and grandchildren. Alternatively, these individuals could also tie up their assets in forms that do not produce income (houses, cottages, hobby farms). They can also place their investments in a holding company, so that they do not personally reap any investment income.

4.7   The Principal Residence Exemption

If clients or their spouses own more than one residential-type property such as a house or cottage, they do not need to decide which property will be designated the principal residence for capital gains purposes until the year that either property is sold or disposed of. A seasonal residence such as a cottage may qualify as the principal residence, since it meets the test of having been occupied for some period of time during the year. (For more information on designating cottages as the principal residence, see Chapter 6, section 3.8.) According to the *Income Tax Act*, as long as the owner, the owner's spouse, or one of their children occupies the vacation property at some point during the year, the property qualifies for the principal residence exemption for some or all of the years of ownership of that property. From a tax-planning perspective, the owner does not have to identify the principal residence until the year that the property is disposed of.

The principal residence exemption is calculated by reference to the number of years that a client has owned the property and the number of years that they designate it as their principal residence for capital gains purposes. The exemption formula is as follows:

$$\frac{\text{Number of years after 1971 designated as the principal residence, plus "1"}}{\text{Number of years after 1971 that the client owns the property}}$$

You should spend some time explaining the exemption formula to a client in order to be able to estimate the future tax liability. When the property is disposed of, go through the following steps:

- Calculate the capital gain by taking the actual proceeds of disposition (or the fair market value in the case of a deemed disposition) and subtracting the selling expenses and the adjusted cost base.

- Apply the principal residence exemption fraction to determine how much of the capital gain is exempt.

- The remainder is the capital gain that must be reported, two thirds of which must be included in a client's taxable income for the year.

Case 7.3   Maximizing the Principal Residence Exemption

Jane and Jim Svensen bought a house in 1980 for $75,000. In 1987 they bought a cottage for $50,000. In 1999 they decided to sell both the house and the cottage and move in with their recently widowed daughter. They sold the house for $275,000 and the cottage for $150,000.

Analysis:

The house could be treated as Jane and Jim's principal residence for 1980 to 1998 inclusive, or 19 years. The plus "1" in the principal residence exemption formula makes the numerator equal to 20. The denominator is all of the years in which the property was owned, or 20 years (1980 to 1999). The fraction therefore comes to 20 over 20, or 100%, indicating that the $200,000 gain on the house will be completely tax-free.

Jane and Jim can designate the cottage as their principal residence for capital gains tax purposes for 1999. Since the cottage was bought in 1987, there were 13 years of ownership up to and including the year of sale (1999). The principal residence exemption portion for the cottage is (1 + 1)/13 = 15.4%. Therefore 15.4% of the capital gain realized on the sale of the cottage will be tax-free under the principal residence exemption.

4.8   Tax Planning for Investment Income

For a given level of risk, different forms of investment returns produce different after-tax yields. Table 7.3 illustrates the after-tax cash flows retained by a taxpayer in the top tax bracket from three different forms of investment income, each of which generates $100 of pre-tax cash flows.

Table 7.3   Comparison of Tax Impact on Different Forms of Investment Income (assuming no provincial surtaxes)

	Interest Income	Dividend Income	Capital Gains
Actual cash flow received	$100	$100	$100
Taxable income	$100	$125	$66.67
Federal tax @ 29%	$29	$36.25	$19.33
Dividend tax credit (13.33% of grossed-up dividends)	n/a	($16.66)	n/a
Net federal tax	$29.00	$19.59	$19.33
Provincial income tax (50% × net federal tax)	$14.50	$9.80	$9.67
Federal surtax (5% × net federal tax)	$1.45	$0.98	$.97
Total taxes payable	$44.95	$30.37	$29.97
Effective tax rates	44.95%	30.37%	29.97%
After-tax cash flows	$55.05	$69.63	$71.03

Because risk and pre-tax returns are rarely equal across the different forms of investment income, comparisons and universal preference rules are hard to establish. Usually, a return in the form of capital gains entails greater risk (for example, stocks) or greater effort (real estate) or reduced liquidity (oil and gas limited partnership units), whereas interest-bearing instruments involve less risk and effort, while offering greater liquidity.

If risk, liquidity, and investor effort were equal across all forms of investment income, then investors would increase their demand for assets that offered the most lightly taxed returns, thereby bidding up their prices and reducing their pre-tax returns. For example, suppose the government exempted family cottages or second homes from capital gains tax (similar to the principal residence exemption). The investor demand for such properties would go up and the pre-tax rates of return would go down. The tax benefits would be capitalized in the asset prices.

Although the lower capital gains tax rate and deferral until realization increase the after-tax returns on investment, they have very little impact on the risk of such capital investments. Easing the restrictions on the use of capital losses might be a better incentive for risky investments, since such measures reduce risk. A taxpayer who can shield capital losses with realized capital gains or other forms of income (if allowed) is at less risk of losing money on such losses than the taxpayer who cannot take advantage of the loss.

For example, an individual in a 40% tax bracket investing in a $10,000 capital property may have a maximum downside risk of only $7,320.00 computed as follows:

$$\$10,000 - [40\% \times .67 \times \$10,000] = \$7,320.00$$

The reduction in downside risk depends on the ability to set losses against other income. Most taxpayers, however, cannot use capital losses, since capital losses can be offset only against capital gains. The time value of money reduces the value of any loss that cannot be used immediately to offset taxable gains. Having to carry forward any net capital losses rather than using them immediately increases the risk of investments generating such losses.

Since the capital gains tax is generally triggered only when an appreciated capital property is sold, taxpayers are usually reluctant to sell such assets. This lock-in effect deters investors from switching into new and potentially more productive investments because doing so would be subject to taxation. For example, it may not be a good idea to switch investments from capital property that appreciates at a rate of 8% to another that appreciates at a rate of 9%, since the tax levied on the sale of the first property will reduce the after-tax amount available to invest in the second property.

Case 7.4 Hanna's Lock-in Effect

Hanna Barlow wants to buy a painting for $20,400. The painting is expected to appreciate 10% per year. She has only $3,750 cash on hand; however, she owns 1,000 shares of Abacan Resources Inc., which she bought for $10 a share and which has a current market price of $20 a share. Abacan pays a constant cash dividend of $1 a share per year, and the share price is expected to grow at the rate of 8% a year for the next 20 years.

Up to now, Hanna has re-invested the dividend income in a money market fund yielding 5% a year. Abacan does not qualify for the dividend tax credit. Hanna has a marginal tax rate of 50% (combined federal and provincial). This rate is expected to remain constant. Hanna plans to cash in all her investments 20 years from now. Should Hanna buy the painting or retain the Abacan shares? (Ignore RRSP issues for this question.)

Analysis:

Alternative 1: Hanna buys the painting

Sells 1,000 shares of Abacan:

Proceeds 1,000 @ $20	= $ 20,000
Tax $0.67 \times [20,000 - 10,000] \times (1\text{-}50\%)$	= 3,350
After-tax proceeds	$ 16,650

Use proceeds to buy the painting, and sell painting in 20 years:

Proceeds from painting $20,400 \times (1.10)^{20}$	= $137,241
Tax on capital gain $0.67 \times (137,241 - 20,400) \times 50\%$	= $39,142
After-tax proceeds	$98,099

Alternative 2: Hanna keeps the Abacan stock

Invest the $3,750 in money market = $3,750 [1 + [(1 - t)5\%]]^{20}$ = 6,144
Reinvest dividends

PMT	=	500 = $1000(1 - t)$
n	=	20
i	=	2.5% = 5\%(1 - t)$
Comp FV_{20}	=	$ 12,772

Sell stock 20 years from now:

Proceeds $20,000 (1.08)^{20}$	= $ 93,219
Tax on capital gain $0.67 \times (93,219 - 10,000) \times 50\%$	= ($27,878)
After-tax proceeds	= $ 62,012

Total after-tax proceeds if Hanna keeps the stock

$6,144 + 12,772 + 65341	= $ 84,257

For any given asset, taxpayers have an incentive to convert heavily taxed forms of income into lightly taxed forms of income, even if it means giving up a few percentage points of yield. For example, a top-tax-bracket taxpayer lending mortgage funds to a home-buyer might be better off demanding the return in the form of half the appreciation on the house (capital gains) rather than in regular interest payments (100% taxable).

Most tax planning related to investments involves achieving large, immediate tax deductions while realizing smaller, more distant taxable assets. Borrowing to invest (the interest expense is 100% tax-deductible immediately) in capital properties (future capital gains are only 2/3rds taxable) is the most frequently used tax planning strategy. Another strategy is inflating the selling price of a capital property while compensating the buyer with cheap financing to allow the seller to convert interest income to capital gains. Such capital gains can also shield capital losses that might otherwise have to be carried forward. However, the General Anti-Avoidance Rules (GAAR) of the *Income Tax Act* could trigger tax on such transactions by deeming the capital gains to be interest income.

Some financial institutions have tried unsuccessfully to create products and services that convert highly taxed forms of income into lightly taxed forms of income. A few years ago, several American banks offered higher-than-market interest rates on tax-sheltered Individual Retirement Accounts (the American equivalent of RRSPs) if the customer also bought a fully taxable Guaranteed Investment Certificate (GIC) at below-market rates of interest. The United States tax authorities caught on and disallowed such arrangements.

4.9   Flow-Through Shares

Flow-through shares can provide attractive investment returns in addition to tax savings. In general, flow-through shares are shares of a corporation issued to an investor, who provides funds to the corporation, usually a Canadian resource company, for exploration or development work. Tax deductions generated by the work or acquisition are flowed through to the investor and deducted from the investor's income.

Typical deductions include Canadian Exploration Expenses (CEE) and Canadian Development Expenses (CDE). The CEE is 100% deductible while the CDE is 30% deductible on a declining balance basis. Flow-through shares usually provide a tax deduction to an investor equal to the amount invested in the shares. The tax deduction does not usually come all at once, but is spread out, usually over three years, with the largest part of the deduction coming in the first year.

Flow-through shares are automatically acquired with an adjusted cost base of zero, which means that any sale of the shares will give rise to a taxable capital gain. Flow-through shares offer several tax planning opportunities for:

- Clients who have capital losses to use up. Flow-through shares that provide a capital gain in the future can be used to offset those capital losses.

- Clients who have realized large capital gains. Flow-through share tax deductions can offset some or all of the taxable capital gain.

- Clients who have made an RRSP or RRIF withdrawal. Tax deductions from flow-through shares can offset the taxable income created by the withdrawal.

- Clients who earn more than $53,000 and are at risk of having their Old Age Security benefits clawed back. Tax deductions from flow-through shares can reduce the clawback of Old Age Security benefits by reducing a client's net income.

- Clients who have maximized their RRSP contributions and have no additional RRSP contribution room. Flow-through shares can provide additional deductions with a similar effect.

4.10   Stock Option Plans

Some employers offer stock option plans as an employee incentive. Generally, employees who qualify for a stock option plan can buy shares of the employer's company (or a related company such as a subsidiary) at a price that is less than the current fair market value of the shares.

Before looking at the tax consequences of stock options, it is useful to review some basic terminology. A stock option is "granted," which means that the company gives the employee the right to buy shares in the company. Buying shares under a stock option is called "exercising" the option. The price at which the shares are purchased is called the "exercise price" and the date on which the shares are purchased is the "exercise date."

Some companies charge an administration fee to employees for participating in a stock option plan. This is similar to the price paid by an investor buying an equity option (although the rationale for the charge is administration costs, not profit, as it is for sellers of equity options).

The rules governing the tax treatment of employee stock options apply only to stock options that are received by a taxpayer in the course of employment. If the taxpayer is a shareholder as well as an employee (for example, in an owner-managed company), it is important to determine whether a stock option has been granted as a result of employment or as a result of being a shareholder.

Employees do not get any taxable benefit simply by being eligible to buy stock under a stock option plan. There are tax consequences only if the employee actually buys shares under the plan. The nature and timing of the tax consequences depends on whether the options and the employee are eligible. There are also tax consequences if the employee transfers or disposes of rights under a stock option plan to someone who is not a relative for less than the amount the employee paid the company for those rights.

Tax Treatment Prior to February 27, 2000

Up to the February 27, 2000 budget, employees were deemed to have received income from employment when they exercised an option relating to shares of non-Canadian Controlled Private Corporations. The value of the benefit was the difference between the fair market value (FMV) of the shares at the time of exercise and the exercise price plus any amount (fees) paid for the option. The employee was allowed to deduct one-quarter of the deemed benefit from income that year if:

- the exercise price was not less than the share's FMV on the date the option was granted;

- the employee deals at arm's length with the employer; and

- the shares are common shares that meet specific criteria.

The employee's cost base of the shares equaled the share's FMV on the exercise date. When the employee sold the shares, only gains accrued since the exercise date were included in the capital gains calculation.

If the employer was a Canadian-controlled private corporation (CCPC) with which the employee dealt at arms-length with, taxable benefits were only recorded when the shares were sold rather then when they were bought as a result of the exercise of the options.

Tax Treatment after February 27, 2000

The February 27, 2000 budget proposed that eligible employees be able to defer the income inclusion from exercising eligible stock options for publicly listed shares, subject to an annual $100,000 limit, for options issued after February 27, 2000. The $100,000 limit applies to the fair market value of the underlying shares at the time the options are granted. It is proposed that the income inclusion be deferred until the earlier of the time the employee disposes of the shares, dies or becomes a non-resident. This brings the tax treatment of options relating to non-CCPCs on a similar footing to employee options on shares of CCPCs.

As well, since the budget also proposed lowering the inclusion rate for all capital gains from three-quarters to two-thirds, the employee deduction for qualifying stock options was increased from one-quarter to one-third.

An eligible option is one which:

- the share to be acquired is an ordinary common share;

- the share is of a class of shares traded on a prescribed Canadian or foreign stock exchange; and

- the total of all amounts payable to acquire the share, including the exercise price and any amount payable to acquire the option, is not less than the fair market value of the share at the time the option is granted (otherwise there is a taxable benefit in the year the option is exercised).

As well deferral of taxation of the employment benefit arising from the exercise of an employee option will depend on the employer having an arrangement in place to ensure that:

- the employer, or an agent of the employer, can monitor compliance with the $100,000 limit; and

- the related employment benefit and the stock option deduction can be reported on an information slip in the year the share is disposed of.

Eligible employees are those who at the time the option is granted:

- deal at arm's-length with the employer and any related corporation; and

- are not specified shareholders (specified shareholders are generally those who own 10 per cent or more of a company's shares).

Case 7.5   Clever Idea Co.

Clever Idea Co., an eligible company, grants stock options to certain key employees under the following terms:

"Qualified employees may purchase up to 5000 common shares of Clever Idea Co. per year for each of the next four years on January 1, starting in 2001 at $10/share (which was the fair market value when the options were granted).

On January 1, 2001, Anna Lee, an eligible employee, exercises the option, purchasing 5000 shares. The fair market value of the shares at that time was $15.

On January 1, 2002, Anna sells 5000 shares at $25/share on CDNX, and buys 5000 additional shares under the stock option plan.

What are the tax consequences for Anna?

Analysis:

1. Since the fair market value of the shares in each of the four years is less than $100,000, Anna will be able to defer the income inclusion from exercising all the options.

2. In taxation year 2002, Anna will have a taxable capital gain of two-thirds of $75,000.

Stock Options Exercised after Employment Ceases

These rules apply even if a taxpayer exercises an employee stock option after ceasing to work for the employer that granted the option.

4.11   Employee Loans

To help employees take advantage of employee stock option plans, some companies offer employee loans. Generally, a loan received from an employer is not included in income for tax purposes, unless the employer charges interest below the rate that would have been negotiated between arm's-length parties. If the interest on the loan is below this prescribed rate, then a benefit is included in the employee's income equal to the interest at the prescribed rate, minus any interest the employee paid on the loan during the year or within 30 days after year-end.

The deemed interest applies whether or not the loan is outstanding at year's end. In other words, even if a low-interest loan is outstanding for only part of the year, the employee has a deemed benefit. Also, if the loan is subsequently forgiven for an amount less than the outstanding loan, the employee is deemed to have received an employment benefit that must be included in income.

However, if the employee uses the loan to buy shares under a stock option plan and he or she holds the shares to earn investment income, the employee can deduct the deemed interest expense, including the portion that was calculated as a taxable benefit.

Case 7.6   Ray's Employee Loan

Bright Company offers a stock option plan as incentive to certain key employees. Ray Fernandez would like to participate in the plan, but lacks the funds. In 2000, the board of directors of Bright Company agrees to lend Ray $20,000 interest-free so he can exercise his stock options. Assume the prescribed rate for 2000 is 6%. What are the tax consequences for Ray of taking the loan and using it to buy shares?

Analysis:

Since the loan is in the year 2000, Ray will have a taxable benefit from employment equal to $1,200. However, since Ray used the loan to buy shares, he can deduct the deemed interest expense as a carrying charge. For tax purposes, therefore, the effect of the interest-free loan to Ray is neutral.

4.12   Limited Partnerships

A partnership is not a separate legal entity, like a corporation. Instead, as outlined in Canada Customs and Revenue Agency's Interpretation Bulletin IT-90, a partnership is a legal relationship between persons carrying on business in common with a view to profit. A partnership also does not offer limited liability like a corporation. Partners are generally jointly and severally liable for partnership debt.

However, in the 1970s, provincial legislatures amended their *Partnership Acts* to extend the protection of limited liability to a new category of partnership, the limited partnership. A limited partnership has two types of partners:

- **General partners** are responsible for managing the underlying partnership business. Although general partners have unlimited liability, they may form a corporation to limit their liability.

- **Limited partners** are liable only to the extent of their underlying investment and do not participate in management.

Under the *Income Tax Act*, partnership income is calculated at the partnership level. However, the resulting income is taxed, not within the partnership, but in the hands of the partners.

If a partnership has losses in the first few years of operation, it may be desirable to have an individual hold the underlying investments in the limited partnership. The individual partner's share of the partnership losses can be deducted against his or her other sources of personal income, subject to certain restrictions.

On the other hand, if the partnership earns income, it may be desirable to have the investor registered as a corporation. The income can then be taxed within the corporation, which will benefit the individual investor.

Because of this flexibility, limited partnerships may offer advantages over corporations as investment vehicles. Limited partnerships can easily be transferred to a corporation when appropriate. A number of tax shelters have been structured as limited partnerships because of the flexibility offered by this arrangement. However, the "at risk" rules of the *Income Tax Act* limit the losses that a limited partner can claim against the amount of his or her original investment.

Clients should consider the following criteria in deciding whether or not to invest in a limited partnership:

1. Liquidity and cash flow. Many limited partnerships are long-term investments vehicles that require a commitment by the investor to forgo short-term cash flow for several years. Although some limited partnerships are publicly traded, most are not and therefore the liquidity may be less than that of other types of investments. A

limited partnership may not be ideal for certain investors, such as retirees, who rely upon investment returns from their portfolio for living expenses.

2. Control. As a limited partner, the partner has no control over the partnership business. All control is in the general partner's hands. The investor therefore needs information about the general partner. Does he or she have a credible history? Is he or she trustworthy? How will he or she be paid?

3. Risk. In general, limited partnerships carry a higher risk of loss than other, more conservative type of investments such as GICs. Limited partnerships may be in businesses such as films, leasing, agriculture, real estate, research and development, oil and gas exploration and development, or an investment businesses such as mutual fund sales, all of which have varying levels of risk.

Tax Considerations of Limited Partnerships

A primary reason for deciding whether or not to invest in a limited partnership is the tax situation. The investor must consider the following points:

Reporting the income or loss from the partnership

If limited partners expect losses from the underlying partnership business, they may choose (subject to the reasonable expectation of profit and "at risk" rules) to have such losses deducted against their other personal income sources to the maximum of the "at risk" amount.

If they expect taxable income, it may not be desirable to have such income taxed personally. Accordingly, it is essential to specify who will hold and buy the limited partnership units.

Calculation of adjusted cost base of the partnership interest

The adjusted cost base (ACB) of a partnership interest is calculated using the rules outlined in section 53 of the *Income Tax Act*. Various additions and deductions must be taken into consideration in calculating the ACB of the partnership interest. The ACB of the partnership interest will determine the ultimate capital gain or capital loss when the limited partner finally disposes of the partnership unit.

The ACB of a limited partner's partnership interest is calculated in the following way:

- the partner's original investment;

- **plus** the taxable income allocated to the partner for any year ended before the determination time;

- **minus** any losses for income tax purposes allocated to the partner as well as any withdrawals of capital by the partner.

According to detailed rules found in subsections 40(3.1) through 40(3.19) of the *Act*, if the ACB of a limited partner's partnership interest is negative at the end of any fiscal period of the partnership, the partner will realize an immediate capital gain. This can provide immediate negative consequences to a limited partner.

For example, if Pierre LeBlanc invested $5,000 in XYZ Limited Partnership in year 1, had a $5,000 taxable loss in year 2, and made a $2,000 withdrawal in year 2, his ACB would be negative $2,000. That means that Pierre would have a capital gain of $2,000 that he would have to include the amount in his personal income tax return in year 2.

The "at risk" rules

The "at risk" rules are found in section 96 of the *Income Tax Act*. Under these rules, losses from a limited partnership can be claimed by the limited partner against other income (that is, used as a tax shelter) only to the extent of a taxpayer's investment in the partnership that is at risk of being lost if the business venture of the partnership fails. This amount is calculated under subsection 96(2.2) of the *Act*. Normally the limited partnership reports this amount on the T5013 supplementary receipt issued to investors.

For example, Phyllis Cheung becomes a limited partner of XYZ Limited Partnership by investing $5,000 for her limited partnership units. Her "at risk" amount is $5,000. If her share of XYZ's losses exceeds $5,000, she will be able to deduct only $5,000 on her personal income tax return in the year that the loss is incurred.

In many cases, limited partners of a limited partnership have losses that exceed their "at risk" amount. Section 96 of the *Act* restricts their claimable losses to the amount that is "at risk" as described above. However, limited partners can keep track of the losses that exceed the "at risk" amount and may claim such losses against future limited partnership income. These losses can be carried forward indefinitely further to the rules as outlined in subsection 111(1) of the *Act*.

If, say, Phyllis had losses from XYZ Limited Partnership of $12,000, she could not claim $7,000 of these losses, but she could carry them forward indefinitely and apply them against future limited partnership income.

Disposing of a partnership interest

If a limited partner chooses to dispose of his or her partnership interest, a capital gain or capital loss may arise depending on the fair market value and the ACB of the interest at the time of disposition. Capital gains are calculated as follows:

Fair market value of partnership interest – ACB of partnership interest = capital gain

Interest deductibility

In many cases, a limited partner may borrow funds to make the original investment for the limited partnership units. Is the interest on the debt deductible?

Limited partners must meet two conditions under paragraph 20(1)(c) of the *Act*:

- there must be a legal obligation to pay interest;

- the amount on which the interest is payable must either be borrowed money used to earn income from a business or property or an amount payable for property acquired to gain or produce income from the property.

In a limited partnership, the source of income is the underlying activities of the partnership, not the partnership itself. Therefore, the partnership's activities determine the purpose of the loan and ultimately determine whether or not the interest incurred is deductible.

Transfer of a partnership interest to a corporation

In many cases it may be desirable to transfer the business of a limited partnership to a corporation. In these situations, under the provisions of subsection 85(2) of the *Act*, if the partnership assets are transferred to a taxable Canadian corporation, the partners receive shares of the taxable Canadian corporation.

If the rules under subsection 85(2) are met, the limited partner will receive the shares on a "rollover" basis and thereby defer the income tax consequences of transferring the partnership assets until he or she disposes of the "new" shares of the corporation.

Cumulative net investment loss (CNIL)

The deduction of limited partnership losses increases an individual's cumulative net investment loss. Accordingly, this affects the individual's ability to claim the available $500,000 capital gains deduction on qualified small business corporation shares or qualified farm property under section 110.6 of the *Act*.

Other

Many other tax rules need to be considered when dealing with limited partnerships. Many of these rules are anti-avoidance rules, which are in the *Income Tax Act* to prevent abuse. Investors should be aware of these rules and seek competent tax advice.

Tax Filing and Limited Partnerships

A limited partnership must report its income or loss and distributions and report the "at risk" amounts by March 31 of the year following the partnership's December 31 year-end.

Case 7.7   Jennifer's Limited Partnership Investment

Let us consider the following facts for Jennifer Kochalski, who wants to invest in Oil and Gas Limited Partnership ("O&G"):

Jennifer's original cost of limited partnership units in O&G	$10,000
Jennifer's share of O&G's loss in year 1	$14,000
Jennifer's share of O&G's loss in year 2	$ 3,000
Jennifer's share of O&G's income in year 3	$20,000
Jennifer's disposal proceeds after selling units in year 4	$40,000

Analysis:

Assuming that Jennifer's "at risk" amount in year 1 is equal to her original investment of $10,000, she could claim $10,000 of the $14,000 loss on her personal income tax return for year 1. The remainder of the loss, $4,000, would be carried forward indefinitely.

In year 2, she could not claim any of the $3,000 loss, since her previous year's loss claim has already been equal to her "at risk" amount. However, she can carry the $3,000 loss forward indefinitely. Her total limited partnership loss carry-forward now equals $7,000.

In year 3, Jennifer would report the $20,000 limited partnership income from O&G on her personal income tax return but would claim the $7,000 losses that she is carrying forward to reduce her taxable income from the partnership to $13,000.

In year 4, she sells her O&G partnership units. Her taxable income from the partnership is computed as follows:

Disposal proceeds	$40,000
Less: ACB ($10,000 – 14,000 – 3,000 + 20,000)	($13,000)
(computed at end of year 3)	
Capital gain ($40,000 – $13,000)	$27,000
Taxable capital gain (2/3rds of $27,000[5])	$18,000

---

[5] The February 27, 2000 budget proposed lowering the inclusion rate for all capital gains from three-quarters to two-thirds.

A limited partnership is a flexible investment structure that may appeal to many investors. However, because of the complicated tax rules and investment risks, a limited partnership investment is usually appropriate for sophisticated clients only. In all cases, investors should obtain competent investment and tax advice before investing in a limited partnership.

4.13   Business Losses

Business losses occur when revenues from carrying on a business are lower than the allowable expenses incurred to earn income. Business losses differ from other types of losses such as farming and fishing losses or capital losses in their nature, limitations, and use. Business losses are the most common type of non-capital loss.

Business losses can be used to offset income from other sources, such as income from employment, thus reducing taxable income. Losses that cannot be used in the current year can be carried forward or back, to be applied to a future or a past tax year. Business losses must be claimed by the taxpayer carrying on business.

The allowable business investment loss (ABIL) is a specific type of loss that can be used to reduce taxes. It permits specified investment losses in small business corporations to obtain favourable tax treatment. Of course, any business investment should be based on sound investment principles, not on the ability to deduct losses. ABILs are claimed by the taxpayer who made the investment.

Tax Consequences of Business Losses

Business losses have advantages relative to other types of losses because they can offset other (non-business) income, thus reducing income taxes payable. There are, however, limits on the use of business losses, as well as consequences relating to their use.

Business losses must first be used in the year they occur. They are set against other income such as employment income, investment income (interest or dividends), or the taxable portion of capital gains. In the case of dividends, the loss must be applied to the gross amount of the dividends before the dividend tax credit is applied.

Using losses reduces the level of earned income, which is the figure used to calculate RRSP contribution limits. Also, the taxpayer should consider the effects of using business losses on non-refundable tax credits, particularly those that cannot be used in another year or transferred to a family member.

Allowable business investment losses (ABILs) are designed to encourage investment in Canadian business. These are generally losses resulting from the purchase of shares or from loans made to a small business corporation that meets specific conditions imposed by Revenue Canada. If the loss results from the sale of shares or debt, the sale must have been to a non-arm's-length purchaser.

The ability to use ABILs against other income, as opposed to capital gains, depends on the use of capital gains exemptions in previous years. Revenue Canada rules prevent claiming capital gains exemptions and writing off ABILs against other income.

Tax Filing Rules and Carry-Over Provisions

Business losses that cannot be used during the current tax year can be carried forward seven years or back three years. The taxpayer can choose which year to apply the losses against.

A business loss incurred in the current year is reported on the personal income tax return (T1). Filing the appropriate form (T1A) to carry back losses to a previous tax year can use up any remaining losses, or losses can be carried forward to be filed with future tax returns.

Under ABIL rules, two thirds of the business investment loss may be written off against other (non-capital gain) income. The ABIL can also be carried back for three years and carried forward for seven years.

Tax Planning Implications and Methods

Business losses are deductible only if there is an expectation of profit from the business. Consistent losses are likely to be challenged by Revenue Canada.

If a business is incorporated, its losses cannot be used against income from other sources. The losses of a corporation must be offset against income earned by the corporation. As a result, many businesses start out as unincorporated, when losses are more likely, and incorporate later.

Because losses can be carried forward or backward, they can be used to reduce income in years in which the taxpayer is taxed at the highest marginal tax rates. The taxpayer may choose to apply the losses to one or more years in order to reduce the marginal tax rate paid in each.

Unlike other business losses, ABILs do not expire, but can be converted to capital losses if not used within the seven-year period. They can be applied against income taxed at the highest marginal tax rate. To ensure that ABILs are used before they must be converted to capital losses, the taxpayer may defer some expenses or accelerate income.

Some business expenses can be carried forward and claimed in a future tax year, such as home office expenses and capital cost allowance. Home office expenses may not be used to create or increase a loss that could be applied to other income.

Taxpayers who use losses should consider the impact on earned income and therefore RRSP contribution limits as well as the ability to use various tax credits.

Case 7.8   Bob's Non-Capital Business Losses

Bob Porter has employment income and also operates a home-based gardening business. His net income from employment was $60,000, and his business expenses for tax purposes exceed revenues by $8000. As a result, Bob has a non-capital business loss of $8,000. This amount can be used to reduce his taxable income to $52,000.

Analysis:

Because of the business loss, Bob's earned income dropped, and his RRSP contribution limit for the next year also dropped, from $10,800 to $9,360. However, using the losses may have also decreased his marginal tax rate.

In this case, Bob was able to use the entire amount of the business loss to reduce his taxable income in a single year. Had he not been able to do so, he could have carried it forward or back. Bob's gardening business must have a reasonable expectation of profit, and not be merely a hobby, or the expenses and therefore the loss may be disallowed.

Case 7.9   Paula's Allowable Business Investment Loss

Paula Gluckstein is a manager in a large company and her income for the most recent tax year is $100,000. Her friend Ashley has a small business corporation in which Paula has invested $12,000. When Ashley's business unexpectedly goes into bankruptcy, Paula's business investment loss is $12,000. Her allowable business investment loss (ABIL) is two thirds of that amount, or $8,000. She can use this amount to reduce her income from employment and other sources to $92,000.

Analysis:

When Paula's earned income included the business loss, there was no impact on her RRSP contribution limit, since she was permitted the maximum contribution before and after deducting the ABIL. Given Paula's level of income, there is also likely to be no change in her marginal tax rates. If Paula had used a $5,000 capital gains deduction last year, the ABIL would be reduced by that amount.

4.14   Trusts

A trust is a legal relationship that has developed under common law. It separates the legal title of assets from the beneficiaries of those assets. From a tax perspective, trusts own assets, report income, claim tax credits, deduct losses, and pay income tax. There are two major types of trusts.

- **Testamentary trusts** are created as a result of the death of a person. The trust is established as a result of the direction of a will.

- **Inter vivos trusts** are created by a person during his or her lifetime.

Anyone may set up either a domestic or offshore trust. Offshore, or foreign trusts, refer to trusts that are not resident in Canada. The trust may be based in a tax-favourable jurisdiction (usually known as a "tax haven"). Canadian residents are taxed on their worldwide income, regardless of its source. Therefore, ignorance or poor advice about the rules for foreign trusts, as with other offshore structures, could be costly.

Trusts are used to control how assets are distributed during one's lifetime or after death. They have long been used to transfer wealth between generations and to make provisions for a spouse, minor or adult children, and non-family members such as long-time employees or companions. Increasingly, trusts are being used for income splitting and bypassing probate.

To set up a trust, a document addressing details such as settlor, beneficiaries, trustee, responsibilities, and limitations is created.

- The **settlor** of the trust contributes assets to the trust. These assets become the property of the trust.

- The **trustee** is the person or organization who holds title to the assets and administers them on behalf of the beneficiaries.

- The **beneficiary** or beneficiaries of a trust are those for whom the assets are placed in trust. They may receive income or capital from the trust.

The trust document may specify how income or capital gains are to be distributed to the beneficiaries, or it may leave those decisions to the trustee. The trustee, who may be a financial institution or individual, has specific legal responsibilities and may be sued by beneficiaries if problems arise. Trusts are legal documents that require professional advice in their structure.

A wealth manager with a strong knowledge of international tax should handle offshore trusts.

Tax Consequences of Trusts

Under 1999 proposals, a foreign trust is considered a "specified foreign trust" by Revenue Canada and treated as though it were resident in Canada if the beneficiary is Canadian or if the trust document permits the addition of a Canadian beneficiary in the future. American IRA accounts, foreign mutual fund trusts, and certain pension-related trusts are not included in this treatment.

When assets are placed into a trust, ownership is transferred to the trustee. The transfer of ownership must be final. If the assets generate income or gains, they are subject to tax. Trust beneficiaries pay tax on income they receive. In general, the tax paid depends on whether the money earned in a trust is income, capital gains, or dividends.

Testamentary trusts pay tax at marginal tax rates like individuals, so income splitting benefits may arise. However, an inter vivos trust pays tax at the top marginal tax rate.

When a settlor contributes an asset, and transfers legal title to the asset to the trustee, a disposition is deemed to have occurred, and a capital gain may result for the settlor.

Foreign assets have recently come under additional scrutiny in Canada. A trust based in foreign jurisdiction cannot avoid paying Canadian tax. Foreign reporting requirements, along with substantial penalties for taxpayers and advisors, are imposed for non-compliance.

Special rules for foreign trusts apply to new residents of Canada. These rules exempt them for five years from tax on trusts that they set up before their arrival in Canada. Distributions made to Canadian resident are taxed, but any income not distributed remains in the trust and is not subject to Canadian tax. After five years, the assets of the trust can be brought into Canada tax-free.

Tax Filing Rules

A Canadian resident who has transferred assets into a foreign trust or received a distribution or loan from a foreign trust must file an information return. The income of a foreign trust may be fully taxable in Canada, whether or not distributions are made to the Canadian beneficiary.

Attribution rules, which attribute income to the contributor rather than the beneficiary, may apply. The attribution rules are of particular concern if the trust has been set up for the benefit of a spouse or minor children. Additional rules may apply to the tax-free transfer of property between spouses, either using an inter vivos trust or a testamentary trust. These should be discussed with a tax specialist.

Deemed disposition occurs when property is treated as though it were sold, when in fact it is not. This occurs when assets are transferred to a trust, as well as every 21 years for existing and new trusts.

A rule introduced nearly thirty years ago requires a deemed disposition of trust assets every 21 years, which older trusts were able to defer until 1999. The "21-year rule" has a number of exceptions, but generally requires trusts to report income, losses, or capital gains from the deemed disposition of all capital property, land, and foreign resource properties. Taxable capital gains may result from the deemed disposition.

A new rule, dubbed the "kiddie tax," is an attempt to reduce the opportunity for income splitting with children under 18 who are beneficiaries of dividends from a private corporation. These dividends are taxed at the highest marginal tax rate. Although the new rule limits the opportunity for income splitting with minor children, and therefore tax savings, other benefits of the trust continue to be valid.

Tax Planning and Trusts

One of the most important aspects of setting up a trust is choosing a reliable trustee. For an offshore trust, trustee fees and administration costs may be a consideration. Some international financial institutions will not consider acting as trustee for trusts with a value of less than $1 million.

In providing for a disabled beneficiary, the arrangement known as "preferred beneficiary" may be useful. When a disabled person is designated as the preferred beneficiary, accumulating trust income is taxed in the hands of the beneficiary, at potentially lower tax rates, but the income amounts remain in the trust. This option is available only for beneficiaries who are disabled.

Special risks exist for offshore trusts, including currency fluctuations, political changes, and jurisdictional and legal problems. Because offshore transactions can be conducted in greater secrecy, and the parties to the transactions are operating at a distance from each other, there is a greater potential for fraud. It is important to know the parties involved, especially offshore advisors and trustees.

Trusts in which the assets were contributed by the beneficiary or relatives of the beneficiary may be taxed as though income was paid to the beneficiary, even if no distributions have been made. This could be significant in the case of an offshore inter vivos trust paying Canadian tax at the top marginal tax rate. However, if the contributor does not live in Canada and the trust meets certain guidelines, only distributions to a Canadian beneficiary attract Canadian tax. New rules exist, and some of them remain untested by the courts, so an experienced advisor is highly recommended.

Case 7.10   Intergenerational Transfer of a Family Business

Sally Gardiner has built a successful business over the past 23 years and is interested in giving the company to her adult daughters while retaining control. Sally is concerned that unexpected events, such as the divorce of one of her daughters, might reduce their eventual control of the company, so she sets up a trust with her daughters as beneficiaries. The shares are structured to permit Sally to maintain control, and growth shares are put into the trust. Sally appoints herself trustee.

Analysis:

The trust is an inter vivos trust and therefore taxed at the highest marginal tax rate. If the shares held by the trust do not pay dividends or allocate income, the tax burden may not be large. Sally will have a deemed disposition of the property placed in the trust when she establishes it. This may result in a capital gain on her own personal return. The timing of this transaction should therefore be carefully planned.

Under the new arrangement, Sally can maintain control over the trust assets, future growth will occur in the shares held in trust, and the trust will pay tax at the highest marginal rate on any income. Meanwhile, the assets can be kept out of divorce or other litigation, as well as her estate. Trust assets do not form part of the estate and therefore are exempt from the probate process. If Sally wants to be a beneficiary as well, she would need to ensure that the trust is structured correctly to avoid having it overturned.

Case 7.11   Caroline's Offshore Trust

Caroline Dieter's Swiss grandmother has died, leaving $500,000 to her in a testamentary trust. The will established the trust in an offshore jurisdiction, with Caroline as beneficiary. Caroline lives in Canada.

Analysis:

If Caroline's grandmother never lived in Canada, distributions from the trust are taxable in Caroline's hands as a Canadian resident. Caroline should pay attention to currency risks and to the quality of the trustee, likely a financial institution.

If Caroline's Canadian grandmother had set up the trust, the grandmother would have a deemed disposition of property placed into the trust. Reporting requirements would need to be met when the assets were transferred to the trust and when any loans or distributions were made from it.

The income in the offshore trust would probably be subject to Canadian tax, whether or not it was paid out to Caroline. The eventual death of the grandmother would not affect the assets already in the trust, which would continue to require reporting and tax payments. If Caroline was a new resident of Canada, she could avoid paying tax on the income inside the trust for five years, and it could then be paid to her tax-free.

5.0   Taxation and Mutual Funds

5.1   The Adjusted Cost Base of Mutual Funds

Keeping track of the adjusted cost base (ACB) of mutual funds is important, since it can reduce overall capital gains tax liability. T3 information slips from the mutual fund company report all the interest, dividends, foreign income, and realized capital gains distributed during the year. Regardless of whether these amounts are withdrawn or reinvested, they are taxable and must be reported as income.

In most cases these amounts are reinvested, which increases the cost base. The higher cost base must be deducted from any proceeds of disposition in calculating capital gains. Failure to increase the cost base results in the distributions being taxed twice.

For example, Richard Gottschalk buys units in a mutual fund for $9,000 in 1997. It earns dividends of $500 in 1997, $600 in 1998, and $500 in 1999. He sells his units for $11,000 in 1999. The annual dividends were reinvested and taxed each year, as reported in Richard's T3 slips. The ACB of this fund would be $9,000 + $500 + $600 + $500 = $10,600. When he sells it, he has a capital gain of $400, of which 2/3rds or $267 is taxable. Any buying or selling costs would reduce this gain somewhat. A capital loss arising from the disposal of a capital property must be declared, but not necessarily claimed, in the year in which it occurs. The allowable capital loss—2/3rds of the total loss—can be carried back three years or carried forward indefinitely against taxable capital gains. The best year to claim the loss would be the one in which accrued gains are realized and taxable income (and therefore the marginal tax rate) is likely to be highest.

5.2   Taxation and Churning inside Mutual Funds

About two-thirds of mutual funds are held in taxable or non-registered accounts. Fund managers are evaluated and compensated on their pre-tax yield performance, and therefore often pay less attention to way taxes erode that yield. Taxes are incurred by portfolio turnover or "asset churning." Churning has the greatest effect on after-tax returns, even though management expense ratios attract more scrutiny in the financial press.

Turnover within a portfolio leads to realized capital gains being distributed annually rather than accumulating over time. The difference is reflected in the fund's net asset value. Turnover may be irrelevant if the funds are held inside an RRSP; otherwise, asset churning triggers taxes that erode investors' returns. On the other hand, low-turnover funds may build up a large deferred tax liability that may be inherited by new investors in the fund.

How much of the yield is eroded by turnover? In a 1996 article in the *Canadian Investment Review*, M. Thorfinnson and J. Kiss showed that an 8.5% increase in turnover reduced after-tax returns by about 1.2%, while turnover rates of 35% and 80% reduce after-tax returns by 2.5 and 3%, respectively.[6] A 1999 study by R. Geisthardt for the Investment Funds Institute of Canada showed that a 25% increase in turnover represents a yield loss of 189 basis points.[7]

Churning is one reason why even mutual fund managers with sound investment strategies have a hard time outperforming an index fund. Portfolio Analytics Ltd. of Toronto developed PAL TRAK software to compute the tax-efficiency ratio of mutual funds based on the individual asset holdings of funds (http://www.paltrak.com).

In a *Financial Post* article published in 1997, S. Heinrich reported the difference between pre-tax and after-tax returns of 10 Canadian equity funds as of March 31, 1997, computed by PAL TRAK. The results are shown in Table 7.4.[8]

Table 7.4   Pre-tax vs. After-tax Returns of Selected Mutual Funds

	1-year pre-tax return (%)	1-year after-tax return (%)
Altamira Resources	2.0	-2.77
20/20 RSP Aggressive Fund	7.2	-0.51
Fidelity Capital Builder	8.4	0.57
Multiple Opportunities	14.1	3.05
Altamira Equity	8.0	2.63
C.I. Canadian Growth	6.4	2.58
AMI Private Cap Equity	26.8	14.93
Allstar AIG Canadian Equity	20.6	12.34
Cornerstone Canadian Growth	12.7	6.61
Pret et Revenu Canada	20.2	12.22

Many of the funds lost on an after-tax basis relative to pre-tax ranking because they earned taxable interest income on the cash balance held in equity funds. Pre-tax and after-tax returns may also diverge because of unrealized gains or losses accrued within the funds that are acquired by an investor. When investors sell their funds, they are liable for any unrealized gains accrued within the funds before they acquired them. (Conversely, investors could also benefit from any unrealized losses accrued before they acquired them. Unrealized losses make it possible for funds to have an after-tax return that exceeds pre-tax return.)

---

[6] Thorfinnson, M. and J. Kiss. "The Overlooked Piranha." *Canadian Investment Review*, vol. 9, no. 3 (Fall 1996):17-21.

[7] Geisthardt, R. "The Tax Consequences of Investment Turnover in Mutual Funds." Essay submitted to the Investment Funds Institute of Canada, University of British Columbia, 1999.

[8] Heinrich, S. "High turnover can be costly for taxable funds." *Financial Post*, May 6, 1997, p. 27.

6.0   Inflation and Taxes

For the most part, the *Income Tax Act* implicitly assumes a zero inflation rate. The tax base thus consists of nominal incomes. Deductions are also specified in nominal terms. For example, the old RRSP limit of $3,500 (for taxpayers who were also part of the employer's registered pension plan) was established in 1970 and remained in place until 1990. During this period, inflation eroded most of its impact.

Credits and tax brackets are indexed for inflation of more than 3% a year. Such half-measures lead to "bracket creep" or an increase in real tax liability for the same level of real income. "Bracket creep" occurs when individuals find themselves in a higher tax bracket after a few years of receiving cost-of-living increases, even though their real purchasing power has not increased.

The February 27, 2000 budget proposed to reinstate full indexation effective January 1, 2000, for all amounts that were presently partially indexed.

The biggest impact of inflation is on investment income. Taxing nominal interest income may result in a hidden tax on wealth, as shown in Table 7.5.

Table 7.5   Interaction of Inflation and Taxes

Year	Pre-Tax Nominal Rate	Tax @ 45%	After-Tax Nominal Rate	Inflation Rate	After-Tax Real Rate
1981	22%	10%	12%	13%	-1%
1991	11%	5%	6%	5%	1%
1999	4.5%	2.0%	2.5%	0.5%	2.0%

Similarly, taxes on nominal capital gains may be punitive if the gains are largely caused by inflation. The only tax break offered is the ability to deduct nominal interest expense, thus providing incentives to be levered during inflationary periods.

7.0   Pension and Retirement Plans

Recent pension and retirement plan reform measures have largely accomplished government objectives by:

- eliminating differences in tax incentives for various types of retirement plans;

- giving taxpayers more flexibility in the timing of their retirement savings;

- limiting tax incentives for high-income earners.

The various plans converge in their tax treatment by the imposition of a single limit of either $13,500 or 18% of the taxpayer's earned income (whichever is less) for all tax-assisted retirement plans. This limit is adjusted for inflation, and includes contributions by taxpayers as well as their employers. Taxpayers with identical earned incomes thus have identical tax incentives for any combination of Registered Pension Plans (RPPs) and Registered Retirement Savings Plans (RRSPs).

Upper limits for both RRSPs and RPPs are monitored and enforced by Revenue Canada's pension plan registration procedure. The limits restrict the maximum annual pension benefit to 2% of the average of the member's best three years of remuneration, multiplied by the number of years of service, or $1,722.22 for each year of service, whichever is less.

Since dividends are not considered earnings for pension purposes, small business owners and significant shareholders may need to trade off the preferential tax treatment of dividends against their corrosive effect on future pension benefits. In other words, they can draw a larger salary from the business, pay higher taxes on the amount withdrawn as opposed to taking it out as a dividend, but receive earnings for future pension plan benefits.

Unlike CPP and spousal RRSPs, RPPs do not allow pension benefits to be split between spouses. If the spouses have significantly different marginal tax rates, then income splitting may be worthwhile. This can be accomplished by reducing RPP benefits and increasing the corresponding RRSP contribution room. Bear in mind that any combination of RPPs and RRSPs share a cumulative limit of $13,500 or 18% of earnings, whichever is less.

8.0   Registered Retirement Savings Plans

Registered Retirement Savings Plans (RRSPs) act as individual pension plans. One of the government's objectives in establishing RRSPs was to offer taxpayers who are not members of employer-sponsored pension plans the same tax incentives to save for their retirement as those who are. Individuals can also augment their employer-sponsored plans with RRSPs, within certain limits.

RRSP contributions within certain limits are fully deductible from taxable income, and withdrawals are fully taxable. Any income or capital gains earned on funds or properties sheltered by an RRSP are not taxed until they are withdrawn. When they are withdrawn, however, the nature of the returns earned is not preserved. Therefore, withdrawals of returns accrued in the form of capital gains are taxed in the same way as returns earned as dividend or interest income.

Case 7.12   Registered vs. Non-Registered Investments

Cynthia and Martin Shewchuk each have $3,000 of savings this year. Both are in the 40% tax bracket (combined federal, provincial and surtaxes). Cynthia invests in a non-RRSP corporate bond yielding 10%. Martin borrows an additional $2,000 to invest a total of $5,000 in an RRSP bond fund of equal risk, which also yields 10%. Four weeks later, Martin receives a tax refund of $2,000 ($5,000 RRSP contribution × 40% tax rate) which he uses to repay his $2,000 loan. How much accumulated savings would each one have available for consumption 20 years from now?

Analysis:

Savings: $3,000 (Cynthia)

RRSP principal: $\dfrac{\$3,000}{1-0.4} = \$5,000$ (Martin)

Short-term loan: $5,000 – $3,000 = $2,000

Tax refund to repay loan: 40% × $5,000 = $2,000

RRSP investment: $5,000(1.10)^{20} \times (1 - 0.4) = \$20,183$

Non-RRSP investment: $3,000(1.06)^{20} = \$9,621$

Martin pays 40% in tax when he withdraws the funds, but they have grown substantially in the meantime. After 20 years the original $3,000 is worth $20,183 after taxes.

Cynthia on the other hand has much less at the end of 20 years. Since the annual 10% is taxed, she only has 6% to reinvest for compounding purposes. The fact that Cynthia can use the $9,621 directly without having to pay the 40% tax on it as it is with Martin, doesn't come close to making up for the tax-free compounding.

(These calculations assume that marginal tax rates would be 40% at the end of 20 years.)

There are three areas in which tax makes a difference:

- principal amount;
- compounding rate;
- liquidating tax.

8.1   RRSP Planning Opportunities

Spousal Spins

A spousal spin involves withdrawing from the RRSP of a lower-income spouse and investing the after-tax amount in an RRSP of the higher-income spouse to get a bigger tax refund. This strategy is appropriate when the higher-income spouse has a lot of contribution room but no current or expected cash flows to make the contributions, and the lower-income spouse has some RRSP investments, but very little income.

For example, suppose Mark Singer has $20,000 in an RRSP. He withdraws $5,000 from his RRSP in December 1999 and pays a 10% withholding tax. Mark's wife Anne will lose about $4,428 in spousal tax credit for 1999 ($5,000 income – $572), and will owe about $1,130 in additional taxes ($4,428 × 17% × 1.5 = $1,130). They might also lose some child tax benefit if they have children who are still minors.

Anne could use the $5,000 from Mark's RRSP to contribute to a spousal RRSP, and get a tax refund of $2,400 (that is, 48% of $5,000), yielding a net family benefit of about $1,200 (= $2,400 – $1,130 loss of spousal tax credit). Mark gets his $5,000 RRSP balance back as a spousal RRSP. However, Anne has lost $5,000 of her RRSP contribution room.

Since RRSPs are considered "property" in the *Income Tax Act*, attribution rules may apply when one spouse gives money to the other to invest in a property. This can be avoided if Mark uses his withdrawal to pay down the mortgage, thereby allowing Anne to save her cash for the spousal RRSP contribution. This process can be continued each year until Mark's $20,000 RRSP balance has been used up.

Spousal plans become normal RRSPs after the end of the second calendar year-end. A spousal plan set up in 1999 thus becomes Mark's own plan in 2002. The two-year holding period rule applies to all spousal plans for a particular person; setting up a separate spousal plan for each year thus does not resolve the attribution rule issue.

Case 7.13   Bill and Susanna's Spousal Spin

Bill Ratcliffe, 25, and Susanna Mackie, 45, are a married couple. Susanna is a partner in a law firm and makes $100,000 a year. Bill has no income and stays home to take care of the house. Bill has accumulated $20,000 in his RRSP. Because of their extravagant lifestyle, Susanna was unable to save enough cash to contribute to her RRSP and therefore has been accumulating unused RRSP room. She will probably never use all of her available RRSP room. Bill and Susanna live in a province with a provincial tax rate of 50% of the federal basic tax (ignore federal and provincial surtaxes).

Basic Personal Exemption = $6,456

Married credit = $5,380

Federal tax brackets: 17% for taxable income up to $29,590;

26% for taxable income between $29,590 and $59,180

29%. for taxable income > $59,180

Analysis:

Bill withdraws $6,456 from his RRSP. Bill will pay no tax, as his tax liability will be offset by his personal tax credit. If the withholding tax applies, Bill will receive a refund once he filed his tax return. He then "gives" the $6,456 to Susanna. Attribution can be avoided if Bill uses the money to pay for household needs or other personal expenditures, rather than Susanna paying these expenses.

Susanna then makes a spousal RRSP contribution of $6,456. This will result in $(29\% \times 1.5) \times \$6,456 = \$2,808$ tax refund. However, Bill will have enough taxable income (from his withdrawal) to eliminate the married credit of $5,380. This results in a loss of tax savings of $\$5,380 \times (17\% \times 1.5) = \$1,372$. The net gain from this strategy $2,808 – $1,372 = $1,436.

Next year, the couple can use the same strategy, until Bill's RRSP is depleted. A withdrawal above $6,456 would not be as advantageous, as Bill will start to pay tax at that point.

Early, Continuous, and Over-Contributions

For most RRSP contributors, the deferral of tax on investment income is more important than income tax refunded by Revenue Canada. Sheltering investment income from taxes means that income can be compounded at pre-tax rates of return. This can have a dramatic effect on the amount accumulated over time.

For example, annual savings of $5,000 over 30 years would grow to $566,416 if invested at an after-tax rate of return of 8%. The same contributions would grow to $2,173,725 if compounded at the pre-tax rate of 15% (that is, a marginal tax rate of 46.6%). In this case, compounding at pre-tax rates, yields accumulated savings almost four times greater than the savings accumulated by compounding at after-tax rates.

Thus it makes good financial sense to contribute the maximum possible to RRSPs. This policy should be pursued by both old and young, including those who claim not to be concerned about retirement. Other than liquidity reserves or planned short-run expenditures, taxpayers should not hold non-registered financial investments unless they have exhausted their RRSP contribution room.

The argument in favour of compounding can be extended to justify contributions at the beginning rather than at the end of the year. For example, annual contributions of $5,000 made at the beginning of each year would grow to $2,499,784 after 30 years at a 15% rate of return. The same contributions would grow to only $2,173,725 if invested at the end of each year.

The difference of $326,059 also represents the approximate amount forgone at the end of 30 years when a single annual contribution is missed. Thus, it is important to make regular and continuous contributions, even though legislation allows unused RRSP deduction room to be carried forward indefinitely. The cumulative difference is largely due to the permanent loss of the tax-sheltered investment income on the single contribution missed, and more important, the loss of tax-free compounding on that amount over the 30-year period.

The power of compounding may also make the $2,000 lifetime over-contribution worthwhile, even though the amount is not deductible from taxable income, and is taxed when withdrawn. If over-contributions are left sheltered in the plan for at least 15 years, the benefits of compounding at pre-tax rates of returns outweigh the cost of double taxation. Furthermore, over-contributed amounts can be deducted in future years when a taxpayer cannot make a regular contribution, as long as there is contribution room.

If however over-contributions are left sheltered for less than 15 years, the costs of double taxation will typically outweigh the benefits of compounding at pre-tax rates. Please see Appendix 7.3 for an example illustrating this point.

8.2   Why So Few People Contribute to RRSPs

Although the argument for investing inside RRSPs is convincing, only 61.4% of Canadians have RRSP accounts.[9] The pool of unused contributions is estimated to be approximately $170 billion.[10]

---

[9]   Bell, A. "More Canadians own RRSPs, study says." *The Globe and Mail*, July 10, 1999, p. B8.

[10]   Galloway, P. "Catch-up loan bridges shortfall." *Financial Post*, February 14, 1998, p. 39.

Statistics Canada reports also indicate that growth in RRSP contributions has significantly declined in recent years. Just over 6 million Canadians contributed $26.6 billion to their RRSPs in 1998, a 4% decrease from the $27.7 billion contributed in 1997, despite a 4.6% increase in employment income over the same period. In contrast, the annual growth in RRSP contributions was in excess of 10% during much of the 1990s.[11]

It is important for financial planners to understand why people do not pursue this tax break more aggressively. If it is because they are unaware of the financial implications of their choices, then you should try to educate them. Here are some reasons why people do not invest in RRSPs:

- They see current consumption as more important than future consumption.

- They think they will have more money later (not likely to be true).

- They believe that government schemes will continue to support them.

- They do not appreciate the value of tax-free compounding.

- They believe that tax rates upon withdrawal will be high, thereby making RRSPs not as attractive.

- They believe that since their current tax rates are low, RRSPs are not as attractive.

- They believe that rates of return outside RRSPs are greater than they really are.

- They think that since equities are tax-favoured outside RRSPs, there is no reason to invest inside RRSPs.

- They see paying off a mortgage or other debts as a higher priority.

- They consider RRSP-eligible investments too restrictive (for example, the foreign-content restrictions).

- They believe that transaction costs for RRSPs are too high (which may be true for self-administered RRSPs).

As a wealth manager, you should be able to respond to all of these assumptions and encourage your clients to make the best use of RRSPs.

---

[11] Bell, op. cit.

9.0   Paying Down a Mortgage vs. Contributing to an RRSP

The choice between contributing to an RRSP contribution and paying down a mortgage or other non-tax-deductible consumer debt is one of the most common decisions a client will face. Mortgages are normally the single largest debt a client will assume, and the longer the client has a mortgage the more interest he/she will pay. While that would seem to argue for a decision to pay down the mortgage at every opportunity, it is also true that building retirement assets is as important, and the earlier the client begins saving for retirement the more money he/she will save.

While there are no clear answers, the following are some factors to consider.

In support of paying down a mortgage:

- If the client's mortgage interest rate is significantly higher than the RRSP return, paying down the mortgage may be the best thing for the client to do;

- The fact that a client can carry forward unused RRSP deduction to later years may make paying down the mortgage more attractive.

In support of contributing to an RRSP versus paying down a mortgage:

- If the client's income is high one year (marginal tax rate also high), a contribution to an RRSP would reduce his/her tax liability which may outweigh the interest savings from paying down the mortgage;

- The further the client is from retirement, the more valuable RRSP contributions are, since the money has a longer period to benefit from tax-free compounding.

Often some combination of the paying down a mortgage and contributing to an RRSP is the best solution. One way of doing this is by making an RRSP contribution and using the tax refund to pay down the mortgage.

If this is done, the client should try to:

- make their RRSP contribution early in the year;

- time mortgage payments to coincide with the timing and frequency of pay cheques (biweekly, monthly, etc.).

These procedures will enhance the after-tax family net worth. If it makes more sense for some clients to pay down the mortgage rather than make RRSP contributions, you may face a conflict between serving your clients' best interests and meeting short-run performance targets for products that you are supposed to be selling. Suggesting the mortgage pay-down alternative would create shortfalls in both the RRSP and the outstanding mortgage targets.

However, looking after your clients' best interests and pointing out ways in which they can maximize their after-tax family net worth will create a more affluent, satisfied, loyal, and growing clientele. The focus on sound relationships is also likely to reduce the chances of competing wealth managers luring your clients away with more appropriate financial advice.

Please refer to Appendix 7.4 for an example of the types of calculations necessary for determining the best course of action with respect to either paying down a mortgage or making an RRSP contribution.

10.0   Borrowing to Make RRSP Contributions

Clients often ask wealth managers if they should borrow to contribute to a RRSP if they have not saved enough to contribute from their own money.

Generally, this strategy only makes sense if the client can repay the borrowed funds within about a year, or if the client's income for the current year falls into a higher tax bracket than usual. Otherwise the non-deductible interest that the client pays on the loan, may negate the tax benefits of his/her contribution. The argument against longer-term borrowing (over a year) to make an RRSP contribution is strengthened also by the fact that since 1991, taxpayers that do not make their maximum allowable RRSP contribution in one year, can carry it forward to another. Since that time it has not been a "use it, or lose it" proposition.

Of course borrowing is attractive if the tax refund can be used to pay down some or all of the loan. This is particularly true in cases where a financial institution offers special rates for RRSP loans and gives clients enough of a repayment deferral to allow the client to receive his/her tax refund.

11.0   Tax Planning for Small Business Owners

Tax planning is also an important consideration for small-business owners. Taxes on income, capital, payroll, and sales paid by most small businesses are passed on in various degrees to customers (in the form of higher prices), employees (in the form of lower wages), and shareholders (in the form of lower returns). These taxes are a cost of doing business and small business owners must take them into account to remain competitive.

Business owners who consider taxes an uncontrollable cost may not be giving taxes sufficient consideration in their day-to-day decisions. For small businesses to remain competitive in their product, labour, and capital markets, effective tax planning must be incorporated into all business decisions.

Effective tax planning may require small business owners to consider the tax position of not only the firm itself, but also those of all parties with which it contracts—customers, suppliers, employees, shareholders, and partners. Restructuring these transactions may improve the positions of all contracting parties at the expense of Revenue Canada. The following examples illustrate some tax-motivated strategies and transactions that allow small business owners to increase not only their firms' after-tax profits but also their personal net worth.

11.1   Maximizing Deductible Interest and Other Expenses

Interest on borrowed money is deductible for tax purposes only if the debt was incurred in order to earn income from a business or property.

Revenue Canada traces loans to confirm that the loan was actually taken out for business purposes. It will not accept the argument that residential mortgage interest should be deductible, if the owner had sufficient savings to pay off the mortgage but then borrowed for business. However, it is possible to use savings to pay off the residential mortgage or other personal loans, and then borrow for business purposes using the house or other personal assets as security to obtain a favourable rate.

In the absence of other securities, financial institutions may consider a life insurance policy for the small-business owner as an appropriate security for a loan. Life-insurance premiums can be deducted from business earnings if the financial institution requires the policy as a precondition to lending. Interest payments on such loans are generally tax-deductible if the proceeds of the loan are used to earn business income.

11.2   Incorporation and Tax Deferral

Canadian Controlled Private Corporations (CCPCs) pay a reduced tax rate of about 22% (in most provinces) on the first $200,000 of active business income and 45% on any income over $200,000. Incorporating a business can yield an annual tax deferral of up to $56,000 if the income was earned by an individual with a personal marginal tax rate of 50% (that is, [50% – 22%] × $200,000 = $56,000).

This benefit is a tax deferral rather than a permanent tax saving, since additional taxes will eventually have to be paid by the owners when they receive dividends. However, the benefit of the tax deferral increases with the period of time that the earnings remain in the corporation rather than being distributed.

The main tax disadvantage of incorporating a business is the inability to offset business losses against other personal sources of income. Business losses incurred in an unincorporated entity can be used to offset employment income for the current or previous year. Therefore, a sound tax planning strategy is to postpone incorporating a business until it becomes profitable, to avoid trapping the initial losses inside the corporation.

If the non-capital losses from previous years are in danger of expiring unused inside a corporation, then small business owners may postpone capital cost allowances, which will allow them to report higher incomes that can absorb the losses. Postponing capital cost allowances when income is below the $200,000 limit and deducting more when income exceeds $200,000 is also a sound way of ensuring that more income is taxed at the favourable rate of 22%.

11.3   Salary/Dividend Mix

Owners of incorporated businesses have a choice of drawing a salary or receiving dividends to pay for personal expenses. Since only the first $200,000 of active business income enjoys the favourable rate, it is usually wise to accrue bonuses for the small business owner for amounts over $200,000, to avoid double taxation. Revenue Canada does not seem to question the reasonableness of the bonus amount, as long as it is actually paid out to the small business owner. Any accrued bonuses must be paid within 179 days after the corporation's year-end.

A $75,000 salary or bonus may be advantageous, since it allows the small business owner to make the maximum RRSP contribution room (18% × $75,000 = $13,500). Salaries also avoid minimum tax liabilities, while potentially triggering higher payroll taxes compared to dividends.

Income splitting can be accomplished by paying dividends to family members who have invested into the corporation. Dividends are also preferred over salary if the cumulative net investment loss is expected to reduce the small business owner's ability to claim the capital gains exemption.

11.4   Combined Employment and Business Income

If an individual has both employment income (reported on the T4) and business income, it may make sense not to incorporate the business. Canadian Pension Plan (CPP) contributions are deducted from employment income and reported on the T4. Adding non-incorporated business income (T2124) may not trigger any additional CPP contributions if the contributions through employment income have reached the ceiling. However, the employer's portion of the CPP contributions would not be avoidable if the individual received the same amount as employment income. Although any employee contributions beyond the ceiling are refunded, Revenue Canada keeps the employer's portion, which can add up to more than $1,000 a year.

11.5   Capital Gains Crystallization

Every individual who is a Canadian resident throughout the year in which assets were distributed is eligible for a lifetime capital gains exemption of $500,000. The exemption can be used to reduce or eliminate tax liability on the small business owner's sale of shares. Using this exemption may be a sound idea, given concerns that the capital gains exemption may eventually be repealed.

Crystallizing involves transferring the shares of the operating company to a holding company, thereby increasing the shares' cost base. This allows the small business owner to enjoy substantial future tax savings when the shares of the corporation are eventually sold to a third party. The capital gain is reflected in the higher cost base of the shares of the operating company, now held by the holding company.

In order to crystallize the capital gains exemption, the corporation must meet the criteria for a Qualified Small Business Corporation. If the corporation does not currently meet the standards, there are steps the corporation can take. For example, investment assets may need to be held personally by the owner rather than by the corporation to maintain its qualified status. Holding investment assets personally rather than in a corporation may also avoid Cumulative Net Investment Losses that can hinder the small business owner's ability to claim the capital gains exemption.

11.6   Estate Freezing and Multiple Capital Gains Exemptions

An estate freeze is an effective succession-planning tool that works by splitting income and capital gains among family members. In a typical estate freeze, a small business owner exchanges his or her common shares in the corporation for redeemable, retractable preferred shares that have a redemption value equal to the fair market value of the common shares the owner has given up.

Family members can buy the available common shares at a low price and thereby benefit from any future growth in the corporation. As long as the corporation continues to meet the criteria for a Qualified Small Business Corporation, each family member who owns shares will be eligible for his or her own $500,000 capital gains exemption.

If the small business owner wants his or her family members to benefit from the corporation's growth without holding common shares directly, he or she can set up a family trust with the family members as beneficiaries. Each beneficiary will be eligible for the capital gains exemption, as long as the shares held by the trust qualify as Qualified Small Business Corporation shares.

11.7   Selling or Buying an Incorporated Business

The owner of an incorporated small business can transfer ownership of the business to a new owner by selling either its shares or its assets. The purchaser will likely prefer buying the assets in order to enjoy the higher future capital cost allowance deductions arising from the higher market costs assigned to the depreciable property. However, the vendor would probably prefer to sell shares in a bid to qualify for the $500,000 capital gains exemption. Negotiations on this issue may lead to a sale of shares, but at a lower price so that both parties to the transaction share the tax benefits.

11.8   Shifting Expenses across Time Periods

The marginal tax rate of the firm may change because of operating losses or the use of tax incentives. Small businesses anticipating lower effective tax rates in the future can increase their current expenditures, for example, by increasing their advertising efforts, thereby potentially shifting taxable income from the current high effective tax rate period to a future low effective tax rate period when the medium to long-term benefits of advertising are realized.

Appendix 7.1

The Time Value of Money

Let us take a few minutes to look at the concept of the "time value of money". What that basically means is that a dollar held or received today is worth more than a dollar received next year, or at a later date, because today's dollars can be invested to generate some type of return. This concept is especially important to wealth managers who must attempt to estimate, calculate and match various cash flows for years into the future.

Calculating Future Value of a Present Amount

The money that you have today is worth more than money that you will be receiving in the future because of the interest that you can earn by putting that money in a savings account or investing it in other securities. This becomes even more important when you introduce the concept of compound interest where the interest earned actually starts earning interest itself.

Let us suppose that you have $10,000 and you deposit it into a guaranteed interest account and just leave it in the account making no future contributions. Then at any point in time after today the balance in the account will grow to a value known as the future value of a present amount (the $10,000).

The formula for calculating this amount is:

$$FV = P(1 + i)^n$$

where:

FV = the future value

P = the principal amount

i = the periodic or annual interest rate

n = the number of time periods or years

We can see from the formula that the future value is simply the sum to which a dollar amount invested today will grow given an appreciation rate. Let's look at an example. Assume that you deposited $10,000 for four years into a savings account that pays annual interest of 8%.

$$FV = \$10,000\ (1 + .08)^4$$
$$= \$10,000\ (1.3605)$$
$$= \$13,605$$

As we can see, $10,000 invested at 8% for 4 years will be worth $13,605 at the end of the four-year time horizon.

Virtually all financial calculators can do this calculation for you. There are also future value tables that make this process very easy. More complete future value tables are available at the end of this appendix.

To properly use the future value tables you simply look along the top to find the proper value of "i" and then search down the column until you find the "n" that you are looking for. In this case, we find 8% for 4 periods = 1.3605, the same value derived from doing the calculation. Now you simply multiply your principal amount by the factor found in the table to get the future value.

Future Value Factors

N	8%	9%	10%	11%	12%	13%	14%
1	1.0800	1.0900	1.1000	1.1100	1.1200	1.1300	1.1400
2	1.1664	1.1881	1.2100	1.2321	1.2544	1.2769	1.2996
3	1.2597	1.2950	1.3310	1.3676	1.4049	1.4429	1.4815
4	**1.3605**	1.4116	1.4641	1.5181	1.5735	1.6305	1.6890
5	1.4693	1.5386	1.6105	1.6851	1.7623	1.8424	1.9254
6	1.5869	1.6771	1.7716	1.8704	1.9738	2.0820	2.1950

Notice that all of the factors have a value greater than "1" which represents the premium paid for future dollars.

Either the tables or the formula will allow you to determine the future value of any amount of money provided that you know the interest rate (I) and the number of time periods (n).

Calculating Present Value of a Future Amount

Think of present value as future value in reverse. In this instance, you assume that you already know the future value of your investment, and want to know what your starting principal will have to be in order to reach your goal in the desired amount of time. In other words, present value is the value in today's dollars assigned to an amount of money in the future, based on some estimated rate-of-return over the long-term.

The formula for present value is simple; just take the formula for future value and solve for the starting principal:

$$PV = FV/(1 + r)n$$

Notice that we've substituted "PV" for "P" in the previous formula. Conceptually, all we are doing is bringing a predetermined future amount back to present.

For example, lets say that you need to have $10,000 in 5 years and you can get an 8% return for that period of time. The question now becomes "How much do I need to invest today at 8% to end up with $10,000 in five years"?

$$PV = FV/(1 + i)^n$$
$$PV = 10000/(1.08)^5$$
$$PV = 10000 / 1.4693$$
$$6,805.96 = 10000 / 1.4693$$

Therefore you would need to invest $6805.96 at 8% for 5 years to get your desired $10,000.

Again, virtually all financial calculators can easily do this calculation for you. As there are future value tables, there are also present value tables that make this process very easy. More complete present value tables are also available at the end of this appendix.

To properly use the present value tables you simply look along the top to find the proper "i" and then search down the column until you find the "n" that you are looking for. In this case, we find 8% for 5 periods = .6806, which is approximately the same value derived from doing the calculation. Now you simply multiply your principal amount by the factor found in the table to get the present value.

Present Value Factors

Periods	8%	9%	10%	11%	12%	13%	14%
1	.9259	.9174	.9091	.9009	.8929	.8850	.8772
2	.8573	.8417	.8264	.8116	.7972	.7831	.7695
3	.7938	.7722	.7513	.7312	.7118	.6931	.6750
4	.7350	.7084	.6830	.6587	.6355	.6133	.5921
5	**.6806**	.6499	.6209	.5935	.5674	.5428	.5194
6	.6302	.5963	.5645	.5346	.5066	.4803	.4556
7	.5835	.5470	.5132	.4817	.4523	.4251	.3996

Note that all of the present value factors are less than one. Therefore, when multiplying a future value by these factors, the future value is discounted down to present value.

You can also use the present value concept to estimate the effects of inflation by computing the real purchasing power of present and future sums. To do this, just use an estimated rate of inflation for the "i" in the calculation or in the table.

On occasion, wealth managers will know the present principal amount and the amount that the client will need at some point in the future. Therefore the wealth manager will have to find the interest rate required for the principal amount to become the future amount. Again the formula is simple: solve the future value formula for "i":

$$i = \left(\frac{FV}{PV}\right)^{\frac{1}{n}} - 1$$

The interest rate (i) is often called the "discount rate" when it is the variable that you are solving for, and you are assuming that the future value is a given.

Solving for either the present value or the interest rate may seem like an archaic way of doing things, but these are very useful calculations, especially for comparing different investments. For example, suppose that instead of putting your $10,000 in the bank you decide to invest it. You have a choice between an investment that promises to triple your money in five years or an investment that promises to quadruple your money in seven years. Which of the two investments offers a better return? To determine this we must solve for "i".

Investment 1

$$i = \left(\frac{FV}{PV}\right)^{\frac{1}{n}} - 1$$

$$i = \left(\frac{30000}{10000}\right)^{\frac{1}{5}} - 1$$

$$i = 1.2457 - 1$$

$$i = .2457 = 24.57\%$$

Investment 2

$$i = \left(\frac{FV}{PV}\right)^{\frac{1}{n}} - 1$$

$$i = \left(\frac{40000}{10000}\right)^{\frac{1}{7}} - 1$$

$$i = 1.2191 - 1$$

$$i = .2191 = 21.91\%$$

Therefore from the information given, Investment 1 is a higher yielding investment than investment two.

Annuities

An annuity is defined as an equal, annual series of cash flows. The annuity cash flows may be equal annual payments, equal annual receipts, equal annual deposits or equal annual withdrawals. Notice that the key in all of these examples is "equal" cashflows. Each payment is also assumed to occur at the end of the period.

Future Value of an Annuity

The future value of an annuity is another way of asking, "How much money would I have after a given number of years if I invest a certain amount regularly?" The future value of an annuity is based on regular equal deposits or investments at the end of each period for a certain number of periods and allowing those cash flows to grow.

To calculate this, you would use the following formula:

$$FVA = A \times \sum_{t=0}^{n-1}(1+i)^t = A\left[\frac{(1+i)^n - 1}{i}\right]$$

As you can see, the formula is fairly tedious to work through. As with the future value and present value of a single cash flow, virtually all financial calculators can easily do this calculation for you. Again, there are tables for working with annuities. Basically, this table works the same way as the other tables you have been using. Just locate the appropriate interest rate and look up the appropriate number of periods, take the factor found and multiply it by the amount of the annuity. There are more complete tables at the end of this appendix.

For example, what would a three-year, 5% interest annuity of $100 per year be worth at the end of the three years? From the table we can find the factor of 3.152. Now multiply that factor by the annuity of $100 to get a future value of $315.20.

Future Value of an Annuity

N	1%	2%	3%	4%	5%	6%
1	1	1	1	1	1	1
2	2.01	2.02	2.03	2.04	2.05	2.06
3	3.03	3.06	3.091	3.122	**3.152**	3.184
4	4.06	4.122	4.184	4.246	4.31	4.375
5	5.101	5.204	5.309	5.416	5.526	5.637
6	6.152	6.308	6.468	6.633	6.802	6.975

Present Value of an Annuity

The present value of an annuity will allow you to calculate the value today of an annuity in the future. In other words, if I invested $100 a month for the next five years, what would the total amount be worth in today's dollars? Again remember that an annuity is based on regular equal deposits or investments at the end of each period for a certain number of periods.

To calculate this you would use the following formula:

$$PVA = A \times \sum_{t=1}^{n} \frac{1}{(1+i)^t}$$

As with the previous calculation for the future value of an annuity, this formula is also very tedious to work through but you can easily do this calculation with most financial calculators. There are also tables to assist you in calculating the present value of an annuity which works the same way as the other tables. Just locate the appropriate interest rate and look up the appropriate number of periods, take the factor found and multiply it by the amount of the annuity.

Let's say that you invested $100 a year at 8% for the next 10 years and you want to know what the total amount would be worth in today's dollars.

Present Value Of Annuity Factors

N	8%	9%	10%	11%	12%	13%	14%
1	.9259	.9174	.9091	.9009	.8929	.8850	.8772
2	1.7833	1.7591	1.7355	1.7125	1.6901	1.6681	1.6467

3	2.5771	2.5313	2.4869	2.4437	2.4018	2.3612	2.3216
4	3.3121	3.2397	3.1699	3.1024	3.0373	2.9745	2.9137
5	3.9927	3.8897	3.7908	3.6959	3.6048	3.5172	3.4331
6	4.6229	4.4859	4.3553	4.2305	4.1114	3.9976	3.8887
7	5.2064	5.0330	4.8684	4.7122	4.5638	4.4226	4.2883
8	5.7466	5.5348	5.3349	5.1461	4.9676	4.7988	4.6389
9	6.2469	5.9952	5.7590	5.5370	5.3283	5.1317	4.9464
10	**6.7101**	6.4177	6.1446	5.8892	5.6502	5.4262	5.2161
11	7.1390	6.8052	6.4951	6.2065	5.9377	5.6869	5.4527

Therefore, $100 per year invested at 8% for the next 10 years would be worth $671 in today's dollars. A more complete set of tables is available in Appendix A at the back of this textbook.

Appendix 7.2

Accelerated Versus Gradual RESP Contributions

Annual contributions of $4,000 will yield government grants of only $4,400 ($400 annual maximum grant × 11 years), whereas $2,000 annual contributions will yield government grants of $7,200 ($400 annual maximum grant × 18 years maximum period). However, if contributions earn an 8% return and withdrawals begin when the student is 21 years old, the accelerated contributions (with its corresponding government grants) will have grown to about $166,000, whereas the gradual contributions (with the larger government grant) will accumulate to only about $129,000 assuming contributions are made at the beginning of the year.

Comparison of Accelerated and Gradual RESP Contributions

RESP with Accelerated Contributions	RESP with Gradual Contributions
$4,400 PMT, 10 N, 8 i, FV_{10} = $68,840	$2,400 PMT, 18 N, 8 i, FV_{18} = $97,071
$68,840 PV, 11 N, 8 i, FV_{21} = $160,510	$97,071, 3 N, 8 i, FV_{21} = $122,281
$2,400 PV, 10 N, 8 i, FV_{21} = $5,181	$2,000 PMT, 3 N, 8 i, FV_{21} = $7,012
FV_{21} = $160,510 + $5,181 = $165,691	FV_{21} = $122,281 + $7,012 = $129,293

Where:

PMT = payment made for each period

PV = present value

N   = number of years

i   = interest rate

FV_x = future value at year x

Appendix 7.3
RRSP Over-Contributions

Peter George has made the maximum contribution to his RRSP every year. This year he is considering taking advantage of the $2,000 over-contribution option. The pre-tax yield on the investment he is considering is 10% and he plans to retire 10 years from now. His marginal tax rate is 52% and is expected to be the same at retirement. Is it worthwhile for Peter to over-contribute?

Analysis:

The question can be answered using the following equation, in which the left-hand side represents the cost of over-contributing and the right-hand side the benefit of over-contributing:

$$A[1 + (1 - t)R]^n = A (1 + R)^n (1 - t_n)$$

where

A = income

T = marginal tax rate

t_n = marginal tax rate at end of period n

R = pre-tax yield on investment

N = number of compounding periods

Cost of over-contributing = $\$1[1 + (1 - 0.52)0.10]^{10} = \$1.5981$

Benefit of over-contributing = $\$1(1 + 0.10)^{10} (1 - 0.52) = \$1.2450$

Since the cost of over-contributing is greater than the benefit of over-contributing, it is not worthwhile for Peter to over-contribute to his RRSP.

100K @ 12% (1%) 25 yrs (300 m)

∴ PMT = 1053.^{22}

Reduce mort by 1k → Time ↓ from 300 to 282.^{7}

17.3 months less

∴ 17.3 × 1053^{22} = $\boxed{18304.1^{96}}$

2000k FU = 19783.^{7} less 50% tax

= $\boxed{9891.5^{4}}$

Appendix 7.4

Paying Down a Mortgage Versus Contributing to an RRSP

Yasmin Kassam, 40, plans to cash in her lump-sum RRSP when she retires and move back to Kenya at 65. She has a $100,000 outstanding mortgage with a 25-year amortization period at 12% a year (1% a month). She can earn an annual pre-tax yield of 9.6% (0.8% a month) on her money market fund, and her marginal tax rate is 50%. She has sufficient RRSP contribution room and is trying to choose between paying down her mortgage by $1,000 or investing (a leveraged amount of) $2,000 in an RRSP. What will be the value of each alternative when Yasmin turns 65?

Analysis:

In these calculations, we will assume a constant marginal tax rate.

Option 1: Pay Down Mortgage

Using a financial calculator:

Current monthly mortgage payments:

Key	Touch	Display
100,000	PV	100,000
300	n	300
1	i	1
CPT	PMT	$1,053.22 mortgage payments per month

Months required to pay off mortgage if PV is $1,000 less:

Key		*Touch*	*Display*
99,000		PV	99,000
1053.22	+/-	PMT	1053.22
1		i	1
CPT		n	282.7 (approximately 283 months)

Therefore, mortgage is paid off 17 months early.

Invest "equivalent-to-mortgage-payments" for 17 months at pre-tax yield of 0.8% per month or an after-tax yield of 0.4% per month and calculate the future value:

Key		Touch	Display
1053.22	+ /-	PMT	1053.22
17		n	17
0.4		i.	0.4
CPT		FV	$18,489 more at retirement

Option 2: Invest in an RRSP

Invest $2,000 now at "sheltered" rate of 0.8% per month until retirement in 300 months:

Key	Touch	Display
2,000	PV	2,000
300	n	300
0.8	i	0.8
CPT	FV	$21,836.83

Cash in RRSP at retirement: $21,836.83 x (1-0.5) = $10,918

Conclusion: Yasmin Kassam is better off paying down the mortgage by $7,571

CHAPTER 8

Estate Planning

1.0   Introduction

Estate planning has become an important facet of managing a client's wealth. In some senses, estate planning is the orderly transfer of a client's assets from one generation to the next. But to the client, estate planning is making the most of what they have achieved over their lifetime so that their beneficiaries receive the most allowed by law, without delay or unnecessary fees and taxes.

Although some clients are reluctant to discuss estate planning, it is key to wealth management. A wealth manager who neglects a client's estate planning issues could be accused of neglecting his or her fiduciary responsibilities to the client. If one of your clients dies without a will, or with a huge tax bill, will the client's beneficiaries feel that you served the client well?

You are involved in the estate planning process from the day you open an account with a client. The estate planning implications start with how an investment account is registered and who a client designates as his or her beneficiary on those investments. In your role as a wealth manager, you need to educate your clients on the importance of estate planning and guide them through the estate planning process. To do this, you also need to understand your clients' family situation and their personal values and your clients need to understand the outcomes of the estate plan they put in place.

It is not necessary to become a specialist in estate planning, but you should be able to identify opportunities for clients, help them solve problems before they happen, and make the necessary referrals to the appropriate tax and legal experts. You will need to understand some legal concepts and tax principles. However, unless you are a lawyer, you should avoid making any statements that would be construed as a legal opinion.

Primary Learning Objectives

By the end of this chapter, you should understand:

- **how to design an estate plan to help clients meet beneficiaries' needs, reduce the costs of dying, and minimize taxes payable after death;**

- **the provincial intestacy rules and how they affect the distribution of the deceased's estate;**

- **how to review a client's will and ensure that it meets the client's intentions;**

- **the executor's role in the estate planning process, including selection, compensation, liability, powers, and the appointment of guardians for minor beneficiaries;**

- **how ongoing spousal and child support may affect the deceased's estate;**

- **the nature and scope of the power of attorney document;**

- **how to deal with probate and strategies to reduce probate fees;**

- **the estate planning features of segregated funds;**

- **techniques to defer or reduce taxes at death;**

- **the appropriate use of trusts and the role of the trustee;**

- **effective planned giving strategies;**

- **how to deal with the transfer of a business to beneficiaries.**

2.0 Approaching Estate Planning Issues with Clients

Estate planning is a difficult topic for some clients. Many people dislike thinking about their own mortality. It is your job to help your clients face estate planning issues pragmatically.

Clients make a number of decisions with a wealth manager that can affect their estate planning, such as naming a beneficiary for an RRSP, RRIF, life insurance, or segregated fund, setting up joint or individual segregated fund policies, or registering an investment account in joint ownership. You can make suggestions that will preserve wealth in an estate. For example, if your clients are grandparents who want to open up an RESP account on behalf of a grandchild, you might suggest that from a tax planning perspective, they would do better to give the money to the child's parents and let them open the RESP.

Before you discuss estate planning with your clients, you need to collect the following information about each client:

- assets and how the ownership of those assets is registered;

- what beneficiaries have been named and their relationship to the client;

- the instructions in the will and power of attorney documents;

- the family situation;

- the client's specific estate planning goals.

Some clients want to leave as large an estate as possible. Others may not be particularly concerned about the size of the estate. Most, however, do not want the distribution of their estate to be handled by the government because they die without making a will.

3.0 Dying Intestate: The Government's Solution

When a person dies without a will, they are considered to have died **intestate**. Each province has its own intestacy legislation that states how the estate is to be distributed among living blood relatives. The provincial formula is like a "plain vanilla will" that is applied the same to anyone who dies without having taken the time to prepare an individual will. A spouse is not automatically entitled to the estate of a deceased, particularly if there are children. However, some provinces protect a surviving spouse (but not a common-law spouse) by:

- giving the spouse an interest in the family home;

- providing an initial preferential share of the intestate estate (ranging from $0 to $200,000 across the country);

- protection under family law, such as in Ontario.

Table 8.1 Summary of Provincial Intestacy Rules	
Surviving spouse with no children	100% of residue of the estate goes to the spouse.
Surviving spouse with one child	Spouse receives preferential share of the residue, if there is one, plus half of the residue of the estate; the other half goes to the child.
Surviving spouse with more than one child	*All provinces except Manitoba*: Spouse receives preferential share of the residue, if there is one, plus one-third of the residue; the children share the remaining two-thirds. *Manitoba*: Spouse receives preferential share of the residue, if there is one, plus half of the residue of the estate; the other half goes to the children.
No spouse, and one or more surviving children	The children share the residue equally.
No spouse, no children, surviving parents	*All provinces except Quebec*: The deceased's parents share the residue of the estate. *Quebec*: Half of the residue goes to the parents and half to any surviving brothers and sisters.
No spouse, no children, no surviving parents	*All provinces except Quebec*: All living brothers and sisters of the deceased share the residue equally. If no brother or sisters are living, all nieces or nephews share the residue equally. *Quebec*: All living brothers, sisters, nieces, and nephews share equally.
No living blood relatives	Estate goes to the provincial government.

Although these distributions may be appropriate for the most basic of estates, they usually involve the payment of additional fees and delays in settling the estate. They also may represent a distribution to family members that the deceased might not have intended. This formula currently does not adequately cover the family situation for individuals:

• living in common-law relationships;

• in second marriages;

• in same-sex relationships;

• with children from a previous marriage or born outside of marriage;

• with children with special needs or circumstances;

- who do not want the provincial public trustee and guardian managing assets on behalf of minor beneficiaries;

- who do not want their children to receive the entire inheritance as soon as they reach the age of majority (age 18 or 19);

- who want to do tax planning;

- who want to ensure their spouse receives the entire estate;

- who want to leave money to charity.

Pointing out the limitations of the intestacy rules will often motivate clients to make an appointment to have their will prepared.

4.0   The Will

Every client should prepare a will and power of attorney documents. To protect yourself, you should put your recommendations to prepare these documents in writing, particularly if the client is unwilling or unable to act on them.

The will outlines the deceased's instructions for:

- the choice of an executor[1] who will settle the deceased's financial affairs and;

- how the assets that flow into the deceased's estate are to be distributed after death.

There are three formats for a will:

- A will written entirely in the testator's (the person making the will) own handwriting and signed. This is called a **holograph** will.

- A will prepared using a pre-printed form or generated using computer software and signed in front of two witnesses (not valid in some provinces).

- A formal will prepared by a lawyer or (in Quebec and British Columbia) a notary and signed in front of two witnesses.

The witnesses should not be people who are mentioned in the will. They should be independent third parties. If a witness is also a beneficiary under the will, the courts can disallow the inheritance, citing "undue influence."

Although anyone in Canada can prepare a will, lawyers are professionals with professional liability insurance. As a wealth manager, you cannot comment on the

---

[1]   In Ontario, the executor is formally referred to as the "administrator of the an estate with a will"; in Quebec, as the liquidator.

wording of a will, nor can you prepare a will on behalf of a client. However, you should ask to see the will and ask your clients to explain their estate plan goals and objectives.

4.1   Assets Covered by a Will and Assets Outside the Estate

Assets covered by the will include those registered:

- in the sole name of the deceased;

- in joint tenancy, whereby each owner has an undivided interest in the asset or property;

- in the name of the deceased's estate.

Not all of the deceased's assets are distributed according to the wording in the will. Assets that do not flow through the estate include:

- those for which there is a named beneficiary, such as a life insurance policy or RRSP;

- those that have been gifted before death;

- those for which the owners are registered as joint tenants with rights of survivorship;

- those held in a living (inter vivos) trust;

- business interests covered by a buy/sell agreement;

- assets covered by a pre-nuptial or co-habitation agreement.

Although these assets are distributed outside the instructions in the will, the estate may still be responsible for paying the final taxes on death.

In considering the distribution of the estate, clients should consider all their assets, not just those covered by the will, so that the estate plan produces the desired results.

4.2   Reviewing the Will to Ensure it Meets the Client's Needs

Some clients think of the distribution of their estate in terms of the before-tax value of the assets. However, they usually want each beneficiary to receive an equal benefit from the estate, after all the taxes and fees have been paid. This goal may not be achieved if the client does not disclose all of his or her assets or has not made a proper estate plan.

Suppose a client, David Napier, wants his entire estate to be distributed equally between his two daughters, Eleanor and Jacqueline. At present, his estate "plan" looks like this:

- His will states that everything is to be divided equally between his two daughters.

- His RRIF, worth $300,000, names Eleanor as beneficiary.

- His life insurance policy, worth $200,000 names Jacqueline as beneficiary. Jacqueline has assured her father that she will use the insurance money to pay the taxes on the estate.

- His investment account, worth $300,000, names Jacqueline joint tenant with rights of survivorship (adjusted cost base $100,000), at the time Jacqueline made joint tenant, they neglected to report potential tax event.(50% of the account in each name)

- A house worth $300,000.

- The executor is an old family friend.

The executor is responsible for making sure the estate pays the deceased's final taxes. The house is the only asset that will flow into the estate and be distributed according to the will. The other assets flow to the daughters outside the will's instructions.

When David dies, Eleanor receives $300,000 from the RRIF. Jacqueline receives $200,000 from the life insurance policy. She may decide to keep it, without using it to pay the taxes. She also gets the investment account worth $300,000.

The house is sold. The $300,000 from the sale would go into the estate. If Jacqueline keeps the money from the life insurance policy, then the proceeds from the sale of the house must be used to pay the taxes of about $230,000 ($150,000 on the RRIF and $80,000 on the taxable capital gains on the investment account), leaving $70,000 to divide between the two daughters. In the end,

Eleanor would receive $335,000 ($300,000 + $35,000)

Jacqueline would receive $535,000 ($200,000 + $300,000 + $35,000).

This is not the outcome David had in mind. To make matters worse (from a planning perspective), this estate plan does not consider that the value of the RRIF and investment account will change, due to market conditions and any amounts the client may spend or save.

When you walk a client through the likely outcomes of an estate plan, they may realize that their current plan will not create the result they want. You will, however, need to be very tactful in pointing out that expecting family members to carry out unwritten instructions may sometimes create unforeseen outcomes.

Although there is often more than one way to design an estate plan to meet the goals of the client, here are a couple of solutions that would provide David with a more equitable estate distribution.

Solution #1: Change the beneficiary on the life insurance to "estate," so that the money will flow into the estate on death to pay the income tax bill.

This is a simple change and is better than the original arrangement, but it does not take into account the fact that the value of the RRIF and investment account will vary over time. It still will not ensure an equal after-tax distribution.

Solution #2: Change the beneficiaries on the life insurance and the RRIF to "estate" and register the investment account in David's name only.

These steps will ensure that all the client's assets flow into the estate. The taxes and fees will be paid out of the estate and the residue remaining could then be distributed equally between Eleanor and Jacqueline. Unfortunately, these steps will increase the cost of probating the will, since the value of the life insurance, RRIF, and investment account are now covered by the will. There could also be possible creditor challenges against the assets in the estate. But if David's over-riding priority is to ensure an equal, after-tax distribution of the estate, no matter what the value of the assets, he may consider the cost of probate relatively insignificant.

All the client's estate planning documents should point in the same direction. When clients are transferring assets to a second or third generation, they should understand the effect of taxes and the changing market values on different types of assets and the ultimate after-tax distribution of their estate.

It is not your job to comment on the legal wording in the will, but you can help a client understand the document. If you spot something in the will that doesn't look quite right, you can recommend that your client check it out with a lawyer.

When you review a client's will, ask yourself the following questions. If you notice any contradictions or issues that have not been dealt with, you can refer the client to a lawyer.

1. Was the will prepared or reviewed by a lawyer?
2. Does it meet the family obligations of the client?
3. Has a backup executor been named?
4. Should a corporate executor be named?
5. How long ago was the will prepared?
6. Have there been any changes in the client's circumstances since the will was prepared?
7. Has it been witnessed?
8. Are the witnesses named in the will?
9. Was the will prepared in the province where the client resides?
10. Has the client asked the named executor/guardian/trustee if they are willing and able to do the job?
11. Do the instructions in the will complement or contradict accounts with beneficiary designations or joint ownership?
12. Does the client understand all the implications of the will?

4.3   Special Clauses in the Will

A will indicates who is to get what and who the executor will be, but additional clauses may be added to:

- give more powers to the executor for administering and investing the assets in the estate;

- appoint guardians for minor beneficiaries;

- establish testamentary trusts;

- enable the executor to make decisions about tax planning on behalf of the deceased and the estate;

- specify compensation for the executor;

- cover various eventualities, such as the client and his or her spouse dying at the same time, or the executor dying before the client dies.

4.4   The Executor (Liquidator in Quebec)

Clients may have trouble getting their wills prepared because they do not know who should be executor of their estate. Clients should appoint a primary executor (or two co-executors) and a backup executor in case the first executor dies before the client does or is unwilling or unable to perform the duties when the client dies.

Some clients ask their spouse or other family members, a close friend, or a professional trustee to perform this important role. The potential executor should:

- be willing and able to do the job when the time comes;

- have the expertise to manage the estate assets, including any business interests, and to deal with Revenue Canada;

- be able to deal with the family members fairly and objectively;

- be able to act for several years if trusts are set up in the will;

- know enough about the testator's financial affairs and the instructions in the will to make an informed decision;

- live in a convenient location (although a non-resident of Canada may be able to do the job, they may be required to post a bond or face other legal or tax implications).

Before anyone accepts the role of executor, he or she should be aware that being an executor carries the potential for personal liability if the executor fails to inform a spouse of his or her legal entitlement under provincial family law or fails to pay the full amount of tax due to Revenue Canada. Some executors wait until they have requested and received a tax clearance certificate from Revenue Canada.

The Wealth Manager as an Executor

Some clients may ask you, their wealth manager, if you would be willing to be the executor of their estate, since you already know the financial details of their lives. They may see you as the best person they know to take on the job. Your answer will depend on your personal willingness to take on the job, the advice of your compliance department, and your relationship with the client.

Your duties as an executor will take time away from your primary role as a financial advisor. You would be responsible for wrapping up the deceased's financial affairs, including everything from arranging the funeral and cancelling magazine subscriptions, to dealing with the Canada Pension Plan and Revenue Canada. Executors must deal with Revenue Canada, lawyers, former employers, accountants, creditors, business valuators, and other interested parties.

Some firms do not allow their wealth managers to accept the role of executor and trustee for their clients. At other firms, the wealth manager may be able to act as the executor, but may not earn commissions from the account while acting in this role. The account would likely be treated as a PRO (non-client) account and subject to greater scrutiny by compliance.

If you agree to be an executor, you will need to manage the beneficiaries' expectations. They will likely want the estate to be settled faster than is possible. If you hope to continue to manage the assets once the beneficiaries receive their inheritance, be sure to take the time to explain the process to them so they will understand what you have to do.

Corporate Executors

The corporate executor might be a trust company, a lawyer, an accountant, or other professional. A corporate trustee may be appropriate in the following situations:

- the financial situation is extremely complex;
- there are family conflicts that will affect the situation;
- the estate will take a long time to settle;
- assets of the estate will be held in trust for several years;
- the beneficiaries may struggle to control certain assets;
- no family member or friend is willing to accept the role.

The client hires the expertise of the corporate trustee to set up a formal investment strategy for the assets in the estate, deal with all beneficiaries impartially, and provide trust services for as long as they are required. The cost of hiring a corporate trustee is the same as naming a family member to do the job, although family members may waive their fee.

In some situations, it may be advisable to name a professional trustee and a family member to act as co-executors. The corporate trustee can provide the professional services and the family member can contribute the family view. In this case, the corporate trustee's fee is likely to remain the same, whether they are named as the sole executor or as a co-executor with a family member. Some corporate executors will not take on the role for a relatively small estate.

The Powers of the Executor

The executor's powers may be broad or very limited. The executor may have the legal authority to:

- distribute assets "in specie" or in kind, to beneficiaries;

- purchase assets for the estate;

- determine if and when estate assets are to be sold;

- make investments they deem appropriate for the estate;

- borrow on behalf of the estate;

- consult and employ agents, including accountants, lawyers, professional trustees, or financial advisors and pay them reasonable compensation out of the estate (not out of the executor's fee).

The executor's investment powers come from the will, and if the will does not assign the executor any specific investment powers, they will be assigned by the provincial *Trustee Act*. Some acts list the allowable investments. Others require the trustee to follow the prudent investor rule, or prudent investor standard of care.

Executors may also be given powers to use their discretion to make tax decisions under the *Income Tax Act* that would benefit the estate, but that are not specified in the provincial *Trustee Act*. These might include the power to:

- make an RRSP contribution to a spousal RRSP before March 1 following the year of death;

- transfer assets to a spouse at a certain cost base and defer the tax on the related capital gains;

- determine which assets, if any, are to be held in a spousal trust.

The Legal List

If the province follows a legal list, allowable investments that can be made by an executor might include:

- federal or provincial government and municipal securities;

- first mortgages for real estate in Canada;

- bank or trust company guaranteed investment certificates;

- bank or term deposits;

- bonds of corporations that have paid annual dividends according to a minimum requirement;

- corporate shares (preferred and common), provided that the dividend paid meets the specific minimum requirement.

Traditionally, the investments in the legal list were considered to be "safe," but as interest rates and dividend yields have fallen, the beneficiaries under some trusts have had to deal with falling incomes. The legal list of investments is conservative, and although it may keep an executor or trustee from speculating, it may not meet the needs of the beneficiaries.

In Quebec, estate administrator may have "simple administrative powers" which allow them to do only what is necessary to preserve the property, or "full administrative powers," which allow them to make investments designed to increase the value of the trust assets. The Quebec estate administrator can invest, according to the *Quebec Civil Code*, in investments for which the "yield and anticipated capital gains are suggested by prevailing economic conditions." The investments include federal, provincial, and municipal government securities, some corporate debt, some real estate, up to 5% of the trust's assets in shares of common or preferred stock, and mutual funds, as long as the portfolio consists primarily of "presumed sound investments."

Prudent Investor Standard of Care

A number of provinces have moved to the prudent investor standard of care test for the investments an executor or trustee selects. Under the prudent investor rule, the investments in an estate or trust must take into account:

- general economic conditions;

- the effect of inflation or deflation;

- tax consequences of the investment strategy;

- expected interest and dividend income and capital appreciation;

- the purpose of any special asset in the trust;

- the need for liquidity, income, or the preservation of capital.

An executor or trustee following this standard of care should have documentation showing that all these factors were taken into account. The documentation would be similar to an investment policy statement, which takes into consideration many of the same factors.

Executor Compensation

Executors are entitled to receive compensation for their work as an executor, whether they are a family member or a corporate executor. The will might specify the compensation to be paid to the executor or the fee may be based on generally accepted norms.

Generally, an executor is compensated based on:

- the value of the assets that flow into the estate (1% to 2.5%);

- the amount of capital distributed (1% to 2.5%);

- income earned by the estate (1% to 5%);

- an amount for being the trustee of a testamentary trust.

The compensation must bear some relation to the work done. Suppose the estate asset is a house worth $500,000. If the executor charged $25,000 for settling the estate, in addition to the fees that were paid to the real estate agent for selling the house, the beneficiaries could challenge the executor fees as being excessive.

4.5   Appointing Guardians for Minor Beneficiaries

Many people prepare a will for the first time after the birth of their first child. The parents want to name someone to assume legal responsibility for the child if both parents die before the child becomes a legal adult. Sometimes they have strong wishes about who should or should not assume that role.

Under the law, the guardian named in the will becomes the temporary guardian of the child or children, and must apply to the provincial court to obtain permanent legal custody. Although the courts are not required to grant permanent custody to the person named in a will, they generally do so, unless there is a good reason not to.

In addition to naming a guardian, the testator might also leave a bequest to that person in recognition of the responsibility they are taking on.

4.6   The Common Disaster Clause

The common disaster, or survivorship clause, provides instructions in the event a client and his or her spouse die close together, such as in a car accident. The will usually states that one spouse must outlive the other for a certain period of time (often 25 or 30 days) before they are entitled to any benefits under the other's will. This provision is designed to minimize probate fees. Suppose a woman died on the first of the month and her husband died on the 15th. Without this clause, the estate of the wife would be settled and any probate fees would be paid before the assets are transferred to the estate of the husband. When the husband died, probate fees would be charged a second time on the same assets.

If clients want to ensure that their family and their spouse's family will benefit equally, their two wills would each state that each family is to receive 50% of the residue of the estate in the event of a common disaster.

4.7   Per Stirpes vs. Per Capita

Most clients leave their estate to their children. Occasionally, a child dies before the parents do. If this happens, the client must consider what they want done with their estate.

If clients leave their children an inheritance on a "per capita" basis, the child must be alive when the parent dies to receive their inheritance. For example, Denis Nagorny has three children. If all three children are alive when Denis dies and the residue of the estate is $300,000, each child would receive $100,000. But if one child dies before Denis dies, the surviving two children would each receive $150,000.

However, Denis may want the inheritance his dead child would have received to be paid to his grandchild or grandchildren. His will would state that the inheritance is to be paid on a "per stirpes" basis. (*Stirpes* means "root" or "stem" in Latin.) In this case, the surviving two children would each receive $100,000 and the remaining $100,000 would be paid to the children of the deceased child.

4.8   Restrictions on Testamentary Freedom

Clients can do just about anything they want for their estate plan with two exceptions:

- They cannot cut a family member out of their will if that person is financially dependent on them at the time of their death.

- They must provide for their spouse according to the minimum required in the province they reside in at the time of death.

If the will fails to provide adequate, ongoing support and maintenance to a financially dependent family member, that person, or his or her legal representative, can apply to the courts for a ruling for continuing support from the estate. In some provinces, a family member is defined as a spouse or child. In other provinces, the definition of family member extends to parents and grandparents. The judgement might include a lump-sum payment to the dependent or ongoing support from the estate, which could effectively freeze the distribution of the estate to any other beneficiaries.

Table 8.2	Provincial Legislation Governing the Inheritance of Dependent Family Members
Alberta	Family Relief Act
British Columbia	Wills Variation Act
Manitoba	Dependant's Relief Act
New Brunswick	Provisions for Dependants Act
Newfoundland	Family Relief Act
Nova Scotia	Testator's Family Maintenance
Ontario	Succession Law Reform Act
Prince Edward Island	Dependants of a Deceased Person Relief Act
Quebec	Code of Civil Procedure
Saskatchewan	Dependants' Relief Act

4.9   Amending or Replacing a Will

Every two or three years, and after any significant event, the will and the estate plan should be reviewed. A significant event might include the loss of a job, a move to another province, the birth or death of a family member, marriage, separation, or divorce. Changes in the provincial legislation relating to estate planning or changes to the income tax rules could also trigger a review.

A client's will can be updated in one of two ways:

- by adding an amendment called a **codicil**, to an existing will;

- preparing a completely new will, which revokes the previous will.

If the change needed is relatively simple and the original will is current, then a codicil would do. Preparing a codicil may be cheaper than preparing an entirely new will. The formal codicil is filed with the original will and needs two witnesses. But if the original will is completely out of date, or if the changes will affect many different clauses in the will, a client might do better to prepare an entirely new will so the instructions are clear.

Once a new will is completed and properly signed, a client should destroy the older will.

5.0   Spousal Rights

Family law governs spousal entitlement unless there is a valid marriage or co-habitation contract. The laws vary across the country, but all share the understanding that a spouse has certain basic legal rights. In Quebec, family law is covered by civil law; in the rest of the country by common law. Clients who move from one province to another should ensure that their estate plan conforms to that province's family laws.

A spouse may be entitled to at least what he or she would have received if there had been a divorce, or to minimum rights to the matrimonial home (which could include the principal family residence as well as any vacation properties). If the will does not provide the spouse with at least the minimum to which he or she is entitled, the spouse can file a claim against the estate, rather than accepting the distribution according to the will.

Under the *Family Law Act* of Ontario, divorcing spouses are entitled to receive an equalization of "net family assets." This also applies on the death of a spouse. If a surviving spouse is not named as the sole beneficiary under a will, and if the estate distribution, plus any death benefit paid under any life insurance policies, leaves him or her less than 50% of the value of the net family assets, the spouse has the legal right to accept the inheritance under the will, or to apply for the equalization payment under the *Family Law Act*.

Spouses may accept an estate plan that provides them with less than their legal entitlement, if, for example:

- the will leaves them more than they require for the rest of their life;

- they have significant assets of their own;

- the family business interest is being left to the children;

- a significant charitable donation will be made with resulting tax savings.

To ensure that a client's estate plan will not be challenged, the couple could prepare a marriage contract along with their wills. As a minimum, the clients' lawyer will advise both parties:

- to act in good faith;

- to disclose their total financial situation to the other;

- to understand their rights and any entitlements they are waiving;

- to obtain independent legal counsel.

5.1   Ongoing Spousal or Child Support

If a client is divorced and paying spousal support or child support, the divorce agreement will indicate whether or not death releases him or her from these obligations. Some agreements explicitly state that death releases the divorced spouse from these obligations and some indicate that the obligation continues against the assets of the estate. The agreement may also require divorced clients to carry sufficient life insurance to cover their ongoing support obligations.

Some older agreements may be silent on this issue. Clients should seek a legal opinion from a family lawyer to determine their exposure. It is possible their estate could face a challenge from an ex-spouse and be required to continue to make payments until the death of the ex-spouse. This could freeze some or all of the assets in the deceased's estate.

5.2   Common-Law and Same-Sex Spouses

Under current laws, common-law and same-sex spouses have no property rights under either intestacy laws or family laws. Common-law spouses may be able to successfully argue for ongoing support as a dependent, depending on the length of the relationship and whether or not children are involved. Clients can avoid messy legal battles by ensuring they make adequate provisions for common-law or same-sex spouses in their estate planning.

6.0   Power of Attorney

The power of attorney document allows clients to decide who will make decisions for them if they are alive but unable to make decisions for themselves. The person named as attorney does not have to be a lawyer and may be the same person named as the executor in the will. The person may be referred to as an attorney, a representative, or a mandatory.

Unless the attorney's powers are limited or restricted by the power of attorney document, he or she can do anything the person could have done for himself or herself, except estate planning. In other words, the attorney cannot write a will on a client's behalf.

In all provinces except Quebec, the power of attorney must contain wording so that it will continue in the event of mental incapacity. Without this wording, the power of attorney document would be revoked if the client becomes mentally incapacitated, a time when the client needs the attorney to speak on his or her behalf.

In Quebec, a Mandate Given in Anticipation of Incapacity allows a client to name another person or trust company to act as the mandatory to make decisions if the client becomes mentally incompetent. Before the mandatory can act on a client's behalf, an application is made to the courts to verify the extent of the individual's incapacity (which may include a psychological and medical assessment).

The power of attorney document can cover finances, personal care, and instructions for organ donation. It may also incorporate the wording for a living will. The mandatory can be given:

- **simple administration powers** to preserve property using a limited group of investments, such as bank deposits, shares, bonds, and investment certificates;

- **full administration powers**, whereby the mandatory can invest in a wider range of investments and selling property, without court approval.

If a client does not prepare a power of attorney document and becomes unable to make his or her own decisions, the provincial public guardian will step in to protect the individual and his or her assets.

7.0   Probate

Not every will needs to be probated. In Quebec, there is no probate. Probate allows the executor to deal with third parties who want court verification that the will is valid and that the executor has the authority to transfer the ownership of assets. Probate may be required for:

- financial institutions (although they may waive the requirement for probate on small accounts);

- a privately held company that is being sold to an outside owner;

- creditors;

- transfers of real estate.

If the will is considered invalid (or one can not be located), the deceased's estate will be treated as if he or she had died intestate.

Provincial probate fees vary from 0 to 1.5% and are based on the value of the assets that are distributed according to the instructions in the will.

The will is probated in the jurisdiction in which a client normally resides. If the client was on holiday at the time of his or her death, the estate would be settled based on the location of his or her principal residence. If the client did not live in Canada but held some Canadian real estate, the will would likely have to be probated in Canada to settle that property.

Table 8.3 Current Probate Fees		
Province	Fees	Maximum
Alberta	$25 for first $10,000 increasing to $6,000 for estates over $1 million	None
British Columbia	No fee for estate under $10,000 $208 for estates between $10,000 and $25,000 $6 for each $1,000 from $25,000 to $50,000 $14 for each $1,000 over $50,000	None
Manitoba	$50 for first $10,000 and $6 for each $1,000 over $10,000	None
New Brunswick	Up to $100 for the first $20,000 and $5 for each $1,000 over $20,000	None
Newfoundland	$75 plus $5 for each additional $1,000	None
Nova Scotia	$75 for first $10,000 increasing to $800 for estate valued up to $200,000, plus $5 for each $1,000 over $200,000	None
Ontario	$5 for each $1,000 up to $50,000 and $15 for each $1,000 over $50,000	None
Prince Edward Island	$50 for the first $10,000 increasing to $400 for estates of $100,000 and $4 for each $1,000 over $100,000	None
Quebec	$0 for notarial will	$0
Saskatchewan	$7 for each $1,000	None
Source: Sandra E. Foster, *You Can't Take It With You: The Common-Sense Guide to Estate Planning for Canadians*, 3rd edition, John Wiley and Sons, 1999.		

Probate fees, or taxes, are based on the value of assets that flow through the will. The basic strategies to minimize these fees involve keeping as much of the estate out of the will as possible. However, some strategies cost more than probating a will.

The strategies to reduce the cost of probating a will include:

- gifting assets;

- registering assets as joint tenants with rights of survivorship;

- naming beneficiaries on registered plans and life insurance;

- creating a trust.

7.1 Reducing Probate Fees by Gifting Assets

If clients make a gift of cash, assets, or property while they are alive, then the asset is not included in the probate fee calculation, because the deceased did not own it at the time of death. If the gift is made to a minor child or a spouse, attribution rules must be followed. (The attribution rules can be found in Chapter 7, Table 7.1.)

In Canada, an adult can make a gift to an adult child or children without being affected by the attribution rules. For example, if a parent wants to write a cheque for $25,000 to an adult child, there are no tax consequences to the parent. Other assets can be given to adult children without the attribution rules, but if there are capital gains at the time the gift is made, the asset is deemed to have been disposed of at fair market value, even if there was no actual sale. For example, John Martin wants to give his adult daughter CIBC shares that cost him $1,000 and are now worth $12,000. According to Revenue Canada, if the value of the property when the gift is made is greater than the value of the property when it was acquired, there is a profit. In this case income tax would be due on $11,000 of profit. If John had given his daughter $12,000 cash, he would not have had to pay tax on it unless he sold the shares to raise the cash. John will have to report and pay the tax on the capital gain in the year he made the gift.

Some clients make gifts while they are alive that have nothing to do with the distribution of their estate on death. These gifts are something they want that beneficiary to receive in addition to what they would receive under the will. Other clients want to advance a beneficiary a portion of his or her inheritance, but do not want this gift to result in the beneficiary receiving more than he or she would have under the will after the client's death.

For example, Donna Merrick has advanced her grandson Stephen $50,000. If Donna wants this amount to be considered as part of Stephen's inheritance in the will, she should include a provision in the will about the advance. The legal term for this type of advance is **ademption**. If there is a provision against ademption, Stephen receives the full share of his inheritance stated in the will, not the inheritance minus the $50,000 previously received.

7.2   Reducing Probate Fees by Registering Assets as Joint Tenants with Rights of Survivorship

When assets are registered as "joint tenants with rights of survivorship" (JTWROS) they do not become part of the estate. On the death of the person who holds title to the assets, ownership automatically transfers to the surviving tenant. Financial institutions require proof of death before they will re-register an account. Quebec does not have this form of asset ownership.

Although this is a relatively commonplace strategy, it is often misused and it can be risky. To start with, as soon as another person is named joint owner of an asset, that person has the rights of ownership, even if that person does not consider the asset to be really his or hers. If one owner goes bankrupt or gets a divorce, the assets registered jointly could be become involved in the bankruptcy or divorce proceedings.

Assets registered as JTWROS do not replace the need for a power of attorney document. If one of the owners becomes mentally incapacitated, the other does not have automatic rights to the account. If there is no power of attorney document for finances (or mandate in Quebec), the province's public trustee and guardian could freeze the incapacitated person's share of the account unless there is a valid power of attorney document.

Although clients want to reduce probate fees, it is important to help them see the cost of probate in relation to the overall costs of settling the estate. Clients should be aware that once they give away assets, the gift is irrevocable and they no longer have exclusive control of that asset.

Clients who are considering JTWROS registration should also understand the following issues.

- **Taxes**: Re-registering an asset as JTWROS involves transferring it from one name to joint names. In the eyes of Revenue Canada, this is considered to be a deemed disposition of a portion of the asset at fair market value. If the joint tenant is a spouse or common-law spouse, the change in ownership takes place at the adjusted cost base and no taxes need to be paid. But if the person is not a spouse or common-law spouse, taxes would be based on 50% of the value of the asset (if there is one owner before and two owners after re-registration). Taxes must be paid on any capital gains incurred in the year of the transfer.

- **True transfer of ownership**: Clients who want to reduce their probate fees or taxes might think they could just re-register the asset into joint names without transferring the rights of probate. Then, as long as everyone understood that it's been done just to get around probate and the other person is not really the "owner," why not? If there was no beneficial transfer of ownership of the property until after death, the asset would still be considered to be the asset of the deceased and its market value would be included in the probate fee calculation.

- **Legal interpretations of ownership**: Some elderly or disabled clients might want a son or daughter to be able to do paperwork and make decisions about a particular asset. Instead of using a power of attorney document, they might try to use JTWROS to give the other person signing authority on the account, but without assigning true joint ownership. In this case, it is not clear that the asset would necessarily be left to the son or daughter after the death of the parent. In a court case in Western Canada, the other siblings successful argued that their parent had not intended to use JTWROS to give extra benefits to one child, and the asset was distributed among the deceased's children according to the instructions in the will.

- **JTWROS vs. spousal trust**: Assets held in trust are not distributed through the estate and are therefore not subject to probate fees. Clients who want to set up a spousal trust to manage the assets on behalf of their spouse, protect an inheritance for children from a previous marriage, or use the testamentary trust for income splitting after their death, should not register those assets as JTWROS. To get assets into a testamentary trust, they need to flow into the will to be covered by the wording of the will. (See Section 10.0 for more information on trusts.)

- **Effects on the third generation**: When clients register an asset as JTWROS with their adult children, they generally assume they will die before their children do. Suppose Rita Marshall has three children, and each child has two children. If Rita dies first, the asset would be shared equally by the three children. But if one of the adult children dies before Rita, and Rita then dies before updating her will, only the two surviving children would share the asset. The children of the deceased adult child would not receive the inheritance Rita intended for them.

While registering assets as joint tenants with rights of survivorship seems to be a simple procedure, it may have undesirable results. In certain circumstances, the use of inter vivos trust, life insurance, or outright gifts would be a better way to avoid probate fees.

7.3   Reducing Probate Fees by Naming Beneficiaries on Registered Plans and Life Insurance

Naming a beneficiary on a registered plan is thought to reduce probate fees. Certainly, if the RRSP is with a life insurance company, the proceeds do not form part of the estate and are not included in the probate fee calculation. For RRSPs held with other financial institutions, the probate issue varies from province to province. For example, in British Columbia, an RRSP with a named beneficiary is not part of the estate.

Many financial institutions are reluctant to name multiple beneficiaries on a registered plan. Although this may seem to be a simple request by a client, designating multiple beneficiaries does not give the plan's trustee any guidance about what to do if one of the beneficiaries dies before the client does. Should the deceased beneficiary's share be reallocated to the surviving beneficiary, or should it become part of the estate of the original owner of the plan? All trustees want to avoid legal issues. But if there are no clear instructions about beneficiaries, the trustee may have to get written consent from everyone who has a claim to the RRSP proceeds. This is why financial institutions tend not to allow multiple beneficiary designations. RRSP and RRIFs set up with life insurance companies, however, do allow for contingent beneficiaries.

7.4   Reducing Probate Fees by Creating a Trust

Assets held in a trust are not subject to probate fees or taxes, because the individual does not own the assets, the trust does. The trust may have wording in it that states how assets are to be distributed, similar to a will.

Assets can be transferred into a living trust, which distributes assets after death, without probate fees. However, the cost of setting up the trust and the ongoing trustee and accounting fees might end up costing more than probate would.

Some couples use a testamentary trust in the following way. On the death of the first spouse, the assets are probated under the will and are transferred into a spousal testamentary trust. The testamentary trust describes how the assets are to be distributed after the death of the second spouse. Because the assets are covered by the instructions in the testamentary trust, and not the instructions in a will, when the second spouse dies, there are no probate charges. As an added bonus, the use of the testamentary trust may provide some opportunities for income splitting.

8.0   Estimating the Client's Final Tax Liability

Canadians do not pay estate taxes. But under the *Income Tax Act*, when someone dies, his or her RRSP or RRIF is treated as if it had been cashed in (including any amount withdrawn under the Lifelong Learning program or the Home Buyers Plan). All capital assets are deemed to have been sold at fair market value immediately before death. The tax owing must be paid as part of the deceased's final tax return. There are a few exemptions on the final tax return:

- The deceased's principal residence is exempt from capital gains tax.

- Certain small businesses and farm properties are exempt from capital gains tax.

- Registered plans (RRSPs and RRIFs) left to a spouse or common-law spouse are not taxed. There are also opportunities for tax deferral if an RRSP or RRIF is left to a financially dependent minor beneficiary.

- Appreciated property and assets with unrealized capital gains left to a spouse, common-law spouse, or a qualifying spousal trust is exempt from capital gains until the surviving spouse disposes of the assets during his/her lifetime, or at the time of death.

- The value of the death benefit on a life insurance policy is tax-free.

A beneficiary who acquires an asset from the estate is assumed to have received it with an adjusted cost base equal to the fair market value immediately before the death of the original owner. A spouse or common-law spouse can assume the original adjusted cost base.

On depreciating assets, such as a building, equipment or machinery, the deceased is deemed to have disposed of that property at the time of his or her death. This will result in a terminal loss or the recapture of the depreciation. If the fair market value of a depreciating asset is greater than the undepreciated capital cost, it is also necessary to include the recapture of the capital cost allowance on the final tax return.

Estate planning to minimize the tax liability begins with estimating how much tax would be due when a client dies. It is helpful to draw up two sets of numbers for your clients, showing the tax liability in the following situations:

- if they died tomorrow, and left everything to their spouse or to a particular beneficiary;

- if they lived to a reasonable old age, and left everything to their spouse or to a particular beneficiary.

Although leaving the RRSP, RRIF, and assets with unrealized capital gains to a spouse or common-law spouse can result in future tax deferral, clients may not want to leave everything to the spouse if they have business interests or children from a previous marriage.

Estimating a client's future tax liability means making assumptions about:

- the rate of return the investments will earn;

- the amount that would be withdrawn from registered assets or investments over the client's lifetime.

It may be useful to have a client's accountant estimate these numbers, particularly if the estate is complex.

9.0   Techniques to Defer or Reduce Taxes

Taxpayers are allowed to arrange their financial affairs, in life and in death, so they pay the least amount required by law. Estate planning can help to defer the tax liability for as long as possible. However, a more important goal is to minimize the tax a taxpayer pays over his or her lifetime. This means considering the tax bracket a client is in today, in retirement, and at the time of death, as well as the tax brackets of his or her beneficiaries.

9.1   Leaving Assets with Unrealized Capital Gains to a Spouse

Assets with unrealized capital gains can be rolled over tax-free to a spouse, common-law spouse, or spousal trust. The asset is transferred to a spouse at the adjusted cost base of the deceased and no tax is paid until the spouse sells the asset or dies.

If the deceased has any unused capital losses, the executor may want to realize enough capital gains before transferring those assets to the spouse to take advantage of the capital losses.

9.2 Naming a Spouse or Common-law Spouse as Beneficiary on RRSPs or RRIFs[2]

There are tax advantages to naming a spouse or common-law spouse as the beneficiary on an RRSP or RRIF. When the original owner of the RRSP or RRIF dies, the full amount of the plan is transferred to the surviving spouse's RRSP or RRIF. If the RRSP names the estate *and* the surviving spouse as the beneficiaries, the executor and the surviving spouse can request that the RRSP be transferred to the spouse.

The beneficiary under a RRIF is similar to the beneficiary of an RRSP, but there is one additional option. A RRIF beneficiary may be designated as a "successor annuitant" and may continue to receive the RRIF payments without having to transfer the RRIF to a new account.

9.3 Naming Financially Dependent Children as Beneficiaries on RRSPs and RRIFs

Parents with a financially dependent child or grandchild under 18 can name the child as the beneficiary. When the annuitant dies, the proceeds from the RRSP or RRIF are used to purchase an annuity that matures when the child turns 18. For example, if the child is 8, the annuity would have an 10-year term.

The income from the annuity is taxed in the child's hands, which is normally at low tax rate. Naming a child as the beneficiary could be a way to put funds in the child's name, possibility for post-secondary education, without paying tax at the surviving spouse's tax rate.

Of course, the annuity proceeds should be paid into a testamentary trust on behalf of the minor child. Otherwise, the public trustee would manage the payments until the child reaches 18, at which time they would be transferred to the child.

When the child turns 18, clients should consider changing the beneficiary on the RRSP or RRIF back to the spouse or common-law spouse to get the maximum tax deferral.

Under certain circumstances, the RRSP can be transferred to an RRSP for a child who is a dependent because of a disability. Although this offers tax savings, it is important to think through the implications of putting the money in the hands of a child who may not be able to manage it.

---

[2] Also applies to same-sex partners

9.4   RRSPs on Marriage Breakdown and Death

In the event of a separation or divorce, RRSP and RRIF funds may be transferred to the other spouse's RRSP, RRIF, or RPP on a tax-deferred basis as long as such transfers are governed by a court judgement or written separation agreement. Attribution rules do not apply in the event of a marriage breakdown, thereby giving contributors access to the funds.

In the event of a planholder's death, RRSPs (matured or otherwise) can be transferred to a spouse on a tax-deferred basis. Most provinces allow the spouse to be named as a beneficiary of the proceeds, either in the plan documentation or in the will.

The tax-deferred transfer of RRSPs between spouses consists of two steps:

- the proceeds are physically transferred to the spouse;

- the spouse shelters the proceeds in his or her own RRSP.

A low-income surviving spouse may carry out only the first step if he or she needs funds for immediate consumption. Both steps may be carried out if the RRSP proceeds flow to the spouse through the estate as a bequest under the will, or as part of the spouse's share in the estate. The estate does not have to declare the RRSP proceeds in its own return if the executor and the spouse file a joint election for the proceeds to be taxed in the spouse's hands.

If the spouse is not the sole beneficiary of the estate, the executor will need to appraise the plan so that other beneficiaries can receive their entitlements in cash or other assets. The liquidation or net realizable value of the plan will likely be significantly different from the face value, because of the deferred tax liability due upon collapse of the plan.

A young surviving spouse may be able to afford to shelter the plan from tax liability for a long time, thereby retaining or increasing its value. However, the face value of the plan may have to be discounted significantly for an older surviving spouse, since the deemed disposition on death will probably occur within a few years.

The estate of the deceased taxpayer can make a contribution to an RRSP of the surviving spouse, provided it is made within 60 days of the end of the year in which the taxpayer died. Such a contribution can often result in significant savings to an estate.

If the planholder is unmarried, the entire lump-sum proceeds are deemed to be part of the deceased's income in the year of his or her death. This outcome can be avoided if the proceeds are left to dependent children or grandchildren. The money will be taxed in their hands, presumably at a lower graduated rate. Dependent recipients can also buy term annuities that will last until they turn 18, thereby resulting in income deferral or income spreading. (Permanently disabled dependent children or grandchildren do not face the 18-year term limitation on the annuity, and can get a full tax-deferred transfer into their own RRSP.)

It is important to seek professional tax advice when drafting one's will so that appropriate bequests are targeted for appropriate individuals. For example, an individual might leave a term deposit to his or her spouse and an RRSP to the children, thereby triggering a tax liability that could have been avoided by arranging the bequests the other way around.

Some people also think that tax liability triggered by an asset will be paid by the recipient of that asset. For example, leaving RRSP proceeds to Jack and the residue of the estate to Jill would result in Jack receiving the gross proceeds of the RRSP, and the estate settling the tax liability at the expense of Jill's residue interest. This may not necessarily be what the person who made the will had in mind. A similar result arises when an individual is given a bequest of an asset (such as an investment portfolio) with significant accrued gains.

9.5 Applying All Unused Capital Losses

Unused capital losses can normally be applied against capital gains only. However, when a taxpayer dies, his or her unused capital losses can be applied against all other types of income reported on the deceased's final tax return or in the year before his or her death.

9.6 Life Insurance

Although life insurance does not defer or reduce the amount of income tax that must be paid on death, it can be used to:

- replace the tax dollars sent to Revenue Canada;

- enhance the value of the estate;

- provide cash to pay the taxes to preserve certain assets in the estate, such as a business or cottage that would otherwise have to be sold.

9.7 Spending More before Death

Although this may seem a rather simple-minded approach to minimizing taxes, you can encourage clients to spend a little more on themselves while they are alive. This would reduce the value of their estate at the time of their death, and possibly their overall tax bill and probate and executor fees.

9.8 Estate Freeze

An estate freeze is one way for a taxpayer to get the $500,000 capital gains exemption for qualified small businesses. The shareholder or related shareholders must hold shares in the corporation and pass the 50% and 90% tests in the two years before the sale of the shares. That is:

- more than 50% of the fair market value of the business assets were used primarily in an active business carried on primarily in Canada (the 50% test), or invested in other small business corporations (or any combination).

- all, or substantially all, of the Canadian-controlled private corporation's assets were used in carrying on active business in Canada (the 90% test),[3] or be shares and debt in other small business corporations(or any combination).

9.9   Farm Properties

A Canadian qualified farm property (including land, a farm partnership, and shares in a family farm corporation) can be transferred to a spouse, children, grandchildren, or great-grandchildren at its adjusted cost base, without triggering taxable capital gains. The farm must be an active farm used primarily for farming and be located in Canada.

A qualified farm may also qualify for the $500,000 capital gains exemption, which will increase the adjusted cost base.

9.10   Falling Market Values after Death

Occasionally, while assets are being held in the estate, their value falls below the value they had when the original owner died. If they do, a tax exception can be used so that the amount of tax paid more closely reflects the actual gains. If the executor sells the investment in the portfolio in the estate's first year at a loss, the loss can be used on the deceased's final tax return.

Suppose an investment portfolio belonging to a client's single aunt was worth $1 million dollars at the time of her death, with an adjusted cost base of $200,000. The taxable capital gain that would have to be included on her final tax return would be $533,280 (66.66% of $800,000). If six months later, the same investment portfolio held in the estate was worth only $800,000, the executor could sell the investments and apply the $200,000 loss to the aunt's final tax return. This would more accurately reflect the value of the estate inherited by the beneficiaries.

---

[3]   For a fuller discussion of estate freezing, see Chapter 10 of the *Professional Financial Planning* textbook published by the Canadian Securities Institute.

10.0 Appropriate Use of Trusts

Although trusts have long been considered a sophisticated estate planning tool, they may not be appropriate for all clients. In estate planning, however, trusts can solve some family needs or be used for tax planning.

The settlor of a trust entrusts assets and property to a trustee on behalf of beneficiaries who are slated to receive income or capital, or both, from the trust.

Trusts can be useful:

- when assets must be managed on behalf of a child or spouse who suffers from disability, mental incapacity, or some other problem that makes it inadvisable to give them money outright;

- for tax planning and some income splitting;

- as part of an estate freeze to realize the $500,000 capital gains exemption available to qualified small businesses;

- to control shares of a corporation by holding them in trust;

- to protect assets from creditors in certain circumstances;

- for planned giving;

- to avoid probate fees;

- to keep the arrangement between the settlor and their beneficiaries confidential.

The wording of a trust document can be as flexible and as creative as a client's needs require.

10.1 Type of Trusts

In estate planning, there are two main types of trusts for Canadian residents in Canada.

- a living, or **inter vivos trust**, where assets are transferred into the trust while the settlor is alive and taxed at the top tax rate;

- a **testamentary trust**, where assets transfer into the trust according the deceased's will after their estate is settled and is taxed at graduated rates;

- a special type of testamentary trust called a **spousal trust**, in which the deceased's spouse is the beneficiary.

The tax implications of trusts were described in Chapter 7, section 4.14.

The Inter Vivos Trust

Any income earned in an inter vivos or living trust is taxed at the top marginal tax rate and the opportunities to split income using a living trust have been reduced over the years.

The attribution rules apply to a living trust. The *Income Tax Act* prevents a taxpayer from using a living trust to move income from his or her own high tax bracket to a taxpayer with a lower tax rate, such as a spouse or minor child. Any income, dividend, or capital gain or loss earned in a trust is attributed to the settlor if the beneficiary of the trust is related to the settlor and is a minor, and the income is not paid out to the minor beneficiary or the minor is not a preferred beneficiary.

However, when the children reach the age of 18, the income does not have to be attributed to the settlor and can be taxed in the name of the adult child. If the adult child has limited income, he or she may pay little or no tax after taking advantage of available tax deductions and credits.

Assets can be put in trust for an adult child if the settlor does not want the child to be able to control the property immediately, but wants the child to be the ultimate beneficiary of that property. For example, when business owners do an estate freeze, they might create shares in the names of their children. But rather than giving the children outright control of those shares, the settlor puts them in a family trust in which the trustees retain control.

Before 1996, an inter vivos trust could classify certain beneficiaries as preferred beneficiaries. Under this arrangement, income earned in the trust could be kept in the trust to grow but it would be taxed as if it had been paid out to the beneficiary. Today, the preferred beneficiary category exists only for beneficiaries who qualify for disability tax credits because of mental or physical disability. The trust income must pay the income to the beneficiary to be taxes at the lower rate. Dividend income and capital gains earned in the trust are eligible for the tax-preferred treatment, even when they are paid out to the beneficiary.

Unrealized capital gains can accumulate in the trust for up to 21 years at a time. Every 21 years the trust must pay tax on the asset as if it had been sold. The trustee must ensure there are enough liquid assets in the trust to pay the tax bill at this point. In some cases, some of the assets of the trust must be sold to pay the tax. In other cases, if the trust document gives the trustee power to make decisions to deal with tax changes, it may be appropriate to distribute some of the trust assets before the 21 years are up.

An inter vivos trust can be set up to ensure the privacy of the settlor and beneficiaries. The contents of a probated will become a matter of public record. If the settlor wishes to leave assets and to keep those assets confidential, he or she might create an inter vivos trust.

The Testamentary Trust

The testamentary trust is created according to the instructions in the deceased's will after the estate is settled. The trust manages the assets on behalf of the income and capital beneficiaries and can be a useful income-splitting tool.

The income earned in a testamentary trust is taxed at graduated tax rates, like a taxpayer. For example, Ben Shelburne leaves $150,000 in trust for his adult child Robert. If the trust assets earned $10,000 in interest income, Robert would pay tax based on the lowest marginal tax rate. Contrast this with the tax Robert would pay if he received a $150,000 inheritance outright and the annual income of $10,000 was added to his other income for the year at the top tax rate. If the trust pays dividend income to beneficiaries who have no other income, the beneficiaries do not have to pay any tax on the first $23,000.

The income splitting available with testamentary trusts means that they can be considered for a spouse, adult children, and minor children. However, the trust document is part of the last will and testament, and creating a trust can increase the cost of preparing the will. Also, each year the trust is required to file its own tax return.

A testamentary trust is a good idea for an inheritance left to a minor child or grandchild, regardless of the potential tax savings, unless the client wants the provincial public trustee to manage the assets until the child reaches the age of majority.

Testamentary trusts could also be considered for adult children who have paid off their mortgage, maximized their RRSP contribution, and want an additional way to save tax. The trust could also protect a child's inheritance in the event of a bankruptcy.

Spousal Trusts

A testamentary trust called a spousal trust can provide for a surviving spouse. If the spouse is the only person entitled to receive income and capital from the trust while he or she is alive, all assets transferred into the trust are tax-free.

In certain provinces, a spouse is entitled to receive his or her share of family property with no restrictions. A spouse who chooses to do so could interfere with an attempt to place all the assets into a spousal trust. This does not mean that the spouse will do so, but the surviving spouse could take 50% of the assets outright. The assets in the trust are distributed according to the trust instructions on the death of the surviving spouse. The assets could be paid outright or divided into trusts for children or other beneficiaries.

A spousal trust that pays any income or capital to a non-spouse is considered to be "tainted." If a client wants to set up a trust for his or her spouse and children in a will, he or she should set up a spousal trust for the surviving spouse, and one or more other testamentary trusts for the children.

Traditionally, spousal trusts were set up so that the trustee could manage the assets on behalf of the spouse. Today, the emphasis is on tax savings and protecting the assets in case the surviving spouse remarries.

Suppose Rosalind Samah is concerned that her husband Wayne might remarry after her death and his new wife might spend everything Wayne had inherited from her, leaving nothing for her two children. Rosalind could distribute her estate, one-third to Wayne, and one-third to each of her two children. Alternatively, she could set up a testamentary trust in her will, with Wayne as the income beneficiary during his lifetime, and her children the capital beneficiaries on his death. Wayne could live on the income for the rest of his life. When he dies, the remaining assets in the trust would pass to the children without probate.

Using the spousal trust would also be more tax effective that the one-third, two-thirds distribution for two reasons:

- All Rosalind's estate assets could be transferred into the spousal trust without triggering capital gains tax.

- Since the income earned in a testamentary trust pays tax at graduated tax rates, Wayne may pay less tax than if he received his inheritance outright. If he is in the 50% tax bracket and earns $10,000 a year from the inheritance, he would have to send about $5,000 to Revenue Canada each year. But if the inheritance is left in trust and earns $10,000 in income, the testamentary trust would pay tax at a lower tax rate and he would end up paying only about $2,500 a year in tax.

10.2   The Trust Agreement

The wording of a trust agreement, whether in a separate document for an inter vivos trust, or as part of the will for a testamentary trust, can be as unique as a client's situation. A client can give the trustee full trust discretionary powers to act as he or she sees fit on behalf of the beneficiaries, or specify precisely the powers the trustee will have.

There are two types of beneficiaries:

- **Income beneficiaries** are entitled to receive only the interest and dividend income earned by the assets held in the trust.

- **Capital beneficiaries** are entitled only to the capital, which may become available to them after the income beneficiaries are dead, or may be earmarked for specific uses, such as education.

The trust document may give the trustee the power to allow the income beneficiaries to encroach on the capital and the ability to receive capital out of the trust.

Clients should not scrimp on the cost of drafting a trust document. The legal wording may have to last several generations and a poorly worded trust agreement could be almost impossible to amend.

To amend a trust, a request must be presented to the courts to vary the terms of the trust. It is extremely rare for the courts to grant permission, since they have to consider what would be in the best interests of all those who stand to benefit under the trust, including beneficiaries who have not yet been born.

10.3   The Role of the Trustee

The trustee is expected to act impartially and may have to make difficult decisions on behalf of the beneficiaries. For example, should a trustee maximize the income on behalf of the spouse, or attempt to preserve as much capital for the ultimate beneficiaries, the children? A good trust document should provide guidance on these kinds of decisions. The trustee must also be fair to all the beneficiaries.

The assets in the trust are managed according to the instructions in the trust document, or the provincial *Trustee Act*, which may either provide a legal list of suitable investments or require the trustee to follow the prudent investor rule.

In some wills, the executor of the estate is named as the trustee for all testamentary trusts established by the deceased's will.

11.0   Segregated Funds

Segregated funds provide some estate planning features that are not available with publicly traded mutual funds.

The key estate planning features of segregated funds are:

- The death benefit guarantee, which guarantees to return 75% to 100% of the initial investment, less withdrawals, or the current market value, on the death of the annuitant, whichever is greater. This could be useful for older clients, or clients who are in poor health, who want to invest in the stock or bond market, but do not want to take on an unnecessary risk.

- Creditor protection in certain circumstances.

- In open accounts, avoidance of probate fees or taxes, since a beneficiary can be named. This could be useful in provinces where the cost to probate a will is high.

At some life insurance companies, the segregated fund contract ends when the annuitant dies; other companies allow it to continue.

Three separate "roles" are assigned when a segregated policy is set up:

- The owner of the contract, who has all the rights of the owner, can assign or cancel the policy at any time.

- The annuitant, whose life is used to determine when and if any guarantees are to be paid.

- The beneficiary to whom the investment is paid on the death of the annuitant.

11.1   Market Value at Death Greater than Original Investment

When the owner of a non-registered account dies, if the current market value of the account is greater than the original investment, the profit is taxed as a capital gain.

The way a non-registered account is set up is important, particularly if a couple is involved. When the owner of the account dies, if the owner is not the annuitant, the owner's portion goes to his or her estate. If the account was registered JTWROS, it goes to the surviving owner. If a successor owner has been named, the successor inherits.

When an annuitant dies (who might also be an owner of the account), the proceeds are paid to the named beneficiary. The owner is deemed to dispose of the policy at fair market value, and the estate is responsible for any tax liability. If there are capital gains, they are taxed accordingly and cannot be transferred tax-free to the spouse.

To reduce the tax liability on the death of the first spouse, consider setting up two contracts, one with the husband as the owner and beneficiary and the wife as the annuitant and a second contract with the wife as the owner and beneficiary and the husband as the annuitant. On the death of one spouse, only one policy would be deemed to be disposed of, resulting in half the immediate tax liability.

11.2   Market Value at Death Less than the Guaranteed Amount

If the current value of the account is less than the guaranteed amount, there is no clear precedent on how the difference should be taxed. The life insurance company will pay out the current value and top up the amount to the guaranteed level. If the guaranteed amount was $100,000 and the value at the time of death was $80,000, the insurance company will add $20,000 as a top-up. At some life insurance companies, this top-up is considered part of the original investment, and is not taxable. At others it is taxed as interest income or as a capital gain. If the loss of $20,000 is considered a capital loss, then the interest or capital gain could be offset by the capital loss, with neutral tax consequences.

12.0   Charitable Gifts

A client can make charitable gifts immediately, over time, or after death. When the type and timing of the gift are planned to make the most of the potential tax savings using non-refundable tax credits, a charitable donation becomes a "planned gift." Planned gifts can be incorporated into an estate plan. Some clients may ask for recommendations on the most effective ways to gift assets or property.

Some clients give because they want to support their community or a cause they believe in. Other clients consider planned giving an estate-planning and tax-saving technique. When you review your clients' current tax returns, note any annual charitable gifts. During a meeting with them, you might ask if they ever volunteer their time. It is simple enough to find out if clients are interested in making or leaving a gift to a registered charity. The tax rules establish how much tax a client has to pay. Through charitable gifts, a client can direct some of the tax dollars to charity instead.

12.1   Rules Regarding Charitable Donations

Canada's rules for charitable donations state that the donation itself does not qualify for a tax refund, but the non-refundable tax credit can be used to reduce the tax that would otherwise be payable.

The first $200 of charitable donations claimed in any one year qualifies for a federal tax credit of 17%; amounts over $200 qualify for a federal tax credit of 29%. On top of this amount, a client qualifies for a provincial tax credit that is approximately 50% more.

A charitable receipt does not have to be claimed in the year it is issued. A client and spouse or common-law spouse can pool their receipts on one tax return to maximize their tax savings.

While a client is alive, the charitable receipt can be used in the year the gift is made, or in any of the subsequent four years. The maximum amount of charitable receipts that can be claimed in one tax year is 75% of the individual's net income or, for gifts to Canadian cultural property or to the government, 100% of the individual's net income.

On death, the maximum amount of charitable receipts that can be claimed on the final tax return is 100% of the individual's net income. If this does not include all the charitable receipts, the executor can refile the tax return for the year before the year of death and apply the remaining tax receipts to it, up to the allowed limit.

Some generous clients who make gifts in their wills may accumulate more tax receipts than can be claimed in the tax return filed after they die. They may, however, be reluctant to make gifts while they are alive, in case they need the money for their own needs in their old age.

12.2   Making Effective Charitable Gifts

There are many ways to make effective gifts. When working through strategies for planned gifts, clients should consider:

- when they are ready and willing to give up control of the asset;
- when they can make the best use of the tax receipt;
- the cost of setting up a gift;
- whether or not the gift is revocable;
- if they would like public recognition or if they would prefer the gift to be private.

12.3   A Bequest in the Will

A bequest in the will might read, "I leave $10,000 to Charity X." After the death of the client, the executor would write a cheque from the estate for $10,000. The tax receipt issued by Charity X would be included on the deceased's final tax return.

A bequest made in the will must be specific, and must indicate the amount, or the formula to be used to determine the amount of the gift, as well as the name of the charity. These details cannot be left to the discretion of the executor. For example, the will might indicate that 20% of the residue is to be given to Charity Y, or the amount of the gift should be equal to 30% of the value of the RRSP or RRIF on the date of death and paid to Charity Z.

There are more than 76,000 registered charities in Canada. It is important to use the full and correct name of the charity. Some charities accept donations at the local, provincial, as well as the national level. A client should contact the charity to find out the correct name for the charitable work they want to support, so that the appropriate name can be included in the will. It may also be appropriate to indicate what should be done with the bequest if the charity is shut down or merged with another charity.

12.4   Leaving a RRSP/RRIF to Charity

Clients may suggest that since their RRSPs or RRIFs will be taxed at 50%, they might as well leave it all to charity. If this is what they want, they need to make the gift in two steps to maximize the tax savings.[4] They should:

1. name the estate as the beneficiary under the RRSP/RRIF;

---

[4]   The February 27, 2000 budget proposed to extend the charitable donations tax credit to donations of RRSP, RRIF and insurance proceeds that are made as a consequence of direct beneficiary designations. This puts this form of donation on an even footing with donations made by way of a donor's will.

2. instruct the executor of their will to donate an amount equal to, or a percentage of, the value of the RRSP/RRIF to a charity when they die.

Although this strategy could result in higher probate fees, problems with creditors, or challenges to the will from other beneficiaries, the two-step process will produce a charitable receipt for the amount of the gift.

12.5   In-Kind Donations

Charitable gifts include gifts of:

- capital and depreciable property;

- rights of any kind, including the rights to royalties and income;

- a residual interest;

- a leasehold interest;

- business inventories;

- a life insurance policy.

The amount of the charitable receipt is the fair market value of the gift at the time it is made. Although the donor can claim the charitable receipt for a non-refundable tax credit, a gift of investments or capital property will normally result in a capital gain or loss. The donor is responsible for reporting any capital gain or loss deemed to have been realized on the gift.

Until the end of 2002 (longer if this tax measure is extended), certain in-kind donations qualify for a reduced inclusion rate of 33.33% for realized capital gains (half the normal 66.66%). In-kind donations that qualify include all stocks and bonds listed on registered stock exchanges and all publicly traded mutual funds and segregated funds.

Suppose Colleen O'Hara has $10,000 in cash to donate to charity and asks you to sell $10,000 of stock with an adjusted cost base of $2,000. The taxable capital gain is $5,333 and the tax payable (for the 50% tax bracket) is $2,666.

If Colleen instead transferred that stock from her account with you to the brokerage account of the registered charity, she would have to include only a taxable capital gain of $2,666 and the resulting tax of $1,333.

(Of course, Colleen does not actually have to pay any tax on the charitable donation. She will get a tax receipt for $10,000 in either case for a non-refundable tax credit of up to $5,000, which would offset any tax due.)

Table 8.4: Cash vs. In-Kind Donations to Charity		
Method for making charitable donation	**Stock sold and cash donated**	**Stocks donated in kind**
Amount donated	$10,000	$10,000
Adjusted cost base	$ 2,000	$ 2,000
Capital gain	$ 8,000	$ 8,000
Taxable capital gain	$ 5,333 (2/3rds)	$ 2,666 (33.3%)
Tax due (50%)	$ 2,666	$ 1,333
Source: Sandra E. Foster, *You Can't Take It With You, The Common Sense Guide to Estate Planning for Canadians*, 3rd edition, John Wiley & Sons Canada Ltd., 2000.		

12.6   Life Insurance

If a client changes only the beneficiary on a life insurance policy, no charitable receipt is issued until the insured dies[5]. However, if a client assigns a life insurance policy to a registered charity and the charity becomes the beneficiary of the policy, the amount of the cash surrender value of the policy (less any policy loan outstanding) may qualify for a charitable tax receipt. If a client pays off the policy loan, that amount would also qualify for a charitable tax receipt.

If a client continues to pay premiums on a policy assigned to a registered charity, regardless of whether or not the policy has a cash surrender value, those premium payments also qualify for an annual charitable receipt.

When the proceeds of the policy disposition are greater than the adjusted cost base of the policy, the client will have to include the difference on their tax return.

12.7   The Charitable Remainder Trust

Charitable remainder trusts (CRTs) are a type of inter vivos trust. Although they are not specifically mentioned in the *Income Tax Act*, a number of CRTs have been set up in Canada, mostly with major educational institutions and hospitals. Setting up a trust involves drawing up the terms of the trust, to which the settlor and the charity have to agree, and valuing the assets involved to determine the amount of the tax receipt.

To set up a CRT, the assets are transferred irrevocably to the trust. The income earned on the assets (interest, dividends, rental income, and so forth) is paid to the settlor (the client or the client and his or her spouse) for life. When the client dies, or when the surviving spouse dies, the trust is wound down and the charity receives the remaining value of the assets in the trust.

---

[5]   See footnote 4

The tax receipt (which the clients can use in the year they set up the CRT or any time in the next five years) is based on the present value of the assets the charity will ultimately receive. The present value of the gift takes into account:

- the life expectancy of the donor (and his or her spouse, if appropriate). The older the client, the larger the tax receipt;

- the current fair market value of the assets and the anticipated rate of capital appreciation on those assets;

- current interest rates;

- a discount rate.

The longer it will be before the ultimate ownership of the assets pass to the charity, the more difficult it is to determine the value. If a present value cannot be determined for the gift, then no tax receipt can be issued.

Suppose Helen Taylor wants to reduce her taxes today (or over the next five years). She wants her estate plan to benefit a major charitable organization in her community. She doesn't want all her assets tied up, so she is planning to transfer $500,000 of her estate to a charitable remainder trust. She expects the assets in the trust to earn her about $25,000 in income a year (an annual return of 5.85%, less the annual trustee administration fees of 0.85%). Since Helen is 83 years old, she might receive a tax receipt of about $450,000. If she were younger, the tax receipt would be for a lesser amount.

12.8   Gifts of Cultural Property

Gifts of certified cultural property, such as works of art or artifacts of historical significance, are eligible for a charitable tax receipt. When the item is given to a designated public institution, there is an additional tax credit available to the donors to offset any resulting capital gain realized when the gift is made.

A client should discuss any gift with the receiving institution. He or she will want to ensure that the institution is interested in accepting the gift and that the gift is appraised properly.

13.0   Dealing with a Cottage or Family Business

Helping a family deal with a family cottage or a family business can be difficult. The biggest issues are how to distribute the assets equitably and how to deal with tax liabilities.

Clients may do an estate freeze while they are alive and put the asset into a family trust. However, every 21 years, the family trust faces a deemed disposition for any unrealized capital gains. The have to pay the tax bill, but they do not want to sell the asset to do so. Although a qualifying business may be able to get a $500,000 capital gains exemption for each family member to reduce its taxes, this arrangement cannot be applied to cottages.

Cottages and family businesses cannot be dealt with by one generation alone. The whole family should discuss the matter to determine the most appropriate estate planning solution.

13.1   The Family Cottage

See Chapter 6, Section 3.8.

13.2   A Family Business

Retiring from a family business poses many special issues. One relates to taxation on death. Suppose a client, Sandra Jacobs, has a profitable business. If she leaves the business to her husband Lars, ownership of the business can be transferred tax-free. This makes sense if Lars is willing and able to be active in the business. But if one or more of the children are active in the business, Sandra may want the children to inherit some or all of the business.

If Sandra can perform an estate freeze and take advantage of the $500,000 capital gains exemption for each shareholder in the business, she may be able to minimize the tax due on death. If she cannot reduce the tax bill payable after death, she will need to consider life insurance to provide the funds into the estate to pay the taxes without forcing the sale of the business or other assets in the estate.

If the business represents the significant asset in the estate and Sandra wants to leave it to her children, she must understand spousal rights under family law. She may need to prepare a marriage contract and buy life insurance to provide for Lars. If the business is being left to the children, but not all the children, she will need to determine which of the following is fairer and practical:

• leave the business equally to all the children, even those not active in the business;

• leave the business only to the children active in the business and leave the other children assets or life insurance of similar value;

• give the children the opportunity to buy the business from the estate, using other assets in the estate or using outside financing.

Suppose you have a client, Gary Schwartz, with a wife, three children and a successful, privately held business, which represents a significant portion of his estate. In the event of Gary's death, his wife would be dependent on receiving ongoing income from the business (without working in it). Only one child, Tom, has expressed any interest in carrying on the family business. Gary wants all three children to receive an equal benefit upon his death.

If Gary makes all three children equal voting shareholders in the business but only Tom really knows the business, he could be setting up a disastrous framework for the business. Gary's dilemma is this: should all three children benefit equally from the business for years after his death, when only Tom is actively involved? It might be better to leave the business only to the child that is active in it, and use other assets or life insurance to equalize the inheritance among the children.

Some clients use an estate freeze to crystallize the $500,000 capital gains exemption. Tom would receive the business outright, or with the other two as minor shareholders. Alternatively Gary, if insurable, could purchase enough life insurance (a) to cover the tax liability remaining on any capital gains resulting from the deemed disposition of the business on his death and (b) to pay the two children an amount equal to the benefit Tom receives from the business.

14.0   Assessing Family Needs, Priorities, and Estate Planning Goals

If you are undertaking estate planning for a client, you should ask the client to bring the following documents, if they have them, to your next meeting:

- will;

- power of attorney for finance;

- power of attorney for health care or living will;

- life insurance policies;

- RRSP, RRIF, and pension statements showing the designated beneficiaries;

- investment statements showing the account registrations;

- tax returns for the last two years;

- tax cost basis details to estimate final tax liability;

- pre-nuptial or co-habitation agreements;

- separation or divorce agreements.

These documents, as well as discussions with clients to ascertain their family situation, are the starting point for the estate planning strategies clients can implement to achieve their financial and estate planning goals.

The client's goals may initially conflict with the needs of his or her family. Clients must take the time to consider what they want to happen and to set priorities. Although you can guide the client through the different estate planning strategies and techniques, the final decisions always lie with the client.

15.0   Building the Estate Planning Team

Estate planning may involve a number of different people, including a variety of specialists.

15.1   The Family

Whether or not a client feels comfortable talking about estate planning issues, family members are part of the estate planning team. Families should talk about what they want at the funeral. They should know where to find all the important papers and the original will and power of attorney documents.

Children usually inherit assets or property from their parents' estate. If you take the time and prepare an appropriate estate plan for the parents, it increases the likelihood that the children's assets will remain under your management.

15.2   The Lawyer

Although about 90% of lawyers prepare wills, only a small number specialize in estate and tax planning. When referring clients to a lawyer, choose one who has the expertise the client needs. If the client wants to set up an inter vivos trust for a mentally incapacitated relative, recommend a lawyer who has expertise in this area. Even if the lawyer's hourly rate is higher, the total cost may not be.

You should also prepare a client for the costs involved in preparing the estate planning documents and what to expect when they sit down with the lawyer. Some wealth managers attend these meetings with their clients, to give them moral support. However, the lawyer may want to meet with the client alone as well, to be sure you are not exerting undue influence over the client's decisions.

15.3   The Accountant

Some clients may already have a personal accountant or an accountant who handles their professional or business interests. The accountant will be able to provide the current cost base figures for the estimate of the tax liability. Accountants are normally willing to prepare the pro forma of the tax liability on death.

15.4   The Business Valuator

Clients who have a business that would need to be valued when they die, probably have not yet considered what would happen to the business if they became disabled. If they are working with partner and they cannot determine how best to deal with these issues, a business valuator could provide useful guidance.

Assets may also have to be valued to determine their fair market value at the time of death for the final tax return.

15.5   Estate Appraiser

If the personal assets of the deceased are extensive, or if he or she has an important collection, the estate appraiser will be called in to set a price for the assets, and arrange for a sale or auction, if necessary.

15.6   Funeral Director

Whether the client and his or her executor opt for a simple funeral or a lavish one, the family and executor must deal with someone from a funeral home. To control the costs, some clients plan their own funerals, indicating their wishes for all the services they would like to have. Other clients prepay their funeral; this is more to ensure that all the arrangements have been taken care of, rather than to reap any savings.

15.7   The Gift Planner

Many charitable organizations have staff gift planners who can discuss different planned giving techniques with potential donors. They can provide information on different gift vehicles the client could sponsor directly, include gift annuities and life insurance policies.

15.8   The Grief Counsellor

Grief is a normal reaction to bereavement. Professional help is available for those who need extra support, or who are having trouble coping with their loss. Many funeral homes offer counselling programs to survivors. Many religious organizations also offer programs. Clients can also receive help from a professional psychologist or psychiatrist.

Section III

Investment and Portfolio Management

Once you understand the client's financial planning needs, you are ready to start turning your clients' goals into a portfolio with an asset allocation strategy that will reduce unnecessary risk and offer the potential to earn the rates of return your clients need to achieve their financial goals.

The investment management process includes deciding on an appropriate risk/return tradeoff, setting an asset allocation strategy for your client, understanding the specific managed products within those asset categories, formalizing the process through an investment policy statement, choosing managed products and managed product providers, and finally reviewing and rebalancing the portfolio.

CHAPTER 9

Risk and Return

1.0   Introduction

The risk profile questionnaire found in Chapter 2 will help you as a wealth manager understand the level of risk a client is comfortable with, while the client's financial goals will help you determine how much return is needed. It is the wealth manager's job then to help the client find the right balance between risk and return.

In constructing and maintaining a portfolio, it is essential to measure the rate of return for individual securities and for the portfolio as a whole. This measurement will help you calculate risk levels, determine portfolio performance, and manage the client's expectations.

Modern portfolio management starts with the assumption that the investor is risk-averse. (An investor is said to be risk-averse if, when faced with two alternative investments with the same expected return but different risk levels, he or she chooses the one with the lower risk.) Investors tend to buy lower-risk securities and sell higher-risk alternatives. Over time, as more investors buy the lower-risk security, its price rises, causing its expected return to fall. Meanwhile, the price of the higher-risk security falls, causing its expected return to rise. Eventually the higher-risk security offers a higher return than the lower-risk alternative. This attracts more investors to the higher-risk security.

Securities can be placed into two general categories – riskless and risky.

- A riskless asset is one whose future return is known with certainty. There is virtually no likelihood that the issuer will default on its obligations. The most common example of a riskless security is a Federal Government Treasury bill.

- A risky asset is one that has an uncertain future return. For example, when you buy a share of Imperial Oil stock, intending to hold it for a year, you do not know the final return you will get. Similarly, when you buy a 20-year Canada bond intending to hold it for a year, your realized return is unknown, since you do not know the price of the bond one year in the future.

Primary Learning Objectives

By the end of this chapter, you should understand:

- **the relationship between a security's, or a portfolio's, return and its risk level;**

- **how to measure both single-security and portfolio risk and returns;**

- **covariance and correlation coefficients;**

- **systematic and unsystematic risk;**

- **the risk reduction benefits of diversification.**

2.0   Measuring Returns

You need three pieces of information to measure the return on a security or a portfolio:

- the value of the portfolio or asset at the beginning of the holding period;

- the value of the portfolio at the end of the holding period;

- the starting and ending dates of the holding period.

Using this information, you can calculate the holding-period return (HPR) as follows:

$$HPR = \frac{(\text{end of period value} - \text{beginning of period value})}{\text{beginning of period value}}$$

The holding period can be any length, but one year is usually used in these calculations.

You must also distinguish between the nominal and the real rate of return. The **nominal rate of return** is the rate that is observed in the marketplace, as quoted by financial institutions. The **real rate of return** is the rate that would prevail if price levels remained constant. The **inflation rate** is a measure of the change in price levels; it links these two rates of return.

The real rate of return is calculated by subtracting an inflation premium from the nominal rate of return.

Real Rate of Return = Nominal Rate of Return – Inflation Premium

or conversely,

Nominal Rate of Return = Real Rate of Return + Inflation Premium

You can use these equations to calculate the real rate of return over a given period, using the nominal rate at the beginning of the period and the inflation rate that prevailed during the period. The Consumer Price Index (CPI), published monthly by Statistics Canada, is usually used to determine the rate of inflation.

3.0   Measuring Risks

Although there is no universally agreed upon definition of risk, some principles are generally accepted. Risk can be thought of as *the extent to which the possible realized returns vary from the expected value.*

The way in which returns vary from the expected value is usually expressed as the variance of returns about the mean. Calculating variance involves taking all values above and below the mean. The risk of a portfolio is usually measured as the standard deviation of the portfolio return. The standard deviation is the square root of the variance.

The distribution of returns may be symmetrical, which means that the values below the mean (losses) and the values above the mean (returns) are equal, or it may be skewed to one side or another. Figure 9.1a shows a symmetrical probability distribution. Figures 9.1b and 9.1c show distributions that are skewed to the right and to the left, respectively.

Empirical studies have shown that returns for individual securities measured over short periods of time are almost symmetrical. Over longer periods, security returns tend to be skewed to the right, as in Figure 9.1c, because returns have no upper limit, whereas losses cannot exceed 100%.

Figure 9.1   Possible Shapes for Probability Distributions

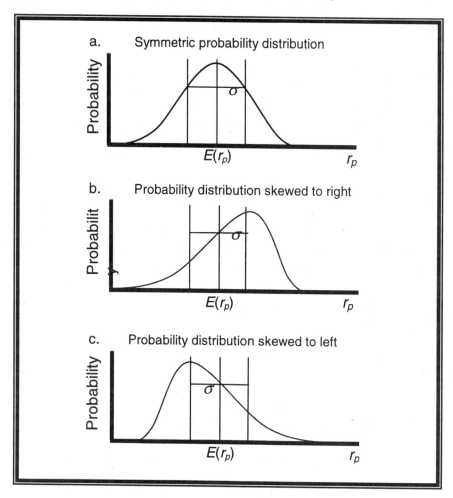

The distribution of returns for portfolios of 20 or more individual securities, however, is very close to symmetrical for all periods. As a result, variance has become a widely accepted measure of risk in portfolio construction.

Risks fall into two categories, systematic and unsystematic, based on the factors that cause a security to fluctuate in value (that is, have different returns) over time:

1. General market conditions. When the economy is doing well, most stock prices move up because of improved profit outlooks, and when the economy is doing poorly, most stocks fall in value. Also, interest rates and inflation rates affect all stocks. The risks that affect all securities and that cannot be eliminated by diversifying a portfolio are known collectively as **systematic risk**.

2. Factors specific to a security. When a firm wins a major new contract, or implements a cost savings plan, its stock value may rise. When a firm suffers an unexpected drop in demand due to a technological innovation, its stock value may fall. These factors

vary from one firm to the next. Moreover, some firms do well when others are doing poorly and vice versa. Company-specific risk, which can be reduced by holding a diversified portfolio of stocks from many different companies, is known as **unsystematic risk**.

Together, systematic risk and unsystematic risk make up the **total risk** of a portfolio.

The notion of risk cannot be considered apart from the length of the holding period. For risky securities, it is important to estimate the expected return and risk level over the same holding period.

4.0   Measuring Single-Security Returns

When calculating returns for single securities, it is conventional to assume that the investor purchases one unit (that is, one bond or one share of common stock) of the security. The purchase price of the security represents the security's value at the beginning of the period. The value of any cash distributions received during the period from dividends or interest is added to the recorded price at the end of the period to obtain the value at the end of the period.

$$r_i = \frac{P_1 + D_1 - P_0}{P_0}$$

where

r_i = *return on security i*
P_0 = *price at the beginning of the period*
P_1 = *price at the end of the period*
D_1 = *cash distribution received by the investor during the period*

This equation assumes that the cash distribution is received at the end of the period. If the distribution is received at some point during the period, then this calculation will understate the actual return.

For example, assume that ABC's common stock is selling for $40 a share at the beginning of the year and for $44 at the end of the year and pays a single dividend of $2 at year-end. The calculated return would be:

$$15\% = [(\$44 + 2 - 40) \div 40] \times 100$$

If, however, the $2 dividend was paid out in the middle of the year, and if the stock price was $42 at that time, the investor could have used the dividend to buy additional shares. The number of additional shares purchased would be:

$$\$2/\$42 = 0.0476$$

The value at the end of the year would then be:

$$\$44 \times 1.0476 = \$46.09$$

and the return for the year would be 15.24%.

To compare different investments, you will need to express returns in terms of one year, even if they are actually paid out over different periods. There are two ways to do this.

1. Suppose you buy a 91-day Treasury bill for $99.26 for each $100 of face value. At the end of 91 days you receive $100. Your 91-day return is:

$$0.7455\% = [(100 - 99.26) \div 99.26] \times 100$$

You can convert this calculated return to a one-year return by multiplying the return by $365 \div 91$ to get 2.99%. This method assumes that you are reinvesting the proceeds at simple interest over the year.

2. If you reinvest the proceeds of your investment in further T-bills to receive the same quarterly rate, your annualized return is:

$$3.01\% = [(1.007455^{(365/91)} - 1) \times 100]$$

Both methods are used under different circumstances. The annual rate quoted by financial institutions for term deposits of less than a year is calculated using the first method. The second would be used to calculate the rate of return for a loan that is quoted as 12% a year compounded monthly (1% per month). The effective annual rate would be:

$$12.68\% = [(1.01)^{12} - 1] \times 100$$

You may also need to compare the returns on different securities that are held for longer than a year. There are two possible methods.

If you have information about individual annual returns, then the simplest method is to calculate the average or arithmetic mean of these returns. If you do not have this information, you will need to calculate the geometric-mean (or time-weighted) return.

Suppose we have the following set of price data for the XYZ Company's shares over five years. In this example, we will assume that no dividends are paid over the period.

Year	Price	Return	(1 + Return)
0	20.22		
1	23.25	0.1625	1.1625
2	22.50	-0.0323	0.9677
3	24.20	0.0756	1.0756
4	25.05	0.0351	1.0351
5	24.62	-0.0160	0.9840

The arithmetic mean return over five years is 0.0450 or 4.5%. This is calculated by adding up the returns and dividing by the number of years:

$$\frac{(0.1625 - 0.0323 + 0.0756 + 0.0351 - 0.0160)}{5} = 0.0450 = 4.5\%$$

The geometric mean return over five years would 0.0427 or 4.27%. This is calculated by multiplying the figures for (1 + Return) and taking the fifth root.

$$(1.1625 \times 0.9677 \times 1.0756 \times 1.0351 \times 0.9840)^{\frac{1}{5}} - 1 = 0.0427 = 4.27\%$$

The arithmetic-mean return can be seen as the average additions or withdrawals that must be made to the portfolio to maintain the initial value intact at the end of each period.

The geometric mean rate of return assumes that all cash distributions are reinvested in the original security. The geometric mean return of 4.27% per year implies that $100 invested in the security at the beginning of the first year will have grown at a compound rate of 4.27% per year during the five-year period.

If the returns are the same in each period, the two methods will produce the same result. Otherwise the arithmetic-mean return always exceeds the geometric-mean return. The results usually differ, because the underlying assumptions differ.

The two methods are used in different circumstances. We will discuss the main use of the arithmetic mean return later in this chapter. The geometric mean return is often used to compare the long-term performance of mutual funds in the financial press.

5.0   Measuring Single-Security Risk

To measure the risk of any individual security, we need to look at the variance of the security's returns. The **variance** is the sum of the weighted and squared deviations from the mean. The deviations must be weighted because each possible outcome has a different probability of occurrence. The **standard deviation** is the square root of the variance.

The variance and standard deviation are referred to as σ^2 (sigma squared) and σ (sigma), respectively.

The following table gives basic data from which we can calculate the variance by multiplying Row 1 and Row 3 and summing up the results.

Probability (1)	Deviation from the mean (2)	Deviation squared (3)	Probability times deviation squared (4)
0.15	17.5%	306.25	45.94
0.30	7.5%	56.25	16.88
0.30	-2.5%	6.25	1.88
0.20	-12.5%	156.25	31.25
0.05	-32.5%	1056.25	52.81
			Variance = 148.76

The variance of the returns on Security X, therefore, is 148.76 and the standard deviation is 12.20% (the square root of 148.76).

6.0   Measuring Portfolio Returns

A portfolio is a collection of individual securities; therefore, the return on a portfolio is a weighted average of the returns on all the securities in the portfolio. It is calculated using the following formula:

$$r_p = w_1 r_1 + w_2 r_2 + w_3 r_3 + ... + w_N r_N$$

where:

rp = the return on the portfolio
wi = security i as a fraction of the total portfolio
ri = the return on security I

Alternatively, the value of the portfolio can be determined at the beginning and end of the holding period. Suppose we have $17,200 invested in a portfolio containing the shares of three different companies, ABC, DEF, and GHJ. The table below shows the number of shares held and the share prices.

Security name	Number of shares	Initial price per share	Dollars invested	Security as a fraction of the total portfolio
ABC	100	$40.00	$4,000	4000/17200 = 0.2325
DEF	200	35.00	7,000	7000/17200 = 0.4070
GHJ	100	62.00	6,200	6200/17200 = 0.3605
			Total = $17,200	Sum of weights = 1.0000

At the end of the period, the value of the shares is:

Security name	Number of shares	Final price	Final value
ABC	100	$46.48	$4,648
DEF	200	43.61	8,722
GHJ	100	76.14	7614
			End of period value = $20,984

The return for each security is:

Security name	Initial price	Final price	Return
ABC	$40.00	$46.48	16.2%
DEF	35.00	43.61	24.6%
GHJ	62.00	76.14	22.8%

We can now calculate the portfolio return:

Method 1: = $(0.2325 \times 16.2) + (0.4070 \times 24.6) + (0.3605 \times 22.8) = 22.0\%$

Method 2: = $[(20984 \div 17200) - 1] \times 100 = 22.0\%$

The contribution of each security to the portfolio's return depends on its individual return and its share of the initial market value of the portfolio.

6.1   Covariance

The variance of a portfolio's return depends not only on how individual security returns vary, but also on the way in which security returns are related to each other. This relationship is known as **covariance**.

If we say that two securities have positive covariance, we mean that when the return on one security increases, the return on the other generally increases as well. However, one may increase only slightly while the other increases by a significant amount. The different rates at which securities rise in relation to each other is expressed by a number called the **correlation coefficient**. The correlation coefficient is a number between −1 and +1.

A correlation coefficient of +1 indicates that the returns on two securities move together at exactly the same rate. An increase or decrease in the return on one security is matched with an identical increase or decrease in the return on the other.

A coefficient of −1 indicates that the returns move in exact opposition to one another. An increase in the return on one is always associated with a decrease in the return on the other, and vice versa.

If the correlation coefficient is 0, then the returns on the two securities are unrelated. The return on one security may increase or decrease while the return on another rises, falls or remains unchanged.

A correlation of 0.5 indicates a moderate likelihood that the returns on two securities will move in the same direction, but movement in opposite directions is possible.

In practice, the correlation coefficients for the securities of different firms, asset groups, and countries range from close to zero to about 0.8.

The variance of a portfolio of securities will equal the weighted average of the variance of an individual security in the portfolio only if every security in the portfolio is perfectly positively correlated with every other security in the portfolio. Otherwise, the portfolio variance will be less than the weighted average of the variances of the constituent securities.

Table 9.1 Rates of Return and Correlation Coefficients for Various Asset Classes, 1981-1998

Year	CPI	T-Bills	Bonds	TSE300	S & P	Gold	Real Estate	Mortgages
1981	12.40	18.41	-2.09	-10.25	-5.56	-32.60	12.02	12.82
1982	10.90	15.42	45.82	5.54	25.94	14.94	-4.87	28.15
1983	5.70	9.62	9.61	35.49	24.16	-16.31	11.12	18.69
1984	4.40	11.59	16.90	-2.39	12.90	-19.19	2.91	11.79
1985	3.90	9.88	26.68	25.07	39.33	5.76	4.15	14.42
1986	4.20	9.33	17.21	8.95	17.19	18.94	12.76	10.93
1987	4.40	8.48	1.77	5.88	-0.89	24.53	17.51	8.74
1988	4.00	9.41	11.30	11.08	7.02	-15.26	14.67	8.31
1989	5.00	12.36	15.17	21.37	27.95	-2.19	14.25	12.44
1990	4.80	13.48	4.32	-14.80	-2.98	-4.60	1.73	11.02
1991	5.60	9.83	25.30	12.02	30.00	2.15	-1.44	19.31
1992	1.50	7.08	11.57	-1.43	18.35	-5.28	0.59	10.08
1993	1.80	5.51	22.09	32.55	14.50	1.68	3.30	11.98
1994	0.20	5.35	-7.39	-0.18	7.44	-1.92	2.53	-0.09
1995	1.70	7.02	26.34	14.53	15.50	-0.45	-1.30	15.30
1996	2.00	5.02	14.18	28.35	24.00	-5.01	-1.93	12.49
1997	1.60	3.20	18.46	14.98	33.36	-43.78		4.48
1998	0.90	4.74	12.85	-1.58	28.58	-9.82		8.44
Mean	4.17	9.21	15.00	10.29	17.60	-4.91	5.50	12.18
Std. Dev	3.12	3.87	11.87	13.92	12.49	16.36	6.84	5.88

Correlation Coefficients (1981 – 1996):

	CPI	T-Bills	Bonds	TSE 300	S & P	Gold	Real Estate	Mortgages
CPI	1							
T-Bills	0.92	1						
Bonds	0.19	0.09	1					
Equities	-0.29	-0.49	0.35	1				
S & P	-0.12	-0.21	0.68	0.66	1			
Gold	-0.21	-0.30	0.37	0.16	0.26	1		
Real Estate	0.15	0.17	-0.05	0.04	-0.34	-0.05	1	
Mortgages	0.60	0.44	0.80	0.25	0.50	0.12	-0.37	1

The data in Table 9.1 generally supports the proposition that higher returns are associated with higher risk. The correlation coefficients show that bonds and T-bills can be added to an equity portfolio to provide useful diversification. T-bills also provide a useful hedge against inflation. Unfortunately, they also provide the lowest rate of return.

Portfolio design has evolved from a general notion of spreading out risk by choosing assets from a variety of industries and market sectors. Portfolio managers pick individual securities that they expect will outperform other similar securities. They combine these with securities from other asset classes, other sectors, and other countries to make the most of each one's return-to-risk trade-offs and covariances.

6.2   Diversification

Assembling a portfolio of several different types of securities (also known as not putting all your eggs in one basket) is a well-known way of reducing risk without sacrificing return. In general, the greater the number of securities in the portfolio, the lower the risk, because their returns will rise and fall at different times and at different rates.

For example, when the return on the market as a whole is 10%, the return on security A may be 8%, the return on security B may be 20%, and the return on security C may be -6%. Equally, when the market return is -10%, security A's return may be -6%, B's may be -25%, while C's may be 7%. When these three securities are combined into a portfolio, the large swings exhibited by security B are dampened by the smaller swings in A and the opposing swings in C. An equally weighted portfolio of the three would give a return of 7% when the market return is 10% and a return of -8% when the market return is -10%.

Figure 9.2 demonstrates the importance of diversification. Annual returns on federal government bonds averaged 7.35% over the 49 years from 1950-98. Although some years saw high returns, several years saw negative returns. If, over the same period, an investor had held a portfolio made up of 85% cash (rolling over 91-day Treasury bills), 5% Canadian stock (as measured by the TSE 300), and 10% U.S. stock (as measured by the S&P 500), the average annual return would also have been 7.35%, but with less volatility. Spreading the investment to more than one asset class and country helps maintain performance, eliminate losses, and make returns more certain.

Figure 9.2

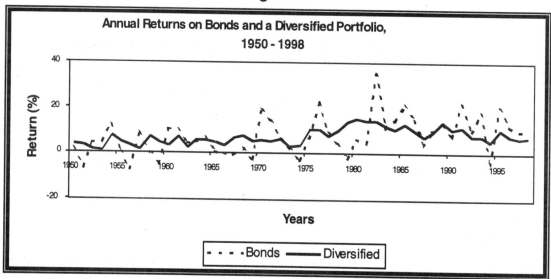

Figure 9.3 shows what happens to a portfolio as it becomes bigger. Risk decreases as the number of different securities in the portfolio increases, until eventually only systematic risk remains. The systematic risk is usually defined by a market index. The market index serves as a performance benchmark portfolio. The purpose of diversification is to eliminate as much unsystematic risk as possible.

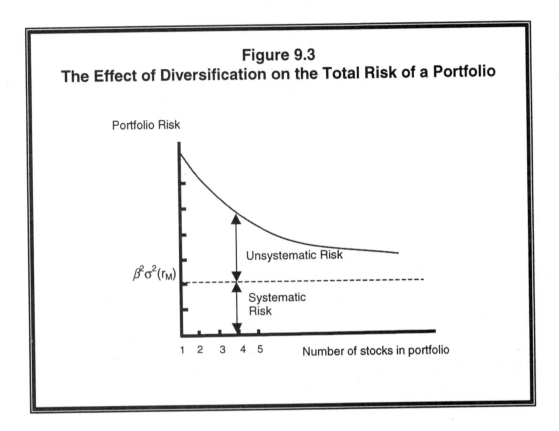

Figure 9.3
The Effect of Diversification on the Total Risk of a Portfolio

How many securities must be included to arrive at a completely diversified portfolio? Studies using a stock market index as the market portfolio and randomly selecting stock to form portfolios have found that:

- About 90% of the maximum benefit of diversification can be achieved with a portfolio of 16 to 20 stocks.

- High beta portfolios (borrowing portfolios) should include at least 30 stocks.

- Low beta portfolios (lending portfolios) need 40 or more stocks.

The smaller the correlation between the returns, the better the diversification. The goal is to keep the average of all the correlation coefficients as low as possible. For example, a portfolio of 5 securities has 10 correlations — between securities 1 and 2, 1 and 3, 1 and 4, 1 and 5, 2 and 3, 2 and 4, 2 and 5, 3 and 4, 3 and 5, and 4 and 5. Even if some of the securities are highly correlated with each other, as long as the rest of the correlations are low, the overall average correlation will be low enough to provide effective diversification.

Finding securities with negative correlation would be ideal, but they are rare within the domestic market. In international investing, however, there are negative correlations among stocks from different countries, so greater diversification is possible.

6.3   Efficient Portfolios

A portfolio is considered to be efficient if, of all the portfolios with the same expected return, that particular portfolio has the lowest risk.

The predicted return on the portfolio is the weighted average of the asset return predictions for all the securities in the portfolio. The weight assigned to each security is the proportion of total funds invested in that particular security. For instance, if one forecasts that Security A will return 10% and Security B will return 12 % over the next year, and 40% of funds are invested in Security A and 60% in Security B, the expected portfolio return is:

$$E(r_p) = (0.4 \times 0.10) + (0.6 \times 0.12)$$
$$= 0.112 \text{ or } 11.2\%$$

Clearly, modifying the investment proportions will affect the expected returns for the portfolio. Dividing investment equally between A and B produces an expected return of 11%, for example.

Variances and covariances are usually estimated using historical returns. Return expectations for different classes of assets and securities may be estimated from historical average returns or determined by the predictions of the portfolio manager. The equations get more complicated, but the procedure remains the same when many securities are involved.

In Figure 9.4, the curve represents the minimum risk portfolio attainable for any desired return. The curve can be sketched by calculating a series of points representing the best possible combination of risk and return for securities in a portfolio. The result is a bullet-shaped curve. The upper part of the curve is known as the **efficient frontier**. Rational investors choose portfolios that lie on the efficient frontier. The upper and lower parts together represent the **minimum variance frontier**. The set of points contained by the frontier is the **portfolio opportunity set**, which includes all possible but inefficient portfolio combinations and arrangements. The point at the left end of the frontier represents the least risky portfolio that can be assembled from risky assets, and is known as the **minimum variance portfolio.**

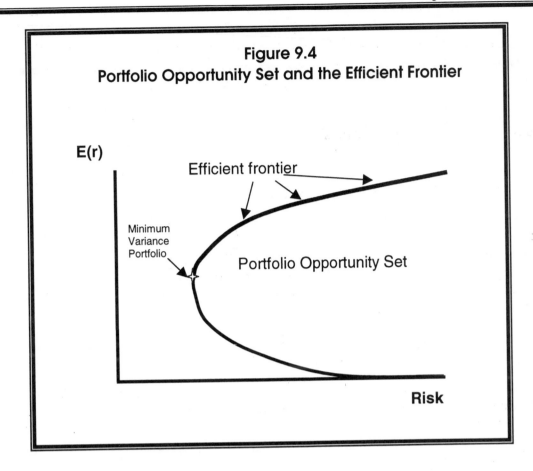

Figure 9.4
Portfolio Opportunity Set and the Efficient Frontier

6.4   Evaluating Diversification

As a portfolio becomes more diversified, its risk and return come to resemble more and more closely the market index, because most of the return variance comes from market fluctuation. Figure 9.5 displays this effect. Perfect positive correlation between the portfolio and the market (that is, a correlation coefficient of +1) indicates that no unsystematic risk is left in the portfolio. Consequently, correlation can be used to measure the degree of diversification achieved by a portfolio.

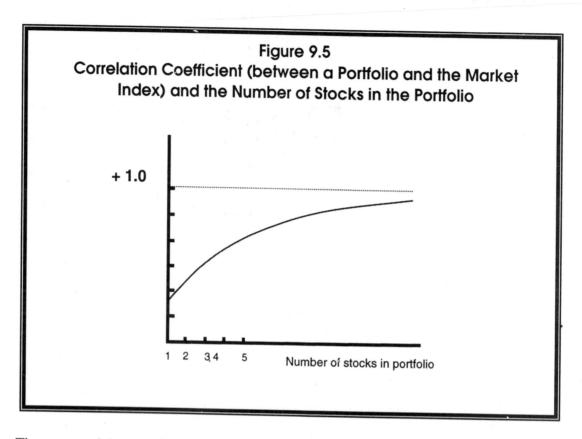

Figure 9.5
Correlation Coefficient (between a Portfolio and the Market Index) and the Number of Stocks in the Portfolio

The square of the correlation indicates the proportion of a portfolio's total risk that comes from systematic risk. A squared correlation of .75, for example, indicates that 75% of the total risk is systematic risk. The rest, 25%, comes from fluctuation in individual securities, or unsystematic risk.

CHAPTER 10

Asset Allocation

1.0   Introduction

The most important part of the investment advisory process is helping a client establish a suitable asset allocation program. Whether the client has a $500,000 portfolio or $50 million under administration, the investment decisions are the same. These decisions are:

- what is the appropriate mix among the various investment classes?

- when should the actual mix be changed?

- when should the target mix be changed?

These approaches to asset allocation are called, respectively, strategic, dynamic, and tactical. When all three approaches are used, they are known as integrated asset allocation.

Primary Learning Objectives

By the end of this chapter, you should understand:

- **the benefits of an asset allocation strategy;**

- **the steps involved in the strategic asset allocation process;**

- **how to implement a dynamic and tactical asset allocation program;**

- **what is meant by passive and active investment strategies;**

- **the implications of the three market efficiency concepts for investment strategy choice.**

2.0   Strategic, Dynamic and Tactical Asset Allocation

Strategic asset allocation is the most important investment decision of the entire investment process. Strategic asset allocation means choosing a long-term target asset mix among available asset classes, also known as the **investment opportunity set**. The goal is to balance market, inflation, and interest rate risk against the desire for enhanced returns.

Dynamic asset allocation involves the periodic adjustment or re-balancing of the actual portfolio weights to ensure that they match the target weights.

Tactical asset allocation involves adjusting the asset classes or sector allocations to reflect current asset class return and sector rotation goals.

Portfolio Design and Maintenance

Asset Allocation or Investment Policy

		Designation
Step 1	Decide which asset classes to include and to exclude from a portfolio.	Strategic asset allocation
Step 2	Decide the normal, or long-term weights allowed in the portfolio.	Strategic asset allocation for each asset class
Step 3	Periodically adjust the actual portfolio weights to reflect target weights.	Dynamic asset allocation
Step 4	Adjust the asset class or sector allocations to reflect current asset class return and sector rotation goals.	Tactical asset allocation

Investment Strategy

Step 5	Select individual products or securities within an asset class to achieve superior returns relative to that asset class.	Security research and selection

---

There are a number of benefits to asset allocation. Studies show that asset allocation, rather than the security selection and market timing decisions, is by far the most important factor in achieving an appropriate total return. It can account for up to 93.6% of the variation in returns on large investment portfolios. Asset allocation is also important because without a clear policy, it is not possible to set goals or measure progress toward those goals.

Wealth managers must analyze the performance of the portfolio and review returns in terms of the relative contributions of investment policy and investment strategy. A properly structured asset allocation program does not drift away from the investment policy and ensures that the investment portfolio continues to reflect the long-term strategic asset allocation policy. Nevertheless, a successful tactical program can also achieve good returns. Dynamic and tactical asset allocation will be discussed later in this chapter.

3.0   Asset Classes

Portfolio design involves forecasting expected returns on asset classes and assessing the risk of these asset classes. This process uses **nominal** returns. Nominal returns are reported in current dollars. If an asset has a nominal return of 3% for the year, but inflation was 4% for the year, the *real* return would be -1% (3 – 4). That is:

Real Rate of Return = Nominal Rate of Return – Inflation Premium

To maintain purchasing power, investors need positive real returns. That means that the nominal returns must exceed the rate of inflation.

Wealth managers need to define available investment opportunities. The conventional approach to defining asset classes is to break them down generally into fixed-income securities and equities, and then refine the breakdown into:

1. **Cash and cash equivalents**: cash and short-term debt securities that are highly liquid and marketable, such as Treasury bills, Certificates of Deposit, or money market mutual funds.

2. **Bonds**: Government or corporate fixed-income securities, or investment funds specializing in fixed-income securities. These securities provide periodic income for spending or reinvestment, some capital preservation, and, depending on the term and issuer, liquidity. Foreign-currency-denominated bonds provide exchange rate exposure.

3. **Domestic and international stocks**: common or preferred shares or investment funds specializing in equities to provide capital appreciation and some dividend income. International stocks provide foreign currency risk exposure and portfolio risk reduction.

4. **Other (gold, real estate, venture capital, and derivatives)**: these products offer capital gains, a hedge against inflation, systematic risk diversification, and portfolio risk reduction.

The traditional approach is to select assets from the cash or safety investments, income investments, growth investments, hedge investments and others, including derivatives, and to determine the normal or long-term benchmark weights for each of the asset classes allowed in the portfolio. The portfolio must be periodically rebalanced as the actual portfolio weights are adjusted to match target weights.

4.0   Strategic Asset Allocation

The asset allocation policy must reflect the client's needs and investment horizons. The wealth manager must consider the client's:

- net worth;
- return objectives;
- risk tolerance;
- investment horizon;
- need for liquidity;
- legal constraints;
- tax position;
- need for income.

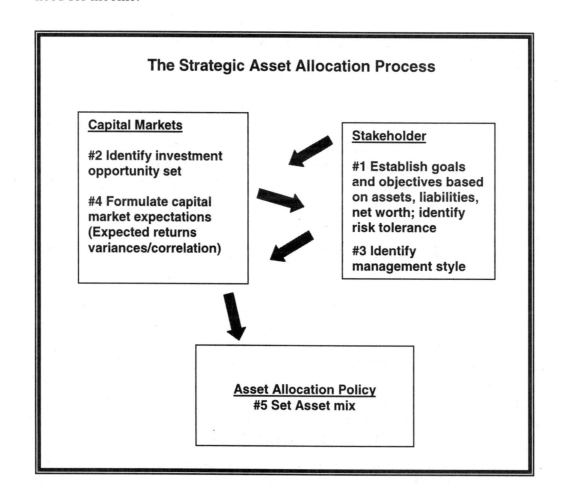

The Strategic Asset Allocation Process

Capital Markets

#2 Identify investment opportunity set

#4 Formulate capital market expectations (Expected returns variances/correlation)

Stakeholder

#1 Establish goals and objectives based on assets, liabilities, net worth; identify risk tolerance

#3 Identify management style

Asset Allocation Policy
#5 Set Asset mix

4.1   Identify the Investment Opportunity Set

Typically, wealth managers can select asset classes from the entire investment opportunity set. In a few cases, constraints on a client or the by-laws and guidelines of a particular managed product restrict certain investments. For example, some managers are not permitted to use derivative products. In other cases, ethical screens prohibit the manager from investing in specific types of companies or securities.

4.2   Determine the Appropriate Investment Management Style

Once the investment opportunity set has been identified, the wealth manager helps determine the investment management style that will best suit the client. Different investment styles include active versus passive approaches, value versus growth, small versus large caps, bottom-up versus top-down, and sector rotation.

The major style decision is whether the manager will use an active, passive, or mixed approach to investing.

Some experts question the value of active approaches to investing. They point to the fact that despite all the work done by fundamental analysts and, to a lesser degree, technical analysts, an investment policy of randomly selecting common shares, buying them, and holding them has returned about 10% to 11% a year over the past 65 years.

Active management involves adjusting the asset class or sector allocations to reflect sector rotation goals. The manager may also alter the mix away from the target weights to capture high returns caused by short-term fluctuations in the returns on certain asset classes and select managed products or individual securities within an asset class to achieve superior returns.

4.3   Develop Capital Market Expectations for the Asset Classes in the Portfolio

The next stage in the process is to develop capital market expectations for the asset classes to be considered in the portfolio mix. These expectations specify the expected returns, as well as the variances and covariances among the various asset classes. These calculations are normally based on historical asset class return results, standard deviations, and correlation matrixes for each asset class adjusted for current economic forecasts. Capital market expectations are normally revised four times a year as new information is released, but they may be reviewed weekly. The sources for forecasts are historic short-, medium-, and long-term asset class returns and economic forecasts.

Returns for the periods 1924-67, 1947-97, and 1961-97 are shown in the following table:

Asset Class Returns, Various Periods				
Period	T-Bills (91-day)	Bonds (long govt.)	Stocks (TSE 300)	Inflation (CPI)
1924-67	NA	6.05%	10.46%	3.16%
1947-97	7.23%	9.22%	11.24%	5.36%
1961-97	7.80%	9.75%	11.99%	4.93%

The typical forecasting period for wealth managers is five years, although adjustments may take place more frequently. After all, long-term investment horizons require short-term reality checks.

4.4   Develop Long-Term Asset Mixes

The next step is to reconcile capital market expectations and risk tolerance to produce long-term asset mixes that reflect optimum portfolios at different risk levels.

5.0   Dynamic Asset Allocation

Once you have determined the long-term policy mix, you need to establish a dynamic rebalancing policy. Dynamic asset allocation refers to the systematic rebalancing, either by time period or by weight, of the securities in the portfolio, so that they match the long-term benchmark asset mix among the various asset classes.

Any rebalancing must reflect changes in capital market expectations, risk tolerances, or client objectives. The asset mix may have drifted away from the target mix because of abnormal returns within asset classes or changing capital market conditions. This kind of drifting away may also be the result of idle cash reserves or impending cash payments or movements in capital markets.

Rebalancing reinforces the integrity of the asset allocation policy; it means that the time and effort spent on establishing the long-term policy was not wasted. It also adds value by counter-cyclical selling and buying and enforces discipline by requiring managers and decision-makers to stick with a policy, even during unfavourable periods.

Rebalancing dampens returns in a strong market period, because the manager may have to reduce holdings of the strongest-performing component of the portfolio. It improves returns in a weak market period, because it is possible to buy weak asset classes at reduced price levels. In a weak market, rebalancing can often be accomplished with derivatives, which require a limited capital outlay and offer leverage. For example, if stock values have risen, it may be more efficient to sell index futures rather than stocks.

The ideal approach is to rebalance based on deviation from target weights in response to price and value fluctuations. For example, a manager might choose to adjust every time the portfolio deviates from the target by 1%. Simulations using past data could be used to set the target points for systematic rebalancing. Although deviation from weights is the theoretically correct approach, the more practical method is temporal rebalancing. This means reviewing the structure and adjusting the portfolio once or twice a year.

6.0　Tactical Asset Allocation

Tactical asset allocation is an active management strategy designed to add value by deliberately departing from the long-term asset allocation policy, but without changing the policy. It attempts to respond to the changing patterns of returns in markets.

Tactical asset allocation is often confused with market timing, but there is a subtle difference. Technically, tactical asset allocation is the process of adjusting a portfolio to take advantage of perceived inefficiencies in the prices of securities in different asset classes or within sectors. A particular tactical asset allocation strategy is short-lived, spanning a few weeks to a few months. Market timing, on the other hand, may result in a change to the long-term strategic allocation policy if a manager decides to increase holdings of an asset class beyond what the current strategic allocation allows.

Managers who use tactical asset allocation believe that an investment policy cannot be static. It makes little sense to pick a 10%/30%/60% cash/income/equity investment policy and stick with it, since the financial environment is constantly changing. They also believe that active shifts can add value.

Tactical asset allocation is also independent of risk tolerances—a change in risk tolerance may affect the strategic asset allocation, but tactical asset allocation assumes a constant level of risk tolerance.

Of course, portfolio revisions and switches incur costs, including commissions and loads, and possibly transfer fees, not to mention the "nuisance costs" of signing documents and negotiating instruments. The cost of acquiring and disposing of investments ranges from 0% for term deposits, GICs, and CSBs to 10% or more for speculative stocks and bonds. Commissions and loads alone do not capture all costs—many securities are subject to an auction, which also includes paying bid/ask spreads. Too much rebalancing might create excessive costs.

7.0　The Efficient Market Hypothesis

The choice between a passive or active investment strategy depends on one's attitude toward the efficient market hypothesis (EMH). This is the theory that current stock prices incorporate both past and current publicly available information. In other words, one cannot expect to earn excess profits by employing conventional analytic techniques using publicly available information. If you believe that markets are efficient, then you will follow a passive investment strategy.

The Efficient Market Hypothesis takes three forms.

- The *weak form* states that past price changes are unrelated to future price changes and that stock price changes are independent of each other. The weak form of EMH suggests that charting and technical analysis are of no value.

- The *semi-strong form* states that all price data plus all other known information (such as earnings, new product developments, financial difficulties) is already incorporated in a security's price. If the semi-strong form of the EMH is correct, then fundamental and technical analysis are ineffective in attempting to earn above-average risk-adjusted returns.

- The *strong form* states that stock prices fully reflect *all* information, both public and confidential. In this case, not only are fundamental and technical analysis pointless in attempting to earn above-average risk-adjusted returns, but also there is nothing to be gained from inside and non-disclosed information.

The EMH was widely accepted for many years until anomalies in security pricing and returns began to surface in the late 1970s. Analysts started to notice some low price-to-earnings multiples. Then researchers documented turn-of-the-year and day-of-the-week trends as well as unexpected performance from small-cap securities and neglected stocks.

Approximately 35 trading and pricing anomalies have been documented. Some market followers believe that chaos theory may explain these effects. In chaotic systems the behaviour of individual elements appears random, but they all—at least partially—follow a set of rules. The recent behaviour of stock prices, including the crash of 1987, has led some researchers to believe that stock price patterns may be chaotic rather than random and that forecasts of future stock prices, including the large, abrupt changes caused by panics and bubbles, are possible.

Managers who accept the pricing anomalies or chaotic view of the world believe that it is possible to find undervalued securities and therefore pursue an active security selection strategy. If they also believe in market timing and that market cycles can be identified, then they will adjust the strategic asset allocation or policy mix by buying or selling Treasury bills and bonds and stocks at different times.

These two approaches—searching for undervalued securities and market timing—need not be implemented simultaneously. For example, wealth managers who believe they can find undervalued securities, but that they cannot time or anticipate asset class return trends, may pursue an active security selection strategy, yet maintain a fixed strategic asset allocation policy.

However, managers who believe in efficient markets, in which security prices reflect all information and economic cycles cannot be accurately forecast, will not spend time searching for undervalued securities or trying to predict economic cycles. Instead, they will take a passive approach to investing, by constructing and maintaining a portfolio in a cost-efficient manner.

Some investors adopt a mixed approach to their strategic asset allocation by apportioning part of their portfolio to active and part to passive investing.

8.0   Asset Mix Ranges for Different Portfolios

A strategic mix is usually ranges from 35%/65% to 65%/35% proportions of debt to equity. The table below shows some typical asset allocations:

Typical Asset Allocations				
	Conservative	Aggressive	Super-aggressive	Defensive
T-bills	10	5	2	12
Mortgages	10	5	5	12
Bonds	45	40	30	35
Stocks (Can.)	20	20	30	15
Stocks (U.S.)	5	10	10	6
Stocks (EAFE)	5	10	20	5
Real Estate	5	10	3	15
Total	100	100	100	100

Wealth managers usually identify a range of portfolios of varying volatility and calculate the expected basis point increments per additional risk for each one.

9.0   Taxes, Inflation and Other Expenses

Taxation and inflation play a role in an investor's choice of investments. To judge the impact of taxes and inflation, consider the historical returns of domestic asset classes. Over a 49-year period, yearly returns on cash averaged 6.27%, on bonds 7.35%, and on stocks 12.17%. The returns seem reasonable, but they do not account for taxes and the changing purchasing power of money.

Although inflation can be accurately measured—it averaged 4.25% a year over the 1950-98 period—information is not available on after-tax returns to Canadian investors over the same period. Because of changing tax regimes, it is impossible to accurately estimate after-tax returns over the past half-century. However, we can estimate. Suppose that from

1950 to 1998 an investor in the top tax bracket retained an average of two-thirds of investment income, paying out one-third to government. The results are shown in the following table.

Average Annual Returns: 1950 - 1998	Before taxes and inflation	After taxes	After taxes and inflation
Cash	6.27%	4.18%	−0.07%
Bonds	7.35%	4.90%	0.65%
Common Stock	12.17%	8.11%	3.86%

The real after-tax return on stock is probably understated because of the historically lower or nonexistent taxes on capital gains and dividends. Nevertheless, this table is fairly indicative of the situation in the last 15 or 20 years. But for bonds and cash (as measured by 91-day Treasury bills) the outcome is even more surprising. After adjusting for taxes, bonds barely maintained their purchasing power and Treasury bills lost in real value.

The effects of taxes and inflation reveal another risk—the risk of not being able to meet future commitments. This analysis suggests that the only way to maintain purchasing power over time is to invest heavily in common stock. Even that may not provide sufficient real return if the investment is restricted to the domestic market.

A taxable portfolio that does not contain a substantial proportion of common stocks may not retain its real value over time. Although other equity investments such as venture capital or real assets such as real estate and precious metals may provide inflation protection after adjusting for taxes, the asset allocation decision should include a significant amount of common stock.

Management fees and expenses must also be considered. For example, money market mutual funds have low management expense ratios (MER) and may be the most efficient vehicle for holding cash. However, the MER on money market mutual funds may be a larger proportion of return than for other mutual funds. Other sources of "riskless" investments, like short-term GICs, should be compared to the returns after management costs on money market mutual funds. Many mutual funds have relatively high MERs but, for small portfolios, mutual funds may be the most efficient way to achieve effective diversification.

"Wrap" accounts are accounts run by professional managers. They typically charge a flat fee (as a percentage of the value of assets managed). A larger minimum investment is necessary for wrap accounts than for mutual funds.

Segregated funds are investment pools offered by insurance companies. The type of vehicle used, whether a wrap account or investment pool, is a function of the size of the investment and the cost of the vehicle. Lower-cost vehicles generally require larger investment amounts

The complete range of managed products, from standard mutual funds to customized separately managed accounts, is discussed in Chapters 11 and 12.

10.0   Client Needs

Portfolio investment style is also determined by clients' current and future cash requirements.

Clients with adequate income who are thinking in terms of future retirement will focus on growth instead of current income. They may hold a smaller proportion of fixed-income investments and hold a larger proportion of common stock. Many managed funds feature long-term capital appreciation as their primary objective.

Other clients may need to generate current income. This usually means increasing the proportion of fixed-income securities in the portfolio and not reinvesting the periodic income. Investors who want to reduce their tax liability may want to invest in preferred shares, which pay fixed dividends, rather than bonds, which pay higher-taxed interest. The higher market price of preferred shares reflects this tax advantage.

It is important to think through the implications of substituting preferred shares for bonds based on tax considerations. Consider two investments with the same level of risk: a bond and a preferred share. The bond has a higher before-tax expected rate of return than the preferred share, but when personal taxes have been subtracted, the after-personal-tax expected returns are similar.

CHAPTER 11

Basic Managed Products

1.0   Introduction

After deciding on an asset allocation strategy for a client, you as a wealth manager must begin the process of helping the client choose managed products within the selected asset categories. The process starts with understanding the range of available products.

Over the past ten years, as more and more Canadians have accumulated liquid assets, managed investment products have proliferated, the most popular being mutual funds. According to the Investment Funds Institute of Canada (IFIC), which counts more than 95% of the mutual fund dealers in Canada as its members, at the end of January 2000, the total of assets under management in IFIC-member mutual funds was $382.7 billion. This compares with $20.3 billion in 1987 and $114.6 billion in 1993.

After experiencing the benefits of professional management through mutual funds and other types of investment funds, investors have gradually turned to other managed products, including segregated funds, realty and income funds, index participation units, hedge funds, wrap accounts, pooled funds, and separately managed accounts.

This chapter will cover investment funds, including mutual funds, segregated, realty, and income funds, and index participation units. Chapter 12 will focus on managed products such as hedge funds, managed futures funds, pooled funds, and separately managed accounts.

Primary Learning Objectives

By the end of this chapter, you should understand:

*   **the differences between open-end and closed-end investment funds;**
*   **various ways investment funds can be structured;**
*   **mutual fund alternatives;**
*   **the differences between active versus passive funds;**

- **the benefits of index participation and index-linked GICs in gaining market exposure;**

- **the unique characteristics of royalty and income trusts.**

- **The benefits of segregated funds.**

2.0   Investment Funds

An investment fund is a company that invests capital. It is similar to a regular corporation in that it raises capital. However, instead of using it to buy plant and equipment and hire employees, the fund invests in securities or other tradable assets with the goal of earning income and making capital gains. Money committed by investors is put into a pool of funds so that the investors own portions of the pool and do not directly own the assets.

Buying shares in an investment fund is often the easiest and most practical method for an investor to diversify, reduce transaction costs, obtain professional management, and get access to markets that would not otherwise be available. Also, some funds hold relatively illiquid assets that they can transform into liquid securities for investors. The advantages of investment funds have proven so popular that most investors now participate in securities markets through investment funds rather than by investing in securities directly. However, investors must ensure that they are not overpaying for the services they receive.

Open-end investment funds, better known as mutual funds, are the best-known type of pooled fund. They share some common features with other pooled investment vehicles and provide the basis against which all other investment funds are measured.

Closed-end investment funds are professionally managed portfolios of securities, precious metals, and other risky assets. They differ from mutual funds in that after the original issue of shares, closed-end funds only occasionally issue additional shares to raise more capital. Moreover, a closed-end fund does not stand ready to buy its shares back from shareholders.

3.0   Mutual Funds

Since Canada's first mutual fund made its initial share offering in December 1932 (Spectrum United Canadian Investment Fund), mutual funds have grown to include about 1,200 funds worth more than $389 billion as of the end of 1999. Individual funds range from under a million dollars to many billions of dollars. The 1990s have seen a phenomenal movement of investors into funds. About 40% of Canadian households invest in mutual funds and hold roughly 46 million accounts.

The distinguishing feature of a mutual fund is that it is a company or trust whose common shares or units are bought directly from the fund and can be sold back to the fund, usually at any time. In certain circumstances, however, purchases and redemptions may be restricted. Funds that hold assets that cannot easily be converted into cash without losing money (such as real estate), usually have redemption restrictions. For example, shares can be redeemed only on one month's notice.

A fund can suspend redemptions or postpone the date of payment for redemptions only with the consent of the appropriate securities commission. On the other hand, a fund may close itself to new investors at any time. This is often done when a fund reaches a size beyond which the management feels it would be difficult to find profitable new investment opportunities.

The price at which a fund buys and sells its shares is the net asset value per share (NAVS). It is calculated by dividing the net asset value of the fund's portfolio, essentially the estimated liquidation value of the fund, by the number of fund shares outstanding:

$$\text{Net asset value per share} = \frac{\text{net asset value of the portfolio}}{\text{number of fund shares outstanding}}$$

Nearly all funds calculate the NAVS daily, using market closing prices, although a few smaller funds calculate weekly to reduce costs. Funds holding assets that do not have price quotes (real estate is the best example) may be valued monthly or quarterly. Investors buy shares at the NAVS plus any applicable sales charge and redeem their shares at NAVS, minus any redemption fee.

3.1   Structure of a Mutual Fund

An investment fund would lose much of its appeal if both the fund and its shareholders were subject to full tax on the same income. Therefore, special provisions are made for investment funds under the *Income Tax Act*. A fund may elect to become a corporation or a trust.

Mutual Fund Corporations

To become a mutual fund corporation, the fund must be a Canadian public company, whose sole business is investing its funds. At least 95% of its issued shares must be redeemable at shareholders' demand.

A mutual fund company is subject to a special 25% tax on taxable dividends received from corporations resident in Canada. It is taxed at normal corporate rates on other income, such as interest and foreign dividends, and on 2/3rds of its net realized capital gains for the year.

Net realized capital gains are the capital gains earned from the sale of securities minus any capital losses incurred by security sales. The special 25% tax is refundable at the rate of $1 for each $4 of taxable dividends paid to shareholders. The tax on net realized capital gains is refundable when the gains are distributed to shareholders as a capital gains dividend within 60 days after the end of the fiscal year or by the redemption of shares at shareholders' request.

Normally, only domestic common and preferred share funds, which get their major source of income from Canadian corporations, use the corporate structure. In this way, the funds avoid paying tax by distributing their income and net realized gains. Otherwise, taxes hurt fund performance, making it difficult to attract investors.

Mutual Fund Trusts

Most funds operate as trusts instead of as corporations and issue units rather than shares. A trust is not liable for income tax if all revenues, including net realized capital gains, but not including operating expenses, flow through to the unitholders. Thus, trusts ensure that all receipts are paid out within the year, since trusts pay tax at the highest rate applicable to individuals. The income paid out to unitholders is considered the recipients' income and recipients are taxed accordingly.

Unitholders have less control than shareholders over the company but, to all intents and purposes, the outcome for investors is the same. Securities commissions across the country apply certain corporate voting rights to trusts. Trusts must call a special meeting of unitholders to seek their approval for:

*   any change in the fund's investment objectives;
*   any increases in the management fee;
*   any change in auditors or fund managers (other than to an affiliate of the current manager);
*   any change in the frequency in the calculation of net asset value.

A trustee is appointed who has clear fiduciary responsibilities. In effect, the shareholder's individual responsibility to vote at annual meetings is transferred to the trustee, who must act as a prudent person in handling the affairs of the trust. Mutual fund corporations must, of course, hold annual meetings.

Corporations, Trusts, and Tax Efficiency

For investors, the difference between corporate and trust structure has tax implications.

A tax-efficient fund works to minimize shareholder (or unitholder) taxes on its distributions.Consider a fund that has net realized capital gains at year-end. The gains must be paid out to avoid taxes on the fund, but the shareholders will pay capital gains tax on the distribution if the shares are not held in a tax advantaged plan. Shareholders would be better off if the fund had not sold the assets, because the gain would be unrealized and reflected in a higher NAVS.

For example, suppose a fund's NAVS is $40 and the fund pays out $1 a share in capital gains. The NAVS will fall to $39. An investor with a 35% marginal tax rate on capital gains has $39.65, since the distribution is worth only $0.65 a share after tax. If the fund had opted not to realize the price increase, the investment would have been worth $40 a share. This fund is not being tax-efficient.

Although net capital gains must be paid out, mutual funds cannot distribute net capital losses to shareholders. For a trust, each tax year is self-contained: what happened in prior years is irrelevant and so, for tax purposes, a net capital loss is gone forever. On the other hand, mutual fund corporations have the benefit of corporate tax law and can carry forward losses to reduce future gains. This improves their tax efficiency relative to trusts.

4.0 Types of Mutual Funds

Mutual funds are distinguished by their basic investment policy or by the kinds of assets they hold. Because assets are not always held according to a fund's objectives (a declared dividend fund might be heavily into growth stocks), the Investment Funds Institute of Canada set up a standard for Canadian mutual fund classification in May 1999. Funds are now classified into 33 categories within five broad groups. These groups are:

- cash and equivalent funds;
- fixed-income funds;
- balanced funds;
- equity funds;
- sector funds.

There are miscellaneous funds that do fit into any of these groups, as well as funds of funds or portfolio funds.

4.1 Cash and Equivalent Funds

As their name implies, these funds invest in near-cash securities or money market instruments—Treasury bills, bankers' acceptances, high-quality corporate paper, and short-term bonds. Government obligations may have a maximum maturity of 25 months, otherwise the maximum is 13 months. However, the dollar-weighted average term to maturity of the portfolio is limited to 180 days.

Canadian Money Market

Canadian money market funds add liquidity to a portfolio, as well as providing moderate income and safety of principal. According to National Policy 39, accepted by the Canadian Securities Administrators, Canadian money market funds must:

- have 95% of assets invested in Canadian short-term investments;

- have dollar-weighted terms to maturity averaging less than 180 days;

- be issued in Canadian dollars.

All the distributions from these funds are taxable as interest income.

A feature of these funds is the constant share value, usually $10. To keep a constant NAVS, the net income of the fund, including accrued interest and amortized discounts net of premiums, is calculated daily and credited to shareholders. The earned interest is paid out as cash or reinvested in additional shares on a monthly (or sometimes a quarterly) basis.

All realized net capital gains are distributed at year-end, so that the fund can keep its tax-free status (all money market funds are trusts). Normally, however, a fund holds its securities until maturity, so realized capital gains or losses are rare. Redemptions are made at the NAVS plus accrued interest.

Although money market funds seem to be similar to a savings account or term deposit, the stability of the NAVS is somewhat misleading. The stable price does not guarantee that all redemptions will be made at that price. Canadian money market funds are not required to mark their portfolios to market, that is, value their securities according to their trading prices in the market. Instead, most funds use the amortized cost method, valuing their investments at cost and then assuming a constant amortization to maturity of any discount or premium they paid, and ignoring the impact of fluctuating interest rates on the market value of the investments.

For example, suppose a fund buys a 10-day Treasury bill at $998.00. Each day the fund unitholders are credited with 20 cents (prorated) and the value of the instrument on the fund's books of account remains at $998.00. Two days after purchase, the claimed value of the instrument is $998.40 ($998.00 plus 40 cents credited to unitholders). But if short-term interest rates go up (and therefore Treasury bill prices fall), the security is probably worth less than this amount.

If the fund has net redemptions at $10 per unit plus accrued interest, too much value is taken out of the fund, leaving the remaining unitholders with an overvalued fund. In other words, a claim on the fund is not worth $10. Those who stay with the fund cannot all redeem at the quoted NAVS of $10, because the net asset value of the fund is overstated. The difference between the amortized fund value and the market value depends on:

- the size of the interest rate change;
- the rate of net redemptions;
- the average term-to-maturity of the portfolio.

Consequently, the worst possible situation is being unable to redeem at NAVS following a rapid and large increase in interest rates. The fund company may bear the burden by forgoing its management fee until the deficiency is rectified. Alternatively, the fund company could add more capital to the fund or even reduce, without compensation, the number of units held by each unitholder on a prorated basis.

For example say a fund has 1 million units outstanding with a NAVS of $10. A sudden large jump in interest rates reduces the fund's value from $10 million to $9.5 million. Because of a large redemption demand, fund management decides to reduce the number of units outstanding from 1 million to 950,000 to maintain true NAVS at $10. The cancellation of 50,000 units is a reduction of 5% of the outstanding units. This means the investor will lose 5% of 500 or 25 units.

Because of the fixed NAVS, day-to-day values are expressed as yields rather than unit values. Funds are required to state their yields in two formats:

- **Current yield** is the nominal annual rate of return from accrued or paid interest during the previous seven-day period. For example, suppose a fund paid 1.75 cents on each $10 unit in the preceding week. The return is:

$$0.175\% = 0.00175 \times (365/7) \times 100 = 9.13\% \text{ a year}$$

  To some degree, the current yield reflects the fact that a fund cannot guarantee the rate at which earnings will be reinvested.

- **Effective yield** uses weekly compounding:

$$100 \times [(1.00175)^{365/7} - 1] = 9.55\%$$

  The nominal yield assumes that the fund will continue to make 0.175% a week for the next year and that distributions will be reinvested.

Normally yield is a forward-looking measure; it provides an estimate of what returns will be under certain conditions. However, the current and effective yield figures may bear little relation to what an investor will earn in the fund, because they describe the recent past, not what will be paid in the future.

Foreign Money Market

These funds invest in the money market instruments of non-Canadian issuers. They also provide opportunities for currency investments. For example, if an investor expects the value of the Canadian dollar to decline against that of the U.S. dollar, buying a U.S.

money market fund places a currency bet without credit risk, because the underlying assets are essentially risk-free.

4.2   Fixed-Income Funds

The goal of fixed-income funds is to furnish a steady stream of income rather than capital appreciation.

Canadian Bonds

At least three-quarters of the fund's portfolio must consist of Canadian-dollar-denominated government or corporate bonds, debentures, and short-term notes, with an average portfolio term-to-maturity of more than three years.

High-Yield Bonds

At least three-quarters of the fund's portfolio must consist of government or corporate bonds, debentures and short-term notes. The remainder of the portfolio will contain bonds with below-investment-grade creditworthiness.

Canadian Short-Term Bonds

At least three-quarters of the fund's portfolio must be in Canadian debt instruments including bonds, mortgage-backed securities, term deposits, and guaranteed investment certificates with maturities between one and five years. At least half of the fixed-income section of the fund must be in instruments with maturities between 90 days and three years.

Canadian Mortgages

At least three-quarters of the fund's portfolio must be in Canadian industrial, commercial, or residential mortgages, including mortgage-backed securities.

Unlike bonds, there is no quote system for mortgage prices, so a different approach to computing the daily NAVS is needed. Mortgage funds run by financial institutions value their holdings by the rate the institution currently charges on new mortgages for the same term. Funds not tied to financial institutions tend to use an average of lenders' rates on similar mortgages. Because lending institutions do not change their mortgage rates daily, the NAVS varies much less for mortgage funds than for bond funds.

Foreign Bonds

At least three-quarters of the fund's portfolio must be in debt securities denominated in a foreign currency and have a dollar-weighted term to maturity of more than one year.

4.3   Balanced Funds

Balanced funds invest in both stocks and bonds to provide a mix of income and capital growth. These funds offer diversification, but unless the manager adds value by shifting investment proportions in anticipation of market conditions, investors might as well develop their own balanced portfolio by putting their money into more than one fund.

Canadian Balanced

At least three-quarters of the market value of the portfolio must be in a combination of Canadian equity and Canadian fixed-income securities. The equity component must be between 25% and 75% of the portfolio and fixed-income and cash together must be between 25% and 75% of the portfolio.

Global Balanced and Asset Allocation

The portfolio must be invested in a combination of equity, fixed-income instruments, and cash and cash equivalents. There are no restrictions on asset weightings. At least 25% of the investment must be in non-Canadian securities.

Canadian Tactical Asset Allocation

These funds use a tactical asset allocation strategy, that is, the portfolio is tilted toward the asset class expected to produce the highest return. The portfolio must combine Canadian fixed-income securities, equities, and cash and cash equivalents. There are no restrictions on the asset weightings.

Canadian High-Income Balanced

At least 25% of total assets are in interest-paying securities and at least 50% in non-interest but income-producing securities.

4.4   Equity Funds

Equity funds are the most popular type of fund and therefore have the most classifications.

50% Total
75% noncash

Canadian Diversified Equity

At least 50% of the total assets and 75% of non-cash assets of the portfolio must be in Canadian equities listed on a recognized exchange. In addition, at least 6 of the 14 TSE 300 sub-indexes must be represented with a weighting equal to at least 50% of the sub-index weighting within the TSE 300.

Canadian Large-Cap Equity

At least 50% of total assets and 75% of the non-cash assets must be invested in companies in the TSE 100. Moreover, the equity weighting must represent at least 2 of the 4 major sub-indexes of the TSE 100. Index funds designed to track the TSE 300, although they meet the large-cap criteria, are excluded from this category. These funds are considered to be in the Canadian Diversified Equity category.

Canadian Dividend

At least 50% of total assets and 75% of non-cash assets of the portfolio must be dividend-paying securities of Canadian corporations, equity securities convertible into the securities of Canadian corporations, or royalty and income trusts (restricted to 25% of the portfolio) listed on a recognized exchange. Dividends and other income must be distributed at least quarterly.

Canadian Small-/Mid-Cap Equity

At least 50% of the total assets and 75% of the market value of equity holdings must be in equities of Canadian companies that have a median market capitalization of no more than 0.2% of the total market capitalization of the TSE 300. This threshold is reviewed annually (as of November 30, 1998, it was $1.4 billion).

U.S. Small and Mid-Cap Equity

At least 50% of the total assets and 75% of the non-cash assets in the portfolio, based on individual market value, must be U.S. equities of companies that have a market capitalization of less than U.S.$6 billion.

North American Equity

At least 50% of the total assets and 75% of the non-cash assets of the portfolio must be equities or equity equivalents of companies in Canada and the United States or have derivative-based exposure to the Canadian and American markets. The U.S. equity component must represent at least 25% of the non-cash assets of the portfolio.

Unlike Canadian equity funds with U.S. exposure, these funds are typically not eligible for RRSPs or RRIFs and may hold up to 100% U.S. equities.

International Equity

At least 50% of the total assets and 75% of the non-cash assets of the portfolio must be equities or equity equivalents of companies outside Canada and the United States, or have derivative-based exposure to such markets.

European Equity

At least 50% of the total assets and 75% of the non-cash assets of the portfolio must be equities or equity equivalents of European companies, or have derivative-based exposure to developed European equity markets. More than one country must be represented in the portfolio at all times.

Japanese Equity

At least 50% of the total assets and 75% of the non-cash assets of the portfolio must be equities or equity equivalents of Japanese companies, or have derivative-based exposure to Japanese equity markets.

Asia ex-Japan Equity

At least 50% of the total assets and 75% of the non-cash assets of the portfolio must be equities or equity equivalents of companies which are located in Asia, excluding Japan, Australia, and New Zealand, or have derivative-based exposure to such markets.

Asia/Pacific Rim Equity

At least 50% of the total assets and 75% of the non-cash assets of the portfolio must be equities or equity equivalents of companies which are located in Asia, Australia, or New Zealand, or have derivative-based exposure to such markets.

Emerging Markets Equity

At least 50% of the total assets and 75% of the non-cash assets of the portfolio must be equities or equity equivalents of companies that are located in emerging markets countries, or have derivative-based exposure to such markets. Any country not considered one of the "developed" countries is an emerging market.

The developed markets are Australia, Austria, Belgium, Canada, Denmark, Finland, France, Germany, Hong Kong, Ireland, Italy, Japan, Netherlands, New Zealand, Singapore, Spain, Sweden, Switzerland, the United Kingdom, and the United States. All other countries are considered emerging markets.

Latin American Equity

At least 50% of the total assets and 75% of the non-cash assets of the portfolio must be equities or equity equivalents of companies located in Latin American countries, or have derivative-based exposure to such markets.

Global Equity

At least 50% of the total assets and 75% of the non-cash assets of the portfolio must be equities or equity equivalents of companies in each of three geographic regions—Asia, the Americas, and Europe—or have derivative-based exposure to such markets.

4.5   Sector Funds

Sector funds invest in specific industries, countries, regions, or trading blocs.

Country-Specific Equity

At least 50% of the total assets and 75% of the non-cash assets of the portfolio must be invested in a specific country.

Science and Technology

At least 50% of the total assets and 75% of the non-cash assets of the portfolio must be invested in equities or equity equivalents of companies primarily engaged in some aspect of science or technology. No geographic restrictions apply.

Natural Resources

At least 50% of the total assets and 75% of the non-cash assets of the portfolio must be equities or equity equivalents of companies primarily engaged in the exploration, extraction, or production of natural resources. No geographic restrictions apply.

Precious Metals

At least 50% of the total assets and 75% of the non-cash assets of the portfolio must be equities or equity equivalents of companies primarily engaged in the exploration, extraction, or production of precious metals. No geographic restrictions apply.

Real Estate

At least 50% of the total assets and 75% of the non-cash assets of the portfolio must be equities or equity equivalents of companies primarily related to or engaged in direct investment in commercial and residential real estate. No geographic restrictions apply.

Properties are appraised once a year, so the NAVS is always somewhat out of date. During falling real estate markets, securities commissions normally approve funds' requests to suspended redemptions. They do so because investors who cash in their holdings at full (overstated) NAVS are better off than those who remain in the fund, who will see their NAVS drop as properties are sold and appraised values catch up to market values.

Specialty

At least 50% of the total assets and 75% of the non-cash assets of the portfolio must be related to a specific sector described in the fund's prospectus.

Miscellaneous

Miscellaneous funds are those that do not fit into any of the other defined fund categories, and are sufficiently unusual not to warrant the creation of a new category. This is considered a residual category.

4.6   Portfolio Funds

Portfolio funds, instead of investing directly in securities, hold other mutual funds. Normally, the constituent funds and the fund of funds are within the same family. There are two main types of portfolio funds:

- those in which the individual investor may choose the asset mix;

- those in which the asset mix is decided by the fund company and is the same for all investors.

Funds of funds offer diversification, the ability to rebalance holdings at the initiative of either the client or the fund manager, and the simplicity and convenience of a single purchase. However, it is not always easy to assess their relative performance and they do not offer the flexibility to pick and choose among a wide range of products.

A portfolio fund structure may have an additional layer of fees: fees for the portfolio fund as well as those for the underlying funds. However, management fees are usually waived at the upper level, leaving the unitholders responsible only for the fees charged by the underlying funds.

Multi-Class Funds

Several companies, including AGF Management Ltd., C.I. Mutual Funds, and AIM Funds Management Inc., offer funds that are structured as fund corporations and consist of multiple classes of shares. Each share class represents a different asset category, many of which have different managers or management teams.

C.I. Sector Fund Ltd. offers a wide choice of classes of shares, including diversified Canadian or global equity markets, regional markets such as Asia, Europe, or Latin America, or industry sectors including resources, health, technology, telecommunications, and financial services.

The benefit of multi-class funds is the ability to switch from one class of shares to another without the switch being considered a sale for tax purposes. The multi-class structure is designed for use in taxable accounts. It is attractive for clients who want to make tactical switches from one region to another or from one industry sector to another without having to pay tax immediately. Since an individual can only defer taxation rather than eliminate it, when the units are redeemed, the client will be taxed on any capital appreciation above the adjusted cost base.

Funds of Funds

Funds of funds are diversified investments for which asset allocation is the sole responsibility of the fund manager. They are, for the most part, simply another form of balanced fund. Their risk and return characteristics reflect the mix of underlying funds and the extent to which the manager maintains a stable or varied mix of the component funds.

A fund of funds might serve either as a diversified core holding or, depending on the mix of funds it holds, as a vehicle that plays a narrower role such as providing the client's exposure to foreign equities.

Since company-managed funds of funds provide the same asset mix to all unitholders, it is important to consider other investments that would complement a fund of funds.

Asset-allocation approaches in company-managed funds of funds vary widely.

- In the portfolio funds offered by Investors Group Inc., the asset mix generally remains fixed. The funds are intended to offer clients a simple, one-stop-shopping approach that provides diversification within a single fund.

- The company sponsoring a fund of funds may have a policy specifying the extent to which the mix of the underlying funds can vary. Examples of this approach are the three Advantage funds offered by Royal Trust, which set out specific restrictions on the mix of assets to be held in the funds.

- The manager of a fund of funds may have discretion to vary the asset mix. An example of this approach is the Dundee Fund of Funds offered by Dundee Mutual Funds. Although the fund has a mandate to invest in a combination of domestic and foreign equity and fixed-income funds, not all asset classes are represented in the portfolio at any one time. In mid-1996, for instance, the management of Dundee Fund of Funds reduced the weighting in the fund of Dynamic Income Fund to zero because of a neutral-to-bearish outlook at the time for the North American bond market. These types of funds of funds can provide the benefits of tactical asset allocation for a client.

5.0   Mutual Fund Styles

Mutual funds are distinguished by product or by style. The two main investment styles are active and passive. These terms were introduced in Chapter 10, and discussed in even more detail in Chapter 13.

5.1   Active Funds

Most funds are active funds, whereby the manager tries to increase returns through selection and timing. Properly executed, these strategies will enhance returns. However, the cost of running a portfolio increases with activity. Management fees must cover trading costs, analysts' expenses and greater compensation for money managers to recognize their skills. Active trading also produces capital gains and reduces the tax efficiency of a fund.

5.2   Passive Funds

Passive portfolio management is consistent with the view that securities markets are efficient — that is, securities prices at all times reflect all relevant information on expected return and risk. The passive portfolio manager does not believe that it is possible to identify stocks as underpriced or overpriced, at least to an extent that would achieve enough extra return to cover the added costs.

Passive fund managers aim to reduce investment management fees using a buy-and-hold system. Most funds use indexing, that is, selecting a market index and replicating it by holding the securities that make up the index in the same proportions as the index-weighting scheme.

Index Funds

The goal of passive mutual fund portfolio management is to track the performance of a relevant target—usually a broad, diversified index such as the TSE 300 or the S&P 500. Sometimes a fund will track a specialized index such as a small-cap index or a growth index.

Usually the index fund invests in the securities that make up the index they imitate, in the same proportion that these securities are weighted in the index. For example, if the chosen index is the TSE 300 and the Bank of Montreal represents 0.75% of the TSE 300, the index fund must include 0.75% Bank of Montreal stock.

Alternatively, the fund may buy a subset of the index securities so that the portfolio is highly correlated with the index. This approach reduces the costs associated with maintaining exact investment proportions in large portfolios.

In either case, index fund performance before the deduction of fees closely mirrors the market averages. The extent to which gross return differs from its index is known as **tracking error**. Global index funds have the highest tracking error, about 1.5% a year, while funds mimicking Canadian or U.S. indexes are normally within 0.20% to 0.25% of the index.

Indexing a portfolio decreases the costs of running the fund. No investment advice is needed, and a computer program can provide all the information needed to keep the fund portfolio on balance. Management fees and other administrative expenses are significantly decreased and average less than half the amount levied by actively managed funds. Nonetheless, there are still management fees and costs and therefore over time, a fund's return is always less than the return on the index it follows.

Index funds are also tax-efficient. Securities are bought or sold only when they are dropped or added to the index, so realized capital gains seldom flow through to fund holders.

Index Funds Using Derivatives

Rather than buying individual securities in proportion to their weighting in an index, an increasingly popular method of building an index fund is through the use of index derivatives. The use of index derivatives is particularly popular among managers of Canadian funds that invest in foreign markets.

These funds provide exposure to foreign markets but remain 100% RRSP-eligible by investing the funds assets in Canadian T-bills. For example, a fund with $100 million to invest might gain exposure to the S&P 500 by entering into $100 million worth of S&P 500 index futures contracts. Aside from the required margin deposit (which may be about 10%—usually invested in U.S. Treasury bills), most of the fund's assets (90%) are invested in Canadian securities (Treasury bills) making the fund eligible for RRSPs. The fund also complies with securities regulation, as 100% of the assets are invested in Treasury bills (in other words, leverage is not used).

Examples of this type of fund are Canada Trust EuroGrowth Investor Series, NN Can-Asian, and Scotia CanAm Growth.

Active Index Funds

The term "index fund" has traditionally been associated with passive management. However, the allure of added return through active management coupled with the appeal of lower operating costs that index funds provide has led to the creation of some partly active index funds.

One type is the enhanced index fund, which moves beyond the buy-and-hold strategy. For instance, the fund holds the securities in a stock index, but the manager may make modest sector adjustments, moving disproportionately into resource stocks when the manager believes that that sector will do especially well. Alternatively, the manager may overload individual stocks rather than sectors.

For most funds, the manager may not deviate too far from index weightings and therefore performance is similar to the index. For example 70% to 80% of the portfolio might mimic the index and the remaining 20% to 30% would be actively managed. These funds have slightly higher management fees than passive index funds. Examples are the InvesNat American Index Plus and InvesNat Canadian Index Plus.

Another form of active indexing is to buy and hold proprietary indexes that have been constructed on the belief that the securities composing the index will outperform relevant benchmarks. For example, a management firm may create an index consisting of the 50 stocks it feels have the greatest potential over the next year. The index is adjusted annually to reflect new information.

A mutual fund passively invests in the index and pays the investment company for doing so. Although the fund is passive, the index is based on active management. Management fees are higher than those for true index funds, but lower than actively managed funds. Royal Canadian Strategic Index, Royal U.S. Growth Strategic Index, and Royal U.S. Value Strategic Index are examples.

6.0   Closed-End Funds

Closed-end funds were the first type of investment fund available in Canada, but the stock market crash of 1929, coupled with the arrival of the more popular mutual fund, almost killed them off. Closed-end funds have since made a comeback, but they are vastly outnumbered by mutual funds.

Funds begin life like regular business corporations, issuing stock (or units, if the fund is a trust) either through initial public offerings or private placements. Outstanding shares trade on an exchange or over the counter like other stocks. Investors buy shares from other shareholders, not from the fund, and sell shares to other investors, not to the fund. Commissions are charged at normal brokerage rates. Some of the closed-end funds listed on the TSE are:

• Canada Trust Income Investment Trust;

• First Australia Prime Income Investment Co.;

• Third Canadian General Investment Trust Ltd.;

• United Corporations Ltd.

Management fees and administrative expenses (which may now include exchange listing fees) are lower than those of mutual funds, because these funds are not advertised or marketed. Closed-end funds also do not need load charges or trailer fees.

Another advantage of the closed-end structure is that money managers have the flexibility to concentrate on long-term investment strategies without reserving liquid assets to cover redemptions. Unlike a mutual fund, a closed-end fund can be fully invested at all times.

The most interesting feature of a closed-end fund is the market price at which it trades. Mutual fund shares are bought and sold at prices based directly on their NAVS. But prices of closed-end shares vary with market forces and, for reasons unknown, most fund shares sell at a discount to NAVS. A few funds sell at small premiums but the typical case is a discount, some in the order of 30% or more. For example, in mid-1999 the four funds mentioned above had the following pricing:

Fund	NAVS	Price	Discount
Canada Trust Income	$9.70	$8.75	−9.8%
First Australia Prime	$11.71	$9.80	−16.3%
Third Canadian General	$20.43	$15.80	−22.7%
United Corporations	$66.90	$44.50	−33.5%

The size of the discount or premium usually varies over time. Sometimes a share moves from a premium to a discounted price or vice versa.

The discount at which most funds trade makes it difficult for new closed-end funds to form. There is little reason for investors to buy new shares when the shares will probably soon be selling at a discount to the price that they originally paid. One variation used to help sell a fund is to give the new fund a stipulated term, such as ten years. At the end of that time, it will be wound up and the proceeds will be distributed to the owners. As the liquidation date approaches, the discount narrows, as share price moves toward NAVS. New Altamira Value Fund, for example, is scheduled to terminate on December 31, 2001, and the proceeds will be distributed to unitholders unless an alternative is approved before then.

7.0   Index Participation Units

One of the most efficient investment products for passive investors is the so-called index participation unit (IPU). IPUs are exchange-traded securities that represent a basket of stocks and that replicate a specific market index. IPUs trade on exchanges just like stocks at a designated IPU-to-Index ratio.

Financial innovators tried for years to develop a tradable basket product that represents a market index. In the 1980s, CIPs (Cash Index Participation Units), VIPs (Value of Index Participation Certificates), and Index Trust SuperUnits, were introduced and failed in the U.S., either because of poor design or because of jurisdictional disputes among regulators, exchanges, and institutions.

The legal securities structure was more accommodating to financial innovation in Canada. The Toronto Stock Exchange introduced Toronto Index Participation units (TIPS) on March 9, 1990. The TIPS structure is sound, and it has served as the model for subsequent IPUs, including Standard & Poors Depository Receipts (SPDRs) based on the Standard & Poor's 500 Composite, and World Equity Benchmark Shares (WEBS) based on Morgan Stanley Capital International indexes.

7.1   Canadian IPUs

S&P/TSE 60 (i60s)

On January 19, 2000 the Toronto Stock Exchange announced a plan to merge the Toronto 35 Index Participation unit (TIPS) and the TSE 100 Index Participation Units (HIPS) with the S&P/TSE 60 Index Participation Units (i60s). The i60s started trading in October 1999. The mergers were completed after the March 6, 2000 market close.

The i60s are units of the S&P/TSE 60 index participation fund. The fund is a trust organized by Barclays Global Investors Canada Limited (BGI), that seeks to match the performance of the S&P/TSE 60 Index—an index that consists of 60 of the largest and most liquid stocks traded on the TSE. The fund seeks to maintain a risk-controlled profile of roughly 15 basis points of tracking error relative to the index. In other words, as with

TIPS and HIPS, its market value should rise and fall in almost exact proportion to changes in the index.

The value of each i60 unit is 1/10th of the S&P/TSE 60 index. If, for example, the S&P/TSE 60 index is quoted at 500, the units sell at $50.00 each. There is a small deviation between the i60 price and the index value, due primarily to accumulated dividends. However, i60s track the index very closely.

Every quarter, unitholders receive dividends paid by the 60 companies that make up the index. Annual expenses for i60s are expected to be about 0.15 to 0.17 percent. By comparison, the annual management fee for some Canadian index mutual funds can be as high as 0.80% or higher. Of course, the investment dealer charges a commission when the units are bought and sold.

Distributions

The i60 will make quarterly distributions that will consist primarily of dividends received by the fund, as well as interest and security lending income less expenses.

There is also the possibility of capital gain distributions. These are gains that result from dispositions of shares from the i60s at a price over cost. Gains are made, for example, when a company included in the i60s is successfully taken over. The event causes a disposition within the i60s basket (deemed or real) that can trigger a capital gain. What actually happens is that the gain is immediately reinvested in the fund on behalf of the unitholder and the number of i60s units is consolidated so that the number of units outstanding remains unchanged. The unitholder therefore has a taxable capital gain (although no actual gain is received) for tax purposes. This capital gain is subject to the 2/3rds inclusion rule. It is added to the unitholder's adjusted cost base, thus reducing the gain (or increasing the loss) that would otherwise be incurred when the units are eventually sold.

7.2   U.S. IPUs

SPDRs

The first U.S. index participation unit version was Standard and Poor's Depository Receipts or SPDRs. SPDR units are traded in minimum increments of 64ths of a dollar, or $.016625. Like i60s, SPDRs are quoted and traded in units representing 1/10th the value of the S&P 500. For example if the S&P 500 index is at 1098.73, the value of one SPDR unit will be US$109.87. The market price will generally be about 0.3% to 0.5% higher.

The SPDR Trust will expire in 2018. The dividends and other distributions of the 500 companies of the S&P 500 are collected and invested by the trust and distributed quarterly to the unitholders.

Mid-Cap SPDRs, introduced on May 4, 1995 are based on the S&P 400 MidCap Index, made up of mid-cap US companies.

Select-sector SPDRs, introduced on December 22, 1998, are sector-specific index products that are subsets of the S&P 500 Composite Index. There are nine different IPUs based on:

- basic industries;
- consumer services;
- consumer staples;
- cyclicals/transportation;
- energy;
- financial;
- industrial;
- technology;
- utilities.

Other IPUs

The NASDAQ-100 shares introduced in 1999 are based on the NASDAQ-100 Index of 100 mid- and large-cap companies traded on the National Association of Securities Dealers stock exchange. The index emphasizes high-tech and Internet stocks.

DIAMONDS, the first financial product based on the Dow, was introduced January 20, 1998. The Dow Jones Industrial Average is a large-cap index of 30 blue-chip companies traded on the New York Stock Exchange.

SPDRs and DIAMONDS are qualified investments for the foreign content component of RRSPs, RRIFs, and Deferred Profit Sharing Plans (DPSPs).

7.3   Global IPUs

Morgan Stanley World Equity Benchmark Shares (WEBS) were launched in May 1996. WEBS replicate specific Morgan Stanley Capital International (MSCI) indexes. The fund is advised by BZW Barclays Global Fund Advisor. There are 17 series, each one tied to a specific MSCI index. The MSCI World Composite index, launched in 1969, is the most widely used world performance index. All MSCI indexes are total return indexes and net dividends (after withholding taxes) are deemed to be reinvested.

WEBS are available for Australia, Austria, Belgium, Canada, France, Germany, Hong Kong, Italy, Japan, Malaysia, Mexico, Netherlands, Singapore, Spain, Sweden, Switzerland, and the United Kingdom.

Country	Ticker	Index	No. of Companies
Australia	EWA	MSCI	49
Austria	EWO	MSCI	24
Belgium	EWK	MSCI	20
Canada	EWC	MSCI	84
France	EWQ	MSCI	74
Germany	EWG	MSCI	69
Hong Kong	EWH	MSCI	38
Italy	EWI	MSCI	55
Japan	EWJ	MSCI	317
Malaysia	EWM	MSCI	76
Mexico	EWW	MSCI	41
Netherlands	EWN	MSCI	22
Singapore	EWS	MSCI	32
Spain	EWP	MSCI	31
Sweden	EWD	MSCI	30
Switzerland	EWL	MSCI	43
United Kingdom	EWU	MSCI	144

8.0   Index-linked GICs

Index-linked term deposits vary considerably, although they have one common feature—each pays a guaranteed basic interest rate plus an additional increment tied to the performance of a single market index or a portfolio of market indexes.

For example, CIBC has introduced three-year and five-year GICs that come in four versions. Each one represents a different mix of GICs, bonds, and equity. The GIC component is tied to the GIC yield, the income component to the CIBC Wood Gundy bond index, and the equity component to the aggregate performance of a Canadian (Toronto 35), an American, a Japanese, and a pan-European (Eurotop 100) market index.

Some pay off based on the closing level of the underlying index. Others base the payoff on the average monthly level of the underlying index. For some products, the investor gets the full increase in the index—for others, only a percentage of the increase. Some are capped and therefore subject to a maximum potential profit.

Financial products aimed at retail investors should be fairly advertised, they should be transparent (investors know what they are and where they fit into a portfolio), their return and risk features should be easy to describe, and they should be relatively simple to value.

Index-linked GICs, however, can be difficult to describe and to value. For example, one GIC offered by a well-known trust company is linked to the markets of the G7 countries.

This exotic product pays a floor rate of interest plus an increment pegged to an aggregate index of G7 markets, subject to a maximum of 35% over a three-year period. A 35% return over three years is 9.1% on an annual compounded basis. Although this is a good return, 9.1% hardly sounds as dramatic as 35%!

It is also difficult to determine where index-linked GICs fit into a portfolio. They look simple, but these products, which are retail versions of "heaven" bonds or structured notes in the derivatives markets, are hard to value. An index-linked GIC is actually a term deposit plus a call option on the market. The equation for valuing call options is known as the Black-Scholes option pricing model, and uses the heat exchange equation. This makes valuation difficult for anyone who is not trained in investment finance.

9.0 Royalty and Income Trusts

9.1 Royalty Trusts

Royalty Trusts (RITs), like pooled funds, hold "portfolios" of assets (natural resources, commodities, or real property) and earn cash flows on these investments. The net cash flows (cash flow minus management fees and administration costs) are passed on to the unitholders in the form of interest and dividends. The market value of the trust at any time should reflect the long-term expected value of the cash flows. Most of these trusts distribute income monthly or quarterly. RITs are RRSP-eligible and are not considered foreign property, as long as the real estate portfolio does not contain more than 25% non-Canadian property.

There are different types of RITs—each geared to different investor incomes, investment and tax needs, and circumstances. The most popular are oil and gas, coal, and iron, although many innovative versions exist, including shipping terminals and hotels.

There are two key valuation and investment considerations:

- cash-on-cash yield;

- the reserve life index.

Cash-on-Cash Yield

The cash-on-cash yield is the current one-year expected payout on the unit, divided by the current unit price. At present, yields range from about 9% to 16%. Needless to say, these are relatively high yields, much higher than those available on bonds and other conventional fixed-income securities. The problem is that this cash-on-cash yield is highly misleading on its own, because it ignores the life of the product.

The cash-on-cash yield has to be measured against the expected life of the property or the reserve life index, calculated by dividing the proven and probable reserves (normally only one-half of the probable are used) by the annual rate of production. Obviously, the shorter the reserve life index, the faster the reserves will be depleted, and the shorter the payoff.

Take the case of Royalty Fund A, an oil and gas royalty trust. The fund's annual distributions are $1.44 a unit or 16.1% based on its current $8.90 price. But, with an estimated reserve life of about eight years, this translates into an internal rate of return (IRR) of about 6.1% a year, if the reserves are not extended.

Reserve Life Index

Estimated annual return is highly sensitive to the reserve life index. For example, if the life is extended to 10 years, the yield will be 9.89% a year. Obviously if management is successful in finding and developing new products and extending the estimated life of the property, values will rise.

Other Factors Affecting Values

Values are also affected by the way in which growth is financed. If it is financed with the sale of new units, the existing unitholders suffer dilution, unless the rate of return on the new projects equals at least the rate of return on the old, relative to the same cost of capital. So there is a "shell game" aspect to RITs that have short lives, since management must keep selling new units, investing in new projects, or expanding existing ones—or face deterioration in unit values.

Royalty income and the amount of the distribution will also vary with the price of the underlying commodity of the fund. The market value will drop if interest rates rise and/or the price of the underlying asset (such as oil and gas) drops. If interest rates drop and the price of the commodity rises, the value will also rise.

RIT prices are therefore a function of:

- cash-on-cash yield;

- estimated reserve life;

- changing interest rates;

- replacement development policies and skills of management;

- the price of the underlying commodity, including exchange rate implications.

Tax Consequences

Unitholders are allocated a depletion allowance, royalty tax credits, or a capital cost allowance on the underlying properties. A portion of the distributions may therefore be tax-deferred, depending on whether there is still a depletion or capital cost allowance pool (every trust is at a different stage).

The following example shows the tax consequences. Suppose an investor buys 1,000 units of Athabaska Oil Sands Trust at $21.00 a unit, receives $3,500 ($3.50 a share) in aggregate, tax-deferred distributions and $4,000 in taxable dividends over time, and then sells the shares for $19.50 a share. The investor will pay the following taxes (excluding commissions):

	Per share	Total
Proceeds of disposition:	$19.50	$19,500
Adjusted cost base: Original Cost	$21.00	
Less: tax-deferred dividends	$3.50	
Adjusted cost base:	$17.50	$17,500
Capital gain	$2.00	$2,000

This would mean a capital gain of $2,000, or a taxable capital gain of $1333.33, since only 2/3rds of the gain is included in income. The $4,000 in taxable dividends will be included in the investor's income in the year received.

9.2   Income Trusts

Income Trusts (ITs) hold portfolios of high-yield, fixed-income securities and earn cash flow on these investments. The net cash flow (cash flow minus management fees and administration costs) are passed on to unitholders in the form of distributions. Most of these trusts distribute income monthly or quarterly. At present, yields range from about 7% to as high as 30%.

The cash-on-cash yield must be measured against the actual performance of the portfolio. If cash-on-cash yields remain steady or rise when the market value of the assets in the portfolio are falling, the market values of the units will decline and the fund will essentially be repaying capital to unitholders. If the fund is badly designed or functions poorly, investors might find themselves in the worst of all possible tax situations: they will have high taxable income because of high-interest income, coupled with declining prices, for which there is little or no offsetting tax benefit.

Some of the newer ITs offer unitholders a continuous right to redeem units. For example, one fund allows unitholders the following privilege:

> Units tendered within five business days of the last day of the month are redeemed as at that final date with payment on or before the eighth business date following the redemption date. Units tendered after that date are redeemed on the last business day of the next month. The redemption price is the NAVPU less the lesser of (i) 4% of the NAVPU [net asset value per unit] and (ii) $1.00 per unit. In February each year the redemption price is the NAVPU without adjustment.

Many income trusts have ambitious objectives: an 8% to 9% annual return target is typical. As with their investment cousins, the royalty trust, some income trusts have been maintaining high distributions at the expense of declining unit values. In other words, they are distributing some capital back to unitholders.

First Premium Income Trust (FPI), which is traded on the TSE, is a typical income trust. It was introduced in June 1996 at a price of $25.00. The fund's objective is to make quarterly distributions of at least 50 cents a unit, which translates into a cash-on-cash yield of 7.7%, based on the current market price. FPI holds a diversified portfolio of Canadian common shares spanning the major industry sectors. The largest allocations at present are to utilities (26%) and financial services (25%). The ten largest holdings are: BCE Inc., Royal Bank of Canada, Bank of Nova Scotia, Imasco Limited, Canadian Imperial Bank of Commerce, Donohue Inc. Class A, Imperial Oil Ltd., Alcan Aluminum, Thompson Corporation, and Manitoba Telecom Services Inc. The fund manager sells (writes) call options against part of the portfolio in order to enhance the income. Covered call writing was discussed in Chapter 6.

10.0   Real Estate Investment Trusts

Efficient diversification means holding securities that normally react differently to market and economic events. One key diversification principle is purchasing power protection, that is, holding assets that guard against unfavourable movements in the inflation rate. Although sometimes subject to severe short-term swings, as investors discovered in 1991, over the long run, real estate has been a great hedge against inflation.

The most convenient investment form is the real estate investment trust (REIT). A REIT is a pool of capital invested in income-producing real estate properties and mortgages. If there are 100,000 units of the REIT outstanding and an investor owns 1,000 units, the investor has 1% of the pool and is entitled to 1% of the distributions (which are based on the income of the fund after expenses and management fees.)

REITs are closed-end funds, which means that their units are publicly traded. For illiquid assets such as real estate, the closed-end structure makes the most sense, because open-end or mutual real estate funds are subject to new money and redemption problems that closed-end forms avoid. (In fact, real estate mutual funds all but disappeared in the 1991-92 real estate collapse because of liquidity problems.)

The typical Canadian REIT distributes about 85% to 95% of its income (rental income from properties), usually quarterly. The taxable income earned by the trust flows through the REIT and is taxed when it reaches the Canadian holders. REIT holders are also entitled to a deduction for the pro-rated share of capital cost allowance (depreciation on the properties). As a result, about 75 to 85% of the distributions are normally tax-deferred. However, the value of the tax-deferred receipts reduces the adjusted cost base of the shares.

For example, if you buy 1,000 units of Real Fund at $15.50 a unit, receive $3,000 ($3.00 a share) in aggregate, tax-deferred distributions over time, and then sell the shares for $17.50 a share, you will have a capital gain of:

$$1000 \times (17.50 - 15.50 + 3.00) = \$5,000$$

before adjustments for commissions. The gain will be subject to capital gain treatment. That means that 2/3rds of the gain or $3333.33 will be included in income and taxed at normal rates.

REITs are RRSP-eligible and are not considered foreign property, as long as the real estate portfolio doesn't contain more than 25% non-Canadian property.

The typical Canadian REIT currently yields about 7% to 8% at present, well above the rates on preferred shares and other fixed-income securities. They do have drawbacks, however. Real estate properties depreciate in value without significant maintenance and periodic renovation and renewal. All or most of the REIT's income is distributed and the capital cost allowance is allocated to the investor, so the investor is really getting his or her own capital back, since the book value of the real estate properties will be steadily depleting. Of course, if the properties are appreciating in value, this could offset the depletion factor. The point is that the long-term income stream is quite variable.

REITs have their place in a long-term investment portfolio. For market timers or tactical asset allocators, REITs are ideal for trying to profit from a poor real estate market.

11.0   Segregated/Protected Funds

Segregated funds are investments or pooled funds sponsored by insurance companies. They are insurance products—technically, "individual variable insurance contracts." At the end of 1998, according to the Canadian Life and Health Insurance Association, an estimated $59.3 billion in segregated-fund contracts were issued by about 40 member firms. As segregated funds are an insurance product, they were discussed in Chapter 6.

Although technically they are pooled or mutual fund investments plus an insurance contract, legally, they are an insurance contract with principal and life insurance guarantees. The investor has no ownership of the assets held in the segregated fund. Instead, the investment is in the form of an insurance contract. The insurance company invests in a pool of assets that meet investors' objectives.

Segregated fund managers have two mandates. The first and overriding one is to avoid loss of investor principal, and the second is to produce a positive rate of return. Segregated funds must provide, as a minimum, a guarantee of at least 75% of the deposits to the contract (less reductions for withdrawals) with at least a 10-year term to maturity. This means that the estate receives the greater of the minimum guarantee (such as 75% or 100%) on the entire net deposit of the investor and the current market value of the fund. Many segregated funds have age restrictions.

Segregated funds also provide creditor protection that mutual funds do not provide. The segregated fund is an insurance contract and belongs to the beneficiary at the death of the fundholder. Another important feature is that as long as a beneficiary has been named, on the death of the original owner the proceeds pass directly to the beneficiary without passing through the owner's estate, thus avoiding probate and legal fees.

Until recently only insurance companies offered this product. Today, mutual fund corporations and financial institutions are offering their own versions of segregated funds. Typically called guaranteed or protected funds, they are available in registered and non-registered forms and a wide range of asset allocations. They also offer principal and death benefit guarantees. Sponsors are marketing existing mutual funds and coupling them with an insurance guarantee rather than creating new mutual funds. So a guaranteed investment fund is just a traditional investment plus an insurance wrapper.

Most of the segregated and guaranteed funds offer resets, which allow the investor to reset the principal guarantee to a higher level and lock in all or part of the profits earned to date. The primary drawbacks of these funds are the costs and their lack of transparency. The typical management expense for the guarantee is 1% a year. To value the product properly, it is necessary to value the guarantee (or put option) to ensure that the price is fair.

CHAPTER 12

Managed Products for the High-Net-Worth Client

1.0 Introduction

In addition to the products described in the previous chapter, investors with significant assets have additional investment options. These options offer enhanced customization, broader diversification opportunities, lower fees, and a higher level of service. Alternative investment strategies, such as hedge funds and private equity funds, are also available to high-net-worth individuals.

These services are not accessible to all investors. Specialist portfolio managers are required on the client's portfolio management team and this level of service is expensive to provide. Firms that serve the high-net-worth market usually specify a minimum account size. In some cases, these requirements are necessary to meet regulatory standards; for example, minimum investment levels in non-prospectus pooled funds.

In this chapter, we will define a high-net-worth investor as one with $500,000 or more to invest. Some firms have even higher minimums for certain products or services, particularly for separately managed portfolios.

Primary Learning Objectives

By the end of this chapter, you should understand:

- **the unique characteristics and advantages of separately managed accounts;**

- **the differences between separately managed accounts and pooled funds;**

- **the features of a wrap account and their advantages and disadvantages relative to other managed products;**

- **the different types of hedge funds and the questions that investors should ask of hedge fund managers;**

- **the different ways investors can gain exposure to managed futures.**

2.0.   Separately Managed Portfolios

In separately managed portfolios, investors own the securities directly. They are available through investment counsel, trust companies, and investment dealers. Minimum investment varies from firm to firm; however, the minimum depends on the diversification requirements of the strategic asset mix, or the firm's desire for exclusivity. The more diversified the mix, the larger the portfolio must be.

Separately managed portfolios provide the greatest amount of flexibility to incorporate an investor's unique needs. This flexibility allows for significant customization in policies and management. Guidelines are set out in a detailed investment policy statement designed to capture the investment objectives, risk tolerance, and other requirements for the management of the portfolio.

Flexibility can be achieved through the selection of asset classes and their ranges, and the exclusion of certain types of securities. Some investors, for example, prefer to hold a portfolio that does not permit investments in alcohol, tobacco, or weapons manufacturers.

2.1   Tax Advantages

Separately managed funds offer three tax advantages:

1. Because investors own the securities directly, the securities are readily saleable or transferable. Investors can manage tax planning by directing gains or losses to be realized. They may choose to donate low-cost base securities to a charitable cause, or to their heirs as part of estate planning.

2. By owning the securities directly, investors can change managers without necessarily triggering capital gains, unlike pooled funds, where investors are required to sell units, which may generate significant capital gains.

3. Fees that are charged to clients are tax-deductible in the hands of clients. By contrast, mutual fund MERs are not tax-deductible, since they are charged to the fund and the funds report their returns on a net after-fees basis.

2.2   Separately Managed Account Fees

Depending on the firm offering the account, the minimum account size may be as high as $3 million or as low as $1 million. Fees are based on a declining scale basis. As an example, a firm may charge 1% on the first $1 million of assets, 0.75% on the next $1 million, and 0.5% on the next $3 million. Custodial fees may add 0.3% to 0.4% to the fee charged.

3.0   Pooled Funds

The goal of pooled funds is to deliver investment management as efficiently as possible. Client money is invested on a "pooled" basis, and each investor owns a pro-rated share of the fund, similar to a mutual fund.

Pools are less expensive to operate than mutual funds, as the cost structure is lower, and they offer greater flexibility, because they are not subject to the same restrictions as National Policy 39, which governs mutual funds.

3.1   Structure of Pooled Funds

Pooled funds are sold without a prospectus. The general structure is similar to that of a mutual fund. Investors hold units in the fund. The units represent the investor's pro-rated share of holdings in the fund.

Another similarity with mutual funds is that the pool allocates interest, dividends, and capital gains through a distribution mechanism. Individuals receive these distributions, usually paid as dividends, at specified intervals.

Unlike mutual funds, pooled funds present the problem of unrealized capital gains. If a pool has significant unrealized capital gains, investors should consider the eventual distribution of those gains. They should also avoid investing in pooled funds just before an expected distribution.

3.2   Portfolios of Pooled Funds

There are two key differences between separately managed portfolios and pooled funds:

- pooled fund investors do not have the same level of control of the investment policy;
- the structure of pooled funds has different tax and transferability implications for the investor.

Investors in a pooled fund all have the same investment policy—the policy of the pool. However, it is possible to create mixed-asset-class portfolios using pooled funds.

The mix of allowable pools and their respective ranges can be customized to allow for tactical asset allocation. However, the sophisticated investor rule may affect the asset mix design, since the client must maintain a minimum level of investment in the pool at all times (minimums are set by provincial securities commissions). To respect these minimums and still create the desired asset mix, various techniques are employed. Investors may use a model portfolio option, or the portfolio can be tilted towards a specific asset class to increase exposure to that market.

The structure of pooled funds is such that investors own units of the pool, and capital gains, dividends, and interest accrue to the fund to be paid out regularly to unitholders as distributions. Each investor receives his pro-rated share of these distributions. The structure provides little flexibility for tax planning. The management of the portfolio can be transferred only by selling units, and these sales are subject to taxes.

The minimum account size for pooled funds is generally less than that for separately managed accounts. Some firms have a minimum size of as little as $150,000. Fees are charged as a percentage of assets, and are similar to those charged for separately managed accounts. Custodial, trustee, legal, audit, and brokerage fees may add 0.2% to 0.5%.

4.0   Wrap Accounts

Wrap accounts or wrap fee programs combine investment management and securities selection with order execution and custodial services. In these programs, the client assigns day-to-day management of an account to a partner, director, or qualified money manager, and gets professional money management and related services.

In the past, wrap accounts were offered as brokerage products, designed to provide wealthy investors with access to private asset management services. Generally, the target market for a wrap account was the client with $100,000 to $500,000 to invest.

Over the past few years, the popularity of wrap accounts has surged for both high-end and mid-market investors as fund companies, banks, and trust companies have introduced their own versions of wrap accounts, with many of the newer products targeting lower-end investors by reducing investment minimums. Examples of wrap programs include the Sovereign program at RBC Dominion Securities Inc., ScotiaMcLeod Inc.'s Pinnacle program, CIBC's Professional Investment Management Services, and AGF Management Ltd.'s Harmony program.

Wrap products range from those that offer little in the way of customization to those that offer a high level of customization. An example of the former is a fund of funds account that is essentially a fund that invests in units of mutual funds. As these funds offer little in the way of customization, they require a lower minimum investment compared to others. At the other end of the spectrum are the separately managed programs that offer a high level of customization and require a higher minimum account level.

Some wrap accounts rely entirely on proprietary products as their underlying investments. Others, such as some mutual fund programs, use a wide range of non-proprietary products.

Wrap programs allow clients to work with an investment advisor to develop an integrated investment strategy. They are suitable for clients who want professional money management of their assets within a customized framework. They do not usually involve active trading, nor are they suitable for investors who want to play an active role in making trades or selecting individual stocks or bonds. Wrap accounts generally provide a vehicle for strategic asset allocation and in some cases act as a form of personal pension plan. In mutual fund wrap programs, the service may involve dividing money among asset classes according to a model portfolio that suits the client's objectives. The account may be discretionary, which means that the client's approval is not required for each transaction, or non-discretionary.

Wrap accounts generally charge the client an annual fee based on the assets under management. The higher the amount invested, the lower the percentage fee tends to be. Some programs have a flat fee, others have lower fees, but charge for transactions. In some cases, a flat fee is charged for a certain number of transactions, and a commission applies to trades above this number. Fees for multi-manager wrap programs tend to be higher than for those for a single management firm.

4.1 Advantages of Wrap Accounts

The main advantages of wrap programs include:

- individualized asset allocation;
- the structuring of efficient portfolios to achieve an optimal return for a given level of risk tolerance;
- enhanced reporting services;
- tax-deductible fees.

For affluent individuals who want a high level of service, wrap accounts provide an alternative to mass-market managed funds. An advisor for a wrap account can ensure that a client's objectives are understood and met, and can customize an account according to the client's needs without being restricted to model portfolios.

Many programs allow advisors to develop optimal asset mixes for clients, using computer-driven asset allocation programs in combination with client questionnaires to come up with an efficient portfolio that maximizes the expected return for a given risk. These asset allocation programs take into account assets and investments held outside the wrap program.

In wrap programs, advisors can get to know their clients well. Long-term professional relationships are encouraged and the client's interests are kept at the forefront. Depending on the size of the account, the fees may be lower than those for mutual funds. Large accounts benefit even more from a tiered management-fee structure.

The asset-based fee structure of wrap accounts provides a fair method of compensating advisors for ongoing service. It also mitigates the potential conflicts of interest between client and advisor caused by transaction-based compensation. With a fee-based structure, advisors have no need to generate transactions to be compensated. Also, because no sales charges or switching fees apply to transactions within an account, the advisor has more flexibility to adjust a client's portfolio without triggering costly sales charges.

Annual fees for traditional wrap programs generally depend on the amount of assets held in the portfolio. Management fees are normally charged separately to the clients' account, rather than built into the management-expense ratios of the underlying funds. If clients have earned capital gains, they may obtain a small tax advantage if the fees are charged separately from the funds.

Separate management fee arrangements charged directly to clients is a clear form of disclosure, as the fees charged appear separately in periodic client statements.

In some wrap accounts, the investment process is simplified by using a limited selection of managed funds for the underlying assets. This gives the advisor more time for client service and customized financial planning. Reporting on wrap accounts is generally more detailed than the client statements issued to regular mutual fund investors.

4.2   Potential Disadvantages of Wrap Accounts

A possible drawback is the limited range of investment-management alternatives available to the client through these programs. If the sponsor of the wrap program and the money manager are in the same firm, a perceived conflict of interest may exist. Proprietary programs tie the client more to the firm than to the broker.

Since wrap accounts are not easily portable from one firm to another, clients or advisors who want to change firms have less flexibility. The advisor also has a diminished role in securities selection, since individual security holdings are based on the recommendation of the wrap program's investment manager, rather than that of the individual advisor.

Wrap accounts may be unsuitable for some investors because of their minimum investment restrictions, which are usually higher than for investments in mutual funds. Investors may also find that wrap programs do not provide an adequate level of customization.

Management fees and expenses may not necessarily be lower than for regular retail mutual funds. Fees may be higher for some wrap accounts than for services offered by private investment counsellors. Within a wrap program, mutual funds are subject to the wrap fees on top of their own management fees. In addition, the funds available to wrap programs may be restricted. For instance, the wrap program may not permit the purchase of front-end-load funds, which tend to have lower management-expense ratios than deferred-sales-charge funds.

4.3   Wrap Accounts for Active Traders

Another variation of the wrap account offered by investment dealers is an account that charges an annual fee that is a percentage of assets and offers a certain number of transactions in return for the fee. These accounts do not provide professional management. For example, an account of $150,000 to $200,000 may get 25 trades without commission by paying an annual fee of 1% to 1.25%. A $1 million account may get 75 trades without commission by paying an annual fee of 0.5% to 0.75%.

Clients can determine the appropriateness of this type of account by estimating the number of trades they are likely to make during the year, and the cost of those trades. Active traders, who like to make their own decisions, benefit the most from this type of account. For buy-and-hold investors, this account may not make sense.

5.0   Hedge Funds

Like mutual funds, hedge funds are professionally managed portfolios of securities. Traditionally, these funds are marketed to high-net-worth, sophisticated investors according to the rules imposed by the securities commissions. With minimum investment requirements generally ranging from $97,000 to $150,000, privately offered hedge funds are less tightly regulated and are generally considered more risky than mutual funds.

Hedge funds are one of the fastest-growing segments of the managed products industry. Assets under management at the end of 1999 were estimated at $300 billion worldwide, spread among 4,000 to 5,000 active funds.

Not all hedge funds are the same. Investment returns, volatility, and risk vary enormously among different funds. Some strategies that are not correlated to equity markets are able to deliver consistent returns with extremely low risk, while others may be as volatile or even more volatile than mutual funds.

Despite the differences, hedge funds share the following characteristics:

• They are mostly structured as limited partnerships, often located offshore.

• Many, but not all, tend to hedge against downturns in the markets.

• They are flexible in their investment options, using short selling, leverage, or derivatives such as puts, calls, options, futures, and so forth.

• They offer their managers performance incentives.

Alfred Jones is generally viewed as the father of hedge funds. In 1949 he established the Fully Committed Fund, the first fund to offer investors value-added hedging (profitable strategies that provide a hedge against a market decline) combined with leverage in a private partnership with performance incentives for the manager.

Broadly defined, hedge funds are privately offered managed pools of capital that invest primarily in financial securities. Fees include performance incentives for managers, and managers usually maintain significant personal investments in the funds. Hedge funds generally fall into either one of two broad classifications, true hedge funds or nominal hedge funds.

5.1   True Hedge Funds

The distinguishing characteristic of all true hedge funds is the maintenance of value added hedging. Value-added hedging seeks to capitalize on disparities in the values of related securities, regardless of the direction of the general market.

There are three main types of true hedge funds:

- Jones model funds;

- arbitrage funds;

- macro funds.

Jones Model Funds

Jones Model Funds are equity funds that maintain a substantial portion of assets within a hedged structure at all times, commonly employing some degree of leverage. Assets within the hedge include equal-value long- and short-stock positions. Assets not within the hedge include "net market exposure," expressed as a percentage of capital. Net market exposure is defined as:

$$\frac{\text{long exposure} - \text{short exposure}}{\text{capital}}$$

This exposure can range from zero to greater than 100% (with leverage) or by going net short, with negative net market exposure, depending on the aggressiveness of the fund.

The concept of net exposure is important. If for every $100 of equity, a fund invested $150 in long securities and $125 in short securities, then $25 is net long the market, creating a net exposure of 25%. If both long and short positions follow the market, and the market declines by 20%, the fund would be down by only 5% (25% of 20%).

Conservative hedge funds usually keep their net exposure and leverage quite low. They maintain long and short positions within a region or an industry sector on a beta-adjusted basis to minimize market risk.

The performance of hedge funds is driven by the ability to add value through stock picking, not market timing or sector rotation. Fund managers try to go long stocks they feel are undervalued and short stocks thought to be overvalued.

Arbitrage Funds

Arbitrage refers to the simultaneous purchase and sale of instruments that are perfect equivalents hoping to take advantage of pricing discrepancies between them to earn a risk-free profit.

Arbitrage funds try to neutralize or minimize the influence of the market, while profiting from fully hedged bets on the relative value between two or more securities. Examples of a hedged bet include:

- going long a convertible security and short the underlying common stock;

- exploiting price differences between related fixed-income securities or derivatives;

- going long mortgage-backed securities while hedging interest rate, volatility, and prepayment risk;

- simultaneously buying a stock in a company being acquired, and selling short the acquiring company (making a bet that the deal will go through).

It should be understood that opportunities for "pure arbitrage" (no risk of losing money), are limited. Most of the arbitrage that hedge funds do is "expectations arbitrage" in which the odds of making money are greater than the odds of losing. In other words, there is an element of speculation in most of these funds. If heavy leverage is used, the risk of holding the fund can be quite high.

Long Term Capital Management (LTCM) is a case in point. The company employed market-neutral strategies designed to exploit small differences between similar securities. An example of one such strategy was the sale of a newly issued ("on the run") 30-year U.S. Treasury bond against the purchase of a similar one, issued previously ("off the run"). As there is little economic reason for these bonds to have different yields, the fund engaged in arbitrage to take advantage of the small actual yield differential between the two, expecting the yields to converge.

LTCM used considerable leverage (30 to 40 times) for this strategy, as well as others that were considered to have little risk. Unfortunately, the Asian and Russian economic crises were unfolding and the price discrepancies that LTCM thought would narrow actually widened to the point at which LTCM could not meet its margin calls. The size of the fund and the amount of leverage used convinced the Federal Reserve Board of New York to bail out LTCM, fearing that a forced liquidation might harm the global financial system.

Macro Funds

Macro funds seek to capitalize on global and regional economic trends that effect securities, commodities, and exchange rates. These funds tend to be aggressive asset allocators, and heavy users of leverage and derivatives to accentuate the impact of market moves. Hedges are used, but leveraged directional bets tend to make the largest impact on performance.

One of the best-known macro funds is George Soros Fund Management. This fund made large bets against the British pound in 1993 and against Southeast Asian currencies in 1997. The Soros fund is considered a true hedge fund because it generally hedges its macro bets with long and short investments in global equity markets.

5.2   Nominal Hedge Funds

Nominal hedge funds are widely regarded as hedge funds because of their traditional structure as partnerships with performance incentives, and because many have a low correlation to the market. Rather than value-added hedging strategies, these funds may use index futures, options, or other derivatives (swaps) to reduce market risk. Nominal hedge funds include:

- **Short funds**, which seek to profit from the short sale of securities thought to be overvalued. A portion of the short sale may be hedged through the purchase of the same security.

- **Special situation funds**, which may buy or occasionally short the securities of companies under bankruptcy or reorganization.

- **Emerging market funds**, which invest, primarily long, in the securities of developing countries.

5.3   Due Diligence on Hedge Fund Managers

As hedge funds are less regulated than mutual funds, it is important for investors to do due diligence. Questions that should be asked of the hedge fund manager include:

- What percentage of the hedge fund manager's own money is in the fund?

- What kind of leverage is used?

- How long has the hedge manager been in business?

- Can the hedge manager provide audited financial statements for the last five years?

- Are derivatives being used for hedging purposes only, or to make speculative bets?

- What kind of concentration is being used in specific stocks?

- Is the hedge manager taking a performance fee as an allocation of net profits or assets?

- Is there a high water mark[1] before the hedge fund manager can take a performance fee?

- If a hedge fund manager is typically charging a 1% annual management fee and a 20% performance fee, is the performance fee taken before or after the management fee charge?

- Can the hedge fund manager provide monthly or quarterly performance numbers for at least five years relative to an appropriate benchmark?

- What percentage of the historical track record is attributable to "hot issues," which can dramatically lift the results in early years when a manager has less money under management?

One way to reduce risk exposure of hedge funds is to package them together in funds of hedge funds. These are similar to a balanced fund of pooled funds in the sense that an investor owns units, the prices of which are based on the underlying market values of each pool of hedge fund. The goal of the additional diversification provided by the combination of alternative strategies is to reduce the overall risk to the fund.

6.0   Private Equity Investments

Investors with sufficient assets may want to consider diversification opportunities offered by private equity. Private equity investors buy shares in companies expected to go public in the near future. Certain investment counsel firms offer exposure to private equity via pooled funds.

7.0   Managed Futures

The managed futures industry is made up of professional money managers known as commodity trading advisors (CTAs) who manage client assets on a discretionary basis using global futures and options markets.

As with the hedge fund market, managed futures have grown tremendously over the past 20 years. In 1980 less than U.S. $1 billion was under administration. By the end of 1999 the amount had grown to U.S. $40 billion.

Compared with traditional equity and bond investments, managed futures offer investors unique return possibilities by going either long or short various global commodity and financial futures. In addition to offering unique opportunities, managed futures have shown on average to have a low return correlation with traditional stock and bond

---

1   A high water mark ensures that a manager will not charge a performance fee until any previous losses have been made up, so that the manager theoretically pays back a portion of the losses by working for free until the investor is whole.

markets. In other words, as part of a comprehensive portfolio, managed futures offer investors the potential for reduced portfolio risk and enhanced investment returns.

Clients can invest in managed futures by:

- buying a managed futures fund;

- opening an individually managed futures account;

- purchasing a futures linked note.

7.1   Managed Futures Fund

A managed futures fund is essentially a mutual fund that invests in the futures market. The fund is considered a security and must be registered with securities commissions and file a prospectus.

Managed futures funds allow investors to participate in a well-capitalized portfolio while limiting risk to the amount of the initial investment. The minimum investment size is generally quite low.

For many managed futures funds, an investment in the fund is really an investment in the ability of the manager to provide superior returns by actively trading futures and futures options contracts (commodity futures and financial futures).

Some funds focus on a particular market segment. For example, the 20/20 Managed Futures Fund's strategy involves determining the "intrinsic value" of individual commodities and making investments when those commodities are trading at significant discounts or premiums. The fund invests only in commodity futures and options, not financial futures, and uses leverage conservatively. Most of its invested capital is in Treasury bills. An investment in this fund is an investment in commodities as an asset class with cycles that tend to run counter to equities.

A managed futures fund usually works something like this. A client invests a minimum amount (say $10,000) in the fund. The futures fund manager invests most of that amount (70 to 75%) in high-quality government stripped bonds that have a par value equal to the $10,000 investment. Since there is a few years to the maturity of the bonds, they can be bought at a discount. If, for example, the strip bonds have five years left to maturity and cost $7,000, the fund manager will use the remaining $3,000 to invest in futures. The $3,000 is pooled in a managed portfolio of futures contracts. Some funds use leverage aggressively; others, like the 20/20 fund described above, take a more conservative approach.

These funds generally have risk control features such as trading policies to limit market exposure and stop trading provisions if the net asset value falls below a certain amount.

7.2 Individual Managed Accounts

An investor who wants some exposure to the futures market but lacks the trading expertise or the time to trade may give trading authority to a trading advisor. This custom-tailored approach, however, has the potential for unlimited loss. During periods of losses, the investor may be required to meet margin calls by adding substantial amounts of additional capital. Most firms that offer these accounts have minimum investment requirements as high as $1 million or more.

7.3 Futures Linked Notes

A futures linked note is similar to an index-linked GIC or note, except that the return of the note is tied to the performance of the futures fund upon which it is based, rather than a particular index. Risk is limited to forgone interest, as the majority of capital is invested in a stripped bond.

The worst that can happen is that investors get their original investment back. In this case, all they would lose is forgone interest. These funds are able to ensure that the maximum loss will be limited to forgone interest by suspending trading in the fund if losses exceed a predetermined level.

CHAPTER 13
Performance Appraisal

1.0　Introduction

Once you have decided on an asset mix for the client, it is time to recommend specific managed products (mutual funds, pooled funds, separately managed accounts, and so forth). In order to do this, you must be able to measure and evaluate managed product performance. For example, the recommended asset mix for a client may include exposure to the U.S. bond market. Several managed products will give clients this exposure. How do you choose? Many wealth managers enlist the services of an investment consultant to search, select, and evaluate various managed products and money managers.

This chapter covers what you should know about performance measurement and evaluation. Measurement involves calculating the return achieved by a single portfolio manager over a certain time period. Four types of transactions are measured— purchases, sales, income, and distribution. Although measuring return sounds relatively straightforward, it can sometimes be quite complicated.

Performance evaluation shows how well a managed portfolio has done over an evaluation period relative to the cost of management. It is both expensive and time-consuming to analyze and select securities for a portfolio, so you must determine if the investment performance justifies the cost of the service. Together, performance measurement and evaluation provide a cost-benefit analysis of a money manager.

Primary Learning Objectives

By the end of this chapter, you should understand:

- **how to value a portfolio;**
- **the concept of benchmarks;**
- **the three categories of indexes;**
- **how to analyze a manager's style;**
- **how to evaluate mutual fund performance.**

2.0   Performance Measurement

Performance measurement involves the calculation of the return realized by a portfolio manager over a time interval called the evaluation period.

In order to calculate returns over the evaluation period, you need to know the portfolio values at the beginning and end of the period and at intermediate dates. Portfolio valuation is not an exact science and measurement errors may occur. A portfolio's value is considered to be the value of the portfolio if the securities were liquidated (or **marked to market**), not including transaction costs. The only fair market value of any security is what it will fetch at the time of sale, so securities are valued at current market value.

It is easy to find the last quoted price for active, liquid stocks, but it can be difficult to determine a price for thinly traded equities. Selling pressure depresses the price of an illiquid stock; if that pressure is significant, the price can fall dramatically. It is even harder to determine the price of less actively traded bonds, particularly those in default. (Although the bid price should be used for bonds, quite often the ask or mid-spread price is used instead.)

Real estate is an excellent example of how market value may differ widely from liquidation value. Appraisals may be as much as a year out of date, the appraisal itself may use stale data, and real estate appraisal is an educated guess at best.

Other questions arise. When does an actual trade take place: on the trade date or on the settlement date? Should accrual accounting or cash accounting be used? When are dividends considered received: on the ex-dividend date or on receipt? These variations do not make an enormous difference to the final values, but each one adds to the uncertainty concerning performance data.

The final evaluation should reflect the total change in wealth. An accurate measure of return will capture both income and capital gains (or losses).

In the simplest case, the market value of a portfolio can be measured at the beginning and ending of a period, and the rate of return can be calculated using the **holding period return** equation introduced in Chapter 9:

$$HPR = \frac{(\text{end of period value} - \text{beginning of period value})}{\text{beginning of period value}}$$

This calculation assumes that the client made no additions to or withdrawals from the portfolio during the measurement period. If funds were added or withdrawn, then the portfolio return as calculated using this equation may be inaccurate.

The measurement of return must minimize the effect of contributions and withdrawals by the client, because they are beyond the control of the money manager. This is best accomplished by using the time-weighted rate of return, which measures the actual rate of return earned by the portfolio manager.

2.1 Time-Weighted Returns

Calculating the time-weighted return requires information about the value of the portfolio's cash inflows and outflows. To compute the time-weighted return:

- calculate the total return on the portfolio up to the point at which a cash flow occurs;

- calculate the total return on the portfolio from the time of that cash flow to the next, or to the end of the period;

- calculate the compound rate of return over time.

If frequent cash flows are involved, many calculations will be necessary. For some portfolios, a weekly or even daily valuation would be necessary. Although this does not present a problem for a mutual fund that must calculate the net asset value of the portfolio each business day, it is time-consuming for other investment managers.

Frequent valuation itself may introduce error, particularly with illiquid securities and asset classes such as emerging markets and real estate. Consequently, although time-weighted return is often used to measure the return actually earned by the portfolio manager, the length of time for sub-period returns varies depending on the portfolio. It may take place monthly, quarterly, or semi-annually. Not valuing between each cash flow introduces bias into portfolio returns.

Although no one set of performance measurement rules applies to all users, the investment management industry is moving toward a standard set of guidelines for measuring performance. Accurate performance evaluation is difficult enough without distortions in constructing and presenting performance numbers.

2.2 Adjusting for Risk

Since return is related to risk, the performance of a portfolio cannot be evaluated on its return alone. For instance, say a portfolio has achieved a 20% return over the course of a year. If we know nothing about the risk of this portfolio, we cannot judge the manager's performance. Its manager may have taken twice the risk of comparable portfolios to achieve this 20% return. If we are to assess performance carefully, we must also take into consideration the risks that were taken in achieving the returns.

2.3   Management Fees and Expenses

An important question is whether performance returns include or exclude management fees. Mutual fund returns are calculated with fees included, but returns on other managed portfolios are usually reported without including fees. The latter reflect the manager's raw performance, not the return of importance to investors.

Measuring returns without subtracting the manager's fees has two important implications.

1. A portfolio manager's performance cannot be compared to other managers' returns, because value added depends strictly on *net* returns that exceed the benchmark return. How can a manager be compared to a group of competing managers, when some managers charge more than others for their services? Even fee structures may differ. In performance-based fee structures, managers' fees are directly related to how well a portfolio performs. In asset-value-based structures, fees are calculated on portfolio size, not performance. These differences make comparison even more difficult. Returns that do not include fees based on performance assessment generally overstate superior performance more than they would for asset-value fees. However, the reverse is true for underperforming managers.

2. When the benchmark is a passive portfolio, whoever is doing the appraisal must ensure that the return includes fees. When we say a manager must add value, we mean *net* added value. Investors want their risk-adjusted returns to exceed the costs of producing those returns; otherwise, why pay for active management?

The level of management fees vary according to the type of fund, the sales commission structure, and whether the fund is actively or passively managed. A money market fund may have a fee of 0.5%, while an actively managed equity fund paying trailer fees might charge 2.5%.

Fees are quoted on an annual basis, but are deducted monthly. The effect of the fees is therefore understated. For example, suppose a fund makes 1% a month or 12.68% a year and the management fee is quoted as 2.4%. It might appear that after management expenses, the fund turns in a performance of 10.28%. However, the fund deducts 2.4 ÷ 12 = 0.2% a month, so that the net return is 0.8% a month or 10.03% a year.

Performance measurement uses returns earned before taxes. This is because tax regimes are irrelevant to most managed money (such as pension funds). Even in taxable situations, revenue streams from active and benchmark passive portfolios are sufficiently similar that trying to adjust for various tax rates is not worth the effort. However, when managers' actions affect the tax burden on portfolio investors, it may be necessary to take taxes into account. For example, in some cases the realized components of return must flow through to investors to avoid taxes being levied on the portfolio. The best example is mutual funds.

Dealing with fees is particularly problematic in measuring the return on benchmark portfolios. Every time the index is rebalanced, transaction costs are incurred. If the benchmark is to represent a legitimate alternative to the portfolio being evaluated, reasonable transaction costs incorporating the initial investment and ongoing rebalancing must be deducted from returns. Without an adjustment for transaction costs, the benchmark would be biased against the manager.

2.4   Operating Expenses and the MER

Administrative expenses of a fund include advertising, auditing, office overhead, legal costs, accounting and bookkeeping, preparing and mailing quarterly shareholder reports and prospectuses, and custodial fees to the financial institution that holds the fund's securities. Funds handle these expenses in different ways. Some pay them out of management fees and some out of the remaining assets of the fund as a separate levy.

The net asset value of a fund is calculated after management fees and administrative costs have been deducted.

The sum of management fees and administrative costs is called management expense. The management expense ratio (MER) is management expense expressed as a percentage of the daily average net asset value of the fund. Past MER values must be presented in the fund's prospectus and annual reports.

Obviously, everything else being equal, investors prefer funds with low MERs because every 1% of MER means 1% less for unitholders. But recent years have seen expense ratios rising steadily because of marketing and distribution costs and increasing compliance and disclosure charges. With MERs reaching over 3%, it is clear that funds have to significantly outperform benchmarks in order for investors to "beat the market."

The following table shows median MERs for mutual fund groups (half the funds within a group had higher expense ratios and half had lower). The impact of expenses can be gauged from Canadian money market funds. At the end of May 1999, 6-month T-bills were yielding 4.7%. An MER of 1% represents more than 20% of that amount. In other words, only 80% of market return flows through to unitholders.

Median Management Expense Ratios (May 1999)

Canadian equity	2.4%	Canadian balanced	2.4
U.S. equity	2.4	Global balanced	2.5
Foreign equity	2.6	Canadian money market	1.0
Canadian fixed-income	1.8	Foreign money market	1.1
Foreign bond	2.1		

3.0   Performance Evaluation

Once you have established a satisfactory measure of performance, the next step is performance evaluation, that is, an appraisal of how well the portfolio has done over the evaluation period. Evaluation compares the managed portfolio to a benchmark and takes into account investment style, cash balances and level of diversification.

3.1   Benchmarks

The term "benchmark" has two meanings in performance evaluation:

* a standard of comparison;

* a specific portfolio used as an index.

Using the TSE 300 Index as the benchmark for a manager fulfils both meanings. However, comparing the return on a managed portfolio with the returns on similar managed portfolios invokes a standard of comparison not associated with a specific portfolio.

Benchmark choice directly affects the way a manager's investment skills are measured. The wrong choice can lead to unnecessarily punishing a good manager or inappropriately rewarding a poor one. A good benchmark fairly evaluates the manager and provides a passive alternative. It must be:

* realistic;

* unambiguous;

* appropriate;

* attainable by the manager;

* specified in advance;

* objectively constructed;

* easy to measure.

There are three main types of benchmarks. They are often referred to as "bogeys" or target portfolios:

* composite market indexes;

* normal portfolios;

* generic investment style indexes.

Composite Market Indexes

Market indexes fall into three categories, according to how they are weighted.

* A **market-value-weighted index** is intended to represent a buy-and-hold strategy. All an investor has to do in order to replicate the returns on the index portfolio is to

buy the securities so that their market value is in proportion to the weights they represent in the index portfolio. In practice, some rebalancing is needed periodically to keep up with the index weights, since those who maintain the index have to adjust for changes in the number of securities outstanding (caused by buybacks, private placements, secondary offerings, and so forth). However, rebalancing requirements are not so onerous that they make the index invalid as a comparison for a passive buy-and-hold strategy.

- In a **price-weighted index**, security returns are weighted by their relative prices. Investors can achieve similar returns by buying an equal number of shares (or bonds if it is a bond index) of each stock in the index.

- **Equally-weighted indexes** place an equal weight on each security in the index. A return similar to that of the index can be achieved by having an equal dollar amount in each security for every period. Security selection is mechanical, but transaction costs may be higher than for an actively managed portfolio. Consequently, equally-weighted indexes are the least desirable of the three weighting schemes.

The weighting scheme determines how an index will behave. Consider two indexes that are made up of all the common stocks on the Toronto Stock Exchange. An index that weighted all stocks equally would be dominated by small firms, because small firms vastly outnumber large firms on the exchange, as they do on all exchanges. However, if the index were based on market capitalization, large firms would dominate, as a few dozen companies account for about half of the exchange's market value. In other words, if the index is market-value-weighted, it will behave like a large-cap index, whereas an equally weighted index would behave like a small-cap index.

The equally-weighted index will also have a lower yield than the market-value-weighted index and will differ in other features so that it has the appearance of a growth index. In addition, the equally-weighted index will probably be more volatile, because small-cap stocks tend to be more volatile than large-cap stocks.

Price-weighted indexes are more difficult to predict. Although large firms tend to have higher stock prices than smaller companies, a price-weighted index will probably be heavy on small caps through sheer weight of numbers. Moreover, stock splits reduce the influence of high-priced stocks. Since stocks that have higher growth rates have higher prices, and because such stocks are more likely to split, they will constantly lose weight within the index.

The widely quoted composite market indexes are the best-known type of benchmark portfolio. They are designed to measure the movements of specified markets. Although they may be very good at what they're intended to do, they may not be suitable for evaluating managers.

Normal Portfolios

A normal portfolio is a specialized benchmark that includes all the securities from which a manager normally selects a particular portfolio. For example, if the manager typically chooses investments from a set of 300 stocks, the manager's performance is compared with the performance of this set.

Generic Investment Style Indexes

Using a broad market index or a normal portfolio index, rather than a narrowly defined benchmark portfolio is appropriate when either:

- the portfolio manager does not have an investment style; or

- the manager practises a mixture of styles that the index mirrors.

When a manager has a particular investment style, benchmarks should reflect that style. Poorly performing portfolio managers often assert that their style is out of favour with the market. Gauging the performance against a style-based benchmark quickly shows the validity of this claim.

Another advantage of assessing skills on a style-adjusted basis is that no style does better than any other all the time. The relative performance of an actively managed portfolio will vary considerably over time, regardless of the manager's skills. Even consistent underperformance or superior performance may say less about the security-selection and market-timing abilities of the manager than about the manager's choice of investment style.

Customized or style indexes have been developed to more closely reflect the behaviour of portfolios that have highly specific return and risk requirements that are not tracked by composite indexes. However, they have their own drawbacks. For example, how are "growth" stocks differentiated from "value" stocks? It can also be difficult to identify the correct index for a particular manager.

Composite market indexes, style indexes, and normal portfolios are all used to gauge managers' skills. Published market indexes are widely available. All stock exchanges produce common stock indexes, and investment houses track bond markets. However, one size does not fit all. Customized indexes have been created to more closely represent managers' investment behaviour and normal portfolios are uniquely designed for managers.

3.2   Active and Passive Management

Evaluation must take into account investment style. In general terms there are two mutually exclusive styles, passive and active. These terms were introduced in Chapter 10.

Active Management

Active managers try to increase return through selection and timing. Selection means looking for undervalued securities. Properly executed, this strategy will enhance returns. But active management comes with a price — increased trading costs. The active money manager also requires higher compensation for his or her selection and timing skills. Therefore the return on the portfolio must be greater than that of a passively managed portfolio if it is to cover these extra costs.

There are essentially four different active equity portfolio management strategies. They are all, in one way or another, market timing strategies:

- **Value**: identifying securities that have a market price lower than their intrinsic value.

- **Growth**: identifying companies that have shown long-term growth in earnings at a rate faster than inflation from one business cycle to the next.

- **Sector Rotation**: a style based on the belief that different sectors of the economy and capital markets perform well during different stages of the economic cycle.

- **Momentum**: a style based on the belief that once a stock has established a trend, that trend is expected to continue for a long time.

Fixed-income investing also has four major strategy categories:

- **Interest rate change anticipation**: an aggressive strategy that positions a bond portfolio to profit from changes in interest rates.

- **Value trading**: a strategy that involves changing the structure of the bond portfolio to find the highest possible yield, while keeping the duration and credit quality constant.

- **Sector trading**: a strategy that involves trading between issues from different market sectors.

- **High yield**: a strategy that consists of buying corporate bonds with high yields and holding them to maturity.

Passive Management

The goal of passive management is to reduce investment management expenses. This is usually accomplished by indexing — that is, selecting a broad or narrow market index and replicating it in the portfolio by holding the securities making up the index in the same proportions as they are weighted in the index itself. Clearly, this method does not require much in the way of trading or managerial expertise, since it can be done with a computer program. Performance appraisal for passive investment involves comparing the return earned on one portfolio with the return earned on one or more other portfolios. This reflects a viable, passive investment alternative while recognizing risk.

One potential problem with indexing relates to regulatory restrictions. In 1999, because of a rapidly increasing stock price, Nortel stock accounted for approximately 17% of the TSE 300. However, the Ontario Securities Commission limits the amount of a portfolio that can be invested in a single stock to 10%. Therefore, every manager who used the TSE 300 as a measuring gauge would have underperformed its benchmark because of Nortel's exceptional performance.

3.3   Cash Balances

Most money managers hold cash on a regular basis, even those who describe themselves as fully invested. In contrast, most investment consultants do not include cash in manager benchmarks. Excluding cash from the benchmark overstates benchmark returns in strongly rising markets, understates it in falling markets, and makes it harder to assess the manager's skill.

Holding cash is a matter of style. Many managers like to keep some of the portfolio in cash. If the investment consultant does not like this, he or she should hire another manager. However, if the investment consultant continues to employ a manager who keeps a cash balance, then the manager's long-run cash position should be considered in his or her performance appraisal.

3.4   Diversification

Judging a portfolio's diversification should be a part of performance appraisal. It is important to know if superior performance may have occurred at the expense of diversification.

Part of managing a portfolio is diversifying to reduce risk as much as possible. Portfolio managers have to ensure that their portfolios do not take on more risk than the portfolio description suggests or the portfolio's mandate allows. Investment consultants, when evaluating portfolio managers, must ensure that managers are indeed abiding by the portfolio's mandate.

Some portfolios become underdiversified. The greater the number of securities held, the more difficult it is to exploit any informational advantage. It is not easy to find dozens of undervalued situations at any one time. Many managers tend to concentrate on fewer securities or on a particular sector. But this is seldom in the clients' interest.

An exception to the need for diversification occurs when a portfolio is allotted to separate managers. The sub-portfolio managers do not need to worry about diversification, as each concentrates on maximizing return in a particular area. In this case the wealth manager or the investment consultant must ensure that the overall portfolio is sufficiently diversified.

3.5   Performance Attribution Analysis

Performance evaluation is concerned with more than determining whether a money manager has outperformed an established benchmark. It is equally important to ascertain *how* the money manager achieved this performance. Was the return achieved by market timing, by buying undervalued securities, or by buying small-cap stocks? The attempt to explain why certain results occurred is called performance attribution analysis.

Case 13.1   Manager Style Analysis

Manager Style Analysis

Anne Brown, a wealth manager, is trying to decide between a growth manager and a value manager for the Canadian equity components of her clients' portfolios. Both managers claim their strength is in sector rotation. At first, she leans toward Manager A because of the strength and consistency of his investment record:

Annual Added Value (versus the TSE 300 Index)

	1998	1997	1996	1995	1994	1993	1992	1991
Manager A	2.0%	3.5%	1.8%	-0.5%	4.1%	1.5%	3.2%	0.9%
Manager B	0.9	3.4	-1.9	1.7	2.8	-2.2	4.8	0.2

Anne performs attribution analysis on the investment results to further understand the sources of added value:

Annualized Added Value (8 years ended in 1998)

	Manager A	Manager B
Stock Selection	2.0%	0.1%
Sector Rotation	0.1	1.1
Total	2.1	1.2

She concludes that although Manager A has a better investment track record, most of his added value has come from security selection rather than sector rotation. In her recommendations to the trustees, Anne expresses two concerns:

1. The addition of Manager A would not provide the intended style diversification to Anne's clients, as his value added is in stock selection instead of sector allocation.

2. Manager A believes that he is good at sector rotation when his real strength lies in security selection. This is a problem, because an investment manager must understand his or her own strengths and weaknesses to be successful.

3.6   Survivorship Bias

Survivorship bias can be found in practically every area of financial research. It arises whenever the past performance of a group is evaluated and the membership of the group has varied over time. Survivorship bias occurs when the performance of surviving members is evaluated rather than that of the entire starting group.

The monthly mutual fund results reported in the financial press provide a good example. Suppose an investor looks at performance over a 10-year period. He or she would tend to avoid funds with returns below the 10-year average (setting aside risk-adjustment issues), but the results do not show the whole picture. These funds have survived at least 10 years and the average does not include the funds that have disappeared along the way. Funds are usually shut down or merged into another fund because of poor performance. If the investor could determine average performance, including those poor results, many of the apparent 10-year underperformers would be seen to be turning in a respectable performance. The longer the historical period under study, the greater the impact of survivorship bias.

Measuring the performance of the survivors of a population overstates aggregate performance, because the elements of the population that have dropped out are usually the ones with the worst performance. Any measure based on the survivors that is used for inferences about the population is biased.

3.7   Other Considerations

Any hiring or rehiring decision must be based on performance, consistency of performance, compatibility of the manager's investment approach with the client's portfolio strategy, and whether or not the manager has met the objectives of the client.

Consistency of Performance

Consistency of performance is very important. Some managers' average performance might appear to be excellent because of one or two periods when they achieved very high returns, but overall they might have lost more often than they won. These kinds of records suggest that the manager's results can be attributed to luck rather than skill. However, a manager who has placed winning bets fairly consistently, although none may have had spectacular results, is less likely to have been merely lucky and more likely to possess skill. In order to measure performance consistency, the performance history has to cover more than a few years.

Compatibility with Client's Portfolio Strategy and Objectives

Selecting a portfolio strategy involves the decision to use active or passive management. Choosing active management leads to further decisions on style and market timing, as described earlier in this chapter.

Even if a manager has outstanding performance, he or she might not be the appropriate manager for a particular client. A manager who has reported excellent investment returns may not be meeting the needs of a client whose objective was to receive as much current income as possible. The excellent performance may have been achieved through capital gains on equities, whereas what was needed was income through fixed-income investments.

3.8   A Few Words of Caution

When you look at performance appraisals of various assets, you should always ensure that the data you are viewing is in fact comparable and is represented in a uniform way. The Association of Investment Management and Research (AIMR) has gone to great lengths to standardize the reporting of portfolio returns.

Nevertheless, you should do the following things when you are viewing asset performance appraisals (this list is by no means exhaustive):

- Read the footnotes and the sources of the raw data and comparative data very carefully. It is especially useful to know if the appraisal was done "in-house" or if it has been conducted by a third-party portfolio measurement service.

- Be aware of the time frames used. It is always best if you get a complete range of time frames to consider, such as 1 year, 5 years, 10 years, and 20 years. This will prevent reporting firms from presenting only their most favourable return periods.

- Look for firms that include accrued income in the numerator of performance calculation, but not in the denominator; they are probably overstating the performance of fixed-income securities.

- Take a close look at what the security in question is being compared to.

- If the information is available, determine how frequently the security or portfolio is valued — the more frequently, the better.

- When you are reviewing the performance of a portfolio manager or portfolio management firm, keep an eye out for reports that "cherry-pick" only the best accounts. Read the footnotes or and note if the firm states up-front that *all* accounts under management were included in the appraisal.

- Be leery of comparisons that don't make sense, such as a straight comparison between international funds and domestic funds.

- If the manager being appraised tries to time the market with asset shifts (for example, between stocks and bonds) or by altering risk levels (switching between cash and riskier assets), you should compare the manager's results with market movements.

4.0   Mutual Fund Performance

If active managers do not earn enough to cover their costs, they are wasting resources and the wealth managers or investment consultants should pursue a passive strategy instead. Wealth managers and their clients need the answers to the following questions:

1. Do fund managers as a group provide superior risk-adjusted performance?

2. Do individual funds and managers outperform their benchmarks?

3. If the answer to question 2 is yes, is it through luck or skill?

The answer to the first question is already known for U.S. based mutual funds. Dozens of studies using a variety of techniques have shown that the average active money manager over time produces risk-adjusted fund returns that are lower than their benchmarks. Most recent studies find some excess returns, but after expenses have been paid, the returns passed through to shareholders underperform the market. Funds may "beat the market," but only to the extent of covering a portion of their costs to investors. The few studies done on Canadian funds agree with the U.S. results. During the late 1980s and throughout the 1990s, Canadian stock fund holders underperformed relative to the TSE 300 and so did Canadian bond fund owners relative to the bond market.

Nevertheless, the answer to question 2 is that individual managers can and do beat their risk-adjusted benchmarks, and sometimes by an impressively wide margin. Although on average the industry as a whole underperforms, in any period some funds will do exceptionally well.

This brings us to question 3. What are the chances that successful managers will continue to be successful, giving investors a chance to spot and exploit their success by buying into the fund? Initial research studies did not detect consistency in fund performance. With new techniques and databases, however, investigators in the early 1990s found some consistency in fund performance, although the strongest conclusion was that losers tend to stay losers, rather than that winners continue to win.

More recent work, though, indicates that persistence is due to style, not skill. Value stocks, for example, may do well for a number of years and when they do, value managers will ride the wave. However, after adjusting for style, the analysis of individual funds does not find any consistent performance that can be attributed to managers' skill. There is no evidence, for instance, that value-managed funds consistently outperform a value benchmark. In sum, past fund performance does not predict future performance in any meaningful way.

Nevertheless, this type of analysis does not determine if there are superior managers. Following fund performance through time can only evaluate the wealth manager's or investment consultants ability to hire superior managers, because of the turnover in managers in a typical fund.

Indirect evidence, however, suggests that successful managers may not really have achieved their results through skill. For instance, Peter Lynch made a lasting reputation for himself managing the Magellan Fund in the 1980s. Nearly every year he beat the benchmark applied by Fidelity and most other observers, the S&P 500. However, Magellan held about one-quarter of its portfolio in foreign stocks, with a considerable proportion in Japan. During the 1980s, Japanese stock soared. Had Magellan's performance been compared to a benchmark with some Japanese market exposure, it is unlikely that Lynch's performance would have been thought notable.

Chapter 14

Formalizing and Implementing the Investment Plan

1.0   Introduction

Once you understand your client's financial planning needs and objectives and the basics of investing, including the types of managed products available, you must formalize the investment plan in an investment policy statement (IPS). The IPS is a customized document that details your investment recommendations.

When the client understands and signs the IPS, you must implement the plan. This process involves selecting managed products within broad asset categories, and then choosing the investment firm that will provide the managed product. The choice of product within a particular asset category will be based on your analysis or that of an investment consultant, using the appraisal techniques described in Chapter 13.

The choice of an investment firm may be an easy one if you work for a firm that restricts its advisors to using the firm's proprietary products. If you have more flexibility in your choice, you will base the decision on cost, efficiency, and the service that the provider offers.

Primary Learning Objectives

By the end of this chapter you should understand:

- **the essential items to be included in the investment policy statement;**

- **the different types of investment management providers in Canada;**

- **mutual funds distribution and fee structures;**

- **how to evaluate investment firms that offer managed products;**

- **when to leave an investment firm.**

2.0   Investment Policy Statement

An IPS establishes and documents a long-term plan for an investment portfolio, and the framework within which investment decisions can be made. The statement articulates the client's investment and non-investment goals and objectives, risk tolerance, and long-term strategy, and establishes guidelines for implementing and monitoring the plan. An investment policy statement will help you and your client stay focused on your agreed-upon objectives. It keeps the investment process intact during periods of market upheaval, when the client may be tempted to let emotion dominate the decision-making process.

The IPS also provides a plan for the investment of future cash flows and establishes guidelines for investing assets in an estate.

The statement should include:

- an explanation of the investor's objectives (such as long-term growth for retirement, while assuming a reasonable level of risk and minimizing taxes);
- the tax status of the portfolio;
- an annual return target;
- the client's risk tolerance, stated in terms of acceptable volatility;
- any specific income needs;
- the client's liquidity requirements;
- any lump-sum cash distributions;
- qualitative and quantitative restraints on the portfolio (for example, a limit on the amount that may be allocated to any one security or industry to ensure proper diversification, securities that are not acceptable such as minimum-quality bonds, or a requirement for socially responsible investing);
- an asset allocation strategy that details the recommended asset mix (the IPS should also mention the importance of asset allocation;
- the criteria for selecting money managers or managed products, including specific qualitative and quantitative requirements (for example, conformity to a specific investing style, a minimum tenure of the current manager, historical performance relative to a representative index or peer group, or fund expense standards relative to a peer group);

- control and review procedures (for example, a process for ensuring adherence to the investment policy and monitoring the effectiveness of the policy, requirements for a monthly or quarterly portfolio report, and specific criteria against which each fund manager or managed product is to be evaluated).

A sample investment policy statement is shown below:

Figure 14.1   Sample Investment Policy Statement

Investment Policy Statement
Mark Brown, Q.C.

Mark Brown is a Canadian citizen, and an Ontario resident.

Investment Objective

To provide a diversified portfolio of securities that produces income and capital appreciation, including securities of Canadian and U.S.-based companies.

Rate of Return Expectations

The primary objective for the portfolio is to achieve a rate of return that will exceed the return achieved by T-Bills plus 3% over the majority of market cycles.

Tax Issues

Revenues from the portfolio will be taxed at the maximum rates:

Interest income	50.29%
Dividend income	33.95%
Capital gains	37.72%

Cash Flow Characteristics

There are no anticipated cash requirements from the portfolio for a minimum of 10 years.

Qualitative and Quantitative Constraints

a) *Asset Classes Eligible for Investment*

From time to time, and subject to this Policy Statement, the portfolio may invest in any or all of the following asset categories. These assets may be obligations or securities of Canadian entities, or securities of U.S. companies.
  i) Publicly traded common stocks, or convertible debentures;
  ii) Bonds, debentures, notes, or other debt instruments of the Government of Canada, government agencies, or corporations;
  iii) Mortgages;
  iv) Private placements, whether debt or equity, of Canadian agencies or corporations;
  v) Guaranteed Investment Contracts or equivalent financial instruments of insurance companies, trust companies, banks, or other eligible issuers, or funds that invest primarily in such instruments;
  vi) Cash or money market securities issued by governments or corporations.

Figure 14.1   Sample Investment Policy Statement
(continued)

b) Specified Restrictions

The portfolio shall invest in a socially responsible manner, consistent with the "Definition of Socially Responsible Investing" statement below.

c) Constraints by Asset Class

Canadian Equities
- i) Maximum in single industry group: TSE weight plus 10%.
- ii) Maximum in single company: greater of 10% or twice TSE weight.
- iii) Maximum of 15% in companies with capitalization of less than $150 million.
- iv) Installment receipts requiring the holder to purchase Canadian common stocks listed on the TSE and the MSE are permitted.

U.S. Equities
- i) Maximum of 10% in a single company.
- ii) Maximum of 10% in companies with capitalization of less than $500 million.

Fixed Income
- i) The minimum quality standard for bonds shall be BBB by a recognized rating agency, or the equivalent in the manager's opinion.
- ii) Not more than 10% of the market value of the portfolio shall be invested in bonds with a rating of BBB, or equivalent.
- iii) Not more than 10% of the market value shall be invested in the securities of one issuer, except issues of or guaranteed by the federal or provincial governments.
- iv) Not more than 20% of the portfolio shall be invested in foreign-currency-denominated issues.
- v) Not more than 20% of the market value of the portfolio shall be invested in NHA mortgage-backed securities. Only "AAA" rated, CMHC-insured mortgages are permitted.
- vi) Private placements that offer high liquidity and otherwise meet all other quality standards of this investment policy, to a maximum of 20% of the portfolio. For this section, a liquid security is a security that (1) has a minimum outstanding size of $125 million; (2) is purchased by a minimum of 10 buyers and (3) is brought to market by a major Canadian investment dealer.
- vii) The duration standard for the portfolio shall be plus or minus one year of the duration for the Scotia McLeod Universe Index.

d) Cash and Equivalent

Money market securities must be rated R-1 or equivalent.
Maximum term of any single investment not to exceed one year.

Figure 14.1 Sample Investment Policy Statement
(continued)

e) *Balanced Portfolio Strategic Asset Allocation Ranges*

ASSET CLASS	MEASUREMENT	MIN	BENCHMARK	MAX
Cash and Equivalent	91 day T-Bills	2%	5%	30%
Bonds, Mortgage & Preferreds	ScotiaMcLeod Universe	10%	25%	50%
Total Fixed Income		15%	30%	60%
Canadian Equities	TSE 300	0%	25%	50%
U.S. Equities	S&P 500	0%	25%	50%
International Equities	MS EAFE	0%	20%	40%
Total Equities		40%	70%	85%

Asset allocation is the single most important step in structuring a portfolio. It is estimated that it accounts for between 80% and 90% of the portfolio's return.

f) *Definition of Socially Responsible Investing*

The portfolio shall not hold securities of any company whose primary activities or a major part thereof contribute to:
  i)   neglecting or destroying the environment;
  ii) affecting the quality of life of individuals through its implication in the tobacco, alcohol, or gambling industries;
  iii) promoting conflict between individuals through its implication in the arms industry (all classes).

The manager shall make all possible efforts to avoid including any securities consistent with the above description. However, should the investor decide, on the strength of any analysis, to exclude securities deemed acceptable by the manager, the investor shall advise the manager to dispose of such securities. The manager shall dispose of them as soon as possible, and such disposition shall have no impact on any assessment of the manager's performance.

g) *Conflict of Interest*

All investment activities must be conducted in accordance with the Code of Ethics and Standards of Professional Conduct adopted by the Association for Investment Management and Research.

h) *Regulatory Compliance*

The portfolio will be managed in accordance with applicable legislation, including the *Income Tax Act (Canada)*.

i) *Services*

The client will get a full portfolio report on a quarterly basis. Personal reviews will occur regularly to review the performance and plan future strategy.

The portfolio report will include a comparison of performance against an appropriate benchmark index, and an assessment of the managed product performance relative to its stated style and to the client's stated objectives.

3.0   Choosing an Investment Firm

When the investment policy statement is complete and signed, and you have decided which managed products to use, you need to choose an investment firm to provide the managed products. You must be comfortable with both the firm and the individual representative or portfolio manager who will be servicing your needs and those of your clients.

If you yourself are a registered portfolio manager or are licensed to deal in securities or mutual funds, you may need only an outside provider for products that your firm does not deal in directly. Most large firms offer all types of investment products and registered individuals within those firms are often restricted to the proprietary products of the firm.

Several large investment dealers, however, have programs whereby investment advisors can recommend external portfolio managers to clients. The advisors can choose from many different styles or combination of styles of investment management across a broad spectrum of assets. Often these firms employ an investment consultant to evaluate money managers. The advisors choose from a short list of managers one who best fits their client's needs.

3.1   Step One: Define Your Client's Needs

If you need to search for a product provider, the first thing you should do is define what kinds of investment services you and your client require. If the investment plans call for order execution only, a discount broker may be all you need. For example, a recommended asset mix that includes exposure to international equity markets may be implemented by buying WEBS index participation units. As you do not need advice from an investment professional to buy them, putting the order through a discount broker would make sense, given the savings in commission. Discount broker commissions are 50% to 80% lower than full-service commissions, depending on the size of the order.

However, if your client has a substantial investment portfolio and you feel that professional money management tailored to your client's needs, objectives, and constraints is required, you should look for a portfolio manager. The manager may be employed by or under contract to an investment dealer, an investment counsellor, a trust company, a division of a bank, or an insurance company.

If your client needs professional money management, but without customization, mutual funds may be the answer. You can choose from many mutual fund dealers and full service dealers.

3.2   Step Two: Compile a Long List of Providers

The next step is determining how to find the managed product providers. One of the best sources is word of mouth from other professionals such as accountants, lawyers, or colleagues.

You can also learn about potential providers by checking out advertisements, attending trade shows, reading industry journals, or visiting websites to identify who provides what services and get a sense of the quality of the service.

Regulators are another valuable source of information. You should contact either the Investment Dealers Association of Canada (IDA) or the provincial regulator to get a list of the registered member firms and dealers in your area.

3.3   Step Three: Select a Short List for Further Investigation

After investigating some of the sources, draw up a short list of potential firms that specialize in the appropriate managed products and that you want to investigate further. At this point you should contact the managers for the firms and find out if their services and fee structures are suitable for the type and amount of business that you are prepared to bring them.

4.0   Buying and Selling Individual Securities

Securities dealers are firms that are registered with securities regulators to buy or sell securities, largely on a commission basis, on behalf of clients and to provide advice to clients about their investments. Many different types of dealers offer a variety of products and services and specialize in different areas.

Some dealers are large national firms; others are small and operate in only one province or territory, or even a single city. Some types of dealers are registered to buy or sell a full range of securities; others are restricted to certain types of products such as mutual funds, scholarship plans, real estate securities, or exchange contracts.

Some, but not all, dealers participate in contingency funds such as the Canadian Investor Protection Fund (CIPF). These funds are not designed to cover losses on investments, but they reimburse (within limits) cash or securities lost when a dealer becomes insolvent.

Some dealers offer clients a full range of trading, research, advisory, and portfolio management services; discount brokers, however, specialize in providing low-cost trade execution services for investors who can make their own investment decisions. These transactions may be conducted on the Internet or using proprietary computer networks. Most electronic trading services introduced to date have been those of discount brokerages catering to do-it-yourself investors.

Generally, electronic-based brokerage services offer incentives to encourage clients to place orders on-line. The incentives include discounts on the posted commission rate or flat-fee transactions, regardless of the size of the order. Electronic trading appeals to knowledgeable clients who want to save money, or clients with large, self-directed accounts who want volume discounts. Additional services such as on-line mutual fund programs can be offered either as part of the basic service, or sold separately to clients on a user-pay basis.

5.0   Discretionary Investment Management

Products that involve discretionary investment management include separately managed accounts, pooled funds, and wrap accounts (described in Chapter 12). These products are provided mainly by investment dealers, investment counsellors, and financial institutions such as trust companies and banks. Fees for professional money management are usually a percentage of the market value of the assets being managed. As the size of the assets increase, the percentage rate of the fee decreases. The greater the level of customization, the higher the minimum investment size required. Custodial, brokerage fees, and administrative fees may be added.

When considering a fee-based service, remember that these fees are usually tax-deductible. Quite often these firms also offer additional perks to their clients, such as no commission on mutual fund transactions, complimentary safekeeping, and premium rates on fixed-income securities.

5.1   Investment Dealers

In addition to buying and selling securities on behalf of clients, investment dealers also offer a complete range of professional money management services to clients, including separately managed accounts, pooled funds, and wrap accounts

5.2   Money Managers (Investment Counsellors)

Money managers are registered with provincial securities commissions as investment counsel or portfolio managers. They provide discretionary investment management services directly to private clients in return for a fee. These services include separately managed accounts and pooled accounts. Most also provide investment management to pension funds and institutions such as foundations and endowments.

Investment counsel firms that serve high-net-worth clients tend not to be household names. They do not advertise much, as they focus on a relatively small market. Examples of companies that provide these services include Bissett and Associates, TAL Private Management Ltd., and Phillips, Hager and North.

5.3   Trust Companies

Trust companies offer discretionary investment management, trust and estate services, retirement planning, and banking services.

6.0   Mutual Funds

Unlike direct securities, such as exchange-listed stocks, which are bought and sold for clients at a central marketplace by all types of registered representatives, the managed-money marketplace is fragmented.

Sponsors of funds may restrict distribution of their products to specific distributors, either proprietary or non-proprietary. The largest single mutual fund sponsor in Canada, Winnipeg-based Investors Group Inc., sells exclusively through its own sales force. Sales may also be restricted by occupational group. The MD Management group of funds is sold only to members of the Canadian Medical Association, their employees and family members. Geographic restrictions may also come into play. The Solidarity Fund, the largest labour-sponsored venture capital fund sold to individual small investors, is available only to Quebec residents.

However, in many cases the lines of distribution are blurring. Bank-sponsored funds, for example, are increasingly available through brokers and mutual-fund dealers. In a few instances, funds distributed primarily by brokers are available through branches of financial institutions.

In early 1996, the Toronto-Dominion Bank pioneered the distribution of non-bank funds at bank branches. In addition to funds in TD's own Green Line family, branch customers can buy selected funds from independent companies. In early 1999, the bank's customers could buy selected funds sponsored by AGF, BPI, Fidelity, Templeton, and Trimark.

The distribution of managed products generally tends to fall into one of two main categories:

- sales through commissioned financial advisors;
- sales directly by the fund company, usually from a retail branch, over the phone or, more recently, via electronic channels such as the Internet.

Most advisor-sold funds are sold on a deferred-sales-charge basis. Those sold by financial institutions, investment-counselling firms, or other direct sellers have generally been no-load funds. There are exceptions, such as Clarica (formerly, The Mutual Group) of mainly no-load funds, sold by Clarica's sales force, and the Atlas family of no-load funds, distributed mainly by brokers of Merrill Lynch Canada.

Whatever the method of distribution, registered financial services professionals who sell managed products must adhere to the Know Your Client rule. They must take into account the client's investment objectives, risk tolerance, time horizon, and relevant personal circumstances, such as age. Increasingly, banks have been providing fund-selection services to their customers. This crossover has further blurred the historical distinctions between "advice" and "no-advice" distributors. Examples of these bank-sponsored services include the CIBC Choice Funds and Scotia Leaders programs.

In the case of commissioned advisors, the primary relationship is between the client and the individual salesperson. In the case of the non-commissioned, no-load companies, the key relationship is that between the client and the fund company, and is less likely to be affected by changes in personnel at the firm.

6.1   Advisor-Sold Funds (Commissioned)

Within the distribution channel that relies on commissioned salespeople, there are two main categories.

1. **The independent or third-party sales forces**: These salespeople operate at arm's length from the fund companies whose products they sell. Those that fall into this category include investment dealers, mutual fund dealers, and financial-planning firms that are involved mainly in selling investment funds. Although some investment firms, such as Merrill Lynch Canada, through its Atlas group of funds, may sell some proprietary funds, most of the sales of these firms are of non-proprietary products.

2. **The proprietary sales forces:** The largest in this group is that of Investors Group, the largest distributor of mutual funds in Canada, which as of the end of January 2000 had 3,800 agents. Clarica (formerly Mutual) Life is another prominent sponsor of mutual funds that relies exclusively on a proprietary sales force. Proprietary sales forces may also be licensed to sell segregated funds, which are insurance contracts similar to mutual funds.

Over the past few years, because of increasing demand by consumers for a wider array of products, proprietary funds sponsors have tended to introduce new products. For example, Investors Group has added new families of funds to its product line that are managed by outside advisors but sold exclusively by Investors agents. In 1997, the Mutual Group(now Clarica) introduced two new families of funds, one managed by AGF Management and the other by Mackenzie Financial.

Chapter 13 describes the operating expenses of a mutual fund, including management fees and administrative costs. In addition to these indirect costs, unitholders also pay direct fees associated with the selling and distribution of the mutual fund units.

Investors may expect to pay the various types of fees for dealing in mutual funds.

Acquisition Fees (Front-End Load)

Some funds levy a sales charge, known as a front-end load. The acquisition fee is not paid to the fund, but is a sales commission given to the selling agent.

The maximum load fee is 9%, although most funds have a lower limit and the actual rate charged is usually below the limit. Only a few funds insist that those who act as selling agents for the fund charge the fund's stated rates. Thus brokers and independent agents normally offer funds at discounted rates. Often the sales charge is arranged on a graduated scale, declining as the amount invested increases. For instance:

- 5% on an initial investment of less than $20,000;
- 4% for $20,000 to $40,000;
- 3% for $40,000 to $80,000;
- 2% on any amount of $80,000 or more.

The load fee quoted by a fund is calculated on a margin basis or "gross investment basis." Thus the fund's selling price is *not* NAVS (net asset value per share) plus a fee that is $x\%$ of NAVS, but instead is set up in the following way:

$$\text{selling price} = \frac{\text{NAVS}}{1-x}$$

With a NAVS of $20 and a load charge of 5%, the selling price (P) would be:

$$P = \frac{20}{1-.05} = \$21.05$$

The commission is thus 5.25% of the amount invested ($1.05/$20). Therefore, someone with $10,000 to invest in a 5% load fund will pay 5% of $10,000 or a $500 sales fee, leaving $9,500 to be invested.

Annual returns quoted by funds do not account for the load. A one-year return after accounting for the acquisition fee, denoted R_a, is calculated in the following way:

$$R_a = R - [x \times (1 + R)]$$

where R is the unadjusted return. With a 5% load charge, a 12% return is reduced to:

$$.12 - [0.05 \times 1.12] = 6.4\%$$

If a fund reports an n-year annual compounded rate of return R, the return after accounting for the load fee can be calculated using the equation:

$$R_a = [(1 - [x/n]) \times (1 + R)] - 1$$

where R_a is adjusted compound return. A fund with a 5% front-end load that produces a return of 12% a year over 5 years, therefore has an annual return of:

$$[(1 - .05/5) \times (1.12)] - 1 = 10.88\%$$

after adjusting for the purchase commission. The detrimental effect of the fee diminishes with time as it is averaged over more years.

Redemption Fees (Back-End Load or Deferred Sales Charge)

An alternative to a front-end load is to charge a redemption fee, called a back-end load or a deferred sales charge (DSC). The DSC declines with the length of time shares are held and may decrease as the size of the investment increases. For example, a fund may have an initial 4.9% redemption fee that falls 0.7% a year to zero after seven years. It is common, though, for the rate to decline very little during the first few years.

There are many variations in the application of this fee. Usually the DSC is based on the current value of the fund, although a few funds use the cost of the original purchase. Several funds that use current value cap their fees at, for example, 9% of the cost of the original purchase.

Although some funds base the redemption fee on the net asset value of the units originally purchased and do not charge for units bought through reinvested distributions, others base the fee on the NAVS of all units redeemed. In this case, the rate for each reinvestment depends on when that unit was purchased. Those bought with recent distributions are subject to the full redemption fee.

Trailer Fees

Front-end and back-end load charges are visible to investors, but back-end load funds and most front-end load funds also levy a hidden fee. Sellers of DSC funds receive 4.5% to 6% of the sale value from the sponsor plus an annual trailer fee of about 0.5% each year that the investor holds the fund. To recover the point-of-sale commission and the ongoing trailer fee, the sponsor charges additional management expense to the fund. The unitholders pay these charges by receiving reduced returns. The DSC is essentially a penalty payment on investors who leave the fund before the sponsor has recovered the commission.

Because competitive pressures have forced front-end loads down to the point at which distributors do not find them profitable, most front-end load funds now pay sales agents a trailer fee. However, since the investor, not the sponsor, pays the initial sales commission, some sponsors levy a lower annual fees on their front-end load funds than on their DSC funds.

Clearly, trailer fees create ongoing sales commissions, because investors pay a distribution charge each year for as long as they are in the fund. These hidden continuing fees can quickly become much more significant to investors' return than the visible loads.

For long-term investors, reducing return by 0.75% to 1.0% a year adds up to thousands of dollars forgone over a 15- to 20-year holding period.

Proponents of trailer fees argue that the trailer compensates advisors who keep people invested and provide continuing advice. Investors who do not need advice or feel that they are overpaying for the quality or amount of advice provided should look for funds that do not pay trailer fees.

Distributor Incentives

The most popular avenue for selling funds is through full-service stock brokerage firms and independent mutual fund dealers. Under this distribution system, salespeople deal with the public and can offer any of the funds available through this channel.

Sponsors who market their funds this way compete with each other for the attention of brokers and dealers by offering creative compensation and incentives. Compensation programs vary, particularly in initial payouts to salespeople from DSC funds. The rate can even vary among the products of the same fund organization. Fund sponsors also provide cooperative advertising and marketing programs for brokers and dealers. Special incentive programs are among the most powerful tools for encouraging salespeople to promote certain funds.

Critics of this approach to selling funds stress the conflicts of interest these programs create for salespeople, arguing that they compromise salespeople's objectivity and responsibility to clients. Sales agents may choose to recommend the funds that reward them the most, rather than the funds that are best for the buyer. Regulatory changes have placed restrictions on compensation and marketing programs and require greater incentive policy disclosure to clients, but this sales avenue remains one of the most controversial areas in the mutual fund industry.

6.2   Direct-Sales Funds (No-Load)

Distributors who sell managed funds directly to clients, without the involvement of a commissioned salesperson, fall into two main categories:
- those who work for financial institutions;
- those who work for other firms such as independent direct sellers.

Financial institutions, including the country's largest banks, trust companies, and credit unions, are among the country's fastest-growing distributors of managed funds. At the end of 1998, for example, the five largest fund companies selling no-load funds were all banks or trust companies. They dominate the direct-sales fund business in Canada, in contrast to the United States, where these types of sales are carried out mainly by independent firms.

Independent direct sellers represent a relatively small, though significant, form of distribution. Among the largest of these distributors is Altamira Investment Services, a noted innovator in products and services for do-it-yourself investors.

Many independent direct sellers of retail investment funds are investment-counselling firms whose core business is institutional or high-net-worth money management, and for whom retail funds are a way to make the most of their expertise. Prominent examples of this type of fund sponsor, which pay little if any compensation to financial advisors, include Phillips, Hager and North and Sceptre Investment Counsel.

Funds that are sold directly to the public are promoted by direct advertising rather than by paying sales agents to find clients. Although distribution expenses are usually lower for no-load than they are for load funds, the added advertising expenditures and staff costs reduce the benefit of commission-free sales.

However, some direct distributors also sell through stock brokers and mutual fund dealers and pay trailer fees to the seller. The fees are factored into fund expenses and therefore paid by all investors, no matter where the fund is purchased. In fact, the fund may not differentiate by seller. An investor buying a no-load fund directly from Altamira still generates a trailer fee; it is simply paid to the fund sponsor Altamira Investment Services. These funds may be no-load but they are certainly not "no sales commission."

A number of unions and associations are also active in the direct sales of investment funds. They offer funds exclusively to members of the organization and their employees and family members. These funds may take the form of conventional mutual funds that are sold by prospectus, or may be structured as pooled funds. The largest sponsor of this type is MD Management, owned by the Canadian Medical Association.

7.0 Evaluating Investment Firms that Offer Managed Products

Three types of firms offer investment services:
- dealers (investment and mutual fund);
- financial institutions (trust companies, banks and insurance companies);
- investment counsellors.

In recent years, banks have been integrating their investment dealer, investment counselor, and trust subsidiaries into units within the bank geared to private clients.

S. Kelly Rodgers, CFA, in her book, "The Insiders Guide to Selecting the Best Money Manager"[1] described the types of questions that a client or wealth manager should be

---

[1]   S. Kelly Rodgers, CFA, "The Insider's Guide to Selecting the Best Money Manager," 1993. Published in Canada.

asking, as part of their due diligence, when searching for an investment firm. The questions include:

7.1   Ownership

Is the firm publicly or privately held?

If privately held, who are the shareholders and what percentage does each own?

Is there any potential for conflicts of interest?

If the firm is independent, will it be able to stay that way?

Will the firm be sold or merged when the founders retire?

7.2   Revenue

Is any of the firm's revenue derived either directly or indirectly from commissions on order execution?

If so, does this create a conflict of interest or bias toward more active trading?

Does the firm provide corporate finance services?

If the firm provides corporate finance services, will this bias the firm's security selection for clients to companies that the firm provides the corporate finance services to?

7.3   Growth Record

Too little or too much growth may be problematic. For an independent firm, too little or inconsistent growth may threaten its survival. A firm that grows too quickly too soon risks a decline in customer service. One large Canadian investment counsellor has estimated that it requires about 20 to 25 hours a year to provide excellent service to each of its clients. Since each year contains about 2,500 working hours, it is easy to deduce the maximum client load that should be taken on.

7.4   Management and Staff Turnover

Find out about the quality and balance of the management team of a firm. The history of staff turnover is probably the most important indicator of a firm's ability to manage itself.

7.5   Staff Remuneration

There are a variety of compensation structures within the investment industry, and it is important to understand what portfolio managers or investment advisors are being paid to do. For example:

- If they are compensated on the basis of total assets under management, they may spend too much time working to bring in new clients and increase assets than they do on servicing existing clients.

- A compensation structure that is tied to performance benchmarks may encourage a portfolio manager to take on higher risks.

- When a firm receives revenue from trading activity, a remuneration package based on total revenue generated may encourage more active trading in the account that is necessary.

8.0   When to Change Investment Firms

S. Kelly Rodgers also identified certain warning signals, above and beyond pure performance, that may warrant looking for a different firm. The decision to change investment firms (and money managers) should not be taken lightly, as changing managers frequently is expensive and reduces the return on a portfolio. Change may also incur custodial and brokerage charges, not to mention the cost in terms of time and energy in choosing an alternative.

However, when the following warning signals are apparent, the risks of maintaining the status quo may outweigh the costs of change. As a result, you may have to make the tough decision to take your client's account elsewhere.

8.1   Inability to Meet Stated Objectives

This problem may arise with small firms that grow too quickly. A firm may start out small and aggressive with a mandate to deliver superior investment returns. In doing well and fulfilling this mandate they attract many new clients and grow into a large firm that is unable to meet the objectives of clients who are seeking flexible, aggressive performance-oriented investment management.

8.2   Turnover in Key Staff

This may be a strong indicator that a firm is having difficulties. You should keep up to date on changes in key personnel within the organization.

8.3   Changes in Written Reporting Packages

Periodic changes in written reports to clients are normal. You should, however, be on the lookout for reporting changes that mask poor investment performance. For example, a change from reporting non-domestic holdings in U.S. dollars to reporting in Canadian dollars may be an attempt to hide substandard investment results.

8.4   Change in Level of Service

The level of customer service may deteriorate if a firm adds clients too quickly or compensates managers on the basis of total assets brought in. It may also be a reflection of internal difficulties within the firm.

8.5   Changes in Trading Activity

Increases in trading activity can be a signal that investment returns have fallen behind the target return and the investment manager is trying to recoup lost ground.

8.6   Change in Investment Style

When investment managers change their investment styles, it is usually for one of the following three reasons:

*   short-term results have fallen behind the benchmark;
*   a firm that has grown dramatically now has so many assets under administration that investments can be made only in the largest and most liquid securities (this is particularly true in Canadian markets);
*   there have been changes in key personnel.

8.7   Increased Frequency of Billings

Mutual funds and pooled funds normally bill fees monthly, in arrears. Separately managed accounts are normally billed quarterly, in arrears. If the frequency of billing is increased, for example from quarterly to monthly, it may indicate that the firm is having financial or cash-flow problems.

Section IV

Practice Management

So far, this course has covered the technical knowledge and skills you need on the job. These skills alone, however, do not guarantee success. You must be able to apply them and manage your practice as well.

This section focuses on the skills you need to run a wealth management practice—from doing appropriate market research, competitive intelligence and business planning, to marketing and gaining a competitive edge.

If you are interested in establishing a practice of your own, understanding these matters will be an essential factor in your success—just as essential as knowing the skills of wealth management itself.

Even if you work for a firm that provides clerical, technical, accounting, and marketing support, you should understand the full range of practice management skills and requirements needed to make a practice successful. Wealth management practices are increasingly being established as businesses within a business. You may be expected to work within an established corporate culture, while establishing and sustaining a successful business within the firm.

CHAPTER 15

Market Research and Business Planning

1.0 Introduction

Whether or not you realize it, in deciding to become a wealth manager, you have already conducted some market research. You knew that someone would pay for your services, and knew what those services would be. You identified potential clients, established how much to charge for your services, and figured out how to deliver those services most effectively.

You did all this to prepare for your current position. However, to make your business grow, you must take a more rigorous approach to market research and business planning.

Primary Learning Objectives

By the end of this chapter you should understand:

- **the types of questions you should be asking in building your market research and competitive intelligence information;**

- **the type of demographic and trend research you need to conduct for your business;**

- **the areas in which you can gain a competitive advantage;**

- **the steps in the business planning process.**

2.0 Demographics, Trends, and Consumer Behaviour

You may have clients that represent a wide spectrum of demographic characteristics, from corporate executives nearing the end of their careers to aging baby boomers administering the estates of their parents to young entrepreneurs on the fast track to high-tech fortunes. Each client has different values, different goals, and different attitudes toward risk and reward. The better that you prepare to address these specific values, goals, and attitudes, the more effectively you can attract and retain clients from across the demographic spectrum.

Priorities change for clients, not just with age and maturity but with changes in family circumstances, growth or depletion of wealth, and concerns about health and lifestyle. By staying attuned to the possibility of change, you can address the changing needs of your clients.

2.1   Understanding the High-Net-Worth Market

According to industry estimates, the wealth of the world's highest net worth clients (those with financial assets of $1 million or more) will grow between 1999 and 2003 by more than 50% to $32.7 trillion. During 1999, the wealth of the nearly six million individuals in this market around the world grew by 12%, to about $21.6 trillion. This growth will be driven, not just by re-invested interest payments, dividends, and capital appreciation, but also by continuing global economic prosperity. In 1999, North American and Western European high-net-worth clients accounted for the majority of this market's overall wealth, about 58% of the total.

High-net-worth clients face a wide range of choices in how they manage their wealth. As a result, they will increasingly rely on wealth managers to help them make decisions. The continuing sophistication of this market is also leading them to use a broader range of products, services, delivery mechanisms, and channels.

The profiles of high-net-worth clients are changing. Earned wealth is increasing faster than inherited wealth. Today's high-net-worth clients are more knowledgeable than those of previous generations, and they take a more active role in managing their wealth. They are information-hungry, comfortable with technology, and able to use more sophisticated financial products.

Solid revenues with high returns are intensifying the competition for their wealth. An increasing number of new advice providers are entering the market. New entrants are targeting the affluent and emerging affluent segments at lower levels of wealth.

These changes have led to a plethora of innovations. Wealth managers are offering a wider and more complex range of new services, including the use of alternative investment avenues, such as private equity funds.

Technology and the Internet are changing the way clients interact with their wealth managers. Although many use the Internet only for information gathering, high-net-worth clients are conducting more transactions electronically, as fears about security diminish, forcing firms that provide wealth management services to make a sustained effort to innovate with the Internet and other services.

Today's wealth managers need to offer the best solutions to their customers, regardless of the source of the products they use. Your value to your clients will depend on your ability to coach and advise, bringing in experts where appropriate.

2.2   Demographics Relating to the High-Net-Worth Market

The word demography is derived from the Greek words for "people" and "writing." Demography is the study of populations: how they grow, how they change, the characteristics of different groups. It has emerged as a popular science in recent years primarily because the influence of the baby boom generation. The people born after the Second World War have the power in sheer numbers to indulge their interests and tastes. Just as this generation influenced popular music and culture in the 1960s, they now influence marketing, finance, and retirement planning.

However, many demographers warn about the danger of focusing exclusively on the needs of the boomers. Although the generations coming before and after the baby boomers are smaller and less influential, they have as much earning, spending, and investing capacity as other demographic groups. In fact, it can be argued that younger people have an even greater capacity to accumulate wealth, because they have fewer competitors.

Affluent clients, defined as those holding more than $500,000 in investable assets, are viewed by many wealth managers, especially those who don't have them as clients, as the profession's Holy Grail. Yet this attitude raises some questions:

- What are the defining characteristics of the high-net-worth client?

- Is building a practice predominantly of high-net-worth clients a realistic goal for most wealth managers?

- Are high-net-worth clients, by definition, a limited market?

- What are their unique issues and needs?

To address these and related questions, we will look at research on the North American High Net Worth Client world that has been made available to CSI from the 1997 VIP Forum Buyer Value Study. Hereafter, the terms "affluent," "wealthy," and "high-net-worth" are used synonymously to describe respondents, all of whom have at least $500,000 in investable assets and personally make decisions concerning financial matters.

Figure 15.1 shows the wealth tier distribution of individuals with more than $250,000 in assets: 21% of these individuals have more than $1 million in investable assets.

Figure 15.2 illustrates the educational levels of individuals with more than $500,000 in investable assets: 81% of these individuals have a college education or higher.

Figure 15.1   Wealth Tier Distribution: Individuals Holding More Than $0.25 million in Assets

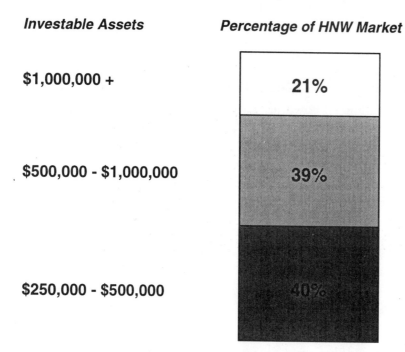

Investable Assets

$1,000,000 +

$500,000 - $1,000,000

$250,000 - $500,000

Percentage of HNW Market

21%

39%

40%

Note: Total investable assets held by surveyed clients include deposits, individual securities, mutual funds, metals, limited partnerships, trusts, investment management accounts, and retirement accounts.

**Figure 15.2:   Education Distribution of U.S. High-Net-Worth Clients[1]
Total Affluent Population**

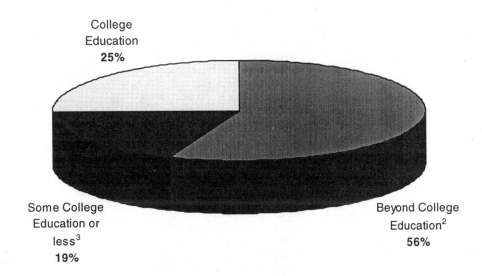

Meanwhile, as baby boomers grow older, they will continue to receive the lion's share of popular attention for at least the next two decades. Consider some of the following statistics:

- The average life expectancy for women in North America has increased to 78 years; for men, it has risen to 72. More people will live beyond the age of 85 in future generations. This will have a significant affect on retirement planning.

- In 1990, one person in eight was over 65; by 2050, one person in five will be over 65.

- Between 1960 and 1994, the number of people aged 85 and over rose by 274%.

- In 1993, the median net worth (assets minus liabilities) of households of older North Americans was $86,300 (over 65). For households headed by people 75 and older, it was $77,000. This is more than double the median household income.

Figure 15.3 shows that the highest proportion of high-net-worth individuals in North America (those with $500,000 or more) are over 65.

---

[1]   Highest level of education completed.
[2]   Includes some graduate school (15.3%), master's degree (26.8%), law school graduate (4.5%), medical/dental school graduate (3.5%) and doctorate (5.0%).
[3]   Includes high school graduate (3.3%) and partial college attendance (16.2%).

Figure 15.3   Age Distribution of High-Net-Worth Clients
Total Affluent Population

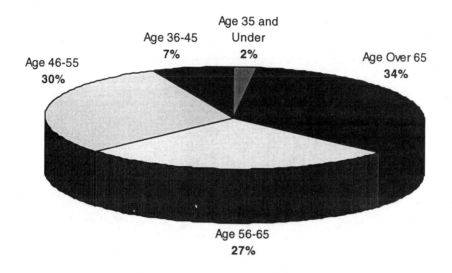

- People aged 45 to 55 spend 17% more money than the average consumer. People 55 to 64 rank second, spending 15% more than the average. People 25 to 34 spend 13% less than the average.

- Most people over 65 own their own homes.

- People over 65 choose products and services based on past experience, price, and quality.

- People over 65 travel more than younger people, and they take longer trips. Preferences include beach vacations (22%), travelling abroad (21%), and cruises (20%).

- Eight out of ten people over 65 are interested in environmental issues.

- The top three hobbies of people over 65 include reading (48%), walking (45%), and cooking (35%).

- Most grandparents see their grandchildren regularly and over half of them buy presents for their grandchildren in a typical month.

- Most are concerned about nutrition, health, and lifestyle, but none of them wants to rely on a product or service that highlights their frailties. They eat out at least three times a week.[4]

---

[4]   Source: Robert Snyder, Senior Vice-President, JWT Specialized Communications.

It's one thing to know that there are a lot of people who will eventually turn 65 and that they spend more money than anyone else on the planet. It's quite another thing to build a business strategy around this or any other statistic. Does this mean that you should focus all your efforts on retired people?

Demographics simply provide a context for understanding marketing. You must interpret them in a way that takes into account your own strengths and weaknesses. Demographic data doesn't affect the fundamental emotions with which most people regard their money and investments, and it's people's emotions, more than the statistical context of their lives, that should determine your strategy and planning.

Some of Canada's largest financial and investment organizations are targeting their marketing efforts at individuals between the ages of 39 and 55 (baby boomers). These individuals are at the height of their wealth-accumulation years, and they have significant responsibilities at home. Their children are growing into adolescence or adulthood, which brings new expenses; their parents are growing older and becoming more frail and financially dependent. As mutual fund companies, banks, and other financial service providers build their marketing efforts around different generations, you have an opportunity to choose the particular rung of the generational ladder that will bring in new business.

2.3   Consumer Behaviour

According to consultant Shirley Roberts of Market-Driven Solutions Inc. in Mississauga, Ont., clients are becoming more knowledgeable and demanding, and they're focusing more than ever on returns from their investments. The challenge for you as a wealth manager lies in relating returns to financial goals, and showing how returns help clients achieve their goals in the long term.

Roberts identifies nine emerging trends of consumer behaviour:

1. As individuals react against the overwhelming trend toward categorizing people (as baby boomers, women entrepreneurs, retirees, and so forth), they're becoming more independent in their thinking and seeking more control over their lives. Financial advisors must improve their communications with their clients to let them know not just what they're doing but why they are doing it. Clients want to set a goal and chart their progress toward achieving it. They won't accept advice at face value, and they will seek a second opinion.

2. Clients understand the tools available for executing a financial strategy and they want to make sure you're using the right ones for them. They also want more sophisticated reports that go far beyond a standard boilerplate monthly statements.

3. Clients want you to reduce their anxiety about financial uncertainty so they can put their time to their own use in pursuit of a higher quality of life. They value their time,

because it's their most precious resource. You must communicate with them to relieve their stress.

4. As clients demand more of their advisors, they will not hesitate to switch if they don't get what they want (relief from anxiety is key). Your survival depends on exceeding their demands. The following chart shows the five most important attributes clients search for when selecting a financial advisor.

Figure 15.4   Top Five Most Important Attributes When Selecting a Comprehensive Provider

$0.5 M - $1.0 M		$1.0 M - $5.0 M		$5.0+ M	
1. Offers consistently high returns	77%	1. Is a trusted advisor	63%	1. Offers consistently high returns	70%
2. Provides solutions to objectives	57%	2. Offers consistently high returns	59%	2./3. Expertise in managing your finances/Wide range of investment services	52%
3. Expertise in managing your finances	52%	3. Provides solutions to objectives	54%		
4. Is a trusted advisor	50%	4. Wide range of investment services	50%	4. Provides solutions to objectives	48%
5. Staff who understand your needs	46%	5. Expertise in managing your finances	40%	5. Is a trusted advisor/ Immediate response to requests	42%

5. Society is growing far less homogeneous, particularly with the growth of ethnic populations. Ethnicity influences individuals' attitudes toward saving, spending, and financial planning.

6. Until they pay off debt, clients will focus on this aspect of their financial lives. They know they have to plan for retirement, and they depend on you to help them achieve their plan.

7. Clients want to have fun, and they seek new and unusual experiences. Not only do they want to talk about new and creative ideas for their financial portfolios, they want you to present them in imaginative ways.

8. They're preoccupied with their health and well-being, and that means a secure retirement.

9. As people stay healthier and more active for longer periods, they will have to rely on their retirement savings for a much longer period than before. You must suggest

creative ways to achieve their financial goals, which includes thinking beyond the framework of conventional investing.

2.4   Women in Perspective

As women feel more at home in the workplace and acquire more power and security, it remains to be seen whether or not financial advisors can direct their marketing efforts specifically at women.

People like to be regarded as individuals first, before they're included in any particular group, whether the group is fifty-five-year-old wealthy white men, educated homosexuals, or female Chinese entrepreneurs.

Nevertheless, women are in the news, and they have become a target for demographic analysis. According to Marti Barletta, president of The Trendsight Group, analysis of women as businesspeople and consumers has revealed some interesting facts:

- Women account for more than 80% of household spending, which in turn accounts for more than half of Canada's GNP. According to Tom Peters, author of *In Search of Excellence,* spending by women in the United States constitutes an economy the size of Japan.

- Women currently own more than one-third of all small businesses, and they are starting new entrepreneurial ventures at twice the rate of men. "Women-owned small businesses are more likely to survive past the critical five-year make-it-or-break-it mark," Barletta says. That is, 65% of women-owned businesses survive vs. 58% for men-owned businesses.

According to financial advisor Patricia Lovett-Reid, the women's market is evolving into distinct groups with specific needs. "Different perspectives on the single woman are now apparent, bestowing unique sales opportunities for investment professionals," she says. "Women are taking more responsibility for their financial futures for several reasons: a stronger presence in the workforce, better education, rising divorce rates, and, increasingly, single parenthood." The problems women have in gaining greater access to the information and expertise necessary to establish a financial plan may be the industry's best opportunity today, she says.

"Considering that one-third of Canadian marriages end in divorce, 82% of single-parent households are headed by women, and that the average woman spends seven years as a widow (compared to two years for men)," says Lovett-Reid, "the need for financial guidance for single women with children is strikingly obvious."

3.0   Information Sources

Read as much as you can. Staying current requires a lot of homework. Sometimes the best sources of information are daily, weekly, and monthly newspapers, magazines and journals—not just the mainstream publications, but specialized ones that may appeal to a specific market. The following is a list and description of where more detailed information may be found:

3.1   Internet

By subscribing to on-line information services and navigating cyberspace, you can find a lot of information about the economic environment. Publishers of industry directories, for example, usually distribute electronic versions of their material. Government sources of information, statistics, and regulations can be reached on-line as well.

3.2   Libraries

Most library systems are linked electronically to computer databases. They also offer a wide variety of directories, industry publications, government statistics, and other resources. There are also many useful books available.

3.3   Chambers of Commerce or Boards of Trade

These organizations compile mountains of valuable information on local markets, industries, spending patterns, income profiles, services, growth rates, and other economic indicators.

3.4   Universities and Colleges

Students in business administration or commerce programs often run faculty-supervised consulting services. For a small fee, the students will conduct a market research program. For straightforward jobs like compiling data and statistics, these services can save you a lot of time.

3.5   Municipal and Provincial Governments

Some municipalities and all provincial governments operate a department dedicated to economic development and research. Most of this research is published in reports that you can use.

3.6 Suppliers

The organizations that provide your company with investment products often have information about markets and consumers you can use in developing a strategy for a client.

3.7 Competitors

Depending on the kind of business you operate and the nature of your relationship with your competitors, you can get good advice, useful insights, and positive encouragement from your peers. Most people feel flattered that others regard them highly enough to ask them to share their wisdom.

3.8 Employees

Your own employees may have significant insights into their industry that no one has ever bothered to ask them about.

3.9 Consulting Firms

If you need an extensive amount of research and you do not have time to do it yourself, consider employing a consulting firm that specializes in market research. Some smaller firms specialize specifically in the financial services industry.

3.10 Clients

Successful clients and potential clients can often provide valuable information based on their own experience. You can ask them: Why do they buy a particular service? How do they decide where to buy it? What qualities do they look for in their supplier? How many suppliers do they use?

There are many ways to listen to clients:

1. **Attending client industry or trade meetings**: At these meetings, you will have the opportunity to listen to clients talk about their challenges, interests and needs. You will learn even more if you attend with a respected client, because you will get immediate evaluation from the client about ideas presented by speakers. Ask your client: Do you agree with what that speaker said? Do you think you'll have to deal with that? What does this really mean for you? These conversations help you understand and interpret what you hear at these meetings.

2. **Client debriefings**: In the best-practice management firms, at points throughout the wealth management process (which is ongoing), the wealth manager sits down with

the client to get the client's feedback on what went well, what did not go well, and how service might be improved. These discussions cover not only the technical quality and success of the project, but also ways to improve communications with the client. They also highlight unresolved issues that may affect your business. Some firms impose a requirement to file a debriefing report, so that ideas for improvement obtained from their clients are formally captured and become part of the intellectual capital of the firm.

3. **Systematic client feedback**: Many firms have a mandatory policy of sending a questionnaire to clients at the end of each project, inviting the client to evaluate the firm. There are three benefits to this practice. First, the questionnaire comes to the client from the firm, not the individual wealth manager, and may solicit comments that the client might not be willing to express face-to-face to the individual manager. Second, the questionnaire helps firms to track their quality performance, and may reveal opportunities for improvement that might not arise in client debriefings. Third, the act of asking for feedback signals to clients a willingness to listen and respond. An example of a client feedback questionnaire is found in the appendix to this chapter.

4. **User groups**: Some firms ask a small group of respected clients to attend periodic meetings, perhaps two or three times a year, to discuss the firm's service offerings in a particular area. These meetings are often held after dinner in a private room at a restaurant. After dinner, the firm presents its plans for developing its practice in the specified area, including the development of new services or enhanced services, and other strategic changes. The clients are invited to comment on the plans, and say whether the proposed strategies make sense from their point of view, and whether or not there are other things that the firm should be considering to improve its practice. There can be no better judge of how the firm can improve the competitiveness of its practice than the clients who will, after all, be the ultimate judges.

3.11   The Value of Information

Using telecommunications, computers and software, individuals can now move more information from one side of the planet to the other in five minutes than a person living in the 1950s could in a lifetime, according to Edward Nazarko, a leading techno-thinker for IBM in Bethesda, Maryland. "Not only that, but you can analyze it."

According to Nazarko, the network economy enables financial professionals to provide a real service to individual investors. "The network economy in the finance environment isn't about being able to offer more kinds of mutual funds," he says. "It's being able to use the healthy variety of stocks, bonds and financial instruments out there, in an optimized, customized fashion, to help an individual person navigate." As a financial advisor, you provide the context. Information itself is not a particularly valuable asset; context is.

4.0　Competitive Intelligence

In addition to understanding your target market, you must also understand the competition and think of ways to differentiate the services you offer.

You can analyze the competition by poring over articles, statistics, and marketing brochures, or by going directly to the source: competitors themselves. Most people feel flattered to answer questions about their own success, and if they're really good at what they do, they'll feel confident enough about their own capabilities to regard you as a colleague, not a threat.

First, you should spend some time identifying the people who are the best in the business, not just in your own city or town, but anywhere in the country. Try to find out in advance what makes them different or special. A call or letter to these people should start off with a compliment such as, "I've been told that you're one of the best financial advisors in the country."

After you've made the initial contact, ask whether or not it would be possible to learn more about their business and if they would be willing to talk to you about their success. You can simply say, "I'd like to hear your story. Would you be able to meet with me now or next week (over the phone or in person) for a few minutes?" Even the most successful people like to have an opportunity to tell their story.

When you have set up a meeting, ask specific questions and let the interviewee talk. Here is a sample of some questions to choose from.

- What do you love about your work?

- What do you dislike about your work?

- What are your biggest concerns each day?

- What do you spend most of your time on?

- Describe a typical day.

- If you had to do it all over again, what path would you take?

- Where would you start?

- Would you share with me your five- or ten-year vision?

Afterwards you should take some time and review the responses. After the appointment, be sure to write a thank-you note. Your letter may even mention the one thing that excited you the most. The interviewee will appreciate the attention to detail and welcome another contact, which could prove to be valuable later.

You can also get information about competitors from current clients. Either in writing or informally, you can ask clients about the services they've received from other financial advisors. What did they like or dislike? The answers will give you a better understanding of your own strengths and weaknesses and identify changes or improvements you can make to your marketing program, including pricing, promotion, and distribution.

You should also be on the lookout for areas where you can gain a sustainable competitive advantage. In other words: in what areas can you provide the best quality, the lowest cost, the most innovation, or the best service?

Analyzing the competition will help you define your own business in customer-based terms and integrate customer satisfaction into organizational goals. "You don't succeed unless you compete," observes Sonny Nwankwo in the *Journal of Consumer Marketing*. "You won't succeed in customer satisfaction unless you regard it as a competitive arena that deserves every bit as much focus as the design and development of your services."

5.0   Business Planning

A business plan should simply and clearly show exactly where you want to go with your business and how you intend to get there.

The first step in planning is defining and understanding objectives. The objectives might be as simple as attracting enough clients over the course of a year to generate a certain level of income. With that simple step, a deadline has been established and an objective set.

With an income goal in place, you then should figure out what asset base and fee structure will yield that income. One way to do that is to decide on an ideal account size and divide that into the desired asset base. This will give you an idea of how many accounts you will have to open.

Next, you must fill in the details of the plan, including defining a target market and analyzing the steps required to attract clients within the stated deadline.

5.1   Defining Objectives

A business plan serves a number of purposes. In stressful or uncertain periods—which will arise frequently as you strive to get your business operating—a plan can serve as a reminder of why you started as a financial advisor and what you hope to accomplish. If you have employees, it can remind them of their role in the success of the business.

The business plan can also be used as a reference guide to keep you on the path to success. Presumably, the business plan can be developed over a period that gives you time to reflect on and think about your goals and strategies. Once you become immersed in the day-to-day running of the business, you will have less time for reflection or strategic thinking. If you have done your initial homework thoroughly, however, you can refer to the plan to make sure you are following the most sensible course.

5.2   Components of a Business Plan

A survey by Charles Schwab & Co. identified the percentage of planners that would have the following components as part of their business plan. They are:

New client acquisition strategies.............	90%
Client retention/relationship building........	90%
Technology expansion........................	71%
Staffing...	61%
Product/service offering......................	59%
Space/facilities planning......................	42%
Succession planning...........................	25%
Mergers and acquisitions....................	14%

A business plan should answer questions raised by individuals such as potential marketers, investors, or lenders. It should reassure them that customers want your product or service, that the business will generate revenues, and that you and your team know what you're doing. This means that you cannot make assertions that you cannot verify with facts.

The process of developing a business plan should force you to answer a number of questions. Depending on the nature of your practice, some of the following questions may not apply to you, but you should consider them all.

1. **The concept**: What service do you intend to provide? (The answer is more complex than you might think.)

2. **The opportunity and strategy**: What is the potential for turning your concept into a business and how do you plan to do it?

3. **The target market and projections**: Who are your potential customers, and how much will they pay for your product or service?

4. **Competitive advantage**: What distinguishes you from your competitors?

5. **The economics, profitability, and ultimate potential returns of your business**: How much do you need to start? Where will the profits come from? How much will your business generate after the initial phase?

6. **The team**: Who are your partners and employees? What experience do they have in the financial industry?

7. **The industry, the company, and its products or services**: Are you focusing on a particular niche? How does your business differ from others in the industry? What exactly are you selling? How will you draw attention to yourself, and how will you build on your initial success?

8. **Market research and analysis**:
   a. **customers**: Who and where are they, what can you do for them?
   b. **market size and trends**: How much in total does the market spend on your service? Is this amount increasing or decreasing?
   c. **competition and competitive edges**: Who are your competitors? How does their service compare to yours in quality, price, image, and other factors?
   d. **estimated market share and sales**: How much of the market do you expect to capture? How much do you need to capture?
   e. **ongoing market evaluation**: How do you plan to monitor changes in the marketplace?

9. **The economics of the business**:
   a. **gross and operating margins**: How have you calculated these figures?
   b. **profit potential and durability**: Once your business is up and running, how much can you expect to earn? How long will those earnings remain at their current level?
   c. **fixed, variable and semi-variable costs**: How much will you be spending on overhead, equipment, wages and salaries, and so forth?
   d. **months to break-even**: How long will it take your business to start making money?
   e. **months to reach positive cash flow**: How long will it take before your company generates more money than it spends?

10. **Marketing plan**:
    a. **overall marketing strategy**: How will you attract the attention of your potential clients? How will you define yourself within your industry and convince potential clients that they need your service?
    b. **pricing**: How did you arrive at your price?
    c. **sales tactics**: Will you reach your customers through direct selling, cold calling, direct mail, or some other method?
    d. **service policies**: Will you provide a special type of service, for example, round-the-clock service? If so, how will you deliver and pay for it?
    e. **advertising and promotion**: How much will you need to spend to establish and maintain your professional identity?

11. **Management team**:
    a. **organization**: What positions have you established for marketing, sales, and other key tasks?
    b. **key management personnel**: Who will carry out these tasks? What experience do they have?
    c. **management compensation and ownership**: How much will you pay your employees?
    d. **other investors**: Has anyone else put money into the business? How much?

e. **employment and other agreements**: Do your employees work on contract? What other means of compensation, such as stock option and bonus plans, have you initiated?

f. **board of advisors**: Who are they? What experience do they have?

g. **supporting professional advisers and services**: Who are your accountants, lawyers, and other advisors who can provide support in building client relationships?

12. **Overall schedule**: How do you plan to build your business over the next five years? What are your critical deadlines?

13. **Critical risks, problems and assumptions**: Identify the conditions that would create the worst possible scenario for your business. How would you deal with this situation, and how will you avoid it if the risk looks possible?

14. **The financial plan**:

a. **income statements and balance sheet**: If your company is up and running, what are its revenues, earnings, and other financial details?

b. **income statements**: What are your realistic expectations for sales and expenses over the next year?

c. **balance sheets**: What are the projected current and fixed assets and projected current and fixed liabilities?

d. **cash flow analysis**: How much money will be coming in and going out of your business? When will these cash flows occur over the next year? For example, how much will you spend on promotion and salaries?

e. **break-even chart and calculation**: What variable and fixed costs and income will be generated by your services?

f. **cost control**: What mechanisms do you have in place to keep your costs predictable?

g. **highlights**: Do you have a unique way of approaching any of these aspects of your business?

5.3   Ongoing Business Planning

Business planning is an ongoing process. A periodic review of your objectives, and the strategies you have adopted to reach them, will keep you focused on the plan and keep you from being distracted by unnecessary and time-consuming activities.

Although it is sometimes useful to conduct formal strategic analysis under the guidance of a facilitator, a number of pre-packaged questionnaires are available to help you conduct your own strategic analysis. The following questionnaire was developed by Deborah Hornberger, President of Hornberger & Associates, a strategic planning company in San Francisco.[5] It will help you assess whether you are giving enough time and attention to the strategic activities that really make a difference in the long run.

---

[5]   Source: Hornberger & Associates (www.hornbergerassociates.com)

Are you, as a wealth manager, keeping your key objectives in focus, for example, or have they been pre-empted by the minutiae—those daily requests that never stop coming across your desk? Are you taking full advantage of new opportunities in your marketplace?

Your Key Objectives

Answer each question yes or no, unless it does not apply to your business:

1. Can you state your three to five most important annual objectives—without looking at your annual plan?

2. Are you positioned to achieve these key objectives?

3. Have you developed a realistic timeline for the major deliverables?

4. Does your staff have the necessary skills, experience, and time?

5. Have you defined the key costs required to achieve each objective and are these expenses budgeted?

6. If you delay implementing any of your key objectives, will you still make your profit projections?

7. Is your competitive information up-to-date on products offered, new product features, pricing servicing channels, and Internet offerings?

8. Are you actively keeping your product line competitive? For example, do you frequently consider repricing, product enhancements, repackaging, or featuring different benefits?

9. Are you constantly capitalizing on market opportunities, such as new trends, mergers and acquisitions, or competitive product changes?

10. Do you have a successful referral incentive program for the employees of your firm?

11. Is your customer information current on new products and services desired, customer satisfaction ratings, and client Internet preferences?

12. Have you specifically defined and activated customer retention strategies?

APPENDIX 15.1
Client Feedback Questionnaire

For each of the following statements about our practice, please indicate whether you: Strongly disagree (1); somewhat disagree (2); neither agree nor disagree (3); somewhat agree (4); strongly agree (5)

You are thorough in your approach to your work	NA	1	2	3	4	5
You show creativity in your proposed solutions	NA	1	2	3	4	5
You are helpful in redefining our view of our situation	NA	1	2	3	4	5
You are helpful in diagnosing the causes of our problem areas	NA	1	2	3	4	5
Your people are accessible	NA	1	2	3	4	5
You keep your promises and deadlines	NA	1	2	3	4	5
You document your work activities well	NA	1	2	3	4	5
Your communications are free of jargon	NA	1	2	3	4	5
You offer fast turnaround when requested	NA	1	2	3	4	5
You listen well to what we have to say	NA	1	2	3	4	5
You relate well to our people	NA	1	2	3	4	5
You keep me sufficiently informed on progress	NA	1	2	3	4	5
You let us know in advance what you're going to do	NA	1	2	3	4	5
You notify us promptly of changes in scope, and seek our approval	NA	1	2	3	4	5
You give good explanations of what you've done and why	NA	1	2	3	4	5
You don't wait for me to initiate everything: you anticipate	NA	1	2	3	4	5
You don't jump to conclusions too quickly	NA	1	2	3	4	5
You involve us at major points in the engagement	NA	1	2	3	4	5
You have a good understanding of our business	NA	1	2	3	4	5
You make it your business to understand our company	NA	1	2	3	4	5
You are up to date on what's going on in our world	NA	1	2	3	4	5
You make us feel as if we're important to you	NA	1	2	3	4	5
You are an easy firm to do business with	NA	1	2	3	4	5
You deal with problems in our relationship openly and quickly	NA	1	2	3	4	5
You keep us informed on technical issues affecting our business	NA	1	2	3	4	5
You show an interest in us beyond the specifics of your tasks	NA	1	2	3	4	5
You have been helpful to me beyond the specifics of your projects	NA	1	2	3	4	5
You have made our people more effective in what they do	NA	1	2	3	4	5
My own understanding of your area has improved from working with you	NA	1	2	3	4	5
Overall, I would rate your service very highly	NA	1	2	3	4	5

CHAPTER 16

Marketing Your Wealth Management Business

1.0   Introduction

Like any successful business, wealth management requires a dedicated approach to marketing, not only to attract new clients but also to retain existing ones. The aim of marketing is nothing more nor less than making sure that your business survives. Some people enjoy marketing; others don't. Those that don't have to force themselves to sit down every week and sell themselves and their business to potential customers. In any case, marketing is not a full-time job for a wealth manager. It's just a tool for keeping one's business in good shape.

Marketing is a way of letting people know what services you offer, and how well you carry them out. Ultimately, if you do your work well, clients will come. The work comes first. Marketing is just a way of telling people how well you are doing your job.

Primary Learning Objectives

By the end of this chapter, you should understand:

- **the various ways you can define your market;**

- **how to gain a competitive edge;**

- **how to approach the pricing of wealth management services;**

- **different ways of promoting a wealth management business;**

- **the importance of updating a marketing plan to reflect new realities in the marketplace.**

2.0   Marketing Plan Checklist

A marketing plan should define how you intend to find enough people to buy enough of what you are selling, for enough money, to ensure a reasonable profit margin. A good marketing plan will help keep your business priorities straight and ensure the most effective route to maximum sales in the market area selected.

When you do not meet your projections, you can refer to the marketing plan to understand why. By always keeping an eye on the goals in a marketing plan, you can ground your dreams in reality. The following questions should be answered in a marketing plan.

- Defining your target market:
    Who are your potential customers, defined by profession, lifestyle, etc.?

- The value proposition:
    What are you selling?
    What customer services will you offer?
    What is special about what you are offering?
    How can it be differentiated from similar services offered by the competition?

- Pricing:
    What is your pricing strategy?
    How have you arrived at your margin?
    How does your price compare to that of your competitors?

- Promotional plan:
    What advertising media will you use?
    What message do you want to get across?
    What budget will you allocate to advertising?
    What is your public relations and sales promotion program?

3.0   Defining Your Target Market

3.1   Targeting by Occupation

Probably the best way to define a potential market is by what people do. This may involve targeting people by occupation, such as surgeons or lawyers. "Many of my best customers are surgeons," says Thomas Stanley, author of *Selling to the Affluent*. "They don't make house calls. They are too busy. So I make house calls. I tell them loud and clear that I cater to surgeons."

People who grow wealthy from their work usually do it with a passion. They spend most of their time at it, they talk about it with their peers, and they enjoy spending time with people who understand what they do and appreciate how well they do it.

3.2 Targeting by Outside Pursuits

Another effective way of defining a market is to target people by what they do when they're not working. It also enables you as a wealth manager to spend time doing something you enjoy, as well. You work more effectively when you enjoy what you do.

Golfers, tennis players, stamp collectors, big-game hunters, skydivers, ballroom dancers—the list is endless. Name a passion, and you'll find people who enjoy sharing the experience. From this group, you can identify five or ten with whom you could build a relationship as a financial advisor. "Every advisor should have a top ten list of mega-prospects who are worth extraordinary wooing," says Dan Richards, author of *Getting Clients, Keeping Clients*.

The best chances of success come from people with whom you share a common interest. In fact, says Richards, "unless you have a common interest that brings you together occasionally, or you went to school together, or you introduced him to computers, he's unlikely to be a prospect."

You should not expect immediate results from your prospecting efforts. It may take months or years for someone to decide on a particular financial advisor.

In the meantime, you should stay in touch. By spending even an hour a week meeting with potential prospects—which adds up to 50 hours a year (assuming a two-week vacation)—playing golf, going to baseball games, attending fashion shows, or meeting for lunch or breakfast, your time is being spent wisely.

Case 16.1   Leads Can Come From Anywhere

Ron Reynolds never expected his childhood passion for hockey would lead to scoring goals in the business community. Growing up in Halifax, Ron had been involved in sports teams supported by a few local businessmen. In fact, he probably would never have had the opportunity to enjoy and learn from the team experience if it hadn't been for the generous sponsors. Raised by a single, working mother, Ron could otherwise not have afforded the luxury of playing hockey. He never forgot those businessmen. He promised himself that he would contribute to a team if he were ever in a position to do so.

When Ron started building his business, he fulfilled that promise and sponsored a youth hockey team. The team became such a hit that fellow entrepreneurs were invited to sponsor other teams in the league and the network of hockey supporters grew. Off the ice, the team sponsors joked about the news, local politics, their respective businesses, and, of course, the latest league standings.

During one of these post-game conversations, one of the new sponsors asked Ron if he would organize some financial planning and retirement seminars at the local

Case 16.1   Leads Can Come From Anywhere
(continued)

community library. As a result, Reynolds ended up with a score of new clients. "Often when we are looking to help out our communities, good things happen which we do not expect or anticipate," he says.

3.3   Targeting by Location

Another target market may live right on your street. It's not impolite or forward for you to tell neighbours what you do for a living. It's called conversation.

If you believe in yourself and in the services that you provide to clients, you should not have reservations about letting neighbours know that you are available if they want to talk to about their financial affairs.

"It's easier to ask a neighbour to do business with you than a total stranger," says Thomas Stanley. "People who live in the same neighbourhood tend to imitate the consumption patterns of their neighbours."

3.4   Building a Network of Professionals

Just as you depend on people for client referrals, people depend on you, too. By spending time with lawyers, accountants, financial consultants, and insurance agents, for example, you can generate referrals for them, a favour that will likely be returned when the occasion arises.

At the very least this allows you to understand their work and the cycles of their business. This understanding helps considerably when the time comes to provide them with financial advice.

Real estate agents should also be part of your network, particularly since people move, on average, every five years. If they move to another city or town, they usually don't take their advisors with them. Real estate agents can provide the names of potential clients who have recently moved into your neighbourhood.

3.5   How to Turn Down Business

In addition to identifying clients you want, it is also important to identify the clients you don't want.

"If you don't need them," observes Nick Murray, "you won't be tempted to take them on just because you need the money." It helps to have enough money on hand to keep afloat for a year, so you won't be tempted to take on a client simply to pay the bills.

The clients whom you should turn away include people who:
- don't have enough money to make it worth your while to work with them;
- have unrealistic goals about the returns they want;
- have no prospects of making more money;
- want to "play the markets";
- have no understanding of financial markets;
- work or play outside your target market;
- complain about your fees;
- compare your advice to other advice they get from newspapers and magazines and point out your shortcomings;
- demand too much of your time and seek short-term results.

Remember, you will be doing them a favour. If you indulge these kinds of clients, you'll be wasting their time too.

In many industries, firms derive 80% of their income from 20% of their clients. That's not to say the other 80% aren't important. But at the bottom of the list, there are probably some clients who are not adding value.

Once a year, you should review your client list and if necessary consider getting rid of the ones at the bottom of the list. "It's dead weight, and it's draining your time, energy and self-esteem," says Nick Murray.

The best clients are those who will help you get where you need to go, and whom you can help in the same way. People who diminish your ability to do a job to the best of your ability stand in the way of success for both you and your clients.

4.0   Value Propositions

4.1   The Wealth Management Plan

At the heart of the value proposition that a wealth manager provides for a client is the wealth management plan presented in the investment policy statement. Everything else revolves around it, including the relationship with the client and the client's family and their present and future financial needs.

"For most clients there will be a gap between future financial needs and likely financial capacity," says author Dan Richards. "The wealth management plan puts those issues on the table and presents an agreed-upon solution. The plan is a vital part of retirement preparation and, more importantly, at the core of the value proposition that a wealth manager provides. A financial plan gives clients the sense that they're in control. They can now sleep soundly at night."

The value proposition begins with fulfilling a dream. It evolves into a practical concept when you as a wealth manager and your client determine exactly how to accomplish it. But it begins with the dream.

To this end, you and your client's vision should match. You can ensure this by asking the client the right questions and listening closely to the answers. The better you know your client, the more completely you can develop a shared vision.

4.2   Adding Value—Going the Extra Mile

You can add value to your relationships with your clients by going beyond the requirements of the job. Added value can take the form of a personal letter explaining more clearly the content of a report from head office. Or it may take the form of a seminar or workshop developed exclusively for a particular group of clients. It may consist of a simple phone call to alert the client to a potential business opportunity.

"Clients migrate to those businesses that provide clear, concrete, substantive value," says Dan Richards. "We must focus on adding value."

It's not enough to execute the tasks of your job with competence and skill. Any financial advisor can do that. If you want to distinguish yourself from the crowd, you have to go the extra mile for your clients. That means going beyond the requirements of the job and providing a service that clients won't forget.

"I am actively involved in five trade/professional organizations that represent the segments of the affluent population that I have targeted," says Thomas Stanley. "I specifically targeted the senior officers of several of these organizations. Some have purchased from me; others have not. But I have done many favours for all of them, such as developing programs and seminars for their demanding members. I have also used my marketing expertise to further the causes of some of these organizations. I was instrumental in initiating a letter-writing campaign designed to influence selected lawmakers in opposing proposed legislation that would adversely affect the industry of which many of my clients are members. They have often reciprocated by asking me to give important speeches at major gatherings. Several have also published my ideas in their national trade publications."

4.3   Gaining a Competitive Edge

The following service enhancements can not only distinguish you from the competition, but also provide clients with an advantage, as well.

Quality

You should know the market, understand what distinguishes average quality from excellence, and know how to deliver the best quality to your clients.

Speed

As an entrepreneurial advisor, you may have an advantage over some of your competitors by making informed decisions and executing them quickly.

Flexibility

Flexibility may involve going above and beyond the call of duty on behalf of a client. It may involve revising a client's financial plan as circumstances change. It may simply involve listening and trying to understand exactly what a client wants and needs.

Competitive Pricing

Although the quality of the service you provide is the most important criterion for clients, the cost of those services is also important. As a wealth manager you may be able to actually reduce the cost of your client's financial services (fees are discussed in more detail in section 5.0).

Personal Service

In 1993, the International Association for Financial Planning asked a sample of American adults what elements they considered most important in their relationship with a financial advisor. The respondents considered returns and performance important: those were selected 24% of the time. They picked expertise, which is related, 18% of the time. But the single most important factor was trust, cited 53% of the time. One in two Americans consider trust the most important element in their relationship with a financial advisor.[1]

Client trust comes from being able to reassure your clients that what happens today will not jeopardize their investments over the long term. Clients can easily learn about what's happening today, says author Nick Murray. But you can give your client information that's far more valuable. "The advisor who's a student of the business can tell people what happened the last time this happened."

---

[1] Source: Dan Richards, *Getting Clients, Keeping Clients: The Essential Guide for Tomorrow's Financial Advisor*. Marketing Solutions, 1998.

You can't possibly earn a client's trust unless you provide personal service that goes far beyond the basic requirements of conducting transactions and providing quarterly reports. The way to gain a client's trust is not with information but with empathy.

Case 16.2   Having Fun Puts Clients at Ease

When it comes to personal service, Liz Palmer goes the extra mile. She often sets up initial meetings in the client's home at lunchtime, then arrives on their doorstep with pizza or chicken wings.

"I try to create a relaxed, fun atmosphere with my clients," says Palmer. "Some clients prefer to come to an office environment, close the door, and discuss their financial future across a desk. I am able to provide that too, but, over the years, I have noticed that my clients appreciate the fact that I come to them, bring a pizza, wings, or whatever. We sit in the rec room and throw around some ideas, admit fears, reveal financial dreams and joke around as well."

Palmer says that spending a couple of hours in an informal setting getting to know each other certainly helps her understand her clients' goals much better. "It's fun, it's relaxed, it's not intimidating and true expectations are revealed," she says.

From the looks on her clients' faces, Palmer says she can tell that clients prefer personal contact as well. She believes that financial planning involves more than one or two visits, and that it's an ongoing process. "If I can make this an enjoyable experience along the way, then ultimately, I won't lose clients and I'll find new ones."

Specialization

You may focus on clients in a certain age group, business sector, or community group. For example, you may be knowledgeable about the particular financial requirements of family physicians or divorce lawyers. However, regardless of your individual strengths, you must specialize in building trust and confidence in high-value clients. This means helping them achieve their financial goals while relieving them of anxiety about their financial future. That's your real specialty.

Innovation

You have an infinite number of opportunities to be innovative on a client's behalf. For example, you may have access to information that would otherwise never reach the client. You can compile an electronic clipping file for each client, and every few months send your clients a summary of information that you know would interest them. You can also provide useful and accessible data such as performance calculations, market comparisons, and performance figures that make it easier for clients to see exactly how a plan is meeting objectives.

5.0 Fee Structures

"The best compensation arrangement—indeed, the only sane one—is the one the client trusts," says Nick Murray. If clients wonder whether you are really trying to help them and their families attain their financial goals or simply earn a commission, it will undermine your trust. This, as Murray says, is to be avoided at all costs.

"All questions/objections regarding compensation are a sign that you as a wealth manager have not finished your work, which is to cause your prospects to see that you represent the difference between lifetime investment success or failure," Murray says. "Your price is only an issue to the extent that your value is still in question."

5.1 Establishing Fees

In a commission-based world, the emphasis is on gathering assets; in a fee-based world, the emphasis is on retaining and growing those assets. This involves a different way of thinking and different skills.

In the long run, fees may be more expensive than commissions. But in the context of helping clients achieve their financial plans, neither structure should present an obstacle to your clients' faith in your ability to help them reach their objectives.

In fact, as we've already discussed, customers have other priorities than price. Although they pay attention to fees, they make decisions based on their faith in your abilities, not on the amount you charge them.

In fact, fees should reflect the quality of service. By charging too little, you may be sending the wrong message.

Only you (or your firm) can determine the right fee structure. But in the process, the fee you charge should contribute to a competitive advantage in at least some of the following ways.

It should:
- ensure that you can compete with other advisors;
- capture your own competitive advantages;
- discourage others from entering your market niche;
- discourage clients who consume your time without paying a fair price for it.

You have to consider these factors in addition to making a profit and covering your costs.

One of the easiest ways to figure out how much to charge a client is to find out how much your competitors charge. Experience in the industry should give you an idea of your competitors' pricing. If not, this information can be gathered through clients, acquaintances, industry contacts, or competitors themselves.

Some potential clients will ask you to adjust fees to meet those of the competition. In most cases, if you have set the fees according to an honest evaluation of the services you offer and your ability to deliver them, you should refuse.

That's not to say that you should never negotiate. But the negotiating should be done in the context of what you as a wealth manager do for your clients and how effectively you help them and their families meet their financial objectives. It should not be done in the context of a competitive battle for the client's business. If you know the value of your services and charge accordingly, you should have the courage of your convictions and stick to the quoted price.

6.0   Promotional Plan

Promotion covers the mix of advertising, public relations, sales promotion, personal selling, and old-fashioned word-of-mouth that will inform clients about you as a wealth manager and your work. Generally, some combination of these promotional tools works best.

When developing a marketing plan, you should consider the size and nature of your target audience. If the market is large, the best way to reach potential clients might be through advertising in a specialty magazine, for example, or an event program. On the other hand, if the target market is a small and highly specific, personal selling might be the number-one approach.

Here's a brief description of promotional options:

6.1   Advertising

Advertising can reinforce your image as a wealth manager and attract new clients. However, it can be expensive and it is not always cost-effective. You should determine, preferably with an advertising specialist, the medium that works best for you. Choices include:

- newspapers;
- magazines;
- television;
- radio (local and network);
- Yellow Pages;
- direct mail;

- billboards;
- telemarketing.

6.2 Public Relations

Less costly than advertising, public relations involves the preparation and distribution of information packages for the media about the business that you are operating. A specialist can help you develop such material. For example, you could write a column for a newspaper or magazine about developments involving finance and investing. You can also write press releases when you win an award or prize, develop a unique product or service, perform notable charity work, or make a substantial donation to a cultural institution. The coverage won't cost anything—although there's no guarantee you'll get coverage at all.

6.3 Seminars and Workshops

Seminars can showcase your knowledge and talents. In the process, they provide an opportunity to solidify relationships with existing clients and develop new relationships as well. These events can also be used to expand and reinforce your network of professional associates by inviting them to participate. "Learn to give excellent seminars," says author Nick Murray. "It's good to make one person at a time like you, but it's very hard work. Making a whole roomful of people like you (not *understand* you; *like* you) is much more efficient and much more fun. [And] the way you say what you say is much more important than what you say."

6.4 Sales Promotions

You may conduct a workshop or seminar with one or more well-known speakers and invite your clients at a nominal charge of, say, $10. If they bring a friend, you can waive the fee.

6.5 Newsletters

Ready-made financial newsletters can be purchased from publishers who will attach your name and photograph. More effective by far, however, is the newsletter that you write and publish yourself. Even a one-page newsletter, sent at regular intervals throughout the year, reminds clients that you're on the job, and gives them something to pass along to a friend or colleague when they make a referral.

6.6   Prospecting

There are many ways to prospect for new clients. Some will be easier for you than others. The best strategy is to pick the prospecting method that you as a wealth manager are most comfortable with, then stick to it.

"Experienced advisors will need to create and/or clear three prospecting hours every day," suggests author Nick Murray. "They have to be the same three hours, and you can't do anything else, including taking incoming phone calls, during those three hours. Prospect, or just sit there. Everything else is an avoidance behaviour."

Just as you tell your clients that they invest for the long-term, that short-term returns don't count so much as disciplined long-term investing, you can tell yourself that prospecting for new clients is a long-term proposition. The rejection encountered today or tomorrow isn't nearly so important as the client who stays for the next twenty years.

One of the best methods of prospecting is through a professional referral network. The following are some of the most other common prospecting methods, as defined by author Dan Richards. Some work better than others, and as a wealth manager you'll find some easier than others to do.

- client referrals;
- cold calls;
- direct mail.

Client Referrals

Probably the best way to attract new clients is to get referrals from current clients. In most cases, the referral is a spontaneous endorsement. Unsolicited testimonials speak volumes about the quality of your work as a wealth manager, and all the money in the world couldn't buy such a believable reference.

During those months and years when you sit back and wait for referrals, however, you should keep occupied by trying to solicit them. At first glance, you might think this approach a little crass. However, all you are doing is asking a client to tell the truth, and to tell it to someone who might become a client. Assuming you have served your clients well, clients feel flattered to be asked for a testimonial. Asking for a referral is a form of compliment. If their endorsement means so much, then it must carry some authority. It's important to keep in mind that, with referrals, as with all efforts to develop a market, the key is doing good work. If clients love the work you are doing for them, they won't hesitate to tell others.

Case 16.3   Client Referrals

In *Getting Clients, Keeping Clients*, Dan Richards explains: "My company developed what we call the Trust Spectrum [to measure the effectiveness of an activity in attracting clients]. The high-trust activities are professional referrals, client referrals, serving as a guest speaker, knowing somebody through community involvement, and meeting people through giving a seminar. At the low end of the trust scale—from the client's perspective, let me remind you—are the mass marketing techniques: direct mail, advertisements, and cold calling.

"Our firm has developed a letter, tied to seminars, that has been more effective in generating referrals than almost anything we have done. Its expressed aim is to solicit feedback from clients in determining the seminars that would be most attractive. That's a valuable enough basis for writing, since you invest time and money in seminars and they should be broadly popular with your client base. In the process, though, you canvass recipients for the names of friends, family, or co-workers who might also appreciate an invitation to the seminars.

"Advisors using this letter have managed to persuade between 25 and 30% of their clients to complete the questionnaire, with one or more names of additional people to be invited to the workshops. Not every client, obviously, gives a name, but many offer more than one. So the advisor receives one potential prospect per response, with a quarter of the client base participating."

Cold Calling

You can't rely on referrals alone, however. Sometimes you have to bite the bullet and go looking for clients. Like quitting smoking, going on a diet, exercising, or cleaning the house, a routine makes the chore easier. Procrastination never works; discipline does. No matter what method of prospecting you choose, you should do it every day, even if, on some days, you make only one phone call or write only one letter.

It helps to include prospecting on a list of things to do each day. When you've done it, you can cross it off the list and feel as if you have accomplished something. And remember, as Nick Murray says, "You can't control outcomes, you can only control your own behaviour."

You can expect to fail, and fail often. Most people will say that they are not interested. Some will say it in a nice way; others won't be so tactful. No matter what happens, it is important for you to regard each failure as a minor victory in an ongoing battle to build a business.

Direct Mail

A direct mail package is designed to inform potential clients about your services. Direct mail can be an effective complement to your overall marketing efforts. It is cost-effective and, unlike mass media advertising, it can easily be targeted to your specific audience. Results can be easily tracked and over time successes from direct mail campaigns can be predicted with reasonable accuracy.

6.7   Keeping Clients

It takes far more resources to attract a new client than it does to retain an existing one. With this in mind, you can follow some straightforward procedures to make sure current clients stay over the long term.

Clients not only want you to perform well today, they also want to feel reassured that you have the knowledge and capability to lead them in the most appropriate direction for the future. Above all, they want to feel that they can trust you with their financial future and that of their family.

If clients feel unhappy, they may or may not say so, unless asked. The only way to find out how satisfied a client feels is to maintain regular contact. Some of the ways of ensuring regular contact include:

- telephoning clients regularly;
- visiting clients at every opportunity;
- scheduling business meetings for breakfast, lunch, or dinner;
- inviting clients to the office;
- sending clients useful articles;
- if possible, referring business to clients;
- remembering their anniversaries and birthdays;
- offering them tickets to local events.

7.0   Marketing Plan Update

The world is changing rapidly, and so is your role. In the context of these changes, you must re-evaluate your marketing plans to address emerging issues that may affect your capabilities and ultimate success.

In their book *Blur: The Speed of Change in the Connected Economy*, authors Christopher Meyer and Stan Davis offer several tips to financial advisors for addressing some recent significant changes on the financial planning industry:

1. Connect everything with everything. Rethink your contact schedule. "Rather than be calendar-driven, might it not be more interesting to be event-driven?" asks Meyer.

"Manage your knowledge of the customer, so that you are connecting to that customer as an individual, rather than as somebody who is scheduled for a call on the third Thursday of each quarter."

2. Be able to do anything at any time. It's Sunday evening and *60 Minutes* has just begun tearing into a major multinational that you as a wealth manager have invested several key clients in. Are you available to answer questions and take direction? "This is going to become a question of individual effort," says Meyer. "Some people put their home numbers on their business cards, and some people don't. If I wake up Monday morning and I've got an overnight e-mail message from my advisor, I'm feeling pretty good about the service he's giving me."

3. Help customers get smarter. Every contact represents an opportunity to teach the client how to better benefit from your service. Meyer goes a step further, though. "If you're making your clients smarter all the time, then every time you talk to them they'll teach you something," he says. Think of the contact as an exchange, one that benefits both you and the client.

4. Extract information from every buy-sell exchange. "What if, every time you had a conversation with a client, you posed five research questions?" asks Meyer. "Not all of your clients are going to be helpful, but I bet you would learn some things."

5. Put emotions into every offer and every exchange. "Stop showing people spreadsheets and start telling them stories," says Meyer. "Instead of showing them all these numbers, say, 'Here's what you'll be able to do'."

6. Virtual location, virtual location, virtual location. A web site is more than an electronic business card. You should include information on your professional track record. A simulation function, allowing clients to examine the potential results of decisions made or not made, is also very useful as is a "frequently asked questions" (FAQ) section to make basic information on investing, taxes, and so forth accessible to clients around the clock.

Appendix A

Future and Present Value Tables

Future Value Factors

N	1%	2%	3%	4%	5%	6%	7%
1	1.0100	1.0200	1.0300	1.0400	1.0500	1.0600	1.0700
2	1.0201	1.0404	1.0609	1.0816	1.1025	1.1236	1.1449
3	1.0303	1.0612	1.0927	1.1249	1.1576	1.1910	1.2250
4	1.0406	1.0824	1.1255	1.1699	1.2155	1.2625	1.3108
5	1.0510	1.1041	1.1593	1.2167	1.2763	1.3382	1.4026
6	1.0615	1.1262	1.1941	1.2653	1.3401	1.4185	1.5007
7	1.0721	1.1487	1.2299	1.3159	1.4071	1.5036	1.6058
8	1.0829	1.1717	1.2668	1.3686	1.4775	1.5938	1.7182
9	1.0937	1.1951	1.3048	1.4233	1.5513	1.6895	1.8385
10	1.1046	1.2190	1.3439	1.4802	1.6289	1.7908	1.9672
11	1.1157	1.2434	1.3842	1.5395	1.7103	1.8983	2.1049
12	1.1268	1.2682	1.4258	1.6010	1.7959	2.0122	2.2522
13	1.1381	1.2936	1.4685	1.6651	1.8856	2.1329	2.4098
14	1.1495	1.3195	1.5126	1.7317	1.9799	2.2609	2.5785
15	1.1610	1.3459	1.5580	1.8009	2.0789	2.3966	2.7590
16	1.1726	1.3728	1.6047	1.8730	2.1829	2.5404	2.9522
17	1.1843	1.4002	1.6528	1.9479	2.2920	2.6928	3.1588
18	1.1961	1.4282	1.7024	2.0258	2.4066	2.8543	3.3799
19	1.2081	1.4568	1.7535	2.1068	2.5270	3.0256	3.6165
20	1.2202	1.4859	1.8061	2.1911	2.6533	3.2071	3.8697
21	1.2324	1.5157	1.8603	2.2788	2.7860	3.3996	4.1406
22	1.2447	1.5460	1.9161	2.3699	2.9253	3.6035	4.4304
23	1.2572	1.5769	1.9736	2.4647	3.0715	3.8197	4.7405
24	1.2697	1.6084	2.0328	2.5633	3.2251	4.0489	5.0724
25	1.2824	1.6406	2.0938	2.6658	3.3864	4.2919	5.4274
26	1.2953	1.6734	2.1566	2.7725	3.5557	4.5494	5.8074
27	1.3082	1.7069	2.2213	2.8834	3.7335	4.8223	6.2139
28	1.3213	1.7410	2.2879	2.9987	3.9201	5.1117	6.6488
29	1.3345	1.7758	2.3566	3.1187	4.1161	5.4184	7.1143
30	1.3478	1.8114	2.4273	3.2434	4.3219	5.7435	7.6123

Future Value Factors

(continued)

N	1%	2%	3%	4%	5%	6%	7%
31	1.3613	1.8476	2.5001	3.3731	4.5380	6.0881	8.1451
32	1.3749	1.8845	2.5751	3.5081	4.7649	6.4534	8.7153
33	1.3887	1.9222	2.6523	3.6484	5.0032	6.8406	9.3253
34	1.4026	1.9607	2.7319	3.7943	5.2533	7.2510	9.9781
35	1.4166	1.9999	2.8139	3.9461	5.5160	7.6861	10.6766
36	1.4308	2.0399	2.8983	4.1039	5.7918	8.1473	11.4239
37	1.4451	2.0807	2.9852	4.2681	6.0814	8.6361	12.2236
38	1.4595	2.1223	3.0748	4.4388	6.3855	9.1543	13.0793
39	1.4741	2.1647	3.1670	4.6164	6.7048	9.7035	13.9948
40	1.4889	2.2080	3.2620	4.8010	7.0400	10.2857	14.9745
41	1.5038	2.2522	3.3599	4.9931	7.3920	10.9029	16.0227
42	1.5188	2.2972	3.4607	5.1928	7.7616	11.5570	17.1443
43	1.5340	2.3432	3.5645	5.4005	8.1497	12.2505	18.3444
44	1.5493	2.3901	3.6715	5.6165	8.5572	12.9855	19.6285
45	1.5648	2.4379	3.7816	5.8412	8.9850	13.7646	21.0025
46	1.5805	2.4866	3.8950	6.0748	9.4343	14.5905	22.4726
47	1.5963	2.5363	4.0119	6.3178	9.9060	15.4659	24.0457
48	1.6122	2.5871	4.1323	6.5705	10.4013	16.3939	25.7289
49	1.6283	2.6388	4.2562	6.8333	10.9213	17.3775	27.5299
50	1.6446	2.6916	4.3839	7.1067	11.4674	18.4302	29.4570

Future Value Factors

N	8%	9%	10%	11%	12%	13%	14%
1	1.0800	1.0900	1.1000	1.1100	1.1200	1.1300	1.1400
2	1.1664	1.1881	1.2100	1.2321	1.2544	1.2769	1.2996
3	1.2597	1.2950	1.3310	1.3676	1.4049	1.4429	1.4815
4	1.3605	1.4116	1.4641	1.5181	1.5735	1.6305	1.6890
5	1.4693	1.5386	1.6105	1.6851	1.7623	1.8424	1.9254
6	1.5869	1.6771	1.7716	1.8704	1.9738	2.0820	2.1950
7	1.7138	1.8280	1.9487	2.0762	2.2107	2.3526	2.5023
8	1.8509	1.9926	2.1436	2.3045	2.4760	2.6584	2.8526
9	1.9990	2.1719	2.3579	2.5580	2.7731	3.0040	3.2519
10	2.1589	2.3674	2.5937	2.8394	3.1058	3.3946	3.7072
11	2.3316	2.5804	2.8531	3.1518	3.4786	3.8359	4.2263
12	2.5182	2.8127	3.1384	3.4985	3.8960	4.3345	4.8179
13	2.7196	3.0658	3.4523	3.8833	4.3635	4.8981	5.4924
14	2.9372	3.3417	3.7975	4.3104	4.8871	5.5348	6.2613
15	3.1722	3.6425	4.1772	4.7846	5.4736	6.2543	7.1379
16	3.4259	3.9703	4.5950	5.3109	6.1304	7.0673	8.1372
17	3.7000	4.3276	5.0545	5.8951	6.8660	7.9861	9.2765
18	3.9960	4.7171	5.5599	6.5436	7.6900	9.0243	10.5752
19	4.3157	5.1417	6.1159	7.2633	8.6128	10.1974	12.0557
20	4.6610	5.6044	6.7275	8.0623	9.6463	11.5231	13.7435
21	5.0338	6.1088	7.4003	8.9492	10.8038	13.0211	15.6676
22	5.4365	6.6586	8.1403	9.9336	12.1003	14.7138	17.8610
23	5.8715	7.2579	8.9543	11.0263	13.5523	16.6266	20.3616
24	6.3412	7.9111	9.8497	12.2392	15.1786	18.7881	23.2122
25	6.8485	8.6231	10.8347	13.5855	17.0001	21.2305	26.4619
26	7.3964	9.3992	11.9182	15.0799	19.0401	23.9905	30.1666
27	7.9881	10.2451	13.1100	16.7387	21.3249	27.1093	34.3899
28	8.6271	11.1671	14.4210	18.5799	23.8839	30.6335	39.2045
29	9.3173	12.1722	15.8631	20.6237	26.7499	34.6158	44.6931
30	10.0627	13.2677	17.4494	22.8923	29.9599	39.1159	50.9502
31	10.8677	14.4618	19.1943	25.4104	33.5551	44.2010	58.0832
32	11.7371	15.7633	21.1138	28.2056	37.5817	49.9471	66.2148
33	12.6761	17.1820	23.2252	31.3082	42.0915	56.4402	75.4849
34	13.6901	18.7284	25.5477	34.7521	47.1425	63.7774	86.0528
35	14.7853	20.4140	28.1024	38.5749	52.7996	72.0685	98.1002
36	15.9682	22.2512	30.9128	42.8181	59.1356	81.4374	111.8342
37	17.2456	24.2538	34.0039	47.5281	66.2318	92.0243	127.4910
38	18.6253	26.4367	37.4043	52.7562	74.1797	103.9874	145.3397
39	20.1153	28.8160	41.1448	58.5593	83.0812	117.5058	165.6873
40	21.7245	31.4094	45.2593	65.0009	93.0510	132.7816	188.8835
41	23.4625	34.2363	49.7852	72.1510	104.2171	150.0432	215.3272
42	25.3395	37.3175	54.7637	80.0876	116.7231	169.5488	245.4730
43	27.3666	40.6761	60.2401	88.8972	130.7299	191.5901	279.8392
44	29.5560	44.3370	66.2641	98.6759	146.4175	216.4968	319.0167
45	31.9204	48.3273	72.8905	109.5302	163.9876	244.6414	363.6791
46	34.4741	52.6767	80.1795	121.5786	183.6661	276.4448	414.5941
47	37.2320	57.4176	88.1975	134.9522	2Q5.7061	312.3826	472.6373
48	40.2106	62.5852	97.0172	149.7970	230.3908	352.9923	538.8065
49	43.4274	68.2179	106.7190	166.2746	258.0377	398.8814	614.2395
50	46.9016	74.3575	117.3909	184.5648	289.0022	450.7359	700.2330

Present Value Factors

N	1%	2%	3%	4%	5%	6%	7%
1	.9901	.9804	.9709	.9615	.9524	.9434	.9346
2	.9803	.9612	.9426	.9246	.9070	.8900	.8734
3	.9707	.9423	.9151	.8890	.8638	.8396	.8163
4	.9610	.9238	.8885	.8548	.8227	.7921	.7629
5	.9515	.9057	.8626	.8219	.7835	.7473	.7130
6	.9420	.8880	.8375	.7903	.7462	.7050	.6663
7	.9327	.8706	.8131	.7599	.7107	.6651	.6228
8	.9235	.8535	.7894	.7307	.6768	.6274	.5820
9	.9143	.8368	.7664	.7026	.6446	.5919	.5439
10	.9053	.8203	.7441	.6756	.6139	.5584	.5083
11	.8963	.8043	.7224	.6496	.5847	.5268	.4751
12	.8874	.7885	.7014	.6246	.5568	.4970	.4440
13	.8787	.7730	.6810	.6006	.5303	.4688	.4150
14	.8700	.7579	.6611	.5775	.5051	.4423	.3878
15	.8613	.7430	.6419	.5553	.4810	.4173	.3624
16	.8528	.7284	.6232	.5339	.4581	.3936	.3387
17	.8444	.7142	.6050	.5134	.4363	.3714	.3166
18	.8360	.7002	.5874	.4936	.4155	.3503	.2959
19	.8277	.6864	.5703	.4746	.3957	.3305	.2765
20	.8195	.6730	.5537	.4564	.3769	.3118	.2584
21	.8114	.6598	.5375	.4388	.3589	.2942	.2415
22	.8034	.6468	.5219	.4220	.3419	.2775	.2257
23	.7954	.6342	.5067	.4057	.3256	.2618	.2109
24	.7876	.6217	.4919	.3901	.3101	.2470	.1971
25	.7798	.6095	.4776	.3751	.2953	.2330	.1842
26	.7720	.5976	.4637	.3607	.2812	.2198	.1722
27	.7644	.5859	.4502	.3468	.2678	.2074	.1609
28	.7568	.5744	.4371	.3335	.2551	.1956	.1504
29	.7493	.5631	.4243	.3207	.2429	.1846	.1406
30	.7419	.5521	.4120	.3083	.2314	.1741	.1314
31	.7346	.5412	.4000	.2965	.2204	.1643	.1228
32	.7273	.5306	.3883	.2851	.2099	.1550	.1147
33	.7201	.5202	.3770	.2741	.1999	.1462	.1072
34	.7130	.5100	.3660	.2636	.1904	.1379	.1002
35	.7059	.5000	.3554	.2534	.1813	.1301	.0937
36	.6989	.4902	.3450	.2437	.1727	.1227	.0875
37	.6920	.4806	.3350	.2343	.1644	.1158	.0818
38	.6858	.4712	.3252	.2253	.1566	.1092	.0765
39	.6784	.4619	.3158	.2166	.1491	.1031	.0715
40	.6717	.4529	.3066	.2083	.1420	.0972	.0668
41	.6650	.4440	.2976	.2003	.1353	.0917	.0624
42	.6584	.4353	.2890	.1926	.1288	.0865	.0583
43	.6520	.4268	.2805	.1852	.1227	.0816	.0545
44	.6454	.4184	.2724	.1780	.1169	.0770	.0509
45	.6391	.4102	.2644	.1712	.1113	.0727	.0476
46	.6327	.4022	.2567	.1646	.1060	.0685	.0445
47	.6265	.3943	.2493	.1583	.1009	.0647	.0416
48	.6203	.3865	.2420	.1522	.0961	.0610	.0389
49	.6141	.3790	.2350	.1463	.0916	.0575	.0363
50	.6080	.3715	.2281	.1407	.0872	.0543	.0339

Present Value Factors

N	8%	9%	10%	11%	12%	13%	14%
1	.9259	.9174	.9091	.9009	.8929	.8850	.8772
2	.8573	.8417	.8264	.8116	.7972	.7831	.7695
3	.7938	.7722	.7513	.7312	.7118	.6931	.6750
4	.7350	.7084	.6830	.6587	.6355	.6133	.5921
5	.6806	.6499	.6209	.5935	.5674	.5428	.5194
6	.6302	.5963	.5645	.5346	.5066	.4803	.4556
7	.5835	.5470	.5132	.4817	.4523	.4251	.3996
8	.5403	.5019	.4665	.4339	.4039	.3762	.3506
9	.5002	.4604	.4241	.3909	.3606	.3329	.3075
10	.4632	.4224	.3855	.3522	.3220	.2946	.2697
11	.4289	.3875	.3505	.3173	.2875	.2607	.2366
12	.3971	.3555	.3186	.2858	.2567	.2307	.2076
13	.3677	.3262	.2897	.2575	.2292	.2042	.1821
14	.3405	.2992	.2633	.2320	.2046	.1807	.1597
15	.3152	.2745	.2394	.2090	.1827	.1599	.1401
16	.2919	.2519	.2176	.1883	.1631	.1415	.1229
17	.2703	.2311	.1978	.1696	.1456	.1252	.1078
18	.2502	.2120	.1799	.1528	.1300	.1108	.0946
19	.2317	.1945	.1635	.1377	.1161	.0981	.0829
20	.2145	.1784	.1486	.1240	.1037	.0868	.0728
21	.1987	.1637	.1351	.1117	.0926	.0768	.0638
22	.1839	.1502	.1228	.1007	.0826	.0680	.0560
23	.1703	.1378	.1117	.0907	.0738	.0601	.0491
24	.1577	.1264	.1015	.0817	.0659	.0532	.0431
25	.1460	.1160	.0923	.0736	.0588	.0471	.0378
26	.1352	.1064	.0839	.0663	.0525	.0417	.0331
27	.1252	.0976	.0763	.0597	.0469	.0369	.0291
28	.1159	.0895	.0693	.0538	.0419	.0326	.0255
29	.1073	.0822	.0630	.0485	.0374	.0289	.0224
30	.0994	.0754	.0573	.0437	.0334	.0256	.0196
31	.0920	.0691	.0521	.0394	.0298	.0226	.0172
32	.0852	.0634	.0474	.0355	.0266	.0200	.0151
33	.0789	.0582	.0431	.0319	.0238	.0177	.0132
34	.0730	.0534	.0391	.0288	.0212	.0157	.0116
35	.0676	.0490	.0356	.0259	.0189	.0139	.0102
36	.0626	.0449	.0323	.0234	.0169	.0123	.0089
37	.0580	.0412	.0294	.0210	.0151	.0109	.0078
38	.0537	.0378	.0267	.0190	.0135	.0096	.0069
39	.0497	.0347	.0243	.0171	.0120	.0085	.0060
40	.0460	.0318	.0221	.0154	.0107	.0075	.0053
41	.0426	.0292	.0201	.0139	.0096	.0067	.0046
42	.0395	.0268	.0183	.0125	.0086	.0059	.0041
43	.0365	.0246	.0166	.0112	.0076	.0052	.0036
44	.0338	.0226	.0151	.0101	.0068	.0046	.0031
45	.0313	.0207	.0137	.0091	.0061	.0041	.0028
46	.0290	.0190	.0125	.0082	.0054	.0036	.0024
47	.0269	.0174	.0113	.0074	.0059	.0032	.0021
48	.0249	.0160	.0103	.0067	.0043	.0028	.0019
49	.0230	.0147	.0094	.0060	.0039	.0025	.0016
50	.0213	.0134	.0085	.0054	.0035	.0022	.0014

Present Value Factors

N	15%	16%	17%	18%	19%
1	.8696	.8621	.8547	.8475	.8403
2	.7561	.7432	.7305	.7182	.7062
3	.6575	.6407	.6244	.6086	.5934
4	.5718	.5523	.5337	.5158	.4987
5	.4972	.4761	.4561	.4371	.4190
6	.4323	.4104	.3898	.3704	.3521
7	.3759	.3538	.3332	.3139	.2959
8	.3269	.3050	.2848	.2660	.2487
9	.2843	.2630	.2434	.2255	.2090
10	.2472	.2267	.2080	.1911	.1756
11	.2149	.1954	.1778	.1619	.1476
12	.1869	.1685	.1520	.1372	.1240
13	.1625	.1452	.1299	.1163	.1042
14	.1413	.1252	.1110	.0985	.0876
15	.1229	.1079	.0949	.0835	.0736
16	.1069	.0930	.0811	.0708	.0618
17	.0929	.0802	.0693	.0600	.0520
18	.0808	.0691	.0592	.0508	.0437
19	.0703	.0596	.0506	.0431	.0367
20	.0611	.0514	.0433	.0365	.0308
21	.0531	.0443	.0370	.0309	.0259
22	.0462	.0382	.0316	.0262	.0218
23	.0402	.0329	.0270	.0222	.0183
24	.0349	.0284	.0231	.0188	.0154
25	.0304	.0245	.0197	.0160	.0129
26	.0264	.0211	.0169	.0135	.0109
27	.0230	.0182	.0144	.0115	.0091
28	.0200	.0157	.0123	.0097	.0077
29	.0174	.0135	.0105	.0082	.0064
30	.0151	.0116	.0090	.0070	.0054
31	.0131	.0100	.0077	.0059	.0046
32	.0114	.0087	.0066	.0050	.0038
33	.0099	.0075	.0056	.0042	.0032
34	.0086	.0064	.0048	.0036	.0027
35	.0075	.0055	.0041	.0030	.0023
36	.0065	.0048	.0035	.0026	.0019
37	.0057	.0041	.0030	.0022	.0016
38	.0049	.0036	.0026	.0019	.0013
39	.0043	.0031	.0022	.0016	.0011
40	.0037	.0026	.0019	.0013	.0010
41	.0032	.0023	.0016	.0011	.0008
42	.0028	.0020	.0014	.0010	.0007
43	.0025	.0017	.0012	.0008	.0006
44	.0021	.0015	.0010	.0007	.0005
45	.0019	.0013	.0009	.0006	.0004
46	.0016	.0011	.0007	.0005	.0003
47	.0014	.0009	.0006	.0004	.0003
48	.0012	.0008	.0005	.0004	.0002
49	.0011	.0007	.0005	.0003	.0002
50	.0009	.0006	.0004	.0003	.0002

Future Value Of An Annuity

N	1%	2%	3%	4%	5%	6%	7%
1	1	1	1	1	1	1	1
2	2.01	2.02	2.03	2.04	2.05	2.06	2.07
3	3.03	3.06	3.091	3.122	3.152	3.184	3.215
4	4.06	4.122	4.184	4.246	4.31	4.375	4.44
5	5.101	5.204	5.309	5.416	5.526	5.637	5.751
6	6.152	6.308	6.468	6.633	6.802	6.975	7.153
7	7.214	7.434	7.662	7.898	8.142	8.394	8.654
8	8.286	8.583	8.892	9.214	9.549	9.897	10.26
9	9.369	9.755	10.159	10.583	11.027	11.491	11.978
10	10.462	10.95	11.464	12.006	12.578	13.181	13.816
11	11.567	12.169	12.808	13.486	14.207	14.972	15.784
12	12.683	13.412	14.192	15.026	15.917	16.87	17.888
13	13.809	14.68	15.618	16.627	17.713	18.882	20.141
14	14.947	15.974	17.086	18.292	19.599	21.015	22.55
15	16.097	17.293	18.599	20.024	21.579	23.276	25.129
16	17.258	18.639	20.157	21.825	23.657	25.673	27.888
17	18.43	20.012	21.762	23.698	25.84	28.213	30.84
18	19.615	21.412	23.414	25.645	28.132	30.906	33.999
19	20.811	22.841	25.117	27.671	30.539	33.76	37.379
20	22.019	24.297	26.87	29.778	33.066	36.786	40.995
21	23.239	25.783	28.676	31.969	35.719	39.993	44.865
22	24.472	27.299	30.537	34.248	38.505	43.392	49.006
23	25.716	28.845	32.453	36.618	41.43	46.996	53.436
24	26.973	30.422	34.426	39.083	44.502	50.816	58.177
25	28.243	32.03	36.459	41.646	47.727	54.865	63.249
30	34.785	40.568	47.575	56.085	66.439	79.058	94.461
35	41.66	49.994	60.462	73.652	90.32	111.43	138.23
40	48.886	60.402	75.401	95.026	120.8	154.76	199.63
45	56.481	71.893	92.72	121.02	159.7	212.74	285.74
50	64.463	84.579	112.79	152.66	209.34	290.33	406.52

Future Value Of An Annuity

N	8%	9%	10%	11%	12%	13%	14%
1	1	1	1	1	1	1	1
2	2.08	2.09	2.1	2.11	2.12	2.13	2.14
3	3.246	3.278	3.31	3.342	3.374	3.407	3.44
4	4.506	4.573	4.641	4.71	4.779	4.85	4.921
5	5.867	5.985	6.105	6.228	6.353	6.48	6.61
6	7.336	7.523	7.716	7.913	8.115	8.323	8.536
7	8.923	9.2	9.487	9.783	10.089	10.405	10.73
8	10.637	11.028	11.436	11.859	12.3	12.757	13.233
9	12.488	13.021	13.579	14.164	14.776	15.416	16.085
10	14.487	15.193	15.937	16.722	17.549	18.42	19.337
11	16.645	17.56	18.531	19.561	20.655	21.814	23.045
12	18.977	20.141	21.384	22.713	24.133	25.65	27.271
13	21.495	22.953	24.523	26.212	28.029	29.985	32.089
14	24.215	26.019	27.975	30.095	32.393	34.883	37.581
15	27.152	29.361	31.772	34.405	37.28	40.417	43.842
16	30.324	33.003	35.95	39.19	42.753	46.672	50.98
17	33.75	36.974	40.545	44.501	48.884	53.739	59.118
18	37.45	41.301	45.599	50.396	55.75	61.725	68.394
19	41.446	46.018	51.159	56.939	63.44	70.749	78.969
20	45.762	51.16	57.275	64.203	72.052	80.947	91.025
21	50.423	56.765	64.002	72.265	81.699	92.47	104.76
22	55.457	62.873	71.403	81.214	92.503	105.491	120.43
23	60.893	69.532	79.543	91.148	104.6	120.205	138.29
24	66.765	76.79	88.497	102.17	118.15	136.831	158.65
25	73.106	84.701	98.347	114.41	133.33	155.62	181.87
30	113.28	136.30	164.49	199.02	241.33	293.199	356.78
35	172.31	215.71	271.02	341.59	431.66	546.681	693.57
40	259.05	337.88	442.59	581.82	767.09	1013.704	1342.0
45	386.50	525.85	718.90	986.63	1358.2	1874.165	2590.5
50	573.77	815.08	1163.9	1668.7	2400.0	3459.507	4994.5

Future Value Of An Annuity

N	15%	16%	18%	20%
1	1	1	1	1
2	2.15	2.16	2.18	2.2
3	3.472	3.506	3.572	3.64
4	4.993	5.066	5.215	5.368
5	6.742	6.877	7.154	7.442
6	8.754	8.977	9.442	9.93
7	11.067	11.414	12.142	12.916
8	13.727	14.24	15.327	16.499
9	16.786	17.519	19.086	20.799
10	20.304	21.321	23.521	25.959
11	24.349	25.733	28.755	32.15
12	29.002	30.85	34.931	39.581
13	34.352	36.786	42.219	48.497
14	40.505	43.672	50.818	59.196
15	47.58	51.66	60.965	72.035
16	55.717	60.925	72.939	87.442
17	65.075	71.673	87.068	105.93
18	75.836	84.141	103.74	128.11
19	88.212	98.603	123.41	154.74
20	102.44	115.38	146.62	186.68
21	118.81	134.84	174.02	225.02
22	137.63	157.41	206.34	271.03
23	159.27	183.60	244.48	326.23
24	184.16	213.97	289.49	392.48
25	212.79	249.21	342.60	471.98
30	434.74	530.31	790.94	1181.8
35	881.17	1120.7	1816.6	2948.3
40	1779.0	2360.7	4163.2	7343.8
45	3585.1	4965.2	9531.5	18281.
50	7217.7	10435.	21813.	45497.

Present Value Of Annuity Factors (Ordinary Annuity)

N	1%	2%	3%	4%	5%	6%	7%
1	.9901	.9804	.9709	.9615	.9524	.9434	.9346
2	1.9704	1.9416	1.9135	1.8861	1.8594	1.8334	1.8080
3	2.9410	2.8839	2.8286	2.7751	2.7232	2.6730	2.6243
4	3.9020	3.8077	3.7171	3.6299	3.5460	3.4651	3.3872
5	4.8534	4.7135	4.5797	4.4518	4.3295	4.2124	4.1002
6	5.7955	5.6014	5.4172	5.2421	5.0757	4.9173	4.7665
7	6.7282	6.4720	6.2303	6.0021	5.7864	5.5824	5.3893
8	7.6517	7.3255	7.0197	6.7327	6.4632	6.2098	5.9713
9	8.5660	8.1622	7.7861	7.4353	7.1078	6.8017	6.5152
10	9.4713	8.9826	8.5302	8.1109	7.7217	7.3601	7.0236
11	10.3676	9.7868	9.2526	8.7605	8.3064	7.8869	7.4987
12	11.2551	10.5753	9.9540	9.3851	8.8633	8.3838	7.9427
13	12.1337	11.3484	10.6350	9.9856	9.3936	8.8527	8.3577
14	13.0037	12.1062	11.2961	10.5631	9.8986	9.2950	8.7455
15	13.8651	12.8493	11.9379	11.1184	10.3797	9.7122	9.1079
16	14.7179	13.5777	12.5611	11.6523	10.8378	10.1059	9.4466
17	15.5623	14.2919	13.1661	12.1657	11.2741	10.4773	9.7632
18	16.3983	14.9920	13.7535	12.6593	11.6896	10.8276	10.0591
19	17.2260	15.6785	14.3238	13.1339	12.0853	11.1581	10.3356
20	18.0456	16.3514	14.8775	13.5903	12.4622	11.4699	10.5940
21	18.8570	17.0112	15.4150	14.0292	12.8212	11.7641	10.8355
22	19.6604	17.6580	15.9369	14.4511	13.1630	12.0416	11.0612
23	20.4558	18.2922	16.4436	14.8568	13.4886	12.3034	11.2722
24	21.2434	18.9139	16.9355	15.2470	13.7986	12.5504	11.4693
25	22.0232	19.5235	17.4131	15.6221	14.0939	12.7834	11.6536
26	22.7952	20.1210	17.8768	15.9828	14.3752	13.0032	11.8258
27	23.5596	20.7069	18.3270	16.3296	14.6430	13.2105	11.9867
28	24.3164	21.2813	18.7641	16.6631	14.8981	13.4062	12.1371
29	25.0658	21.8444	19.1885	16.9837	15.1411	13.5907	12.2777
30	25.8077	22.3965	19.6004	17.2920	15.3725	13.7648	12.4090
31	26.5423	22.9377	20.0004	17.5885	15.5928	13.9291	12.5318
32	27.2696	23.4683	20.3888	17.8736	15.8027	14.0840	12.6466
33	27.9897	23.9886	20.7658	18.1476	16.0025	14.2302	12.7538
34	28.7027	24.4986	21.1318	18.4112	16.1929	14.3681	12.8540
35	29.4086	24.9986	21.4872	18.6646	16.3742	14.4982	12.9477
36	30.1075	25.4888	21.8323	18.9083	16.5469	14.6210	13.0352
37	30.7995	25.9695	22.1672	19.1426	16.7113	14.7368	13.1170
38	31.4847	26.4406	22.4925	19.3679	16.8679	14.8460	13.1935
39	32.1630	26.9026	22.8082	19.5845	17.0170	14.9491	13.2649
40	32.8347	27.3555	23.1148	19.7928	17.1591	15.0463	13.3317
41	33.4997	27.7995	23.4124	19.9931	17.2944	15.1380	13.3941
42	34.1581	28.2348	23.7014	20.1856	17.4232	15.2245	13.4524
43	34.8100	28.6616	23.9819	20.3708	17.5459	15.3062	13.5070
44	35.4555	29.0800	24.2543	20.5488	17.6628	15.3832	13.5579
45	36.0945	29.4902	24.5187	20.7200	17.7741	15.4558	13.6055
46	36.7272	29.8923	24.7754	20.8847	17.8801	15.5244	13.6500
47	37.3537	30.2866	25.0247	21.0429	17.9810	15.5890	13.6916
48	37.9740	30.6731	25.2667	21.1951	18.0772	15.6500	13.7305
49	38.5881	31.0521	25.5017	21.3415	18.1687	15.7076	13.7668
50	39.1961	31.4236	25.7298	21.4822	18.2559	15.7619	13.8007

Present Value Of Annuity Factors (Ordinary Annuity)

N	8%	9%	10%	11%	12%	13%	14%
1	.9259	.9174	.9091	.9009	.8929	.8850	.8772
2	1.7833	1.7591	1.7355	1.7125	1.6901	1.6681	1.6467
3	2.5771	2.5313	2.4869	2.4437	2.4018	2.3612	2.3216
4	3.3121	3.2397	3.1699	3.1024	3.0373	2.9745	2.9137
5	3.9927	3.8897	3.7908	3.6959	3.6048	3.5172	3.4331
6	4.6229	4.4859	4.3553	4.2305	4.1114	3.9976	3.8887
7	5.2064	5.0330	4.8684	4.7122	4.5638	4.4226	4.2883
8	5.7466	5.5348	5.3349	5.1461	4.9676	4.7988	4.6389
9	6.2469	5.9952	5.7590	5.5370	5.3283	5.1317	4.9464
10	6.7101	6.4177	6.1446	5.8892	5.6502	5.4262	5.2161
11	7.1390	6.8052	6.4951	6.2065	5.9377	5.6869	5.4527
12	7.5361	7.1607	6.8137	6.4924	6.1944	5.9176	5.6603
13	7.9038	7.4869	7.1034	6.7499	6.4235	6.1218	5.8424
14	8.2442	7.7862	7.3667	6.9819	6.6282	6.3025	6.0021
15	8.5595	8.0607	7.6061	7.1909	6.8109	6.4624	6.1422
16	8.8514	8.3126	7.8237	7.3792	6.9740	6.6039	6.2651
17	9.1216	8.5436	8.0216	7.5488	7.1196	6.7291	6.3729
18	9.3719	8.7556	8.2014	7.7016	7.2497	6.8399	6.4674
19	9.6036	8.9501	8.3649	7.8393	7.3658	6.9380	6.5504
20	9.8181	9.1285	8.5136	7.9633	7.4694	7.0248	6.6231
21	10.0168	9.2922	8.6487	8.0751	7.5620	7.1016	6.6870
22	10.2007	9.4424	8.7715	8.1757	7.6446	7.1695	6.7429
23	10.3711	9.5802	8.8832	8.2664	7.7184	7.2297	6.7921
24	10.5288	9.7066	8.9847	8.3481	7.7843	7.2829	6.8351
25	10.6748	9.8226	8.0770	8.4217	7.8431	7.3300	6.8729
26	10.8100	9.9290	9.1609	8.4881	7.8957	7.3717	6.9061
27	10.9352	10.0266	9.2372	8.5478	7.9426	7.4086	6.9352
28	11.0511	10.1161	9.3066	8.6016	7.9844	7.4412	6.9607
29	11.1584	10.1983	9.3696	8.6501	8.0218	7.4701	6.9830
30	11.2578	10.2737	9.4269	8.6938	8.0552	7.4957	7.0027
31	11.3498	10.3428	9.4790	8.7331	8.0850	7.5183	7.0199
32	11.4350	10.4062	9.5264	8.7686	8.1116	7.5383	7.0350
33	11.5139	10.4644	9.5694	8.8005	8.1354	7.5560	7.0482
34	11.5869	10.5178	9.6086	8.8293	8.1566	7.5717	7.0599
35	11.6546	10.5668	9.6442	8.8552	8.1755	7.5856	7.0700
36	11.7172	10.6118	9.6765	8.8786	8.1924	7.5979	7.0790
37	11.7752	10.6530	9.7059	8.8996	8.2075	7.6087	7.0868
38	11.8289	10.6908	9.7327	8.9186	8.2210	7.6183	7.0937
39	11.8786	10.7255	9.7570	8.9357	8.2330	7.6268	7.0997
40	11.9246	10.7574	9.7791	8.9511	8.2438	7.6344	7.1050
41	11.9672	10.7866	9.7991	8.9649	8.2534	7.6410	7.1097
42	12.0067	10.8134	9.8174	8.9774	8.2619	7.6469	7.1138
43	12.0432	10.8380	9.8340	8.9886	8.2696	7.6522	7.1173
44	12.0771	10.8605	9.8491	8.9988	8.2764	7.6568	7.1205
45	12.1084	10.8812	9.8628	9.0079	8.2825	7.6609	7.1232
46	12.1374	10.9002	9.8753	9.0161	8.2880	7.6645	7.1256
47	12.1643	10.9176	9.8&66	9.0235	8.2928	7.6677	7.1277
48	12.1891	10.9336	9.8969	9.0302	8.2972	7.6705	7.1296
49	12.2122	10.9482	9.9063	9.0362	8.3010	7.6730	7.1312
50	12.2335	10.9617	9.9148	9.0417	8.3045	7.6752	7.1327

Present Value Of Annuity Factors (Ordinary Annuity)

N	15%	16%	17%	18%	19%
1	.8696	.8621	.8547	.8475	.8403
2	1.6257	1.6052	1.5852	1.5656	1.5465
3	2.2832	2.2459	2.2096	2.1743	2.1399
4	2.8550	2.7982	2.7432	2.6901	2.6386
5	3.3522	3.2743	3.1993	3.1272	3.0576
6	3.7845	3.6847	3.5892	3.4976	3.4098
7	4.1604	4.0386	3.9224	3.8115	3.7057
8	4.4873	4.3436	4.2072	4.0776	3.9544
9	4.7716	4.6065	4.4506	4.3030	4.1633
10	5.0188	4.8332	4.6586	4.4941	4.3389
11	5.2337	5.0286	4.8364	4.6560	4.4865
12	5.4206	5.1971	4.9884	4.7932	4.6105
13	5.5831	5.3423	5.1183	4.9095	4.7147
14	5.7245	5.4675	5.2293	5.0081	4.8023
15	5.8474	5.5755	5.3242	5.0916	4.8759
16	5.9542	5.6685	5.4053	5.1624	4.9377
17	6.0472	5.7487	5.4746	5.2223	4.9897
18	6.1280	5.8178	5.5339	5.2732	5.0333
19	6.1982	5.8775	5.5845	5.3162	5.0700
20	6.2593	5.9288	5.6278	5.3527	5.1009
21	6.3125	5.9731	5.6648	5.3837	5.1268
22	6.3587	6.0113	5.6964	5.4099	5.1486
23	6.3988	6.0442	5.7234	5.4321	5.1668
24	6.4338	6.0726	5.7465	5.4509	5.1822
25	6.4641	6.0971	5.7662	5.4669	5.1951
26	6.4906	6.1182	5.7831	5.4804	5.2060
27	6.5135	6.1364	5.7975	5.4919	5.2151
28	6.5335	6.1520	5.8099	5.5016	5.2228
29	6.5509	6.1656	5.8204	5.5098	5.2292
30	6.5660	6.1772	5.8294	5.5168	5.2347
31	6.5791	6.1872	5.8371	5.5227	5.2392
32	6.5905	6.1959	5.8437	5.5277	5.2430
33	6.6005	6.2034	5.8493	5.5320	5.2462
34	6.6091	6.2098	5.8541	5.5356	5.2489
35	6.6166	6.2153	5.8582	5.5386	5.2512
36	6.6231	6.2201	5.8617	5.5412	5.2531
37	6.6288	6.2242	5.8647	5.5434	5.2547
38	6.6338	6.2278	5.8673	5.5452	5.2561
39	6.6380	6.2309	5.8695	5.5468	5.2572
40	6.6418	6.2335	5.8713	5.5482	5.2582
41	6.6450	6.2358	5.8729	5.5493	5.2590
42	6.6478	6.2377	5.8743	5.5502	5.2596
43	6.6503	6.2394	5.8755	5.5510	5.2602
44	6.6524	6.2409	5.8765	5.5517	5.2607
45	6.6543	6.2421	5.8773	5.5523	5.2611
46	6.6559	6.2432	5.8781	5.5528	5.2614
47	6.6573	6.2442	5.8787	5.5532	5.2617
48	6.6585	6.2450	5.8792	5.5536	5.2619
49	6.6596	6.2457	5.8797	5.5539	5.2621
50	6.6605	6.2463	5.8801	5.5541	5.2623

Section V

Case Study

As a wealth manager you must be a solution provider for your clients. You must lead a team of professionals in helping clients reach their financial objectives. In doing this you must have expertise yourself in the areas of financial planning and investment management, and be able to effectively deal with, educate, and act in an ethical manner with your clients, and also be able to get the most out of the members of your team.

Although you may have sufficient knowledge and client management skills, you still must be able to integrate all the components of what makes a successful wealth manager, into a wealth management plan for your client.

Section V of the text describes a specific case that is designed to bring together the skills involved in dealing with clients, financial planning and investment management.

Wealth Management Techniques

8592123
1947500
YRS 8644 623

45 92940   2,000,000   YRS

2 592122

yn9

C6 644,622

648031
YN3   1,148,026
yn9
~   500,000

SAMPLE CASE: JAMES & LAURA PARKER

James and Laura Parker have just attended a wealth management seminar hosted by your employer, Summit Investment Counsel Inc. A friend of theirs, who is already a client, told them about the seminar which covered financial planning topics ranging from investment management, tax planning, retirement planning and estate planning. It also addressed how to use insurance to protect one's legacy. You are a wealth manager with Summit Investment Counsel Inc. and had been one of the speakers at the seminar. The seminar provided them with "food for thought" and made them realize that they could and should be doing more to get their financial affairs in order. They introduced themselves to you at the end of the seminar to take you up on your offer for a complimentary financial plan.

You meet with the Parkers the following week to gather the necessary information. You agree to develop a financial plan for their review at the next scheduled meeting in three weeks.

James Parker is 53 years old. He owns 50 percent of TNT Tool & Die Inc., a qualifying small business corporation, whose principal business is manufacturing precision aircraft parts for the aerospace industry in Canada, the U.S., and Eastern Europe. James has been in business for five years with his partner William Davis, age 48, who owns the other 50 percent of the company. James has earned a stable salary of approximately $155,000 per year from the business. The original cost of his shares that he bought three years ago was $1,947,500. The book value of his shares has grown at 10 percent per year since they were purchased.

James's wife Laura, aged 50, has been employed with a software manufacturing firm, GrafiX Ltd., for the last five years. The firm is a subsidiary of a large U.S. company. She was recently promoted to the position of vice president of marketing. She earns $105,000 per year. Her remuneration package also includes an employee stock option plan, which allows her to purchase up to 1,000 shares of GrafiX. Ltd. on January 1 of each of the next five years at $20 per share. The current market price of GrafiX is $30 per share. Laura would like to exercise her options on January 1, which is coming up in a month's time, but has heard that exercise will have tax consequences.

James and Laura have two children: Derek aged 30, and Christina aged 19. Christina still lives at home, and is attending university. James and Laura are paying her tuition. Derek has been living common-law with his girlfriend for the last four years. They have a three-year old child. James has committed to paying 50 percent of his grandchild's post secondary education and is not sure whether or not it is better to fund the education costs using an RESP or an in-trust account.

Derek is a history professor at the University of Toronto. He has no interest in going into his father's business. As a result, James, who is looking to retire by age 60, will be looking at selling his share of the business within the next several years. He believes that the book value of the business will continue to rise by 10 percent per year.

The Parkers purchased their current home in May 1991 for $550,000 in Vaughan, Ontario. A real estate agent told them that it could be sold for $750,000 if they were interested in selling it in the current real estate market. They are happy with their home and have no plans to sell it. Of the original amount borrowed from the bank, $150,000 is outstanding today. The mortgage rate is 8 percent, monthly pay with a 25-year amortization.

Although they are entitled to a 20 percent pre-payment of their mortgage on each of its anniversary dates, the Parkers have not yet taken advantage of it. Instead, they have been contributing to their RRSPs. Both James and Laura made their maximum RRSP contributions in 1999. They are also thinking of borrowing funds for their RRSP investments. James and Laura's 1998 Tax Notice indicates that they have unused RRSP contribution room of $67,000 and $42,000 respectively.

Besides their house, the Parkers own a recreation property with a cottage on it. James inherited the cottage from his mother who passed away five years ago. James estimates that the cottage is currently worth about $195,000. It was worth $125,000 when he inherited it. He believes that due to the demand that aging baby boomers will put on recreation properties, the cottage will escalate in value at a rate of at least 10 percent per year. Both James and Laura agreed that they would like their children to inherit the cottage and use it for their enjoyment for many years to come.

The Parkers live very comfortably, and spend just about what they earn. Their current combined expenses, including cottage expenses are $110,000 per year (not including taxes).

James's car, a BMW 740i, was purchased one year ago for $130,000 and is primarily used for business purposes. He believes its current value is around $115,000. Laura has a convertible Saab worth approximately $40,000. Laura paid off her car loan two years ago.

The Parkers left you with copies of their 1998 tax return and statements from various banks/investment companies.

The tax returns showed the following:

	James	**Laura**
Employment Earnings	$155,000	$105,000
CPP Premium	$1,890	$1,890
EI Premium		$1,131
RRSP Contributions	$13,500	$6,500
Charitable Donations	$1,000	$2,000
Dividends		$390
Interest Income	$2,400	$800
Taxes	$60,900	$57,700

The current market value of James and Laura's RRSP and non-RRSP investments are as follows:

	James	**Laura**
Non RRSPs	$250,000	$550,000
RRSPs	$150,000	$130,000

The Parkers currently have their taxable and RSP portfolios invested at the Maple Leaf Bank. They hold mutual funds and GICs, and are generally not interested in being involved with making investment decisions.

Laura currently has both RRSP and non-RRSP investments in mutual funds. She has 80 percent in the Maple Leaf Canadian Fixed Income Fund, and 20 percent in the Canadian Equity Value Fund. Both funds have deferred sales charges.

James has 50 percent of his RRSP and non-RRSPs in GICs at Maple Leaf Bank and 50 percent in the Maple Leaf Canadian Fixed Income Fund.

Laura would like to be able to retire at around the same time as James. The Parkers want to be debt-free by the time they retire. Laura keeps herself in good shape and expects to live to age 85 while James feels he'll be lucky if he makes it to age 78.

Inflation has been very low for the past couple of years, however you agree with James and Laura to assume that inflation until their retirement will be 3 percent.

As they expect to do a considerable amount of travelling James and Laura estimate that they will need to earn about 85% of their pre-retirement, pre-tax income during their retirement years. Laura feels that if she outlives James, she will still need to spend a similar amount due to her likely reliance on some degree of health/home care, and some support of her children and grandchildren.

Although the Parkers have not specifically asked you about estate planning, you feel that this is in order. Overall, they want to leave everything to their children, except for a $1 million dollar donation, which they wish to leave to a registered charity. The Parkers are very involved in their church, and through the church and other organizations have taken an active stance against companies that profit from selling tobacco, alchohol, and gambling services, as well as those companies who are involved in arms industry.

Questions

1. Advise James as to any tax planning opportunities available with respect to minimizing his and/or his family's tax liability when his share of the business is eventually sold. Explain the tax implications of your recommendation. Assume that neither James nor any of his family members have used any portion of the $500,000 lifetime capital gains exemption. As discussed in the case, assume the business has grown 10 percent per year over the past three years. As well assume the business is expected to grow by another 10 percent per year over the next six years.

Answer to Question 1

_____

_____

_____

_____

_____

_____

_____

_____

_____

_____

_____

_____

_____

_____

_____

_____

_____

_____

_____

_____

_____

2. As of February 27, 2000 the tax treatment of employee stock options has changed. Describe for Laura these changes and how they will impact her in the current taxation year and those to follow.

Answer to Question 2

---

3. Distinguish between RESPs and In-Trust Accounts. What are the pros and cons of each. If James were to contribute $2,000 per year to an RESP for 15 years, what would the accumulated balance be? Assume the monies contributed to the RESP will earn 5 percent each year. What would the accumulated balance be if James contributed $2,000 per year to an in-trust account at 5 percent each year? Assume James's marginal tax rate is 40%.

Answer to Question 3

4. James and Laura's mortgage runs for another 16 years (to the month) to James's 69th birthday. Their monthly payments are $1,350 per month.

    a) If instead of making their RRSP payment this year, they used the $20,000 to pre-pay their mortgage, how many months earlier would the mortgage be paid off.

Answer to Question 4 a)

192
154.6

38.4 mo   2 5 9, 200

x 1350 = 51840

    b) What would the future value of the savings be when James turns 69, assuming they could invest the savings at a 6% before-tax annual rate. Assume their marginal tax rate is 50%.

Answer to Question 4 b)

c) If they did make the RRSP contribution instead of paying down the mortgage, how much would the $20,000 be worth when James turns 69. Assume they could invest the $20,000 at the same rate as described in 4 (b).

Answer to Question 4 c)

d) What other considerations should Laura and James take into account before they make a decision on whether to make an RRSP contribution this year or pay down their mortgage?

Answer to Question 4 d)

_____

_____

_____

_____

_____

_____

_____

5. James and Laura are concerned about the tax consequences of leaving the cottage to their children and are seeking your advice. Advise them of the current rules regarding taxation of vacation property and ways in which they could help minimize their heir's tax liability.

Answer to Question 5

_____

_____

_____

_____

_____

_____

_____

_____

6. Laura and James have indicated that they are very active in their church and would like to donate on the surviving spouses' death (presumably Laura) $1,000,000. She asked you for recommendations on how this can be accomplished. Give her 3 recommendations. Discuss the merits of each.

Answer to Question 6

_____

_____

_____

_____

_____

_____

_____

_____

7.   As a wealth manager you should be building a team of experts to help you and your client address financial planning problems such as the ones described above. As well, the team should consist of an individual who can help in the area of investment and portfolio management. List the professionals that should be part of the team and describe the financial planning and/or investment areas they would be covering as they relate to Questions 1 through 6.

Answer to Question 7

_____

_____

_____

_____

_____

_____

_____

_____

_____

_____

_____

_____

_____

_____

_____

_____

_____

_____

_____

James and Laura have completed the following risk profile questionnaire.

Risk Profile Questionnaire

1. Which of the following best describes how you view your investment portfolio?
   a. Seeking to protect account value, which implies low returns and minimal chances for short-term losses.
   b. Seeking moderate returns, which implies moderate chances for short-term losses.
   c. Seeking high returns, which implies high chances for short-term losses.

(a)

2. Which of the following best describes your expectations for your portfolio?
   a. I want a portfolio that will primarily provide me with supplemental income.
   b. I want a portfolio that offers both moderate long-term growth potential and current income.
   c. I want a portfolio that will maximize my long-term growth potential.
   d. I want a portfolio that will make me rich very quickly.

(b)

3. Suppose you had most of your money invested in one mutual fund and your last statement showed that the value of the fund decreased by 2%. (For example, your $100,000 investment was now worth $98,000.) What action are you most likely to take?
   a. Sell all shares of the fund.
   b. Sell some, but not all, of the fund shares.
   c. Continue to hold the shares.
   d. Purchase more shares to take advantage of the low price.

(c)

4. If your tax rate is 50% and the inflation rate is 2.0%, your investments must return at least 4% to retain their purchasing power. With this in mind, which of the following best describes your attitude toward taxes and inflation?
   a. I am primarily concerned with protecting my investments. So I want investments designed to minimize risk and to keep pace with inflation on an after-tax basis.
   b. I want investments designed to moderately outpace inflation on an after-tax basis. I am willing to accept some additional risk to do so.
   c. I want investments designed to significantly outpace inflation on an after-tax basis. I am willing to accept substantial risk to do so.

(a)

The following table lists several different types of investments. For each type, please indicate the status that applies to you.

Type of Investment	Previous or Current Investment Would Invest Again	Previous or Current Investment Dissatisfied	No Previous or Current Investment
Short Term Assets – T-bills, money market accounts, GICs etc.	Yes		
Government bonds or Government bond mutual funds		Yes	
High-Grade Corporate Bonds or Corporate Bond mutual funds		Yes	
Blue-Chip Stocks or Blue-Chip mutual fund	Yes		
Small-Cap stocks or mutual fund			
Hedge Funds			
Derivatives – Futures or Options			

5. The following table shows potential one-year gains and losses for four different portfolios with an initial investment of $250,000. Which portfolio would you invest in?

Portfolio	Potential Low Return	Potential High Return	Potential Average Return
A	-4%	+11%	+7%
B	-8%	+20	+9%
C	-11%	+28%	+12%
D	-20%	+45%	+18%

    a.   Portfolio A
    b.   Portfolio B
    c.   Portfolio C
    d.   Portfolio D

(a)

6. I can tolerate substantial short-term fluctuations in my portfolio value in order to increase the likelihood of long-term after-tax gains that outpace inflation.
    a.   Strongly agree
    b.   Agree
    c.   Neutral
    d.   Disagree
    e.   Strongly disagree

(d)

Part II

The Parkers are planning to retire after the sale of the business, which James hopes will take place six years from now. After that, they plan to have an active retirement. Their goals for retirement include extensive travel and the purchase of a condo in Tuscany. After James turns 69, they expect to enjoy retirement a little more quietly.

You may find the timeline below helpful when considering the questions below.

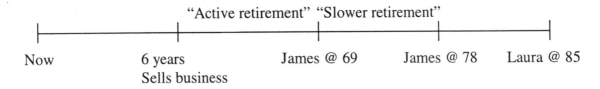

Questions

1. Prior to developing an investment policy statement for the Parkers, what further information should you be gathering (about the Parkers)?

Answer to Question 1

_____

_____

_____

_____

_____

_____

_____

_____

_____

_____

_____

2. How would you charchterize the Parker's tolerance for risk? List 5 different types of risk that the Parkers or any individual should understand about investing.

Answer to Question 2

_____

_____

_____

_____

_____

_____

_____

_____

_____

_____

_____

_____

_____

_____

_____

_____

_____

_____

_____

_____

_____

_____

3. Both Laura and James will continue to make the same level of contributions to their RRSPs until they retire in another 6 years. Assuming a 6% rate of return, calculate the value of their respective RRSPs at retirement six years from now.

Answer to Question 3

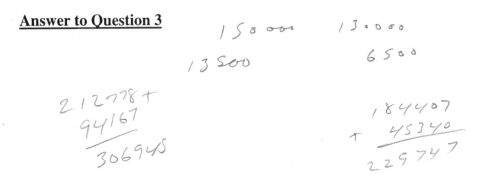

4. The Parkers currently have their taxable and RRSP portfolios invested at the Maple Leaf Bank. Their investments consist of funds and GICs, and they are not interested in being involved with making investment decisions. They currently hold relatively conservative mutual fund portfolios, as follows:

	Asset Allocation (both RSP and taxable)
Laura	
Canadian Fixed Income Index Fund	80%
Canadian Equity Value Fund (DSC)	20%
James	
GICs (at Maple Leaf Bank)	50%
Canadian Fixed Income Fund	50%

Their asset allocation hasn't changed in five years, and they have had several people from Maple Leaf Bank look after their affairs over the years. There has been no regular review of their portfolio.

a)   Aside from whether or not their current investment strategy is appropriate in meeting their retirement needs (this will be covered later on in this case), identify three other risks the Parkers are facing given their current investment strategy.

Answer to Question 4 a)

_____

_____

_____

_____

_____

_____

_____

_____

_____

b)   The Parkers have heard about investment firms that offer separately managed accounts. Advise them on the appropriateness of this type of managed product as it relates to their needs, objectives and constraints.

Answer to Question 4 b)

_____

_____

_____

_____

_____

_____

_____

_____

_____

_____

_____

_____

_____

_____

_____

_____

_____

_____

_____

_____

_____

_____

_____

c)   Identify what considerations should be made for a private investor regarding changing investment service providers.

Answer to Question 4 c)

_____

_____

_____

_____

_____

_____

_____

_____

_____

_____

_____

_____

_____

_____

_____

_____

_____

_____

_____

_____

_____

_____

5. Assume James successfully sells his shares in the business six years from now, and that the shares have grown at a rate of 10% per year.

Use the answer from Part I, Question 1 to complete the table below:

	James	Laura
Proceeds from sale of shares in business	1148024	1148024
Cost of Shares when bought or transferred	486 875	648030
Capital Gain	644,644	499994
Taxable Capital Gains — 16535	429742	φ
Taxes payable (50% marginal rate):	214871	

6. The Parkers' investment portfolios will remain invested before the sale of TNT shares. What will their taxable and RRSP portfolios be worth in six years time. Assume they maintain their current portfolio, which is yielding 3% on an after-tax basis. Use your answer from Question 3 to fill in the value of the RRSP in six years time.

Portfolio	Starting	3% After Tax Growth (6% before tax) for 6 Years
James's Taxable	250000	298 513
James's RRSP	80945	306 945
Laura's Taxable	556 000	656 729
Laura's RRSP	130000	229747
Total Taxable	800 000	955 242
Total RRSP	380 000	536 692
Total		1,491,934

7. The Parkers require 85% of their pre-tax, pre-retirement annual income level for their retirement, and also have the following goals:

Condo in Tuscany: $350,000
Pay off mortgage: $120,000

The Parkers also have the after-tax cash amount from the sale of TNT shares.

$\hookrightarrow$ 2,081,177

a) Discuss whether the Parkers can achieve their retirement goals without using their RRSP's or depleting the capital by maintaining their current investment strategy. Assume that the expected rate of return through their active retirement period will be 7.3%, and that this investment income will be the only income they will be earning.

Answer to Question 7 a)

9 955 242 + 2,081,177 − 350,000 − 120,000 =

2,566,419 × 7.3% = $187,349

need 85% of (155,000 + 105,000) 260,000 = $221,000

b) Notwithstanding your response to a) above, if the Parkers could not achieve their retirement goals through their current investment strategy, what other options could they consider without using their RRSP's?

Answer to Question 7 b)

8. Calculate the expected return for the three portfolios below by filling out Table 8.1, using the following data:

Asset Class	Expected Return	Standard Deviation
Canadian Bonds	6.5%	7.5%
International Bonds	7.2	7.7
Canadian Equities	10.0	16.0
US Equities	12.5	16.6
International Equities	14.6	22.9

Asset Class	Portfolio 1	Portfolio 2	Portfolio 3
Canadian Bonds	80%	25%	5.0%
International Bonds	0%	25%	5.0%
Total Fixed Income	**80%**	**50%**	**10%**
Canadian Equities	20%	10%	20%
US Equities	0%	20%	35%
International Equities	0%	20%	35%
Total Equities	**20%**	**50%**	**90%**

Table 8.1

Asset Class	Portfolio 1 Asset Mix	Expected Return	Standard Deviation	
Canadian Bonds	80.00%	6.5	7.5	5.2
International Bonds	0.00%			
			16	2.
Canadian Equities	20.00%	10		7.2
US Equities	0.00%			
International Equities	0.00%			
Total	**100.00%**		**7.1%**	

Asset Class	Portfolio 2 Asset Mix	Expected Return	Standard Deviation	
Canadian Bonds	25.00%	6.5	7.5	1.625
International Bonds	25.00%	7.2	7.7	1.8
			16	1.0
Canadian Equities	10.00%	10		2.5
US Equities	20.00%	12.5	16.6	2.92
International Equities	20.00%	14.6	22.9	
Total	**100.00%**		**10.5%**	9.85

Asset Class	Portfolio 3 Asset Mix	Expected Return	Standard Deviation	
Canadian Bonds	5.00%	6.5	.325	
International Bonds	5.00%	7.2	.36	
			2.0	
Canadian Equities	20.00%	10	4.375	
US Equities	35.00%	12.5	5.11	
International Equities	35.00%	14.6		
Total	**100.00%**		**14.0%**	12.17

9. Which of the three portfolios shown above is most suitable for the Parkers'? Give at least three reasons to back up your answer. As well, describe at least one drawback to your choice. Finally, what advice would you give to the Parkers alongside your recommendation.

Answer to Question 9

@ 9% not 3% 6 yrs. Tax. Port

= 1,341,680. ↑ assets by 1,341,680 - 955 242

= $386,348 + 2566,419 = 2952857.

So now Retirement I = 2,952,857 × 7.3%

= 215,558 Closer to $221,000

10. Create Investment Policy Statements for the Parker's taxable portfolio for the six-year period leading up to the sale of the business.

Structure your answer according to the policy below:

Investment Objectives & Risk Tolerance

Cash-flow characteristics

Asset Classes Eligible for Investment

Specific Constraints

Asset Mix

Answer to Question 10

_____

_____

_____

_____

_____

_____

_____

_____

_____

_____

_____

_____

_____

_____

_____

_____

_____

_____

_____

11. Are there other investment policy statements that should be created for the Parkers (not individually but as a couple)? If so, identify them. How would they differ from the IPS developed in Question 10, in terms of investment objectives, cash-flow characteristics, assets eligible for investment and strategic asset mix?

Answer to Question 11

SAMPLE CASE: JAMES & LAURA PARKER

Answer Key

Question 1

James can gift half the shares to his children or a trust with his children as beneficiaries. As well he could sell a quarter of the shares to his wife. If he transfers shares to a trust for his children, he should remain the trustee, meaning he retains control of the trust assets (which would likely be an important consideration for his partner who would not want to have to deal with additional shareholders).

For his wife he could also transfer shares to a spousal trust at cost. Capital gains tax would then only have to be paid when those shares are disposed of. This however does not result in maximum income splitting (i.e. the use of all four family member's capital gains exemption). For this example we assume he sells shares directly to his wife.

By gifting and selling 3/4 of the shares to his kids and wife respectively, they all will have the $500,000 exemption to minimize their taxes when the business is eventually sold. James would not have to pay tax on the transfer, as his capital gains exemption will cover it, but would have to pay taxes on his shares when they are sold.

When James sells the shares to his wife he takes back a promissory note from his wife at a market rate of interest.

	Original Cost of Shares	Value of Shares when transferred	James Realized Capital Gain	Value of shares after 6 years	Capital Gain	Taxable Capital Gain
Derek	$486,875	$648,030	$161,155	$1,148,024	$500,019	~ 0
Christina	$486,875	$648,030	$161,155	$1,148,024	$500,019	~ 0
Laura	$486,875	$648,030	$161,155	$1,148,024	$500,019	~ 0
James	$486,875	$648,030 (Not transferred)	0	$1,148,024	$661,149	2/3rds of $644,614($ 661,149 - $16,535)
Total	$1,947,500	$2,592,122	$483,465	$4,592,102		

James uses up all but $16,535 of his $500,000 capital gains exemption when he transfers shares to his children and wife. He must pay tax on 2/3rds of the capital gain (less $16,535) when the shares are eventually sold.

The kids and Laura pay virtually no tax on the sold shares as they get to use their capital gains exemption.

Question 2

Prior to February 27, 2000 employees of non-CCPCs were deemed to have received income from employment when they exercised an option relating to shares of that company.

After February 27, 2000 employees who have stock options will only have to pay tax on any capital gains that arise when the shares are eventually sold subject to a $100,000 annual limit. As the fair market value of the underlying shares is less than $100,000, Laura will only pay tax when she sells the shares that she received by virtue of the option exercise.

Question 3

The major advantages of an RESP are:

– Tax-free compounding of income, dividends and capital gains
– Can be rolled over to RRSP if funds are not used for post-secondary education
– Eligibility for government grants (20% of contribution to a maximum of $400 per year)

The major disadvantages of an RESP are:
– There are limits on contributions ($4,000/year)
– Withdrawals can only be used for post-secondary education. There is a 20% penalty for withdrawing RESPs for any other purpose.

The major advantages of an In-Trust Account are:

– Withdrawals can be used for any purpose benefiting the child
– There are no contribution limits

The major disadvantages of an in-trust account are:

– Dividend and interest income is attributed back to the contributor – capital gains are taxable in the hands of the child
– They are not eligible for government grants
– Not accessible to the contributor

RESP Contribution
FVA (5%, 15 years, $2,400) = $51,789 accumulated after 15 years.
(extra $400 is from government grant)

In-Trust Account
FVA [5%, (1-0.40), 15 years, $2,000] = $37,198

Question 4

a) If the Parkers pay down their mortgage by $20,000 to $130,000, the mortgage could be paid off in 154 months or about 38 months early.

b) $53,745.38 more at age 69.

c) The future value of $20,000 invested at 6% at the end of 16 years will be worth $50,808. After cashing in the RRSP that amount will be worth only $25,404. The Parkers are better off paying down the mortgage.

d) Paying down the mortgage is probably the best strategy due to:
   - The mortgage rate being higher than the RRSP return
   - The Parkers being able to carry forward unused RRSP contribution room to future years
   - The relatively short period of time to retirement. If the Parkers were younger the RRSP contribution would have a longer period to benefit from tax-free compounding.

Question 5

When James and Laura die, there is considered to be a deemed disposition of all capital property immediately before death at fair market value. If there are not enough liquid assets in the surviving spouse's estate to cover the income tax liability, the heirs may be forced to sell the property to pay the taxes.

The Parkers could consider at least two options:

- Purchase of a "joint and last to die" insurance policy that would pay out on the death of Laura the funds needed to meet the tax liability from the deemed disposition of the cottage.

- Transfer ownership of the cottage to Christina so she could take advantage of the principal residence exemption. When the cottage is transferred however James and Laura would be subject to capital gains tax on the increase in value from when the cottage was bought to when it was transferred.

Question 6

- Laura, assuming she is the last to die, could bequest that amount in her will. This is the simplest strategy, but the problem with this strategy is that a bequest of this size may exceed the allowable limit for tax purposes. Instead, both Laura and James may consider spreading out their contributions while they are living.

- Laura may consider leaving an in-kind donation. If she has stocks she may consider bequesting the stocks directly to the charity, where the capital gains inclusion rate is only 1/3rd versus the normal 2/3rds.

- A charitable remainder trust could be set up. For example, Laura and James could transfer their home into the trust. They would get the immediate tax credit based on the present value of the gift, but would retain legal ownership and use of the house until Laura dies. There would be no tax liability on transfer of the house to the trust as it is the Parkers' principle residence.

Question 7

- Lawyer – In the setting up of a trust, or transferring ownership of the cottage
- Accountant for tax planning advice
- Business valuator for valuing James's business
- Gift planner who can discuss various planned giving techniques
- Portfolio Manager to help build the RRSP and taxable portfolios.

Part II

Question 1

In addition to the information that has already been gathered, the wealth manager should find out the following:

- Whether or not there are preferences or constraints regarding the types of investments that the Parkers will invest in.

- Do the Parkers have arrangements in case one of them could not work?

- Does each one have a will?

- Do they have insurance and if so, what types of policies?

- Do they have company pension plans and if so are they Defined Benefit Plan or Defined Contribution Plans?

- How much can they expect from CPP and OAS when they retire?

Question 2

The Parkers are very risk averse.

Five different types of risk:

- The risk of not investing or investing too conservatively
- The risk of not diversifying
- Purchasing power risk
- Interest rate risk
- Currency risk

Question 3

Laura:
RRSP now: $130,000
Annual Contribution: $6,500

For Contributions:
FVA (6%, 6 years, $6,500) = $45,339 accumulated after 6 years.

For Beginning Amount:
FV (6%, 6 years, $130,000) = $184,407

Laura's RSP 6 years from the present = $229,746

James

RRSP now: $150,000
Annual Contribution: $13,500

For Contributions:
FVA (6%, 6 years, $13,500)   = $94,167

For Beginning Amount:
FV (6%, 6 years, $150,000) = $212,777

James's RSP 6 years from the present = $306,944

Question 4

a)   Possible Answers:

1) Issuer default - limit of CDIC coverage on James's GICs
2) Concentration in one market – the Parkers have minimal diversification and so are completely at the mercy of Canadian markets
3) Misallocation of investment strategy – the asset allocation is not being managed and there is no regular review. As a result there is the risk of the portfolio not matching objectives and risk tolerance
4) Lack of stability of personnel at Maple Leaf Bank – low probability that they will recommend a change proactively
5) Purchasing Power risk, particularly as they are holding a significant part of their portfolio in fixed-income investments

b)   The Parkers are suitable for separately managed accounts for the following reasons:

- They are already familiar with professional investment management, as they currently hold mutual funds
- They do not want to be actively involved in making investment decisions, so a traditional broker relationship may not be appropriate
- They need to have their goals, objectives, and risk tolerance embodied in a policy statement
- They need ongoing service from a professional who can effectively guide them in making adjustments to their portfolios as their needs and risk tolerance change
- They can benefit from the lower, tax-deductible fees charged by investment counsellors
- Because the securities are owned directly, they are readily saleable or transferable, which enhances tax planning opportunities
- By owning the securities directly, investors can change managers or firms without triggering capital gains

- In order to open a separately managed account most firms require at least a $1 million minimum. Between the Parkers RRSP and non-RRSPs they would likely have enough.

c) When contemplating a change of investment service providers, an investor should consider the following:

- Any applicable tax implications
- Any additional fees that may be charged, for example, mutual funds that have been sold on a Deferred Sales Charge (DSC) basis
- The ongoing fees or commissions to be charged at the new investment service provider
- Any potential conflicts of interest the firm may be facing
- Firms that are too large may not be able to offer a high level of customer service
- Management style.

Question 5

	James	Laura
Proceeds from sale of shares in business	$1,148,024	$1,148,024
Cost of Shares when bought or transferred	$ 486,875	$ 648,030
Capital Gain	$ 661,149	$ 500,019
Taxable Capital Gains	$ 429,743	0
Taxes payable (50% marginal rate):	$ 214,871	0

Question 6

Portfolio	Starting	3% After Tax Growth (6% before tax) for 6 Years
James' Taxable	$ 250,000	$ 298,513
James' RRSP	$ 150,000	$ 306,944
Lauras' Taxable	$ 550,000	$ 656,729
Lauras' RRSP	$ 130,000	$ 229,746
Total Taxable	$ 800,000	$ 955,242
Total RRSP	$ 280,000	$ 536,690
Total	$1,080,000	$1,491,932

Question 7

a)   If the taxable portfolio is invested at 3% (after-tax) for six years until their "active-retirement" period begins, the Parkers will have a total of $955,242in their combined portfolios (as shown above). The sale of the business will bring them $2,081,177 after James pays taxes on his capital gain arising out of the sale of the business. The Parkers then want to buy a condo in Tuscany ($350,000) and pay off their mortgage that they estimate will have a balance of around $120,000. This leaves them with $2,566,419.

An expected rate of return of 7.30% will only yield them $187,349 pre-tax per year, considerably short of their $221,000 pre-tax stated requirement.

b)   – Take a more aggressive stance towards their portfolio. However, this may conflict with their low tolerance for risk
     – Save more during their working years to put aside for their retirement
     – Lower their retirement goals
     – Sell their house or cottage
     – Draw-down principal to make up the difference between the income earned and income needed

Question 8

Asset Class	Portfolio 1 Asset Mix	Expected Return	Standard Deviation
Canadian Bonds	80.00%	5.20%	
International Bonds	0.00%	0.00%	
Canadian Equities	20.00%	2.00%	
US Equities	0.00%	0.00%	
International Equities	0.00%	20.00%	
Total	**100.00%**	**7.20%**	**7.1%**

Asset Class	Portfolio 2 Asset Mix	Expected Return	Standard Deviation
Canadian Bonds	25.00%	1.63%	
International Bonds	25.00%	1.80%	
Canadian Equities	10.00%	1.00%	
US Equities	20.00%	2.50%	
International Equities	20.00%	2.92%	
Total	**100.00%**	**9.85%**	**10.5%**

Asset Class	Portfolio 3 Asset Mix	Expected Return	Standard Deviation
Canadian Bonds	5.00%	0.325%	
International Bonds	5.00%	0.360%	
Canadian Equities	20.00%	2.00%	
US Equities	35.00%	4.38%	
International Equities	35.00%	5.11%	
Total	**100.00%**	**12.18%**	**14.0%**

Question 9

In terms of return and geographic and currency diversification, Portfolio 3 would appear to be the best fit for the Parkers.

As much of the 12.18% return will come from capital gains (some of which may not be realized during this period), the after-tax return can be roughly estimated to be around 9.00%. If the portfolio grows by this amount, and they can invest at 7.30% for their active retirement years, the income from their investments would be close to $221,000 (actual amount would be $215,547, if the after-tax yield is 9%).

The difficulty with Portfolio 3 is the risk. The standard deviation is considerably higher as compared with the other portfolios, and is not consistent with the Parkers' risk tolerance profile.

Portfolio 2 would generate much less income (also will have a higher tax rate as there is more interest income). However the risk is significantly less, and is more consistent with their risk profile. As well, it does offer diversification between asset classes and some limited geographic and currency diversification.

If the Parkers insist on meeting their income objective for retirement, they may then have to be ready to accept the risk, or as discussed earlier, try and spend more or save less or work down their principal.

The wealth manager should ensure that the Parkers understand the risk in Portfolio 3, and very carefully have them evaluate their retirement objectives.

Question 10

Investment Objectives & Risk Tolerance

The primary objective of the portfolio is to provide long-term growth, at a low to moderate level of risk.

Cash flow characteristics

No need for cash flow from the portfolio.

Asset Classes Eligible for Investment

  i)   Publicly traded Canadian and non-Canadian common stocks, convertible debentures or preferred securities;

 ii)   Bonds, debentures, notes or other debt instruments of Canadian and non-Canadian governments, government agencies, or corporations;

iii)   Mortgages;

 iv)   Private placements, whether debt or equity, of Canadian agencies or corporations;

  v)   Guaranteed Investment Contracts or equivalent financial instruments of insurance companies, trust companies, banks or other eligible issuers, or funds which invest primarily in such instruments;

 vi)   Cash, or money market securities issued by governments or corporations;

Specific Constraints

The portfolio shall not hold securities of any company whose primary activities or a major part thereof contribute to:

a) affecting the quality of life of individuals through its implication in the tobacco, alcohol or gambling industries, or,

b) promoting conflict between individuals through its implication in the arms industry (all classes)

Strategic Asset Mix

See Portfolio 2 or 3

Question 11

Ideally the Parkers should have a total of 5 investment policy statements, including the one described above. They would differ in the following ways:

RRSP IPS Until Age 69

The objective of this portfolio would be moderate growth with low risk. There would be no cash-flow requirements. The foreign content rule would limit the extent to which they could invest in securities outside of Canada. The asset mix could be similar to the one described above.

IPS for the taxable portfolio in their "active retirement years"

The objective of this portfolio would be to provide a level of income that would meet their retirement objectives. They would need regular withdrawals of income from the portfolio. With the inclusion of the proceeds from the sale of the business and using portfolio 3 **up until the time of selling the business**, they could invest the money in a portfolio such as #1 **in active retirement** as it would yield them income of close to $221,000 pre-tax with little risk. Of course the taxes on this portfolio would be higher as compared with the other portfolios due to much of the income being derived from fixed-income investments (i.e. interest income versus dividends or capital gains).

IPS for the taxable portfolio in their "slower retirement years"

The Parkers will still need to draw from this portfolio for their slower retirement years, but will also have income from their RRSP portfolio. As they wish to leave $1 million to the church and want to leave their children and grandchildren in good shape, their primary objective would be to provide a significant level of current income with a modest exposure to growth to help preserve the future purchasing power.

IPS for their RRSP portfolio during their "slower retirement years"

The objective would be similar to the IPS for their taxable portfolio. Regular cash withdrawals according to Revenue Canada mandated minimums would be expected from this account. For both this IPS and the taxable portfolio, Portfolio 2 would be the most appropriate, with its balance between equity and fixed income.

Index

A

accumulators, 2-6
active, 10-5, 13-8
active funds, 11-15
active index funds, 11-17
active managers, 13-9
    growth, 13-9
    momentum, 13-9
    sector rotation, 13-9
    value, 13-9
acquisition fees, 14-11
    front-end load, 14-11
ademption, 8-20
adjusted cost base (ACB), 7-26, 7-27, 7-37, 8-23, 8-24, 8-28
administration costs, 11-23
administrative expenses, 11-18, 13-5
advertising, 16-10
affluent, 15-3
after-tax, 10-10
agent-principal relationship, 4-3
    explicit instructions, 4-4
    express delegated authority, 4-4
allowable business investment loss (ABIL), 7-30, 7-31
annuitant, 8-34
annuity, 5-22, 5-23, 6-5, Appendix 7.1-5, 8-25
    annuity with an escalating option, 6-6
    future value, Appendix 7.1-5
    joint and last survivor annuity, 6-6
    level-paying annuity, 6-6
    present value, Appendix 7.1-6
    single-life annuity, 6-6
anonymous, 2-6
anti-avoidance rules, 7-28
anticipation of incapacity, 8-17
arbitrage funds, 12-8, 12-9
arithmetic mean, 9-6, 9-7
asset allocation, 1-6, 5-23, 5-24, 10-1, 10-5, 11-1, 11-15, 12-5
    dynamic, 10-2, 10-6
    investment classes, 10-1
    market timing, 10-2
    security, 10-2
    strategic, 10-2, 10-4
    tactical, 10-2, 10-7
asset allocators, 12-9
asset churning, 7-37
asset classes, 10-3, 12-2, 12-3
asset mix, 10-9, 12-5, 13-1
asset-value-based, 13-4
Association of Investment Management and Research (AIMR), 13-13

at risk, 7-25 – 7-27, 7-29
attorney, 8-17
attribution, 7-9, 7-10, 7-34, 8-20, 8-26, 8-30
    family loan, 7-13
average tax rate, 7-5

B

back-end load, 14-12
balanced funds, 11-5, 11-9
before-tax, 10-11
benchmark, 13-6
    composite market indexes, 13-6
    normal portfolios, 13-8
    style indexes, 13-8
beneficiary, 7-33, 8-23, 8-26, 8-29, 8-34, 11-28
bequest, 8-27, 8-36
beta, 12-8
bogeys, 13-6
bracket creep, 7-39
burglary, 6-9
business income, 7-49
business losses, 7-30
business plan, 15-14
    components, 15-15
    objectives, 15-14
buy-sell agreements, 6-17, 8-6
    corporate-redemption agreements, 6-19
    cross-purchase agreements, 6-19
    funding, 6-18
    sinking fund, 6-18
    structuring, 6-19

C

Canada Business Corporations, 6-10
Canada Education Savings Grant (CESG), 7-10
Canadian-Controlled Private Corporation (CCPC), 7-22, 7-48
Canadian Development Expenses (CDE), 7-20
Canadian Exploration Expenses (CEE), 7-20
Canadian IPUs, 11-19
Canadian Investor Protection Fund (CIPF), 14-7
Canadian Life and Health Insurance Association, 11-27
Canadian Pension Plan (CPP), 5-26, 7-49, 8-10
capital beneficiaries, 8-32
capital cost allowance, 11-27
capital gains, 7-18, 8-24, 8-27, 8-34, 8-37, 10-10, 11-20
capital gains exemption, 8-28

capital losses, 7-18, 8-24, 8-27, 8-37
cash, 13-10
cash and equivalent funds, 11-5 – 11-7
cash flow, 11-15
cash-on-cash yield, 11-23, 11-25
charitable donations, 8-35
charitable gifts, 8-35, 8-37
    in-kind donations, 8-37
    planned gift, 8-35
Charitable Remainder Trusts (CRTs), 8-38
charitable tax receipt, 8-38, 8-39
child support, 8-17
CIPs (Cash Index Participation Units), 11-19
civil law, 8-16
claims-made policy, 6-16
clients, 15-11
    debriefing, 15-11
    feedback, 15-12, Appendix 15.1-1
    trade meetings, 15-11
    user groups, 15-12
closed-end, 11-2, 11-18, 11-19, 11-26
    real estate investment trust (REIT), 11-26
code of conduct, 4-11
code of ethics, 4-11 – 4-17
    competence, 4-11
    confidentiality, 4-11
    diligence, 4-11
    fairness, 4-11
    integrity, 4-11
    objectivity, 4-11
    professionalism, 4-11
codicil, 8-15
co-executors, 8-11
co-habitation agreement, 8-6
commercial insurance, 6-2
commercial property insurance, 6-9
commissioned, 14-10, 16-9
    proprietary, 14-10
    third-party, 14-10
commodity trading advisors (CTAs), 12-11
common law, 8-16, 8-17
    common-law spouses, 8-17
common-law spouses, 8-17
commuted value, 5-10
company pension plans, 5-9
    Defined Benefit Pension Plan (DBP), 5-9
    Defined Contribution Plan (DCP), 5-9
    Group Registered Retirement Savings Plan
    (GRRSP), 5-9
CompCorp, 6-25
Compensation Corp., 6-25
competence, 4-3, 4-10, 4-11
competition, 15-13, 16-6
Competition Act (Canada), 6-10
compliance, 8-10
composite market indexes, 13-6
    equally-weighted indexes, 13-7
    market-value-weighted index, 13-6
    price-weighted index, 13-7

compounding, 3-10
confidentiality, 4-11
conflict of interest, 4-12, 4-13
    apparent, 4-13
    official duty, 4-12
    potential, 4-13
    private or personal interests, 4-12
conflict of obligations, 4-13
consumer behaviour, 15-7, 15-8
Consumer Price Index (CPI), 9-3
corporate executors, 8-10
corporate-redemption agreements, 6-19
corporate trustee, 8-11
correlation, 9-15, 10-5, 12-11
correlation coefficient, 9-10, 9-16
covariance, 9-9, 9-14, 10-5
covered call sale, 6-30
covered call writing, 6-30
creditor protection, 6-26, 8-33, 11-28
criminal, 6-12
critical illness insurance, 6-4
crystallization, 7-49, 7-50, 8-41
cultural property, 8-39
current yield, 11-7

D

3D, 6-12
    destruction, 6-12
    disappearance, 6-12
    dishonesty, 6-12
death benefit, 8-33
deemed disposition, 7-34, 8-39, 8-41
Deferred Profit Sharing Plans (DPSPs), 11-21
deferred-sales-charge, 14-9, 14-12
Defined Benefit Pension Plan (DBP), 5-9, 5-10
    opting out, 5-10
Defined Contribution Plan (DCP), 5-9
demographics, 15-1, 15-2, 15-7
    consumer behaviour, 15-7, 15-8
    high-net-worth, 15-2
    women, 15-9
dependent, 8-25, 8-26
    disability, 8-25
depreciating assets, 8-23
derivatives (swaps), 11-16, 12-9, 12-10
destruction, 6-12
DIAMONDS, 11-21
diligence, 4-11
disability, 8-25
disappearance, 6-12
discount, 11-18
discount brokers, 14-7
discretionary, 12-5
discretionary delegated authority, 4-4
discretionary management, 14-8
    managed accounts, 14-8

pooled funds, 14-8
wrap accounts, 14-8
dishonesty, 6-12
distribution of returns, 9-3
symmetrical probability distribution, 9-3
distributor, 14-13
diversification, 9-12, 9-13, 9-15, 13-10
evaluating, 9-15
dividends, 7-49, 10-10
divorce agreement, 8-17
downside risk, 7-18
due diligence, 12-10
dynamic, 10-2, 10-6

E

effective yield, 11-7
efficient frontier, 9-14
efficient market hypothesis (EMH), 10-7
semi-strong form, 10-8
strong form, 10-8
weak form, 10-8
efficient portfolios, 9-14
emerging market funds, 12-10
employee dishonesty, 6-12
employee loans, 7-24
employment income, 7-49
environmental harm, 6-11
equally-weighted indexes, 13-7
equity funds, 11-5, 11-9 – 11-12
errors and omissions/professional liability
insurance, 6-3
estate, 8-7
estate administrator, 8-12
full administrative powers, 8-12
Quebec Civil Code, 8-12
simple administrative powers, 8-12
estate freezing, 7-50, 8-27, 8-39, 8-41
estate planning, 8-1, 8-29, 8-35, 8-41
estate team, 8-42
evaluation, 13-2
Executive Pension Plan, 5-15
executor, 8-9 – 8-11, 8-17, 8-18, 8-26, 8-28, 8-33
compensation, 8-13
corporate executors, 8-10
investments, 8-12
personal liability, 8-9
powers, 8-11
standard of care, 8-12
wealth manager, 8-10
executor fees, 8-27
express delegated authority, 4-4
exchange-traded put options, 6-27
exercise date, 7-21
exercise price, 7-21
exercising, 7-21
expectations arbitrage, 12-9

F

fair competition, 4-17
fair treatment of competitors, 4-17
genuine competition, 4-17
fair market value, 7-22, 13-2
fairness, 4-11
family business, 8-39, 8-40
family cottage, 8-39, 8-40
Family Law Act of Ontario, 8-16
family loan, 7-13
family stewards, 2-6
family trust, 8-30, 8-39
federal tax credit, 8-35
fee-based, 12-5
fees, 16-9
fidelity, 6-9
fiduciary, 8-1, 11-4
fiduciary relationship, 4-5
financial phobics, 2-6
financial plan, 16-5
fixed-income funds, 11-5, 11-8
fixed-income investing, 13-9
high yield, 13-9
interest rate change anticipation, 13-9
sector trading, 13-9
value trading, 13-9
flow-through shares, 7-20
Canadian Development Expenses (CDE), 7-20
Canadian Exploration Expenses (CEE), 7-20
capital gain, 7-20
capital loss, 7-20
foreign trusts, 7-33, 7-34
front-end load, 14-11
full administrative powers, 8-12, 8-18
funds of funds, 11-14
fraud, 6-12
fundamental analysts, 10-5
future value, Appendix 7.1-1
futures, 12-11
futures linked notes, 12-13

G

gamblers, 2-6
General Anti-Avoidance Rules (GAAR), 7-20
general partners, 7-25
geometric-mean (or time-weighted), 9-6, 9-7
gifting, 8-19
Global IPUs, 11-21
Morgan Stanley Capital International (MSCI), 11-21
Morgan Stanley World Equity Benchmark Shares (WEBS), 11-21
gross investment, 14-11
Group Registered Retirement Savings Plan (GRRSP), 5-9

growth, 13-9
guaranteed funds, 11-28
Guaranteed Investment Certificate (GIC), 7-20
guardian, 8-13, 8-21

H

health, 15-2
hedge funds, 12-7, 12-11
    arbitrage funds, 12-8, 12-9
    due diligence, 12-10
    Jones model funds, 12-8
    macro funds, 12-8, 12-9
    nominal hedge funds, 12-10
    value added hedging, 12-8
hedges, 12-10
high-net-worth, 12-1, 15-2, 15-3
    affluent, 15-3
    wealthy, 15-3
high yield, 13-9
holding period, 9-5
holding-period return (HPR), 9-2, 13-2
holograph, 8-5
Home Buyer's Plan, 5-7, 5-8, 8-23
homeowners' insurance, 6-3, 6-4

I

in trust accounts, 7-12
inclusion rate, 8-37
income beneficiaries, 8-32
income-deferral, 7-7, 8-26
income splitting, 7-8, 7-9, 7-33, 7-49, 8-23, 8-31
income spreading, 8-26
Income Tax Act, 7-25 – 7-28, 7-39, 7-42, 8-11, 8-23, 8-30
Income Trusts (ITs), 11-25
incorporated small business, 7-50
independents, 2-6
index funds, 11-16
    active index funds, 11-17
    derivatives, 11-16
index futures, 12-10
index futures contracts, 6-31
index-linked GICs, 6-24, 11-22, 12-13
index participation unit (IPU), 11-19
    Canadian IPUs, 11-19
    Distributions, 11-20
    Global IPUs, 11-21
    U.S. IPUs, 11-20
index put options, 6-29
Index Trust SuperUnits, 11-19
Indexing, 13-9
individual managed accounts, 12-13
Individual Pension Plans, 5-15, 7-40
    Executive Pension Plan, 5-15

Shareholder Pension Plan, 5-15
Individual Retirement Accounts, 7-20
inflation, 7-39, 9-3, 10-9
inflation premium, 9-2
inflation rate, 9-2
information, 15-10, 15-12
    sources, 15-10
    value, 15-12
information return, 7-34
inheritance, 8-31
in-kind donations, 8-37, 8-38
innovators, 2-7
insurance, 6-1
    business property insurance, 6-9
    commercial property insurance, 6-9
    covered call sale, 6-30
    covered call writing, 6-30
    critical illness insurance, 6-4
    exchange-traded put options, 6-27
    homeowners' insurance, 6-4
    index futures contracts, 6-31
    index put options, 6-29
    key person, 6-13
    kidnap, 6-12
    life insurance, 6-4
    marriage contract insurance, 6-5
    product recall, 6-12
    property and casualty insurance, 6-9
    ransom, 6-12
    travel insurance, 6-5
    workers' compensation, 6-12
insurance companies, 11-28
insurance policies, 6-16
    claims-made policy, 6-16
    commercial policy, 6-16
    occurrence-based policy, 6-16
integrity, 4-3, 4-10
inter vivos trusts, 7-33, 8-6, 8-29, 8-38
    Charitable Remainder Trusts (CRTs), 8-38
interest, 7-48
interest rate change anticipation, 13-9
internal rate of return, 11-24
intestate, 8-3, 8-4, 8-18
intrinsic value, 12-12
in-trust accounts, 7-7, 7-12
investment, 14-1
investment advisors, 14-6
investment and portfolio management, 1-5
investment classes, 10-1
investment counsel, 12-2
investment counsellors, 14-8
    money managers, 14-8
investment dealers, 12-2, 14-8
Investment Dealers Association of Canada (IDA), 14-7
investment firm, 14-6
investment funds, 11-1, 11-2
    closed-end, 11-2, 11-18
    open-end, 11-2

Investment Funds Institute of Canada (IFIC), 11-1, 11-5
investment income, 7-17, 7-18
    capital gains, 7-17
    dividend income, 7-17
    interest income, 7-17
investment manager, 12-6
investment opportunity, 10-2, 10-5
investment policy, 10-2, 12-3
investment policy statement (IPS), Introduction-4, 14-1, 14-2, 16-5
investment pools, 10-10
investment returns, 12-7
investment strategy, 10-2
investment style, 10-5
    active, 10-5
    mixed approach, 10-5
    passive, 10-5
investor profile statement, 2-13, Appendix 2.1-1

J

Joint Tenants with Rights of Survivorship (JTWROS), 8-20 – 8-22, 8-34
Jones model funds, 12-8

K

key person, 6-13
    contribution-to-profits, 6-13
    cost-of-replacement, 6-13
    funding, 6-14
    multiple-of-compensation, 6-13
kidnap, 6-9, 6-12
kiddie tax, 7-35
know your client rule, 4-6, 14-9

L

leverage, 12-9
Leveraged Deferred Compensation Plan, 5-12
LIF, 5-11
Life Income Fund (LIF)
life insurance, 6-2, 6-4, 6-6, 7-48, 8-2, 8-27, 8-38, 8-40, 8-41
    funeral-expenses, 6-6
    joint and last to die, 6-7
    premium, 8-38
Lifelong Learning Plan, 5-7, 5-8
Lifelong Learning program, 8-23
lifestyle, 15-2
limited partnerships, 7-25
    adjusted cost base (ACB), 7-26
    at risk, 7-26, 7-27

    cumulative net investment loss (CNIL), 7-28
    disposing interest, 7-27
    general partners, 7-25
    transfer interest, 7-28
liquidity, 7-18
living trust, 8-23
living will, 8-18
load, 11-18, 14-14
lock-in effect, 7-18
locked-in RRSP, 5-9 – 5-11
long-term equity anticipation securities options (LEAPS), 6-29

M

macro funds, 12-8, 12-9
managed accounts, 14-8
managed futures fund, 12-12
managed pools, 12-8
managed products, 11-1, 12-7, 13-1, 14-6, 14-9
management fees, 10-10, 11-18, 11-23, 12-5, 12-6, 13-4
management expense ratios (MER), 7-37, 10-10, 12-2, 13-5
mandatory, 8-17
    full administration powers, 8-18
    simple administration powers, 8-18
marginal tax rate, 7-6
market cycles, 10-8
market index, 9-13, 9-15
market research, 15-1
market timing, 3-12, 10-2, 10-8
market value, 8-34, 11-23
market-value-weighted index, 13-6
marketing, 16-1, 16-14
    target market, 16-2 – 16-5
marriage breakdown, 8-26
marriage contract insurance, 6-5
mean, 9-3
measurement, 13-1
minimum variance frontier, 9-14
minimum variance portfolio, 9-14
mixed approach, 10-5
moguls, 2-6
momentum, 13-9
moral behaviour, 4-10
moral character, 4-2, 4-10
moral insight, 4-2
Morgan Stanley Capital International (MSCI), 11-21
Morgan Stanley World Equity Benchmark Shares (WEBS), 11-21
mortgage, Appendix 7.4-1
multi-class funds, 11-14
mutual funds, 7-37, 11-1, 11-2, 11-5 – 11-14, 13-14, 14-9
    active funds, 11-15

active index funds, 11-17
adjusted cost base (ACB), 7-37
asset churning, 7-37, 7-38
balanced funds, 11-5, 11-9
cash and equivalent funds, 11-5 – 11-7
cost base, 7-37
derivatives, 11-16
equity funds, 11-5, 11-9 – 11-12
fixed-income funds, 11-5, 11-8
index funds, 11-16
management expense ratios, 7-37
net asset, 7-37
passive funds, 11-15
performance, 13-14
sector funds, 11-5, 11-12, 11-13
shareholders, 11-4
styles, 11-15
types, 11-5
unitholders, 11-4
value, 7-37
mutual fund corporation, 11-3
mutual fund trusts, 11-4

N

NASDAQ-100, 11-21
National Policy 39, 11-6, 12-3
NAVPU (net asset value per unit), 11-26
net asset, 7-37
net asset value, 13-3, 13-5
net asset value per share (NAVS), 11-3, 11-4,
11-6, 11-8, 11-18, 11-19, 14-11
net market exposure, 12-8
net realized capital gains, 11-3
newsletters, 16-11
no-load, 14-10, 14-13, 14-14
nominal, 9-2, 10-3
nominal hedge funds, 12-10
    emerging market funds, 12-10
    short funds, 12-10
    special situation funds, 12-10
normal portfolios, 13-8
non-capital loss, 7-30
non-discretionary, 12-5
non-proprietary, 14-9
non-refundable tax credit, 8-37

O

objectivity, 4-11
occurrence-based policy, 6-16
Old Age Security (OAS), 5-27, 7-16
    clawed back, 7-16
Ontario Business Corporations Act, 6-10
Ontario Superintendent of Financial Institutions,
6-22

open-end, 11-2
options, 12-10, 12-11

P

Partnership Acts, 7-25
partnership income, 7-25
passive, 10-5, 10-9, 13-8
passive funds, 11-15
passive management, 13-9
pension tax credit, 5-26
    taxation, 5-26
per capita, 8-14
per stirpes, 8-14
performance analysis, 13-11
performance appraisal, 13-1, 13-10, 13-13
    diversification, 13-10
performance-based fee, 13-4
performance evaluation, 13-6
    benchmark, 13-6
performance measurement, 13-2, 13-4
plain vanilla will, 8-3
planned gift, 8-35
pooled funds, 11-27, 12-3, 12-4, 14-8
    protected funds, 11-27
    segregated funds, 11-27
portfolio funds, 11-13
portfolio insurance, 6-21
portfolio manager, 14-6
portfolio opportunity set, 9-14
portfolio returns, 9-8
portfolio valuation, 13-2
power-of-attorney, 5-31, 8-17, 8-21
preferred beneficiary, 7-35, 8-30
premium, 8-38, 11-18
pre-nuptial, 8-6
prescribed rates, 7-13, 7-24
present value, Appendix 7.1-2
price-weighted index, 13-7
principal residence, 7-16
    capital gains, 7-16
private equity investors, 12-11
probate, 8-14, 8-18, 8-19, 8-21, 8-22, 8-27, 8-33,
11-28
product recall, 6-12
professionalism, 4-11
promotion, 16-10
    advertising, 16-10
    newsletters, 16-11
    prospecting, 16-12
    public relations, 16-11
    sales, 16-11
    seminars, 16-11
proprietary, 14-9, 14-10
prospecting, 16-12
protected funds, 11-27
power of attorney, 8-5, 8-17, 8-18

professional liability insurance, 8-5
professional trustee, 8-11
protected funds, 11-28
provincial public guardian, 8-18
provincial tax credit, 8-35
prudent investor rule, 8-33
public relations, 16-11
public trustee, 8-21
purchasing power, 10-10
pure arbitrage, 12-9
put options, 6-28

Q

qualified small business, 5-18, 7-50
qualified farm property, 8-28
Quebec Civil Code, 8-12

R

ransom, 6-12
rate-of-return, 5-4, 9-1, 9-2
real estate, 7-18
real estate investment trust (REIT), 11-26
real rate of return, 9-2
real return, 10-10
rebalancing, 10-6
redemption fees, 14-12
    back-end load, 14-12
    deferred sales charge, 14-12
    trailer fees, 14-12, 14-14
referrals, 16-12
Registered Education Savings Plan (RESP), 5-6,
7-7, 7-10, 7-13, Appendix 7.2-1
    Canada Education Savings Grant (CESG),
    7-10
    family-plan, 7-11
    over-contributions, Appendix 7.3-1
    withdrawals, 7-11
Registered Pension Plans (RPPs), 7-40
Registered Retirement Income Fund (RRIF),
5-21, 5-26, 6-5, 8-2, 8-22, 8-25, 8-36, 11-21
    younger spouse, 5-26
Registered Retirement Savings Plan (RRSP),
5-6, 5-20, 6-5, 7-7, 7-40, 7-45, 8-2, 8-22, 8-25,
8-36, 11-21
    borrowing, 7-47
    compounding, 7-44
    early, continuous, and over-contributions,
    7-43
    maturity options, 5-20
    mortgage vs. RRSP, Appendix 7.4-1
    spousal RRSP's, 7-11
    spousal spin, 7-42
    RRSP vs. mortgage, Appendix 7.4-1
representative, 8-17

reserve life index, 11-24
retirement, 5-16
    choosing a date, 5-17
    emotional issues, 5-30
    from a business, 5-18
    from a partnership, 5-19
    preparing, 5-16
    retirement income projection, 5-17
Retirement Compensation Arrangement (RCA),
5-14
retirement independence calculation, 5-2
return, 9-1, 9-12, 9-14, 13-2
    after-tax, 10-10
    before-tax, 10-11
    distribution, 9-3
    holding-period return (HPR), 9-2
    inflation premium, 9-2
    inflation rate, 9-2
    nominal, 9-2
    portfolio returns, 9-8
    rate of return, 9-2
    real rate of return, 9-2
Revenue Canada, 8-10
rights of ownership, 8-20
risk, 7-18, 9-1, 9-3, 9-12, 10-6, 12-7, 13-3, 13-10
    risk-averse, 9-1
    risk profile questionnaire, 9-1
    risk profile statement, Appendix 2.2-1
    riskless, 9-1
    risky, 9-1
    single-security, 9-7
    systematic, 9-4
    tolerance, 5-23
    total risk, 9-5
    types of risk, 3-5 – 3-8
    unsystematic risk, 9-4, 9-5
risk-adjusted returns, 13-4
risk-averse, 9-1
risk management, 6-21
risk profile questionnaire, 9-1
riskless, 9-1
risky, 9-1
retirement savings, 5-12
    Individual Pension Plans, 5-15
    Leveraged Deferred Compensation Plan,
    5-12
    Retirement Compensation Arrangement
    (RCA), 5-14
    Supplemental Executive Retirement Plans,
    5-16
risk and return, 1-6
Royalty Trusts (RITs), 11-23
    cash-on-cash yield, 11-23
    reserve life index, 11-24
rule of 72, 3-10

S

S&P Canada 60 index (i60), 6-28, 6-29
salary, 7-49
sales, 16-11
same-sex spouses, 8-17
sector funds, 11-5, 11-12, 11-13
sector rotation, 10-5, 13-9
sector trading, 13-9
seminars, 16-11
separately managed portfolios, 12-2
    tax advantages, 12-2
    tax planning, 12-2
security, 10-2
segregated funds, 6-22, 8-2, 8-33, 10-10, 11-27
    annuitant, 6-26
    bypass probate, 6-22
    CompCorp, 6-25
    Canadian Life and Health Insurance
    Compensation Corp., 6-25
    contract holder, 6-26
    creditor protection, 6-22, 6-26, 8-33
    death benefits, 6-22, 6-23, 8-33
    maturity guarantee, 6-22
    maturity protection, 6-22
    reset dates, 6-23
self-directed RRSP, 5-9
semi-strong form, 10-8
separation agreement, 8-26
settlement date, 13-2
settlor, 7-33, 7-34, 8-29, 8-38
shareholders, 11-4
Shareholder Pension Plan, 5-15
short funds, 12-10
simple administrative powers, 8-12, 8-18
sinking fund, 6-18
small business, 7-47
    tax planning, 7-47
SPDRs, 11-21
special situation funds, 12-10
specified foreign trust, 7-33
spousal loans, 7-14, 7-15
spousal rights, 8-16, 8-40
spousal RRSPs, 7-11
spousal spin, 7-42
spousal support, 8-17
spousal testamentary trust, 8-23
spousal trust, 8-21, 8-29, 8-31, 8-32
    tainted, 8-31
Standard & Poors Depository Receipts (SPDRs),
11-19, 11-20
standard deviation, 9-3, 9-7, 10-5
Standard Mortgage Clause, 6-16
standard of care, 8-12
stock option plans, 7-21
    exercise date, 7-21
    exercise price, 7-21
    fair market value (FMV), 7-22
strategic, 10-2, 10-4

    investment opportunity, 10-2
strategic asset allocation, 10-8
stripped bond, 12-13
strong form, 10-8
style indexes, 13-8
Supplemental Executive Retirement Plans, 5-16
survivorship bias, 13-12
survivorship clause, 8-14
systematic risk, 9-4, 9-13, 9-16
symmetrical probability distribution, 9-3

T

21-year rule, 7-34
tactical, 10-2, 10-7, 12-3
tainted, 8-31
tax advantages, 12-2
tax-deductible, 12-2
tax deferral, 7-48, 8-26
tax free roll over, 8-24
tax haven, 7-33
tax planning, 12-2
tax-saving,, 8-35
taxation, 10-9
    after-tax, 10-10
    before-tax, 10-11
    capital gains, 10-10
    dividends, 10-10
    lifetime tax bill, 5-25
    tax-effective portfolios, 5-25
    tax loss selling, 5-25
    tax planning, 5-24
tax-deferral, 7-7
technical analysts, 10-5
term annuities, 8-26
testamentary freedom, 8-14
testamentary trusts, 7-33, 7-34, 8-23, 8-25, 8-29,
8-31, 8-33
testator, 8-5, 8-9, 8-13
theft insurance, 6-12
third-party, 14-10
time value of money, 7-7, 7-18, Appendix 7.1-1
    calculate and match, Appendix 7.1-1
    present value, Appendix 7.1-2
time-weighted returns, 13-3
Toronto Index Participation units (TIPS), 11-19
total risk, 9-5
tracking error, 11-16
trade date, 13-2
trailer, 11-18
trailer fees, 14-12
transaction-based, 12-5
travel insurance, 6-5
trust, 8-22, 16-7, 16-9
trust agreement, 8-32
trust companies, 12-2, 14-9
trust document, 7-33

trust income, 8-30
trust relationship, 4-3
    competence, 4-3
    integrity, 4-3
trustee, 7-33, 8-22, 8-29, 8-30, 8-33, 11-4
Trustee Act, 8-11, 8-33
trusts, 7-32, 8-29, 8-30
    attribution, 7-34
    beneficiary, 7-33, 8-29
    Canadian beneficiary, 7-34
    Capital beneficiaries, 8-32
    deemed disposition, 7-34
    foreign trusts, 7-33, 7-34
    income beneficiaries, 8-32
    income splitting, 7-33
    inter vivos trusts, 7-33, 8-29, 8-30
    kiddie tax, 7-35
    settlor, 7-33, 7-34, 8-29
    specified foreign trust, 7-33
    spousal trust, 8-29, 8-31
    21-year rule, 7-34
    tax consequences, 7-33
    tax implications, 8-29
    testamentary trusts, 7-33, 7-34, 8-29, 8-31, 8-32
    trust agreement, 8-32
    trust document, 7-33
    trust income, 8-30
    trustee, 7-33, 7-35, 8-29
TSE 100 Index Participation Units (HIPS), 11-19

U

unitholders, 11-4
units, 12-4
unrealized capital, 8-24, 8-30, 8-40
unsystematic risk, 9-4, 9-5, 9-13, 9-15
U.S. IPUs, 11-20

V

vacation property, 6-6
value, 13-9
value added hedging, 12-8
value propositions, 16-5 – 16-9
    investment policy statement, 16-5
    wealth management plan, 16-5
value trading, 13-9
variance, 9-3, 9-7, 9-10, 9-14, 10-5
VIPs (Value of Index Participation Certificates), 2-6, 11-19
volatility, 3-11, 9-12, 12-7
vulnerability, 4-5 – 4-7

W

weak form, 10-8
wealth-accumulation, 15-7
wealth management plan, 16-5
wealth management process, 1-1, 15-11
    formalizing and implementing the plan, 1-8
    formulating the plan, 1-3
    investment and portfolio management, 1-5
    monitoring and re-balancing, 1-9
    understanding the high-net-worth client, 1-2
wealth manager, 8-10, 15-2, 15-3
wealthy, 15-3
wealth tier, 15-3
weighted average, 9-14
will, 8-5, 8-9, 8-18, 8-27, 8-32, 8-36
    codicil, 8-15
    clauses, 8-9
women, 15-9
workers' compensation, 6-12
World Equity Benchmark Shares (WEBS), 11-19, 14-6
wrap, 10-10
wrap accounts, 12-4, 12-5, 14-8
wrap fee, 12-4
wrap programs, 12-5, 12-6